# The Modern Brass Band

For Muriel

# The Modern Brass Band

From the 1930s to the New Millennium

ROY NEWSOME

ASHGATE

Published by
Ashgate Publishing Limited
Gower House
Croft Road
Aldershot
Hants GU11 3HR
England

Ashgate Publishing Company
Suite 420
101 Cherry Street
Burlington, VT 05401-4405
USA

Ashgate website: http://www.ashgate.com

**British Library Cataloguing-in-Publication Data**

Newsome, Roy
   The modern brass band : from the 1930s to the new millennium
   1. Brass bands – Europe – History  2. Brass band music – History and criticism
   I. Title
   784.9'094

**Library of Congress Cataloging-in-Publication Data**

Newsome, Roy.
   The modern brass band: from the 1930s to the new millennium / Roy Newsome.
        p. cm.
   Includes bibliographical references (p.      ) and index.
   ISBN 0-7546-0716-X (hardcover : alk. paper) – ISBN 0-7546-0717-8 (pbk : alk. paper) 1. Brass bands – Great Britain – History. 2. Brass band music – History and criticism. I. Title.

   ML1331.N495  2006
   784.9'0941'0904–dc22

2005005492

ISBN 0 7546 0716 X (Hbk)   ISBN 0 7546 0717 8 (Pbk)

Printed on acid-free paper

Typeset in Sabon by J.L. & G.A. Wheatley Design, Aldershot, Hants.

Printed and bound in Great Britain by TJ International, Padstow.

# Contents

**Appendices**

# List of illustrations

# Foreword

Until recent times the world of brass bands has been inadequately supported by authoritative literature, other than the weekly and monthly magazines which faithfully report and comment on passing events. With one or two notable exceptions, such books as have been written on the subject have done little more than scratch the surface of a cultural phenomenon both rich in achievement and meaningful in social history. In part, the reason for this is that the authors have tended to be enthusiasts whose observations on the scene have been made from the touchlines or exponents whose writings reflect their own limited experience.

Roy Newsome, author of *The Modern Brass Band*, a welcome and overdue addition to the genre, is of a different breed. Steeped in bands from the ground floor up, his insatiable quest for detail and balanced judgement in presenting what, in lesser hands, could be boring lists of facts and figures has, as in his earlier work *Brass Roots* (1998), provided players, students and aficionados of the present day and of generations to come with a comprehensive in-depth account of brass banding from 1930 to the end of the century.

The reader will follow the fortunes of bands great and small, conductors whose influence varied from local to regional and even, for a special few, to international significance, and cameos of a selection of outstanding instrumentalists of the period. Of special interest is the scholarly account of banding during and immediately after the days of World War II, and the effects of sweeping social changes that followed, not least the impact of modern technology. Given his unique role in post-war banding, Roy Newsome is well equipped to assess the impact of the burgeoning youth band scene which revitalised an ailing band movement, and the explosion of brass banding throughout Europe – not forgetting its emergence in Japan and resurgence in the USA.

For readers of my age group, this timely book refreshes what are but dim and distant memories and adds a great deal that we did not know. Comprehensive, packed with statistical details but user-friendly, it is the product of diligent research, a staggering depth of knowledge and the author's total dedication to a life-consuming hobby.

Peter Wilson

**Peter Wilson**

In 1991 Peter Wilson joined the illustrious group of recipients of the Iles Medal – presented for outstanding service to bands.

His life in bands began at the age of eight, when he started learning to play the cornet. A dozen or so years later he was playing solo euphonium with the then highly successful Scottish CWS Band. Later he took an interest in conducting, was runner-up in the National Association of Brass Band Conductors' first competition for conductors, and conducted a number of Scottish bands. He was also, at around this time, the dynamic secretary of the NABBC's Scottish centre, where he established a series of short courses for young conductors.

Peter Wilson moved to London in 1971, where he became the organising secretary of the National Brass Band Championships. Six years later he relinquished this position, becoming the managing editor of the weekly journal *British Bandsman* and managing director of the Rosehill Music Publishing Company.

He was also, at this time, in demand worldwide as a brass band adjudicator. In May 2000 Wilson retired from the editorship of *British Bandsman* after almost 24 years' service. He continued, however, in a consultative capacity and also maintained his interests in the publishing business, where he was constantly introducing new and exciting composers to the world of the contesting brass band.

# Preface and acknowledgements

This book is in some ways a follow-up to my *Brass Roots*, published in 1998. It is, however, complete in itself and though there are occasional references to the earlier book, familiarity with that is not a prerequisite to a reading of this.

The year 1936 was the break-off point of *Brass Roots*, primarily because it marked a century of published brass band music; but it was also the year when Crystal Palace, home of one of the brass band world's most prestigious competitions, was gutted by fire. Further, it was the year in which the final work in a series of test pieces by major British composers appeared[1] and the year in which William Rimmer, a leading band conductor and composer, died. In *The Modern Brass Band* I re-examine the year 1936 and also look back on the events and prevailing conditions during the final years covered in *Brass Roots* before moving on to a study of brass bands in the remainder of the twentieth century.

## Sources

One major source of information has been my own experience, having being born into a family which had connections with brass bands going back several generations. Though taking piano lessons from the age of six, I was keen to join a band and at the age of ten was allowed by my father to begin learning to play the cornet. I had no particular aspirations beyond wishing to become a 'useful' member of the town band but when, a decade or so later, I found myself conducting that same town band – frankly, because no one else would do the job – it seemed that I had found my niche. It led to me studying music more seriously and in time I became a respected conductor, fortunate enough to be offered appointments with leading bands.

I also passed the necessary examinations to become a school music teacher and was able to develop teaching skills alongside my conducting. The two disciplines complemented each other and when, in 1967, the first full-time course in higher education specifically for band musicians was instituted in Salford, I was offered the post of 'Head of Band Studies'.

---

[1] This was the suite *Kenilworth* (Bliss).

I already held the influential position of resident conductor of Black Dyke Mills Band and the two posts meant that for most of my waking hours I was involved in something to do with brass bands, becoming personally acquainted with prominent figures of the time and involved in all aspects of banding. Thus, from humble beginnings in the 1940s and 1950s, I gained experience in higher circles of brass banding in the 1960s and beyond.

Apart from the few available books on, or referring to, brass bands, the growing number of booklets published as bands reach their centenary or some other landmark, and contest and concert programmes, many of which are in my personal collection, the main source of information up to 1956 has been copies of *Brass Band News* (*BBN*), located in the Band Musicianship Research Archive of the University of Salford. This was published from October 1881 by Wright & Round of Liverpool, a company which, in 1885, became a leading publisher of brass band music.

I have also referred to *British Bandsman* (*BB* – founded 1887) and, where appropriate, added extra material found there. With the demise of *BBN* the *BB* became the principal primary source. Copies of this are kept in the offices of the *British Bandsman* in Beaconsfield and at the Colindale Branch of the British Library. I have also had access to the personal copies of Mr Roy Horobin of Sunderland, to whom I am most grateful, as these enabled me to continue my research from home. Supplementary material comes from *The Conductor* (the quarterly magazine of the National Association of Brass Band Conductors), a full set of which is located in the Salford Archive, and from past copies of the *British Mouthpiece* and *Brass Band World* (*BBW*), located in Salford University's Adelphi library. Later copies of *BB* (from the late 1960s) are also held in this library. Other magazines referred to are *Sounding Brass*, copies of which are in the writer's collection; *Brass Band Review*, a short-lived magazine published in the 1970s, copies of which are in the Salford Archive; and a later publication called *Brass Review*.

Reliance on these magazines does create problems. Many topics are mentioned almost en passant. At the time, readers would have been familiar with the points made; but several decades later, it sometimes requires the Sherlock Holmes touch to deduce what is being referred to. Some events are previewed and not mentioned again, whilst others are referred to briefly, after the event, with little detail. Inevitably, some events are not mentioned at all. Rarely are actual dates given and the date of the appointment of a conductor or instrumentalist is ascertained in some cases merely through the report of a contest, concert or broadcast.

For social conditions and changes during the 1930s I found A.J.P. Taylor's *English History 1914–1945* helpful. This also covers the events of World War II. However, *The People's War* by Angus Calder proved to be a most comprehensive guide to this period and I was able to relate much of the information in *BBN* to the immense detail provided by Calder.

## The structure of the book

*The Modern Brass Band* begins with a description of conditions during the 1930s and the war years, and how they affected brass bands; Part One covers this period. Part Two, 'Times of Change', takes us through to 1980 and includes a detailed look at the all-important matter of contests. This is a huge area and I make no apology for examining it in some depth. It has often been referred to as the 'lifeblood' of the banding movement. Though some would take issue with this, there can be little doubt that it has helped keep brass bands at the forefront of amateur music-making, providing the incentive to strive for higher standards and spawning the composition of a substantial repertoire of original music which has extended the skills of players while making ever-increasing musical and technical demands. Success in contests has also helped with public relations, either in the community to which the band belongs or with the sponsoring company.

Throughout the twentieth century the most prestigious contests have been the National Brass Band Championships (the 'Nationals'), held in London, and the Belle Vue September contest, held in Manchester until 1996. In the 1930s, there were competitions at Belle Vue[2] at four different times of the year (February, May, July and September), catering for bands at various levels of competence. The one for the highest class of band was that held in September. It was formerly referred to simply as the 'September', but in 1955 became known as the 'British Open Championships'. The 'Open' has always tried to attract the best bands, inevitably meaning many entrants from some regions and few, or none at all, from others. Of the other former Belle Vue contests, only the 'May' has survived. Known as the 'Spring Festival' this provides the opportunity for 'promising' bands to seek entry into the British Open Championships.

The Nationals were held at Crystal Palace up to 1936. All classes of band competed on the one day, those in the highest competing for the One Thousand Guinea Trophy. After the Crystal Palace was burned down in 1936, the Nationals moved to Alexandra Palace. Two years later World War II caused their cessation but they were reinstated in 1945 under the auspices of a national newspaper, the *Daily Herald*. Now there were

---

[2] Belle Vue was the name of an amusement park on the outskirts of Manchester, with gardens, a boating lake, a large zoo, fairground rides such as the 'big dipper' and 'ghost train', and the King's Hall in which the principal contests were held.

regional qualifying events – known as 'Area' contests – to determine which bands would participate in the Finals. Bands in the highest section, generally referred to as the championship section, competed in the Royal Albert Hall, London, in most years, whilst other finalists played at Belle Vue up until they were moved to London in 1954.

'Repertoire' is another large topic and would require a whole book to do it full justice. I have, therefore, been able merely to scratch the surface, but have reviewed the work of the principal composers and arrangers. For brass bands 1960 was something of a watershed. Concert repertoire and presentation had become rather stagnant. The problems were addressed in the 1960s in preparation for unprecedented advances in the 1970s and beyond. In the 1980s repertoire became the driving force and played a major role in the further evolution of brass bands during the final years of the century. A discussion on the changing patterns of engagements, broadcasting, recordings and the advent of television brings Part Two to a close.

Part Three, 'The Years of Maturity', covers the last 20 years of the century and demonstrates how, following changes and developments in earlier years, brass bands were ready to become a major musical force, not only in Britain, but also overseas. Dates given in the part titles are only a general guide; some aspects discussed will begin earlier than the stated parameters of a particular chapter whilst others will go beyond.

The 'Overseas Developments', discussed in Part Four, were somewhat slow starters. The Salvation Army (SA) was the first major 'exporter' of British-style brass bands. These were established in Australia, New Zealand, Canada, America and several European countries during the late 1880s and early 1890s. Secular band music had been introduced in the Dominions during the middle years of the nineteenth century by British regimental bands; however, it was largely the immigrants from Britain settling there from the late 1840s onwards who were responsible for the formation of amateur bands comparable to those left behind in the 'old country'. Not until the post-war years did European countries take any serious interest in the British-style brass band. Holland was the first to do so, shortly after the war, but European interest did not become widespread until the later 1960s. The progress towards a thriving European brass band movement is discussed in some detail.

There were a few isolated examples of British-style brass bands in the USA during the 1960s, but not until the following decade did a 'movement' emerge. The same happened in Japan, but rather later and, to date, on a smaller scale. Nevertheless, though perhaps not truly worldwide, the brass band as it is known in Britain has been one of the most significant success stories in British post-war exports.

## Pounds, shillings and pence

When mentioning prize-money or fees in the years before decimalisation of British currency in 1971, I have used the prevailing £. s. d. notation rather than adopting the usual system of conversion. Today, all that needs to be known is that there are 100 pence (pennies) in the pound, but pre-decimalisation there were 240 pence (shown as d.) in the pound, with 12d. in the shilling (s.) and 20s. in the pound (£). The following should help clarify this:

| | | | | |
|---|---|---|---|---|
| £1 | = | 100p. | = | 20s. |
| | | 50p. | = | 10s. (10/-) |
| | | 25p. | = | 5s. (5/-) |
| | | 10p. | = | 2s. (2/-) |
| | | 7½p. | = | 1s. 6d. (1/6) |
| | | 5p. | = | 1s. (1/-) |
| | | 2½p. | = | 6d. |

One further complication lies in the use of the guinea. This was worth £1 1s. (21/-). Therefore, five guineas were worth £5 5s., 20 guineas worth £21 and 1000 guineas worth £1050.

There are many acronyms in the text. The general policy is to give the full name first of all, followed by its initials; thereafter, in the main, the initials only are used. A comprehensive list of these abbreviations is provided for the convenience of those readers who may not be familiar with them.

Finally, I have had some difficulties with the use of the word 'band'. It is quite obviously a singular noun and in general I have treated it as such. However, there are times when it seems to imply 'bandsmen' and I hope I may be forgiven for occasionally gliding into the plural mode to accommodate this.

## Acknowledgements

I wish to place on record my thanks to Roy Horobin (mentioned above), to the University of Salford for allowing me access to its archive and libraries, and to Peter Wilson for writing the Foreword and also for his many helpful suggestions. Rachel Lynch and Heidi May, both of Ashgate, have been particularly helpful with advice on the format of the book, and I am especially grateful to Mary Murphy for painstakingly reading the script and making innumerable suggestions for improving the detail. Many others have offered useful tips. These include David Read, Geoffrey Whitham, and Hugh Johnstone – with his encyclopaedic knowledge of the Scottish brass band scene, Tim Mutum and Frank Andrews. I am grateful to all of these and also to the many others who have been prepared to talk to me about the book and its contents.

Above all, I wish to thank my dear wife, Muriel, for her life-long support of my careers in bands and education. *The Modern Brass Band* is humbly dedicated to her.

Roy Newsome
May 2004

# Abbreviations

| | |
|---|---|
| ABBA | Association of Brass Band Adjudicators |
| AGM | Annual General Meeting |
| AOMF | Alexander Owen Memorial Fund |
| ARP | Air Raid Precautions |
| ATC | Air Training Corps |
| BA | Bachelor of Arts |
| *BB* | *British Bandsman* |
| BBC | British Broadcasting Corporation |
| BBCM | Bandmastership [Diploma] of the Bandsman's College of Music |
| BBHT | Brass Band Heritage Trust |
| *BBN* | *Brass Band News* |
| BBO | Brassband Berner Oberland |
| *BBW* | *Brass Band World* |
| BCM | Bandsman's College of Music |
| BFBB | British Federation of Brass Bands |
| BNFL | British Nuclear Fuels Ltd. |
| CBE | Commander (of the Order) of the British Empire |
| CBSO | City of Birmingham Symphony Orchestra |
| CD | Compact disc |
| CISWO | Coal Industries Social Welfare Organisation |
| CNE | Canadian National Exhibition |
| COBBA | Council of Brass Band Associations |
| CWS | Co-operative Wholesale Society |
| EBBA | European Brass Bands Association |
| ENSA | Entertainments National Service Association |
| EP | Extended play (gramophone recording) |
| EYMS | East Yorkshire Motor Services |
| GSM | Guildhall School of Music, London |
| GUS | Great Universal Stores |
| ISB | International Staff Band (of the Salvation Army) |
| ITV | Independent Television |
| JSVB | James Shepherd Versatile Brass |
| LGSM | Licentiate of the Guildhall School of Music |
| LP | Long-playing (gramophone) record |
| LPO | London Philharmonic Orchestra |
| LSO | London Symphony Orchestra |
| MBE | Member (of the Order) of the British Empire |

| MU | Musicians' Union |
| NABBA | North American Brass Bands Association |
| NABBC | National Association of Brass Band Conductors |
| NBBC | National Brass Band Club |
| NBBCC | National Brass Band Contesting Council |
| NCB | National Coal Board |
| NCC | National Contesting Council |
| NJBB | National Jugend Brass Band (National Youth Brass Band of Switzerland) |
| NLBBA | National League of Brass Band Associations |
| NSBA | National Schools Band Association |
| NSBBA | National Schools Brass Band Association |
| NWBBA | North West Brass Bands Association |
| NYBB | National Youth Brass Band |
| NYBBS | National Youth Brass Band of Scotland |
| NYBBW | National Youth Brass Band of Wales |
| NYO | National Youth Orchestra |
| OBE | Officer (of the Order) of the British Empire |
| PhD | Doctor of Philosophy |
| PJBE | Philip Jones Brass Ensemble |
| PRS | Performing Right Society |
| QEH | Queen Elizabeth Hall |
| RCBB | River City Brass Band |
| RNCM | Royal Northern College of Music |
| RAF | Royal Air Force |
| rpm | Revolutions per minute |
| SA | Salvation Army |
| SABA | Scottish Amateur Band Association |
| SP&S | Salvationist Publishing and Supplies |
| TBS | Tokyo Brass Society |
| TUC | Trades Union Congress |
| VAT | Value Added Tax |
| VE | Victory in Europe |
| VJ | Victory in Japan |
| WMC | World Music Concourse (Kerkrade) |
| YBS | Yorkshire Building Society |
| YTV | Yorkshire Television |

# Part One
# Bands and Banding to 1945

# CHAPTER 1

# Introductory overview

This chapter provides some general background to the socio-economic and political situation in Britain as it impacted on bands during the 1930s and through the war years. Though strictly a working-man's activity the brass band enjoyed the patronage of many owners of factories and coal mines, and of other members of the wealthier classes. It was, therefore, affected by social conditions and events of the times. The mining dispute of 1925, for example, had a massive effect on colliery bands and its effect was felt throughout the 1930s.[1]

Radio arrived in the 1920s, with the British Broadcasting Company licensed in 1922 and superseded, in 1926, by the British Broadcasting Corporation (BBC). Brass bands benefited enormously from this. Television appeared in 1936, but had little impact until after the war.

The principal newspapers were the *Daily Mail*, *Daily Express* and *News Chronicle*, with *The Times* and the *Daily Herald* on the political flanks. The latter was to play an important role in post-war banding as sponsors of the National Brass Band Championships from 1945 to 1964. Though privately owned, it had been a socialist newspaper from its inception in 1912. By 1929 it was under the joint ownership of Odhams Press and the TUC. Odhams formed their own brass band but were to take a wider interest when, in 1964, as owners of the Sunday newspaper *The People*, they became, briefly, sponsors of the National Championships.

The 1930s are often referred to as the 'Hungry Thirties'. Unemployment was rife, peaking at three million. With it went poverty, malnutrition and ill health. Yet for those in work wage rises were accompanied by a fall in the cost of living, whilst family planning and stability in the birth rate brought further security. Smaller families changed the role of women, more of whom went out to work. They now had equal voting rights with men and in due course their emancipation meant that many played alongside husbands, sons and fathers in brass bands.

There were important developments in the service industries – hotels, restaurants and entertainment. Bands, being part of the entertainment

---

[1] With a decreasing demand for coal, pit owners decided that miners should work longer hours for lower wages. The miners refused, coining the slogan, 'Not a minute on the day, not a penny off the pay'. Other unions rallied to their aid, resulting in the General Strike. This lasted from 5 to 12 May 1926, but whilst others returned to work the miners stayed out. Ultimately it was the choice between starvation for their families or acceptance of the new conditions which drove them back.

business, benefited, with concerts in parks, halls and theatres. For some there were summer tours, broadcasts and gramophone recordings.

Mortgages and hire purchase helped with ownership of houses and cars, though few bandsmen enjoyed these luxuries. However, some leading car manufacturers sponsored a brass band, largely as a social activity for the workforce. Morris Motors Band was the first, being formed in Cowley in 1924. Roads built during the 1920s helped with the development of road transport. A million cars were registered by 1930, but for most people the bus was the principal form of transport. This became the normal means of travel for bands, displacing earlier reliance on railways. Some bus companies formed brass bands.

As city centres depopulated in favour of outer suburbs, so new shops and factories were built close to the new housing. Factories were powered by electricity, with raw materials and finished products transported by road. They created environments for the formation of new bands. By the mid-1930s electricity in homes was becoming common. It also helped make bandrooms more civilised, with heat and light readily accessible.

Along with these developments came the demise of music halls and theatres, and a decline in attendance at church and chapel. Such changes were not restricted to entertainment and religion, however; the cotton, woollen and shipbuilding industries all suffered severe hardships. Foreign competition and modern machinery meant mass unemployment in many regions rich in brass bands. The means test reduced, or even removed, many workers' unemployment benefits. Some bandsmen were deemed to be working when attending rehearsals or band engagements and dole money was withheld on those days.[2] Unemployment had a devastating effect. Yorkshire and parts of Scotland were badly hit, but for the cotton workers of Lancashire, the miners of South Wales and the heavy engineering and shipyard workers in the North East it was catastrophic. Bands in these regions had no money and many disbanded. In the *Brass Band News* (*BBN*) of February 1936, the Bury (Lancashire) correspondent wrote, 'If ever there was a stricken area this is one'. This was echoed in March by the Westhoughton correspondent with the words: 'This district has been very badly hit industrially, but our bandsmen are very optimistic about the future.' The optimism was somewhat misplaced as the same scribe reported in June that '100 miners have been laid off at the only colliery left in the district'.

Demonstrations and hunger marches were common and brass bands played their part in these. The most famous was the 1936 march from

---

[2] The means test was an investigation into the financial resources of a family. In the early 1930s it became almost an 'inquisition', adding to the poverty and hardships of the unemployed. Unemployment benefit, often grudgingly paid by local councils, was known as dole money. Those who received it were said to be 'on the dole'.

Jarrow where, following the closure of a local shipyard, 80 per cent of the town's work force had become unemployed. On reaching London the marchers, whose object was to present a petition to Parliament, went to the House of Commons where, though they were cordially received, the petition was rejected.

In 1937, parts of Scotland, South Wales, West Cumberland and Tyneside were designated 'special areas', and attempts were made to create work in alternative industries. However, some families had already moved in search of better conditions. Many bandsmen migrated, and bands in southern England benefited from an influx of players from Wales and the North.

## World War II

The League of Nations had been created in 1920, but in 1932 Germany withdrew from membership, followed by France two years later. With Hitler now the Führer, in 1935 conscription was introduced in Germany and undertones of war were causing concern. In Britain, trenches were dug in London's parks, anti-aircraft guns mobilised, air-raid sirens tested, gas masks distributed and plans made for the evacuation of children. Aircraft were produced at an increasing rate from 1938, and by the following year factories were making tanks and guns.

A recruiting campaign for Civil Defence and the Territorial Army was launched in 1938, and in July and August 1939, *BBN* referred to the fact that many young bandsmen were serving in the militia. It appealed to the authorities to let them continue their musical training alongside military duties, pointing to the morale-boosting effect of bands in times of war.

Conscription had already been introduced, men aged 20 and 21 being called into the militia for six months' training. Thus, bands were losing players – temporarily as they thought – even before the war. Once war was declared, these losses became permanent. Immediately, 18- to 21-year-olds had to register, then the upper age was gradually increased, reaching 40 by June 1941. On registration, men on essential war work were exempted from military service; others, unless medically unfit, were in uniform within weeks.

Civil Defence covered a range of activities, many performed by members of the ARP.[3] At the outbreak of war a million and a half men and women were already involved, mostly part-time volunteers, many of them bandsmen. Initially the ARP looked after air-raid shelters, created temporary hospitals and prepared to deal with casualties resulting from air raids. Numerous buildings, including some bandrooms, were converted

---

[3] These were initials for Air Raid Precautions. Members were said to be 'in the ARP'.

into makeshift hospitals. Other Civil Defence organisations included the Auxiliary Fire Service, ambulance workers, special constables and demolition units. Thousands of bandsmen were involved in one or more of these. From September 1940 people also took turns as 'fire watchers' – watching throughout the night for signs of danger to buildings.

Hitler's troops marched on Poland on 1 September 1939 and two days later Britain and France declared war on Germany. But even though young men were being conscripted and civil defence forces mobilised, while factories turned to producing war-time essentials, children were evacuated and the nation plunged into a 'black-out' for fear of lights being seen by enemy aircraft, this period was called the 'Phoney War'.

It seems to have come as a shock to the brass band world to find the country at war. Nor was the size of the task appreciated. Some of the comments in the October *BBN* are worth noting. The Shropshire correspondent stated:

> From now, brother bandsmen, we shall be taking part in a different fight than the one on the contest field . . . By smashing this terror, we shall bring freedom to the German workers, and enable them once more to pursue the divine art of music.

To some the cancellation of the September contest was apparently a greater inconvenience than the war itself. For example, the Manchester and District correspondent felt:

> It was indeed very unfortunate that, owing to the disturbing national circumstances caused by a mad outlaw, the great historical September Brass Band contest had to be postponed.

On a more aggressive note, the Clydeside correspondent's opinion was that 'The mad dog of Europe has had his way, and now must be destroyed'.

Many young bandsmen were already in the Territorial Army; thousands were now drafted into the regular army and sent to France. Those left behind were doing civil defence work and working long hours if they were on essential war work; bands were plunged into turmoil. Where there was player shortage, 'pairing up' of bands was recommended, along with the intensification of training new players. Bands which had junior groups or learners' classes were at an advantage; many of those which survived were made up of men too old for military service and boys not yet old enough. Some disbanded, badly hit by a combination of call-up and war work; others survived by 'borrowing' each other's players.

Evacuation was now having an effect, with boys and girls in the danger zones being sent to safer environments. The conductor of Marsden School Band reported in *BBN* that a number of evacuees were anxious to join his band. Another correspondent stated that his son had been evacuated to Blackpool, but the boy had his instrument with him and was hoping to join a band. There must have been many such cases. One in particular was that of Denzil Stephens, who had played euphonium in a Salvation Army (SA) band in Guernsey. Following the German occupation he was evacuated, first to Wigan, then to Halifax where he entered and won a talent competition. In the audience was a member of the famous Black Dyke Mills Band, who arranged an audition for him.[4] The outcome was that, after a few months' private tuition, Stephens joined the famous band. His career is outlined later (see Chapters 7 and 11).

In Britain as a whole, entertainment came to a standstill on the outbreak of war but was soon restored. Bands were therefore able to participate in or organise concerts, arranged both for raising funds for charities and as a means of entertaining troops and factory workers. Some works bands, being on essential war work, could find jobs for their members, thereby maintaining high standards

Nevertheless, many engagements were cancelled, the Nationals were abandoned and the 'September' postponed. There was a petrol shortage, reduced train services and, of course, the black-out. Yet the band movement survived, contributing enormously to the war effort through concerts and patriotic marches, by providing entertainment and helping boost morale.

In 1940, Belle Vue ran its May contest as usual. However, this was the last major event before the big turn-around in the fortunes of war. The June issue of *BBN* announced further cancellations, amongst them Belle Vue's July contest.

Fewer people were now prepared to attend functions. A contest had been held in Edinburgh but, disappointed at the attendance, the Clydeside correspondent wrote:

> In my opinion the knock-out blow was delivered by 'old nasty' himself, who chose that week-end for the extension of his beastly aggression to the Low Countries, and put travelling out of the minds of many who consider Edinburgh a danger spot.[5]

The same correspondent noted that many bandsmen were working 12 hours a day, seven days a week – a reflection of the intensification of overtime in key industries.

Serious political miscalculations led to Neville Chamberlain resigning as Prime Minister and a new government being formed under Winston Churchill. This happened on 10 May 1940, the date on which Hitler's attack on the West began, with the occupation of Belgium and The Netherlands. He was also marching on France, heading for the Channel ports. Calais fell on 27 May and between then and 4 June the evacuation of Allied troops from Dunkirk took place. On 14 June the Germans

---

[4] See Taylor, 1983, pp. 96–8.
[5] *BBN* June 1940, p. 6.

captured Paris. Eight days later France capitulated and Britain stood virtually alone.

The next phase of war was the air raids, with German bombers attacking strategic targets. This began in earnest on 10 July 1940 with the bombing of convoys in the Straits of Dover. The first major attack on a British city came when, on four successive nights, bombers flew over Merseyside. On the final night 160 fires were started in Liverpool, home of *BBN*.[6]

London's Blitz began on 7 September, with an attack on the docks in the East End in which 430 civilians died, a further 1600 were seriously injured and thousands left homeless. This was the first of 76 raids, the attacks continuing relentlessly between September and the following May. Perhaps unaware of this, some months later, the *BBN* Manchester correspondent wrote:

> On Sunday, December 22nd and Monday, 23rd, we had to experience in Manchester . . . the worst blitz ever experienced. The wings of death and destruction never ceased to fly over and kept us wondering whose turn it would next be to go under. Most of the instruments of Baxendale's Old band went under but they are an enterprising band, and soon will be afloat again, I hope, for their band is the best in the City.[7]

Things were now looking desperate for Britain. As early as 11 September 1940 barges were amassed on the other side of the Channel, ready to ferry the German invasion force. Churchill likened the situation to the sailing of the Spanish Armada and appealed to all to be ready to do their duty – whatever it might be. Four days later the Germans launched what they anticipated would be the final onslaught, but as their bombers crossed the English coast they were fiercely attacked by Spitfires and Hurricanes. Further damage was inflicted on London but the battle in the air now turned in Britain's favour and on 17 September Hitler postponed his planned invasion. The Blitz continued, but the so-called Battle of Britain had been won.

In the October issue of *BBN* the Manchester correspondent, writing of the Belle Vue September contest, said:

> [It] will go down in history as the most critical musical event ever held at the historical Belle Vue Gardens, for whilst our British workmen's bands were competing for musical honours, those ruthless barbarians the Germans, were flying over London with their instruments of torture and destruction, dropping bombs.

There were many attacks in the provinces, often directed at factories. One of the most devastating was launched in November 1940 on Coventry,

---

6 Calder 1992, p. 154.
7 *BBN* February 1941, p. 2.

which suffered extensive damage in a ten-hour onslaught. Almost a third of its houses were demolished, a large section of the city centre destroyed and over 550 people killed. In addition, 21 factories were hit, 12 of them involved in aircraft manufacture. The one-year-old City of Coventry Band, though badly affected, was not deterred. The secretary had this to say:

> A broadcasting engagement is expected early in the new year, when we hope to prove to all that this recent brutal air attack on this City has not damped our spirit. We have been bombed out of two bandrooms, but as all the instruments and equipment were at the bandsmen's homes no loss has been sustained.[8]

There were also raids in Scotland, one of the most vicious being in Clydebank, home of Scotland's leading band, Clydebank Burgh. Here all but seven of some 12 000 houses were damaged, leaving 35 000 people homeless. In the April 1941 *BBN* a correspondent wrote:

> In answer to numerous enquiries, and to allay the fears of friends everywhere, Clydebank Burgh Band announce with great satisfaction that, so far as is known at present, no casualties have occurred amongst their players or committee. Material damage has, however, been considerable, and to a self-supporting band such as theirs, is very serious indeed. Their library of music, accumulated over their fifty years of existence, is almost completely destroyed, and as it contained many priceless gems, in manuscript, or long since out of print, the loss here is worst of all, for instruments, uniforms, stone and lime, etc., can be replaced, given the necessary money.

The official Clydeside correspondent confirmed that individual members had lost their all through the complete destruction of their houses, leaving them 'nothing but what they stand in'.

An editorial in the April 1941 issue stated that *BBN*'s premises were still intact, that business was as good as could be expected and that the firm was carrying on 'in spite of all the frightfulness that Hitler and his gangsters have inflicted on our city'. Other towns and cities were also bombed as the 'Phoney War' became the 'People's War'. In the country as a whole, by June 1941 more than two million houses had been damaged or destroyed and by September more civilians than military personnel had been killed. Even so, casualties were lighter than expected, mainly because of the widespread use of various forms of air-raid shelter – literally anything from a kitchen table to an underground tube station.

Band news from the capital was sparse, but a correspondent in *BBN* of November 1942 wrote: 'several bands around the North and East of London have been completely wiped out in the great London blitz, and they are almost void of bands around here.'

---

8  *BBN* December 1940, p. 3.

Early in 1940 yet another group of volunteers was assembled, to watch for signs of invasion and to harass the enemy if this happened. An appeal was made in May and within six weeks almost a million and a half men had volunteered. There were few weapons but the men armed themselves – with pick-axes, crowbars, fish knives, dummy rifles and anything else with which they might confront an enemy. The force was known initially as the Local Defence Volunteers, but in a speech on 23 July Churchill referred to it as the 'Home Guard' and this became its official name. Initially, bands helped with recruiting and led parades. Later, Home Guard bands were formed. Uniforms were provided and rehearsal facilities sometimes offered.

Halifax Home Guard Band was the first such band to broadcast, being 'on the air' in January 1941. It had been formed with the aid of instruments and former members of two local bands, along with the conductor of one of them, Tom Casson. Halifax remained one of the most successful of Home Guard bands and it was through a correspondent, 'Guardsman', writing of this band, that the following came to light:

> There has been much talk of the Home Guard bands being disbanded. It will therefore be of interest to know that this is not so. Mr Casson, conductor, has received the official statement on the matter, viz., that there is no objection to Home Guard bands providing the members are trained men and open to serve as combatants and the said bands are not upheld by the battalion funds.[9]

The Blitz subsided in May 1941, but though Britain was given some respite the war raged in other parts of the world and its effect on the lives of the British people became progressively more serious. Players continued to be called up and membership of civil defence organisations still affected rehearsals. However, the authorities had realised that working 12 hours or more per day for seven days a week merely led to illness, fatigue, and absence from work, and by now 60 hours was normally the maximum working week. Therefore, some bandsmen had more free time.

The war was now being fought in Russia and in the Middle East – many former bandsmen serving and dying in this theatre of war. Here the German commander Rommel, the 'Desert Fox', outwitted and frustrated the Allies until Field Marshall Montgomery was given command of the Eighth Army in August 1942. Two months later, in the battle of El Alamein, 'Monty' and his army inflicted the first major defeat on Rommel. This was seen by many as the turning point of the war and, for the first time since its outbreak, church bells were rung to herald the news.

In June, Hitler marched on Russia and Churchill immediately offered assistance. Churchill had, for some time, being wooing America, but the

---

9 *BBN* February 1942, p. 3.

only help he extracted was 'lend-lease', through which supplies could be delivered to Britain but payment not demanded until after the war. So far America had refused to fight, but when Japan bombed its naval base at Pearl Harbor in December 1941 it found itself in a war of its own. Germany then also declared war on America and the stage was set for the formation of the 'Grand Alliance' – Britain, Russia and America – the Allies. Britain was now no longer alone; the 'People's War' had become World War.

The war at sea intensified. Hundreds of thousands of tons of shipping were sunk, tens of thousands of merchant seamen losing their lives. This greatly reduced imports, leading to increased prices, shortages and rationing. March 1943 was the worst month, 477000 tons of Allied shipping being sunk but only 12 enemy submarines destroyed. However, another turning point was reached in July with the sinking of 37 submarines.

On the 'home front' there were frequent National Savings campaigns; fund-raising projects included 'Wings for Victory', 'Salute the Soldier' and a 'Spitfire Fund'.[10] Later campaigns included 'War Weapons Week' and 'Warship Week'. Bands were heavily involved in these. Annual 'Holidays at Home' programmes,[11] introduced in many towns, were not only a means of replacing the 'away' holidays which had been on the increase in the late 1930s, but were also a means of reducing spending. These programmes usually included a number of band concerts, talent-spotting competitions and even brass band contests, all of which enabled bands to 'do their bit' for the war effort.

The BBC launched a 'V for Victory' campaign, with a 'time signal' used to fill gaps between programmes, in which the rhythm of the Morse code sign for 'V' (. . . –) was tapped out on timpani. Beethoven's Symphony No. 5, permeated by this rhythm became, despite its Teutonic origins, a symbol of ultimate British victory. Churchill reinforced the message with his famous two-fingered sign of the letter V, whilst brass bands played 'Themes from the Fifth Symphony'.

Gardening now became an issue as, with imported goods in short supply, householders were asked to grow their own vegetables. Allotments were acquired and lawns and flowerbeds turned into potato patches in a 'Dig

---

[10] The cost of a Spitfire (one of Britain's most successful fighter planes) was estimated at £5000 and anyone – an individual, a group of people or a town – could 'buy a Spitfire' by donating this amount. Towns vied with each other as to which could buy the largest number and over a million pounds per month was contributed. This was probably the most successful money-raiser of the war.

[11] Large towns organised open-air events during the summer months to discourage families from travelling to the seaside for their annual holidays. These programmes became known as 'Holidays at Home'.

for Victory' campaign. *BBN*'s Birmingham correspondent bemoaned the fact that gardening was becoming yet another excuse for non-attendance at rehearsals.

On a more serious note, the same correspondent stated that two local bandsmen were reported missing in France, whilst the Worcestershire scribe mourned the death in action of a bandsmen from his region. In contrast, the Warwickshire correspondent told of a local bandmaster being awarded a medal for bravery. Early in 1941 it became known that the secretary of a band in the South had been recommended for the award of the George Cross.[12] Inevitably, however, there were regular reports of bandsmen being killed, wounded or taken prisoner.

Bands were now benefiting from their learners' classes. More and more boys and girls were joining senior bands, more and more learners' classes becoming junior bands. Young women also now featured in the news, many joining the classes.

Conditions on the home front deteriorated further in 1942. Supplies from the Far East were cut off, resulting in a scarcity of rice, tea, sugar and rubber. Food was already rationed and further waves of rationing during the first half of the year affected even more necessities. Clothes rationing was intensified and a so-called 'utility' range of garments introduced. Similarly, a shortage of wood led to the introduction of utility furniture. There was severe overcrowding in houses. House-building was at a standstill despite many houses having been destroyed by bombs; thousands which had been due for demolition in 1939 were still occupied.

Coal also became a problem. Many miners were either in the armed forces or working on munitions. Those left behind were growing older and weaker, so young men with mining skills working in other industries were made to return to the mines. British Summer Time became an all-year-round war-time feature in an attempt to save energy, with the introduction of 'Double Summer Time' during the summer.

Transport and travel by road was either difficult or impossible, with petrol in extremely short supply and issued only on proof of need. The total cars in circulation were down to less than half the pre-war number, while bus companies were both short-staffed due to conscription and hampered by the shortage of spare parts. There were no services after 9 p.m. in most areas. The railways had suffered through bombing and, despite using old stock, were short of locomotives and carriages. All of this seriously affected the mobility of bands as well as of individual members.

---

12  This was a medal awarded for outstanding heroism shown by a civilian. It was instituted by King George VI in September 1940 and was equivalent to the Victoria Cross, the highest award for military gallantry.

However, most families were better off financially through full employment, and family incomes were up as a result of overtime and the earnings of women. By 1942, though the cost of living had risen 43 per cent since 1938, average earnings had increased by 65 per cent. With fewer goods to buy saving was relatively easy. People were, however, spending more money on entertainment. The cinema was the most popular form and many saw at least two films per week. Competition from the cinema was often cited as one reason for a decline in attendance at band concerts.

Another form of entertainment was provided by ENSA (the Entertainments National Service Association). This organisation was formed just before the war and by 1946 was said to have given over two and a half million concerts to the forces and to industry. Some brass bands were used by ENSA.

Listening-in to BBC radio programmes increased considerably during the early war years. Amongst programmes of interest to bandsmen were *Music While You Work*, broadcast twice daily; *Works Wonders*, a lunchtime programme broadcast live from works canteens featuring talented workers, often members of brass bands; and *Workers Playtime*, a variety show which sometimes featured a band, especially if the works being visited had one.

The fuel crisis continued in 1944, partly because conscription meant fewer coal merchants, but in addition pits were producing insufficient coal. From 1943 young men of conscription age could volunteer for the mines instead of going into the forces but few took this option. In December it was decided to force the issue and from 1944 one young man in ten was sent to a coal mine. Those so conscripted, which included many bandsmen, were called Bevin Boys.[13]

The fledgling aircraft industry produced 120 000 aeroplanes during the war years. Some factories formed their own brass bands, the most famous being that of the Fairey Aviation Works in Stockport.

In January 1944 a new series of air raids was targeted on London. This 'Little Blitz' was but a prelude to the more devastating attacks by pilotless planes – the V1s. The first of these came during June and, for about a fortnight, 100 were launched daily. Literally flying bombs, they were aimed in the general direction of the target and flew until they ran out of fuel. Nicknamed 'doodle-bugs', they approached with a menacing roar, gave a splutter as the engine cut out and then, after a few moments' silence, swished to earth and exploded. By the end of August 80 per cent were being destroyed before they got through, but the remainder had killed

---

[13] These involuntary mineworkers were named Bevin Boys after Ernest Bevin, the then Minister of Labour, who was responsible for the scheme.

over 6000 – mainly Londoners. From September an even more deadly weapon was used, the V2 – a rocket which moved at such a high speed that it could not be intercepted. Within weeks, more than 1000 had exploded on Britain, killing or maiming people and destroying buildings.

Despite all the problems, by mid-1944 bands were looking to the future with confidence. Some were even advertising for players in anticipation of bandsmen returning from the war.

News from the battle zones was still not good, however, with many bandsmen missing, killed or taken prisoner. Nevertheless, many felt that the war was now as good as won. Landing craft, floating harbours and amphibious tanks were being made in preparation for the anticipated Allied invasion of France which began on 6 June 1944 – 'D-Day'. In the early hours of that morning British and American parachutists dropped into France. Seaborne troops followed and it was fortuitous that, as they advanced, they were able to neutralise the launching pads of V1s and V2s. Paris was liberated on 25 August and by September parachutists were pushing into Germany. In April 1945 Hitler reputedly committed suicide and on 7 May Germany surrendered unconditionally.

When Victory in Europe was declared on 8 May – VE Day – it had been anticipated for some time and was celebrated with vigour. Church bells were rung, bands played, and there was dancing and partying in the streets, with floodlights, bonfires and fireworks. Demobilisation of the armed forces was an immediate task, though conscription continued. Most conscripts served for about two years, though many bandsmen signed on as 'regulars' for three so that they could play in a military band.

It only remained now to bring the war in Japan to an end. This was essentially America's war, but Britain had been involved and many British soldiers were held by the Japanese as prisoners of war. The end was precipitated by the dropping of two atomic bombs, one on Hiroshima on 6 August and the other, three days later, on Nagasaki. The capitulation of Japanese forces was accepted on 2 September, when VJ Day was celebrated. World War II was finally at an end.

At home, housing was an enormous problem and a world shortage of food meant that rationing continued. Britain was virtually bankrupt and, whilst exports were low, government spending was high. Nevertheless, the mood of the British people was positive, and, to quote A.J.P Taylor: 'The spirit of the nation had changed. No-one in 1945 wanted to go back to 1939. The majority were determined to go forward and were confident that they could do so.'[14] However, servicemen returning from hostilities anticipating a grand new life were confronted with a country in dire straits. The winter of 1946–47 produced some of the worst weather for over half

---

[14] Taylor, A.J.P., 1975, p. 600.

a century and aggravated the fuel shortage. Unemployment rose, the standard of living fell and there were many strikes.

## Contests

As was pointed out in the Preface, contests are an essential part of the study of brass bands. The number of these peaked in the 1890s at well over 200 per year, but subsequent numerical decline did not diminish their importance. The early 1930s were difficult years for bands, but by 1936 conditions were improving. Concert opportunities for better bands were increasing and spaces left by their absence from local contests were filled by lesser bands.

The National Championships and the series of contests at Belle Vue formed the back-bone of contesting; the destruction of Crystal Palace by fire in 1936 was seen by bandsmen as catastrophic and the restoration of the Nationals at Alexandra Palace was warmly welcomed. With the onset of war the Nationals were suspended, as they had been in 1914. Some of the Belle Vue contests continued, but on a smaller scale.

Much information about Belle Vue contests is to be found in the results sheets which were published annually at the conclusion of the September contest.[15] In addition to this contest, which attracted the best bands, a July contest was inaugurated in 1886 to cater for bands of a slightly lower standard, the winner being invited to compete in September. In 1922, a single-section May contest was introduced, extended to four sections from 1931. From 1933 yet another contest was organised – for mission, school and small bands – taking place in February. By 1936, therefore, the sequence of contests at Belle Vue was as follows:

| | |
|---|---|
| February | Open to bands which had not won a prize at Belle Vue, 1931–35 |
| May | Class A, Class B (2 groups), Class C and Class D |
| July | Class A, Class B |
| September | Championships |

Twenty-seven bands competed in February, whilst the May contest attracted no fewer than 120. The July contest was smaller, with a total of 27 bands, but also incorporated a marching contest. Twenty competed in September, making a total of 194 bands playing at Belle Vue during 1936 – a typical figure.

---

[15] I do not know when these were first published, but the earliest in my collection is dated 1934. The last one appeared in 1973.

On the outbreak of war the February and July contests were suspended. There were five classes in the 1939 May event, reduced to four in 1940 then, from the following year, to three. In 1940, 44 bands participated, the winner of Section A receiving an invitation to the 'September'. A year later, the war having intensified considerably, only 24 competed. In 1943 this rose to 31 and the top three prizewinners were invited to the 'September'. The 53 entries of 1944 reflected improving conditions and the 1945 May contest attracted 58.

In August 1942 the first Belle Vue Marching Contest took place. It attracted 11 bands but, more significantly, a crowd estimated at 10 000. There were two sections and bands marched around the speedway track playing their contest march. On arriving at the adjudicator's box they moved into formation, still playing. They were assessed for deportment whilst on the march and for playing when they reached the box. At the conclusion all bands processed round the arena, formed up as one huge ensemble and played a short programme prior to the announcement of results. The 1943 event attracted only ten bands so in the following year there were additional classes, for bands from the Air Training Corps (ATC); 32 bands attended. However, the popularity of the marching contests waned and they survived only until 1948.

The Belle Vue 'September' was Britain's premier contest from its inception in 1853 until the end of the century. From 1900 it vied with the National Brass Band Championships. On the outbreak of war in 1939 the contest was first cancelled but then reinstated and held on the last Saturday in September, breaking forever the tradition of holding it on the first Monday. Only nine bands competed, but there were 13 in 1940 and, with improvements in war-time conditions, 15 played in 1941. One of the most enthusiastic receptions of the day went to City of Coventry, appearing after its recent Blitz ordeal and earning a creditable 3rd prize. Bands had the choice of one of three test pieces, all of which had been previous 'September' tests.[16] In 1942 entries went up to 19, with a choice of two tests. It was noted that several boys were now playing with these top bands.

Twenty-one bands played in 1943, the test piece being Denis Wright's arrangement of *Themes from Symphony Number 5* (Beethoven). In 1944, entries included three bands from South Wales, reflecting rising standards in that region, and, for the first time since 1938, a new test piece was specially composed, Maurice Johnstone's *The Tempest*.

John Henry Iles (1871–1951),[17] a Bristol-born businessman and amateur musician, initiated the National Brass Band Championships at Crystal

---

[16] The choice was between Brahms's *Academic Festival Overture*, Geehl's *Robin Hood* and Keighley's *The Crusaders*. The 1942 tests were *Pageantry* (Howells) and *Lorenzo* (Keighley).

[17] See my *Brass Roots*, p. 65, for an outline of Iles's introduction to brass bands.

Palace in 1900. He was the most dominant influence in the brass band movement during the 1930s, being administrator of the Crystal Palace Band Festival, all the Belle Vue contests (Belle Vue having come under his ownership in 1925), and owner of *British Bandsman* and the publishers R. Smith & Co. It was through Iles that the operatic selections of former years were replaced by new, specially-composed test pieces commissioned for major contests – from 1913 at Crystal Palace and from 1925 at the 'September'.

One of Iles's many interests was the Worshipful Company of Musicians, in which he had held the position of Master. In 1947 he founded the Iles Medal of the Worshipful Company, to be awarded annually for services to the band movement. (Appendix A lists recipients of the medal.)

He was a wealthy man with investments in various fields, in particular, the manufacture of fairground equipment. His wealth was often the cause of envy – even of suspicion – but his resilience, imagination and organising ability helped bands through times of trouble. Unfortunately, Iles himself was destined for difficult times. He regarded the film industry as an area of huge potential growth and invested in it heavily, but found it less lucrative than he had anticipated. His financial losses were such that in 1938 he was declared bankrupt. Undeterred, he set about making enough money to pay off his debtors.[18] He also weathered the storm caused by the destruction of the Crystal Palace, re-establishing the National Championships at Alexandra Palace. Iles remained a larger-than-life figure, organising the brass band movement from his office in London and appearing at all major events. He maintained two of Belle Vue's contests and guided *BB* and R. Smith's through the war years, being bombed out on several occasions.[19] As the end approached he looked anxiously for help to reinstate the Nationals as he was unable to bear the cost of mounting a new series himself. To his relief, the *Daily Herald* became sponsors.

The National Brass Band Championships, under the guidance of Iles, had developed alongside the Belle Vue series and at the last one to be held at Crystal Palace, in 1936, more than 200 bands competed in seven sections, all on the one day. The attendance was the largest since the 1914–18 war and the contest was followed, as was customary, by a massed band concert. Massed items were conducted by Iles himself, and there were contributions by some of the individual bands. The scale of the event was summed up by Iles in the souvenir programme:

> Over 5,000 musicians, belonging to 208 brass bands, will be heard by an audience expected to number over 60,000 at the National Band Festival to-day. This year's entries constitute a new high record. The

---

[18] Hailstone, 1987, p. 212.

[19] Ibid., p. 217.

instruments alone used in this mammoth musical event are worth £250,000. The uniforms worn by the bandsmen are valued at another £50,000 at least . . .

Iles also underlined the nationwide scope of the event – 36 English counties were represented, with nine bands from South Wales and two from Scotland. As 1936 drew to a close, there came the shocking news that Crystal Palace had burned down on the night of 30 November. Iles successfully reorganised the Nationals at the Alexandra Palace in 1937 and 1938. There were then no further Nationals until 1945.[20]

## Youth

During the mid-1930s there was a growing awareness of the importance of encouraging youth participation in bands, with youth sections in solo contests, special prizes for youths in contests which had no junior section and at the Belle Vue February contest a silver medal for the youngest player. The North of England was the principal domain of the earliest wave of junior bands, some of which were attached to schools and not involved in the competitive scene. Those which did compete were either independent or else spawned by a senior band where contesting was viewed as one of banding's principal activities.

The most successful of the early school bands seems to have been Yorkshire's Marsden Senior School, claimed to be the first ever school brass band. Formed in 1931, it began contesting in 1933 and its first success was at Belle Vue's 1935 February contest. In the following June, despite having 'fed' a number of boys into local bands, it was still 30-strong. All members were trained by the conductor, Tom Eastwood.

In 1939 Tom F. Atkinson[21] was running classes for the Bradford Education Authority. In the December *BBN* he wrote:

the Bradford Education Committee has taken the lead for the whole country in instituting instructional classes at day schools on all instruments. Lessons are free to scholars, are held following school

---

[20] For one who came into the brass band world purely by chance, Iles certainly had a profound effect on its progress. He was awarded the OBE in the King's Birthday Honours list of 1944, being the first brass band personality to receive such an award. His death was announced in *BB* of 2 June 1951.

[21] Tom F. Atkinson (b. 1899) was born into a Salvation Army family in Port Glasgow, where he played with a number of SA bands. He moved to Bradford and in 1923 became bandmaster of Great Horton SA Band. Transferring into secular banding, he took over as conductor of Bradford Victoria Band in 1936, when the former Bradford City Temperance Band adopted this name. In addition to his work with the band and his pioneering work in school instrumental teaching, Atkinson became an influential administrator and a respected adjudicator.

hours, each class being limited to six students to ensure really intensive tuition, and already scores of children are busy learning to play piano, strings, wood wind [*sic*] and brass instruments. I have six classes spread between two of the leading Secondary schools and other schools are clamouring for attention.

Separate to all this, Tom Atkinson's brother, Arthur, formed a boys' band in April 1940. By the end of 1941 he was in the forces but the band was making good progress. Known as the Bradford Boys' Band, it was regularly in the news, participating in annual concerts in the city and many fund-raising events for various charities. Arthur found positions in senior bands for his boys as they reached 16 and was proud of the fact that all leading bands in the district had ex-Bradford Boys' members within their ranks. He also had an interesting policy in that every boy spent some time playing a bass instrument, which both helped keep that section full and resulted in some boys taking permanently to the bass. He felt that even those who returned to their smaller instruments had improved their sounds through having played a larger one.[22]

In January 1940 it was announced that Lancashire's famous Besses o' th' Barn Band was to form a class for the teaching of musical theory and practice. The bandmaster, J.C. Wright, would take charge. Here was the embryo from which the highly successful Besses Boys' Band was to develop. This band was founded on 11 October 1943, Wright was appointed conductor, senior members of Besses gave private lessons and by May 1944 more than 60 boys were being taught.

## Organisations

### *The AOMF Scholarship*

The Alexander Owen Memorial Fund (AOMF) Scholarship was instituted in 1922 in Manchester, following the death of Owen in 1920.[23] Its object was to perpetuate his name by providing scholarships for promising young brass instrumentalists, awarded periodically to the winner of a competition

---

[22] Bradford Boys' Band was disbanded in 1967 and Bradford Youth Band formed. This was wound up in 1976 when Arthur Atkinson reached his 75th birthday. To try to reduce confusion it is necessary to explain that there were two Tom Atkinsons and two Arthurs. The senior member of the four was Tom F. Atkinson; it was his brother, Arthur, who was the key figure in the development of Bradford Boys Band. However, Tom F. Atkinson had two sons named Arthur and Tom, both fine euphonium players. Young Arthur played with Black Dyke for a time, whilst young Tom became a professional tubist.

[23] Owen was an early pioneer of brass bands. For some details of his life and career, see Newsome, 1998, pp. 54–7.

comprising musical theory, sight-reading tests and the public performance of an *air varié*.[24] The theory section posed most difficulties, good players often failing because they had neglected theoretical studies. Eighteen was the maximum age for entry and the Scholarship provided fees for two years' tuition from a teacher of standing. There were also certificates: the winner received the Alexander Owen certificate, whilst candidates placed second and third were awarded the Edwin Swift and John Gladney certificates respectively. (Gladney, Swift and Owen were three of the conducting pioneers of the brass band movement, known collectively as the 'Great Triumvirate'.[25]) Thomas Keighley, an organist, composer and teacher, was the first director of examinations.

There were constant funding problems. In 1936, the competition itself showed a net profit of a mere £6 12s. 10d. There were 16 candidates in 1938, and a summary of the accounts showed a balance of £63 6s. 5d., some two pounds lower than a year earlier, underlining the low level of support. Expenditure of £31 14s. 6½d. included £12 2s. in tuition fees.[26] Hardly a king's ransom!

The first war-time Scholarship did not take place until 1942. It was won by Miss Gracie Cole, making history by being the first lady competitor. (A list of winners of the AOMF Scholarship is to be found in Appendix B.)

*The Bandsman's College of Music*

The AOMF's Scholarship was the first serious attempt within the brass band movement to address the educational needs of its members. A sister organisation, the Bandsman's College of Music, appeared a decade later. It had no permanent premises but held examinations twice per year, generally at a school or in a band's rehearsal rooms. It was founded in 1930 with Sir Granville Bantock as President, the first examinations being held in Manchester in 1932.

As with the AOMF, Thomas Keighley was the first director of examinations. The principal award was the diploma of BBCM – Bandmastership [Diploma] of the Bandsman's College of Music. Candidates were required to pass a preliminary scoring test before proceeding with the examination, which comprised a written paper, a viva voce, a practical demonstration on a brass band instrument and tests in conducting. There was also a series of graded examinations for brass band instrumentalists.

---

24  This was a solo comprising an extended original introduction leading to a well-known tune – the 'air', or 'theme'. This was followed by a set of variations.

25  For details of the 'Great Triumvirate' see Newsome, 1998, pp. 48–57.

26  *BBN* March 1939, p. 4.

The BBCM flourished, but though many conductors attempted it few passed in the early years. There was an impressive list of examiners for the various centres, all of whom were unpaid. Two more advanced diplomas were introduced during the later 1930s – the ABCM (Associateship) and the LBCM (Licentiateship). Requirements for the Associateship were similar to those for the BBCM, but demanded higher standards. For the Licentiateship there was also a paper on canon and fugue, and an original composition was required. Spring 1937 saw the award of three BBCM diplomas and the first of a relatively few ABCM successes. The 1940 examinations produced one successful BBCM candidate but there were no examinations during the next few years due to the effects of the war.

## Local Associations

From as early as the 1890s bands within certain geographic regions formed themselves into associations. The Southern Counties Amateur Bands' Association appears to be the oldest, dating from 1893. Others followed and by the outbreak of World War II there were at least ten. Their chief function was to organise contests for member bands and to formulate appropriate rules. Several associations were formed or re-formed in the immediate post-war years. The Lancashire Brass Band Association became one of the most active. Ted Buttress (see 'Personalia') became the publicity executive of what, by 1951, had become the North West Brass Bands Association (NWBBA), with over 100 member bands. It negotiated a policy with Lancashire County Council whereby bands could apply for financial assistance. Through this scheme suitable conductors were paid on the same basis as teachers of night-school classes.

More associations were formed during the 1950s. Though most worked independently, neighbouring bodies could work together. For example, in Wales from 1956 there was a Welsh Association with affiliations from the South Wales & Monmouth, West Wales, and North Wales associations. A similar group came together in 1957 with the formation of the Yorkshire Federation of Brass Band Associations, linking the Halifax, Harrogate, Huddersfield, York and West Riding associations.

## The National Brass Band Club

Founded in 1925, the National Brass Band Club (NBBC) aimed 'to foster and facilitate the musical aspirations of those interested in Brass Bands, and to further their social welfare and musical advancement'. During the 1930s the Club instituted a code of practice for controlling the use of 'borrowed' players (no more than two at one time) and decreeing that bands should wear uniform and sit in concert formation.[27]

Unfortunately, some bands refused to abide by the code whilst others, trying to be fair, found themselves unable to compete because of a shortage of players or uniform. A contesting band which was under strength could either withdraw from the contest, play with less than a full band, or cheat. Judging by the letters column of *BBN*, cheating was rife. The uniform rule also created problems for bands which could not afford to buy uniforms for new members.

### The National League of Brass Band Associations

In 1934 the NBBC instigated the setting up of a National League of Brass Band Associations (NLBBA).[28] A list of 'matters arising' at meetings included such things as protests to the Performing Right Society (PRS) at the fees which bands were being asked to pay, discussions about borrowed players, 'poaching' and the feasibility of transfer fees, and protests to those municipal authorities which had reduced the number of band engagements or cut fees. There were also appeals to education committees to form instrumental classes and to the BBC for more broadcasts. The League ran 'inter-association' contests in 1936 and 1937, but they received scant support.

Amongst League business in the final pre-war months were representations to the railway companies for travel concessions, consideration of a scheme to obtain professional tuition for bands in remote areas and a discussion about adjudicators. Associations were asked to draw up lists of approved adjudicators and it was suggested that an Adjudicator's Association be formed.[29] By December 1939 it was recognised that the war was preventing some of the League's schemes from reaching fruition. However, in 1942 they launched a campaign in conjunction with the ATC for the formation of bands. Spare instruments were requested, along with the services of suitable volunteers to instruct the cadets. Liaison went well and links were also established with other youth organisations. During 1944 the League secretary corresponded with the Ministry of Labour regarding bandsmen who became Bevin Boys. An agreement was reached that, after training, they would be posted to a colliery where there was a brass band.

In 1945 proposals were discussed for an adjudicators' training scheme, the possibility of publishing a League Journal and the institution of a

---

[27] Brand, 1979, pp. 80–81.

[28] More detail about the origins of the NBBC and the National League is to be found in Cook, 1950, pp. 118–20.

[29] It was to be 60 years before an adjudicators' association was formed (see page 209).

series of theory examinations. Despite these initiatives, the League had little impact and, notwithstanding an announcement early in 1953 that it had decided 'to continue activities', the NLBBA came to an abrupt end in 1956 with a terse announcement saying that it had been dissolved.

## The National Association of Brass Band Conductors

During 1943 the NLBBA formed a National Association of Teachers and Conductors. A year later this was superseded by a National Association of Band Conductors. A further change took place in the spring of 1946 when this was dissolved and re-formed as the National Association of Brass Band Conductors (NABBC).[30] The well-known orchestral conductor Sir Adrian Boult was the first President and J.H. Iles the first Chairman. Founder members included Harry Mortimer and other leading figures of the movement. A quarterly magazine, *The Conductor*, was first published in July 1946. The objects of the Association were:

(a)   To promote the interests of Members of the Association and to provide an effective organisation of such persons
(b)   To organise and promote Conferences and Conventions of its members at which by Lectures and Discussions the progress of the cause may be fostered.

The executive council undertook responsibility for the constitution, membership, the organising of conventions and anything else of a national nature. The forming of regional centres began immediately; they were numbered chronologically in order of formation. No. 1 Centre, covering London and the Southern Counties, was announced in the first edition of *The Conductor*. The January 1947 edition announced the formation of No. 2 – the Northern Centre; No. 3 – the Midlands Centre, followed closely; the Western Centre (No. 4) appeared in May 1950 whilst South Wales (No. 5) was founded in 1952. The last centre to be formed, the Scottish, did not materialise until 1959.

## Conclusion

The 1930s brought mixed fortunes to brass bands as they did in other areas of life. Whilst, particularly in the middle of the decade, the better bands enjoyed a wave of exciting engagements, broadcasts and the making

---

[30] An interesting article on the origins of the NABBC by S.A. Early appeared in *The Conductor* of July 1959, p. 10. In the Spring issue of 1996 Ray Clark gives an account of the Association's history, from its origins until the 50th anniversary, celebrated in 1966.

of gramophone recordings, others struggled. In Lancashire, for example, many bands were badly affected by the slump in the cotton industry and the closure of mines. A group of six Lancashire bands had, between them, won 15 prizes at the 'September' between 1930 and 1935; the combined success of the same bands in the later 1930s were a 2nd prize in 1939 and a 6th in 1938. Many others struggled, with standards dropping as contesting became a luxury they could not afford.

The war years were even more difficult for bands, and it is to their credit that so many survived. The worst of the war was, of course, the Blitz, during which the loss of life and property was devastating. Despite the perpetual exodus of players to the forces, those left behind were kept busy, though there was little new music and no possibility of obtaining new instruments. Most bands stuck faithfully to the wearing of uniform – tunics which buttoned up to the neck, trousers with a coloured stripe down the seams and peaked caps. As new ones could be bought only at the expense of giving up coupons from the personal clothing ration, alteration and make-do-and-mend became the general policy, with purchase only in the case of absolute necessity.

The training of young players was crucial – both boys and girls. Once they were reasonably proficient, youngsters had ample opportunity to play – not only with their own band, but also with others within the vicinity; there were always vacancies. Contests were few and far between and often took on the nature of an entertainment rather than serious competition. Engagements were boosted by the constant round of 'war efforts', when bands were called upon to lead processions or to participate in fund-raising ventures.

The Home Guard was a blessing, saving many bands from extinction and providing outlets for players whose bands had folded. The BBC was another blessing as it provided paid engagements for the better bands, giving them an incentive to produce worthwhile programmes heard by thousands of people – sometimes millions, the world over. Many bandsmen felt that dance bands were given too much airtime. This was reflected by the Clydeside correspondent of *BBN* in April 1944. Worried about changing musical tastes, he expressed the hope that bands would not 'pander' too much to these, maintaining that 'swing music will ultimately begin to pall, and straight, or real, music come into its own again' – a common sentiment amongst older bandsmen.

From early 1945 there was a growing realisation that it was only a matter of time before victory came. Plans were formulated for the rebuilding and consolidation of the brass band movement. The activities of several of the organisations formed before the war came virtually to a standstill during the period of hostilities but most were up-and-running again either by the end of the war or shortly afterwards. Even though it was not completely finished until September, the rebuilding process was under way early in the year. Bands were responding to the victory celebrations and preparing for the return of those servicemen lucky enough to have survived.

# CHAPTER 2

# Bands and personalities

The early 1930s were difficult years for many bands, though the difficulties varied according to the economic climate in different regions. Paid engagements were scarce at first but became more plentiful, peaking in 1938. By then, however, war was becoming ever more imminent, confidence was falling and the nation had more serious things on its mind than band concerts.

The phenomenon of poverty living alongside affluence was reflected in the band world – some bands struggling, others enjoying an upturn in their fortunes. To illustrate the contrasting situations of bands in the 1930s, the plight of some bands from the North East are looked at briefly prior to a more in-depth examination of some of the more affluent ones.

There were many colliery bands in the North East, most supported from miners' social funds. The strikes of the 1920s had a chilling effect. North East bands which actually perished included Marsden Colliery, winners of the Nationals in 1925 but disbanded in 1930, and Hebburn Colliery, the 1904 Nationals winners, who were wound up in 1932. The two leading bands from the region between the wars were St Hilda's and Harton collieries. Harton, which had the distinction of being the first colliery band to win the 'September' (1919), though remaining a leading band locally for some years, never regained its former position nationally.

Following the closure of the pit in 1927, St Hilda's became a professional band, touring in the summer and playing for Bertram Mill's Circus during the winter. In May 1936 it opened its summer season with a nine-day engagement at Eastbourne, and closed it at Southport in October. However, the increasing popularity of the cinema led to fewer engagements. Further, a growing shortage of good young players made it difficult to maintain the band's high standards and at the end of 1937 the proprietor closed the band down. Though the demise of St Hilda's could not be attributed solely to the closure of the pit – it survived for a further decade – that was the start of its troubles.

### The 'Top Ten' bands – 1930–45

The criterion for selecting the best bands for consideration in this chapter has been their success at the two principal contests – the Belle Vue 'September' and the Nationals. In selecting them a 'league table' was assembled in which three points were awarded for a win, two for second place and one for third, during the years 1930–45 (Table 2.1). The bands are discussed here in the order in which they appear in the table.

*Table 2.1  The 'Top Ten' bands, 1930–45*

| | | Prizes won | | |
| | | 1st | 2nd | 3rd | Points |
|---|---|---|---|---|---|
| 1 | Foden's Motor Works | 7 | | | 21 |
| 2 | Black Dyke Mills | 1 | 5 | 4 | 17 |
| 3 | Fairey Aviation | 5 | 1 | | 17 |
| 4 | Abram/Bickershaw Colliery | 2 | 3 | 3 | 15 |
| 5 | Brighouse & Rastrick | 4 | | 2 | 14 |
| 6 | Wingates Temperance | 2 | 1 | 3 | 11 |
| 7 | Creswell Colliery | | 3 | 2 | 8 |
| 8 | Besses o' th' Barn | 2 | | | 6 |
| 9 | Munn & Felton's | 1 | 1 | | 5 |
| 10 | Slaithwaite | 1 | 1 | | 5 |

Virtually all members of the leading works bands in the 1930s were employed by their respective companies and were able to take time out of work for band engagements. Of course, if the player fell short of expectations he was not only out of the band, he was also out of work! Formed in 1900, Foden's Motor Works Band quickly came to the fore, with six major titles to its credit by 1915 and a 'September' hat-trick of wins (1926–27–28). In the nine years from 1930 to 1938 Foden's became National Champions seven times, including a unique double hat-trick, winning in 1930, 1932–33–34, being barred[1] in 1935 then returning to win in 1936–37–38.

As with other leading bands, contesting was but a small part of the band's activities. In 1936 Foden's spent five weeks in South Africa, giving two concerts per day at the Empire Exhibition in Johannesburg. In fact, Foden's spent most of their summers during the 1930s fulfilling extended engagements. These consisted primarily of week-long bookings. During August 1938 the band again played at the Empire Exhibition, but this time rather closer to home, in Bellahouston Park, Glasgow.[2] This was a

---

[1] We shall meet this phenomenon periodically. For reasons now lost in obscurity, three successive wins in a major brass band championship means that the band concerned is not allowed to compete in the following year. It is said to be 'barred'.

[2] The Exhibition this year lasted from 16 May to 15 October and featured either brass or military bands every day (*BBN* February 1938, p. 6).

vintage year, with a Royal Command performance at Windsor (where Foden's played for King George VI, Queen Elizabeth and the two princesses – Elizabeth and Margaret).

Such cheerful times, however, were to end. A dark war-cloud hung over Britain during the summer of 1939 and though Foden's fulfilled its annual round of engagements up to the end of August, including eight week-long engagements, a projected week in Hyde Park during September was abandoned on the declaration of war.[3]

Leading bands owed much of their success to their respective conductors and Foden's was no exception. A conductor attached permanently to a particular band was, during this era, known as the 'bandmaster' – a title commonly used in military bands. Some conductors specialised in contest preparation; working with a number of bands, they became known as 'professional conductors'. John Gladney, Edwin Swift and Alexander Owen, mentioned above, were three famous nineteenth-century 'professionals'. In the early years of the twentieth century the most successful professional conductor was William Rimmer (see 'Personalia'). On Rimmer's retirement from conducting, in 1909, William Halliwell (1864–1946) took his place as the most successful professional, securing, between 1910 and 1936, a record 27 major titles with his bands – 17 at Belle Vue and ten at Crystal Palace. The Belle Vue wins included two hat-tricks – one with Foden's (1926–27–28), and the other with Brighouse & Rastrick (1932–33–34). Halliwell had further successes with Black Dyke, Wingates and Munn & Felton's, and also conducted Clydebank Burgh. Following the Foden's hat-trick, he magnanimously suggested that its bandmaster, Fred Mortimer, should conduct in future contests.

The Mortimer family was the most successful and most influential family in banding. Fred Mortimer (1879–1953) had begun his conducting career in Hebden Bridge, Yorkshire, coming under the influence of both Rimmer and Halliwell. In 1910, at the suggestion of the latter, the family moved to Luton where Fred took charge of Luton Red Cross Band. There were three sons – Harry, Alex and Rex, all destined to become famous. Within four years Britain was at war and Fred Mortimer was in the army. After the war, with Halliwell as professional conductor, Mortimer senior as bandmaster and the sons all playing members, Luton became the leading band in the south of England and the only band from that region to win the National Championships – in 1923. Again at Halliwell's instigation, the family moved north to Sandbach in Cheshire to form the heart of Foden's Motor Works Band. Alex was the first to go, in 1924, followed by the rest of the family in early 1925. From 1929 Mortimer senior took over as the conducting supremo at Foden's, leading the band to its seven

---

3  Littlemore, 1999, p. 76

wins at the Nationals during the 1930s. Following the Belle Vue hat-trick he was invited to adjudicate at the next September contest. He was so alarmed at the noise from the fairground that he refused to take his band to Belle Vue again unless something was done about it – which, of course, it was not.

Despite his phenomenal achievements Fred Mortimer was no great conductor, but as a band trainer he had no equal and his influence on his sons was enormous. Alex was a fine euphonium player and he and his brother Rex were later to make their marks as conductors. The eldest son, Harry Mortimer (1902–91), was now becoming a significant musical figure. He played trumpet with the Hallé, Liverpool Philharmonic and the BBC Northern orchestras and also undertook some adjudicating at band contests and music festivals. Aged 37 when war broke out, he was well poised to take a leading role in the world of brass bands and, in fact, was to take over from Halliwell as the leading conductor. Additionally, in 1942 he became the Supervisor of Brass and Military Bands at the BBC.

One of the bands that Harry Mortimer would conduct in future years was the Yorkshire-based Black Dyke Mills Band. The history of this band goes back to 1855 when John Foster, a mill owner and amateur french horn player, took over the ailing village band of Queenshead (later called Queensbury), provided it with new instruments, uniforms and a rehearsal room, and renamed it Black Dike Mills Band (contemporary spelling). The band achieved early success, winning a mammoth band contest at Crystal Palace in 1860. By 1930 it had won the 'September' contest on ten occasions, and Crystal Palace (the series founded in 1900) twice. It was also in great demand for concerts and had toured Canada and the USA in 1906. Black Dyke remained one of the most consistently successful bands.

A 1938 report in *BBN* concerned a young trombonist, Jack Pinches. Pinches was a famous name at Black Dyke, a number of family members having played there. Family connections within brass bands have always been strong. Jack, who was then 15 years old, was the son of Harold Pinches, Black Dyke's principal cornet player from 1912 to 1926. Jack had joined Black Dyke Juniors[4] at the age of 11. In July 1937 he joined the seniors on second trombone, becoming principal trombone player in 1938[5] and the latest addition to Black Dyke's young team of key players, which included the 23-year-old cornet and euphonium soloists Harold Jackson and Rowland Jones. Jackson had first played cornet at the age of

---

[4] This band was formed in the 1880s. It was junior in status rather than in the age of its players.

[5] Later, Pinches became a Bevin Boy, working as a miner at Carlton Main Frickley Colliery, where he also played in the band. After the war he became principal trombone of the BBC Symphony Orchestra.

eight, joining a local band conducted by his father and graduating to solo cornet at 12. Three years later he became principal cornet player at Harton Colliery. It was here that he first came under the influence of William Halliwell on whose recommendation he became principal cornet player of Black Dyke, in 1934. Following a short spell with Besses, he served in the Royal Air Force during the war, but became a leading trumpet player in various London Orchestras in later years.[6] Jones was Welsh and had played euphonium since the age of 12.[7] He had a fine singing voice and in band concerts, having played a euphonium solo, his encore would generally be vocal. He later became a principal tenor at Sadler's Wells. It is remarkable that these three Black Dyke soloists became professional musicians. All were from families with brass band pedigrees, were taught initially by family members, and had no college training.

Jackson's successor as Black Dyke's principal cornet player was the 17-year-old William (Willie or Bill) Lang. Both Jackson and Lang were interviewed by the author, television producer and band historian, Arthur Taylor.[8] Lang had vivid memories of Black Dyke. All the members except three (including himself) worked in the mills; before he was allowed into the band, Lang's employer was contacted to ensure that he could take time off work for band duties as, like Foden's, Black Dyke was regularly on tour during the summer months. Lang tells how profitable this was. Most players earned less than £2 per week normally, but were paid £1 per day when with the band. Out of this they would pay about £1 7s. 6d. per week for full board and were therefore much better-off, as well as leading a more agreeable life away from the mill. All players received equal pay, though the soloists received annual retaining fees – Lang thought it was £30 for solo cornet, £20 for solo euphonium and £12 for solo trombone.

Each of these are key positions within a band. In addition to being the leaders of their own particular sections, the players are required to perform specific solo passages in the music played and are also regularly featured as stand-up soloists. The principal cornet player is a particularly important member of the team, being equivalent to the leader in an orchestra and often forming a link between the conductor and other band members. Collectively, this trio of soloists has a great influence on the status of a band, and successful conductors owe much to their effectiveness.

Both Foden's and Black Dyke, though remaining at the forefront of brass bands during the war in terms of broadcasts and concert engagements, chose not to attend contests. It is therefore difficult to compare their

---

6  Featured in the 'Profile' column of *BBN* in March 1938, p. 4.

7  Featured in the 'Profile' column of *BBN* in August 1938, p. 4.

8  Taylor, 1983, pp. 76–80. For this book, *Labour and Love*, Taylor interviewed a cross-section of brass band people of all ages and of all levels of experience. He then assembled a fascinating book, described as 'An Oral History of the Brass Band Movement'.

wartime musicality with that of their contemporaries. However, each remained in great demand. Both companies were involved in essential war work.

During the latter part of the 1930s Britain was building up its air force. Reference is made in *BBN* of April and May 1939 to new bands being formed at RAF schools and depots, and at aeroplane factories. Based near Stockport, Fairey Aviation was to become the parent company of a very famous brass band. In its fiftieth-anniversary booklet of 1987, Frank Smith, the first bandmaster, described how it came about. During 1937 Smith was one of Britain's million or so unemployed. Conductor of a local brass band, he learned that at the nearby factory of Fairey's there was 'every kind of sports club but no brass band' – despite having 14 bandsmen on the payroll. Smith visited the factory and spoke to the manager about forming a band. He was sympathetic and promised to talk to Sir Richard Fairey and the directors. Within a week Smith not only had a job, but also a mandate to contact the bandsmen, form a band and give a concert for the directors. Following this, it was agreed that Smith should hire extra players, obtain music and instruments, and give regular lunch-time concerts to entertain the workforce.

Success soon came the band's way. Engaging Harry Mortimer as professional conductor later in 1937, and entering the Belle Vue contests in 1938, they won 3rd prize in Class A in May, improving on this with a win in July, thereby qualifying to compete in September against the cream of bands.

With three wins and a 2nd prize at the 'September' between 1941 and 1944, Fairey Aviation established itself as the most successful war-time contesting band. Fairey's and Mortimer also enjoyed the distinction of winning the first post-war Nationals in 1945, now the *Daily Herald* National Championships. Being attached to an aircraft factory helped considerably, the essential nature of war work aiding the maintenance of a stable band of good players.

The Fairey Aviation works were located just south of the Lancashire coalfield, which boasted several colliery bands. One of these had been formed by the Abram Coal Company in 1919, Abram being a small village near Wigan. The managing director was Augustus M. Hart. Industrial relations at the pit were amicable and the ability to play a brass instrument was an advantage to anyone seeking employment.[9] In 1934 Hart's son became managing director of the company and president of the band. He was Lieut. Col. Ernest Hart, known as 'the Major'.[10] The band steadily

---

9  Information about the band and its history can be found in Keith Hollinshead's booklet, *The Major and His Band, the Story of Abram/Bickershaw Colliery Band.*

10  Of Hart, Harry Mortimer wrote: 'Just in case you were brought up on a surfeit of Victorian melodrama where the pit-owner was the villain of the piece, let me tell you about

improved under William Haydock, a talented local conductor. In 1935 Abram took 3rd prize at the 'September' and 6th at Crystal Palace, in the following year moving into second place at Belle Vue. December 1936 saw a change of name as Abram Coal Company had become part of Bickershaw Colliery.

Star players were enlisted and Major Hart took a personal interest in the band's progress. Bickershaw Colliery appeared in the prize lists as 3rd prizewinner at Belle Vue in 1937 and as runner-up to Foden's at the 1938 Nationals. Fred Mortimer had been engaged to conduct on this occasion but, following a dispute with Hart on the eve of the contest, he walked out and conducted only Foden's – which won the contest. Conducted by Haydock, Bickershaw's 2nd prize was no mean achievement considering that this was the year in which Foden's completed its double hat-trick.

By the time of the outbreak of war Bickershaw had a fine reputation for its concerts. Its wartime record at Belle Vue consisted of two 1st prizes, a 2nd, a 3rd and two 4ths. As coal mining was a reserved occupation, jobs could be found and Major Hart was very generous as far as the band was concerned. When it came to engaging high-quality players money was no object.[11] Third prize in 1944 was a disappointment and in an all-out bid for supremacy Hart engaged Harry Mortimer to conduct at the first post-war 'September' in addition to taking Fairey Aviation. However, Bickershaw was once again placed third.

Following the end of the war the band's fortunes took a turn for the worse. The new Labour government nationalised the coal industry with the result that, while Bickershaw won the 1946 'September', Major Hart realised that before 12 more months had elapsed he would no longer own the colliery. Early in 1947 he was, in his own words, 'sacked', as the National Coal Board (NCB) took over. The new management quickly discovered that additional money was being paid to bandsmen and this was stopped. Hart found alternative rehearsal facilities and paid the bandsmen the extra cash, but a 5th prize at the 1947 'September' was a disappointing reward for his efforts. He then presented each player with his instrument and uniform, thereby ensuring that the NCB would not get hold of them. Suddenly, Bickershaw Colliery Band had gone. The impact on Hart's health was significant, with tragic results. In the early hours of

---

Colonel Hart. Every morning he donned his boots and went down the shaft to see how things were going. He knew every man by name, and knew their lives intimately. An employee's wife who had given birth would look forward confidently to a bouquet of flowers from the boss – often it was the only grand bouquet any of them would receive all their lives' (Mortimer, 1981, p. 77).

[11] No actual figures have been quoted, but all band members were paid retaining fees in addition to their weekly wages. Leading players were, reputedly, receiving substantial handouts.

23 September 1950 he walked to a railway line near his home and was killed by a train. He was 59 and at the inquest into his death the jury returned a verdict of 'suicide whilst of unsound mind'.

Works bands were, in effect, owned by the company. Uniforms, instruments and music were provided. Most importantly, employment could be found for players. The opportunity of a secure job was a priceless incentive to a working man so these bands had enormous advantages. Nevertheless, there have always been unsponsored bands able to 'hold their own'. Brighouse & Rastrick is one. It made history in 1929 by winning both the July and September events at Belle Vue in the same year.[12] Then came the hat-trick – in 1932–33–34 (under William Halliwell) – and, following the statutory 'bar', a further win in 1936. Probably for financial reasons, Brighouse did not attend Crystal Palace during this period and with Foden's not competing at the 'September' the two great contesting bands of the era did not meet in either of the main events.

Though able to accept weekend bookings, unlike the works bands, Brighouse was only rarely able to take engagements which entailed a week or more away from work. In *BBN* of October 1937, Jimmy Squires, secretary, publicity agent, and second trombone player discussed the financial problems of a town band, maintaining that striving for money to keep the band afloat helped create a good atmosphere. He estimated that it cost on average £550 per year to maintain the band. It had been fortunate in that the ladies' committee had raised £400 during the previous 18 months.[13]

In the 1930s Brighouse was the most successful of all public subscription bands. During the war years, though not enjoying the same degree of success it still maintained a good standard, with prizes at five out of the six Belle Vue contests. It also made regular broadcasts and played in some high-profile concerts.

Wingates Temperance Band, another unsponsored group, was based in Westhoughton, Lancashire. It was formed in 1873 and was under the tutelage of William Rimmer for some 20 years, during which time it became the first band to win both the September and the Nationals in two successive years (1906–07) – the 'double-double'. Despite intense local financial problems, it maintained its position with the leading bands during the early 1930s, winning the Crystal Palace contest in 1931, the Belle Vue in

---

12 This feat, known as the 'double', has been achieved only twice in the history of the contest – in 1890 by Batley Old and in 1929 by Brighouse & Rastrick.

13 Bands such as Brighouse & Rastrick were known as 'public subscription' bands and they relied heavily on regular subscribers to help with the expense of running the band. Many also formed a 'ladies' committee'. This was not a committee as such, having no jurisdiction over band matters, but was an informal group of wives, mothers and friends which organised fund-raising events for the band's benefit.

1939 and several other prizes at both contests. Wingates also remained a popular concert and broadcasting band.

Located in Derbyshire, Creswell Colliery was another band which made a mark in the 1930s. Formed in 1899, it had won the September contest in 1925. Its best performances during the 1930s were at Crystal Palace, with 2nd and 3rd prizes in 1933 and 1935. Band members worked at the colliery and, along with some of the bands discussed earlier, they regularly undertook week-long engagements. During the war years Creswell was able to keep its players through essential work in the coal-mine. Its wartime Belle Vue record included 2nd prizes in 1940 and 1944 and a 3rd in 1943.

Yet another unsponsored band, Besses o' th' Barn Band takes its name from the Lancashire village in which it is located. It has one of the most colourful of all brass band histories, going back to 1818, when it was formed as Clegg's Reed Band.[14] During the early years of the twentieth century 'Besses' embarked on two world tours, each lasting over a year, playing in Canada, the USA, Hawaii, the Fiji Islands, Australia, New Zealand and South Africa. Alexander Owen was the conductor at this time.

Besses remained one of the elite bands throughout the 1930s despite modest contest results. Though unsponsored, in 1932 Besses visited Canada on a tour lasting from 13 August to 17 October, primarily to play at the Canadian National Exhibition (CNE) in Toronto. A concert programme in the writer's collection states that Besses gave 112 concerts and travelled 10 980 miles on this tour.[15] Besses won the September contest in 1931, but then had only limited success until, in 1937, it won again – for the fifth time in its history. Nevertheless, its name appeared in the top six places at Belle Vue six times during the 1930s and there were plenty of concert bookings. Besses faced massive problems during the war and survived mainly through the creation and success of Besses Boys Band (see page 19).

Though most industrial regions in England, Scotland and Wales boasted healthy brass band movements, many of the best bands were situated in Northern England. Exceptions included Creswell Colliery and the Northamptonshire-based Munn & Felton's of Kettering. This firm was part of the Northampton footwear industry. Its band was formed in 1933 'from the remnants of a Salvation Army ensemble'.[16] According to Bert Sullivan, a renowned euphonium soloist and one of the band's founder members, two Felton brothers left the Salvation Army group, taking six

---

[14] Clegg was the name of a local manufacturer in the cotton business. There were three brothers, one of whom played keyed bugle in the original band.

[15] From a concert in the Mayfield Cinema, Whitefield, on 24 November 1957.

[16] Taylor, 1979, p. 137.

other members with them to help form the new band. It was the Feltons who backed it, helping bring fame to the company. There were two star players in the original band: Sullivan himself on solo euphonium and Elgar Clayton (see page 146), the principal cornet player. Gradually the band acquired other experienced players, always giving them work which was unimportant so that they could be spared when the band went on tour. Stanley Boddington, a former SA cornet player, was appointed bandmaster from the outset. The band made rapid progress, winning the second section at Crystal Palace in 1934, only the second year of its existence, and taking the title 'National Champions' a year later. Munn & Felton's were also runners-up in 1938. They suffered considerably during the war years, however, and were unable to compete in any contests.

In 1929 the respected but much-feared local musician Noel Thorpe[17] was appointed professional conductor of Slaithwaite Band, a typical small-town band based near Huddersfield. It was largely thanks to his autocratic teaching style that the band prospered. The first important success was winning the second section at Crystal Palace in 1933. Many prizes were won at local contests, but there was a leap forward in 1937 when the band won Belle Vue's July contest and, at its first attempt, took 2nd prize at the 'September', narrowly missing the 'double', but winning a year later. These results placed the band in the front rank and many prestigious engagements came its way. Its glory days were short-lived, however, as it was hard hit by conscription on the outbreak of war.

## Bands with regional reputations

A number of regions spawned bands which enjoyed local contesting success. Yorkshire, with its long tradition of brass bands, had no shortage of good players or conductors. It was the foremost region in the 1930s, but many good bands were unable to break into the ranks of the elite because of the predominance of Black Dyke and Brighouse & Rastrick. Carlton Main and Grimethorpe Colliery bands were in this category, each earning a 2nd prize at Belle Vue (Carlton Main in 1942 and Grimethorpe in 1945). Yorkshire Copper Works Band, established in 1936 at the factory in Stourton, Leeds, attracted good players and won Belle Vue's July contest in 1937, but faced similar problems.

The Midlands also saw the emergence of some successful bands, in particular City of Coventry. This was formed in 1939, following a quarrel between Coventry Salvation Army Band and Headquarters. Despite

---

[17] Noel Thorpe died in 1970 at the age of 81. His obituary in *BB* (19 September 1970, p. 4) provides a detailed account of his 50 years in brass bands.

wartime problems, it quickly established itself as a contesting band, coming fifth at Belle Vue in 1940 and taking 3rd prizes in the following two years. Ransome & Marles Works Band, based in Newark-on-Trent, was not formed until late 1937 and so had little time to establish itself before the war.

In the South, Luton Red Cross Band, as mentioned above, was the only Southern band to win the Nationals. In the 1930s it appeared in the top six at the two major contests seven times. Enfield Central gave more than 100 broadcasts and secured 4th prize at Crystal Palace in 1937. Hanwell Silver appointed J.C. Dyson, a highly-successful Yorkshire band trainer as its bandmaster in 1929, won the London and Home Counties Association contest in nine successive years up to 1935 and was a regular broadcasting band. Morris Motors Band, also heard regularly on the air, was dormant during the early war years, but from 1943 gave lunch-time concerts in the works canteen.

The early and mid-1930s were difficult times for Wales due to problems in the coal mines. The Rhondda Valley was the main home of Welsh banding. Parc & Dare,[18] based in Treorchy, was a band with a history, but during the early 1930s it struggled for survival. Several players were in other parts of the country, busking, whilst those left behind lived below the breadline. By 1938 things were improving and 'Parc' was again appearing at local contests. A few miles down the Valley, the village of Ton Pentre was home to Cory Workmen's Silver Band. Cory's manufactured mining equipment so this community also suffered. Like Parc & Dare, the band already had a history of success but was dormant during most of the 1930s. It was, however, quite active during the war years.

The most successful Scottish band over the long term was Clydebank Burgh, with 15 Scottish Championship titles to its credit. It was a regular broadcasting band and in demand for concerts. Scottish CWS Band, formed in 1918 and well established by the outbreak of war, won its eighth Scottish Championship title in 1938. It also achieved 2nd prizes at Belle Vue in 1933 and 1934, could be heard regularly on radio and was in demand for concerts throughout Scotland.

For a variety of reasons (local economic climate, few contests within the region, no strong banding tradition, and so on) no other part of England was particularly rich in contesting bands during the 1930s. Durham perhaps showed most promise, with an upturn in the fortunes of some of its colliery bands; while Cornwall, somewhat remote in pre-motorway days, had two relatively successful bands – Camborne Town and St Dennis.

There were many disbandments during 1938, a reflection of the economic problems which persisted in certain areas. Some bands closed

---

[18] These were the names of two coal mines in the village of Cwmparc.

through loss of sponsorship or funds, others through lack of players. Lancashire in particular was experiencing difficulties. Well known at the time, Crosfields Soap Works, based near Warrington, was disbanded – without warning. The South West Lancashire correspondent of *BBN* broke the news in February:

> Very few who heard the once famous Crosfields give their recent broadcast had any idea that they were listening to the last performance of the band; not even the bandsmen themselves dreamed it would be the last occasion on which they would play together.

The same correspondent also pointed out that out of an entry of 200 bands for the Nationals, only eight were from Lancashire.

## Denis Wright

A few leading personalities from this era have already been mentioned and others are referred to in 'Personalia'. One who warrants special mention is Denis Wright OBE (1895–1967). His first encounter with brass bands was when he composed the winning entry in a competition, organised by J.H. Iles in 1925 to find a test piece for the Nationals. Wright's piece, now long-forgotten, was called *Joan of Arc*. Its composer very soon became deeply involved in band matters. In 1931 he relinquished his job as a schoolmaster to become General Music Editor for Chappell & Co. but from July 1936 he worked for the BBC, forming a band section within the music department. Here he was responsible for brass and military band broadcasts, in connection with which he used his skills to 'modernise' brass band repertoire. Much band music up to this time had been written for outdoor performance and was inappropriate for broadcasting. Wright made many transcriptions and arrangements in an attempt to correct this deficiency. Also in 1936, Wright became Honorary Director of Examinations for both the AOMF Scholarship and the Bandsman's College of Music, following the death of Thomas Keighley. He was regularly involved in adjudicating and guest-conducting.

Wright introduced many innovations. Two, both introduced in 1939, concerned the seating arrangements of players. He was anxious to get the best possible balance of sound through the microphones when 'on air' and to this end devised what became known as 'broadcast formation': with lower cornets and trombones to the conductor's right, upper cornets and flügelhorn to his left and all instruments with upward-pointing bells – horns, baritones, euphoniums and the basses – in front of him, in three rows. The second seating innovation was introduced at a massed band concert which Wright conducted in Skegness. Up to this time, bands participating in these events sat separately. Now they were treated as one large composite band with, for example, trombones grouped together, solo cornets together, and so on.

In 1933, Wright wrote articles on scoring for *The New Musical Educator*.[19] Two years later saw the publication of the first edition of his *Scoring for Brass Band*, the most successful of a number of books, which became the standard textbook on the subject. From being a complete outsider, Wright had become an influential figure. He was awarded a Doctor of Music degree by Edinburgh University in 1940. In 1942, he moved into the overseas music section of the BBC but this in no way diminished his enthusiasm for brass bands, or of his work with them outside the BBC. Wright was also a founder member of and one of the driving forces behind the NABBC.

## Conclusion

The 1930s was a time of change for brass bands and their music. The early years saw great problems in some regions, but most were overcome by 1937. Conditions peaked in 1938 but then waned, partly due to the bands' music and presentation becoming perceived as old-fashioned, but also with the prospect of war looming. Though many bands closed down, the growth of new industries and new communities led to the formation of some new ones.

An important trend was apparent during the final pre-war years – the emergence of female band members. This was not a total innovation, but was quite rare pre-1940. Gracie Cole (see page 83) was the name which first appeared with any degree of regularity. She was a cornet player at Firbeck Colliery (Yorkshire) and in 1938 was regularly winning solo competitions and making guest appearances. There were also several mentions of Betty Anderson (see 'Personalia'), a tenor horn player from Leicester. Both were to achieve fame as the male-dominated brass band gave way during the war to 'mixed company'. The war years were, of course, immensely difficult. However, those bands which survived were able to contribute to the quality of life of the rest of the population.

---

[19] Grace, 1945.

# CHAPTER 3

# Engagements, broadcasts and recordings

## Concert engagements

Following depressing times for many bands during the early 1930s, the year 1936 saw an upturn in their fortunes. Leading bands had been regularly engaged to play at holiday resorts but now engagements for all bands were more plentiful.

From around May there was a literal explosion in the number of band concerts. Foden's opened the London season in Hyde Park, playing two concerts per day for a week. Callender's Cable Works (see Glossary) were also busy, fulfilling week-long engagements in London, Southport, Glasgow and Dunfermline. Southport was a popular centre for brass band concerts, as the 1936 engagement list in the June issue of *BBN* illustrates:

| | |
|---|---|
| 30 May–6 June (Whit week) | Munn & Felton's |
| 7–13 June | Brighouse & Rastrick |
| 14–20 June | Black Dyke |
| 28 June–4 July | Wingates Temperance |
| 5–11 July | Foden's |
| 12–18 July | Pendleton Public |
| 26 July–1 August | Callender's Cable Works |
| 9–15 August | Vancouver Boys |
| 30 August–5 September | Harton Colliery |
| 20–26 September | Irwell Springs |
| 27 September–4 October | St Hilda's |

Morecambe was also popular, with full week visits by several bands; Scotland was a favourite venue and Scottish enthusiasts turned out in droves to welcome their favourites. Foden's, Munn & Felton's, Black Dyke and Callender's all played there during July. Reciprocal visitors included Clydebank Burgh, which played in the London parks, and Scottish CWS – playing at a Co-op Exhibition in Newcastle. Creswell Colliery spent a week in each of four venues – Worthing, Hyde Park, Alton Towers and Tunbridge Wells – plus ten days in Eastbourne and a fortnight in Brighton. Many places also offered individual engagements.

The pattern of engagements for 1937 was similar. This was the Coronation year of George VI and Queen Elizabeth and May proved to be exceptionally busy as, in addition to the usual engagements, there were extras due to the royal occasion. Several new bands were formed and business boomed for instrument makers, uniform manufacturers and music publishers.

At the Empire Exhibition in Bellahouston Park Glasgow in 1938, 50 famous bands were each engaged on a weekly basis between May and October. This had the unfortunate consequence that the Southport programme was significantly curtailed, never to be the same again – an early warning of impending decline. However, Manchester, celebrating its centenary, had some 295 band concerts in its eight parks. Other 1938 engagements included an appearance at Windsor Castle by Foden's, and Clydebank providing the music at the launch of the world's biggest ocean liner, the *Queen Elizabeth* – launched by the Queen herself.

Local bands played in parks, on Whit walks, at carnivals, flower shows and a host of other outdoor engagements. In a Jubilee Souvenir booklet published in 1942 by Slaithwaite Band its summer schedule was summed up thus:

> Throughout its fifty years' existence Slaithwaite Band has been bound up with the everyday life of the community – led its Whitsuntide processions, carnivals and gala days; taken part in Remembrance Day services, Drumhead services and 'Sings', arranged its own very popular carnivals and brass band contests, ushered in Christmas in the time-honoured manner, and enlivened many a summer evening with the strains of a lilting march.

This was typical of the activities of many local brass bands.

Whit walks took place in many parts of the country, though Lancashire seemed to be the only county where both Whit Monday and Whit Friday[1] were celebrated. The largest procession was in Manchester; here, in 1936, the Friday event featured over 20 bands, each leading its own particular Sunday school. From Oldham, stretching east into Yorkshire, every village had its own celebration, churches and chapels of different denominations engaging bands for their individual processions. The afternoon saw sports for the children and dancing for adults, with music provided by the band.

There were many other processions, including the annual Durham Miner's Gala.[2] That of 1936 saw over 100 bands leading the various miners' lodges. Armistice Day parades were, of course, ubiquitous. In these, the band led civic and military dignitaries to the parish church for a service,

---

[1] This is the Friday after Whit Sunday, that is, the Friday in Whit week.

[2] This, also known as the 'Miner's Picnic', was a high-profile political demonstration held annually in the county of Durham.

followed by a visit to the cenotaph, the laying of wreaths and the sounding of the 'Last Post'.

Band Sunday, usually the first Sunday in May, took on a variety of forms. *BBN* told of one band that took it very seriously, at Crewkerne in Somerset. Here, the band paraded through the town to the parish church, leading the singing during the service. After lunch it visited a hospital and local almshouses, and during the evening played in the market square. The day was summed up thus: 'A topping day – beautiful weather – splendid enthusiasm in band and public alike – finally, a good collection for funds'.

Playing at football matches gave bands their largest audiences. They would play before kick-off and again at half-time, some marching on the pitch, others playing from a convenient place in the stands. The opportunity to watch a match free of charge was quite a perk for band members keen on football.

Bands had mixed fortunes in 1939. However, one prestigious engagement came the way of the Callender's bands in the Summer of that year. The correspondent 'Observer' sent the following report to *BBN* in June:

> I was one of the 60,000 . . . present at Ken Wood [*sic*] (Hampstead Heath) to hear Callenders' massed Bands of about 55 performers perform in connection with the London Music Festival. Before the fireworks were due to start and whilst still daylight the bands entertained the crowd with special music . . . The musical director was Tom Morgan, and I noticed such personages as Toscanini (the great conductor) who went up to congratulate the bands, which was a nice gesture; also Adrian Boult and Kenneth Wright, etc. Truly a splendid tribute to our brass band movement and a great triumph for the bands and their conductor.

There were, nevertheless, complaints that some London park engagements were allocated to orchestras and dance bands. Foden's and Black Dyke both toured Scotland, but with reduced schedules. Southport made yet further cuts and summer band engagements were now clearly on the wane. Never again was there to be such a bonanza as bands had enjoyed up to 1938.

## The war-time years

Early in 1940 bands were busy with concerts, playing for the troops and raising funds for charity. Several bands in mining, shipbuilding and industrial areas were still at full strength; some gave regular lunch-time concerts to fellow workers.

However, many park concerts were cancelled. Manchester abandoned its park programmes from the outset. Leicester announced that because many children congregated round bandstands the Council felt that, should there be an air raid, the risk was very great, and its later park concerts were cancelled.

Reports by *BBN*'s London correspondent had appeared regularly up to September 1939, after which they were quite rare. There were, however, two reports of activity. One concerned a Home Guard band based in Dagenham. Formed 'from scratch' in April 1940, it had completed 12 park engagements and given several concerts, as well as fulfilling Home Guard duties. The other report was from Callender's. Though not quite in the London area, this band was feeling the effects of the Blitz. Nevertheless, they were giving charity concerts and entertaining the workforce with concerts in the canteen.

The Blitz ended in May 1941 and there was a slight upturn in the number of park engagements offered. Wigan, Bradford, Halifax and Huddersfield were amongst those towns that benefited. Edinburgh and Glasgow corporations both sanctioned concerts, but only for local bands. However, Manchester concerts were again cancelled, as were those in some other cities. Clydebank had been booked to play in the London parks, but this booking was cancelled.

From 1942 things generally looked more promising. Bands were invited to quote for Sunday engagements in several locations and Clydebank this year did play in London, with 14 concerts and a broadcast. In many towns park engagements were more plentiful. 'Holidays at Home' projects were now widespread, creating further engagements.

There was also a renaissance in Scotland. Glasgow Corporation overturned its music subcommittee's recommendation not to have any park concerts and booked several bands. There were also Sunday concerts in Edinburgh and Stirling, and Wednesday and Saturday concerts in Dunfermline.

Due to travel restrictions most concerts were local. Permission was needed from the Traffic Commissioner before hiring a bus and one Sheffield band had prepared for a Belle Vue contest only to find that it could not obtain the necessary permission. Conversely, Cory in South Wales reported a busy season. Somehow solving the travelling problem, it fulfilled week-long engagements in Hyde Park, Walthamstow and Weston-super-Mare, plus various 'Holidays at Home' engagements.

News of park concerts in 1944 was varied. In Glasgow a professional light orchestra had been formed to play in the parks, reducing the number of band performances; whilst Sheffield featured only one brass band during the whole season. On the other hand, Manchester opened its bandstands from Whit Sunday. Clydebank booked its usual week in London but expected cancellation because of the flying bombs. Remarkably, the band fulfilled the engagement, playing to surprisingly large audiences. All programmes were played in full, even during alerts. Following one evening concert in Hyde Park, however, the band played at a group of air-raid shelters but, returning to their places of lodging later on, 14 bandsmen found themselves without billets as a result of enemy bombing.

Massed band concerts became very popular during the war. One of the earliest took place in Manchester in April 1940 in aid of the AOMF Scholarship. Giving their services were Bickershaw, Wingates and Fairey's; Sir Granville Bantock conducted.

Two high-profile concerts took place in 1942, one in London and the other in Manchester. The London event was at the Royal Albert Hall and was in aid of the Red Cross. It featured Black Dyke, Besses and Foden's, plus the renowned soprano Dame Eva Turner. Sir Adrian Boult was guest conductor and the programme was given a patriotic flavour by the inclusion of *Land of Hope and Glory*. Denis Wright's arrangement of *Themes from Symphony No. 5* (Beethoven) was premiered, its 'V for Victory' motif adding to the fervour. The Manchester concert was announced thus in the March *BBN*:

> The playing of the Massed Bands . . . electrified the great audience at the Royal Albert Hall and to these famous bands has been added Fairey Aviation Works, the winners of Belle Vue's last championship. Thus over one hundred brilliant players will be massed and give some thrilling and outstanding performances.

The Beethoven arrangement was again performed and the audience was invited to join in the singing of the *Hallelujah Chorus*. In all, 7000 people attended and £500 was donated to 'Mrs Churchill's Red Cross Aid-to-Russia Fund'. Another Belle Vue Sunday afternoon event, in November, featured the four prizewinners from the 'September'. In the North East a massed band concert took place in Middlesbrough Town Hall, when four local bands combined in a concert in aid of a 'Prisoner of War' fund, whilst Brighouse, Creswell and Grimethorpe united in the City Hall, Sheffield, for a concert in aid of the RAF Benevolent Fund.

The Victoria Hall in Hanley became a regular venue and in 1943 two massed band concerts took place there. An innovation at the first was the appearance of Frank Phillips, the famous BBC newsreader. He was to have a long association with brass bands as compere to some of the most prestigious events, of which this was possibly his first. Here he not only looked after the announcements, he also sang.[3] A later concert took place

---

[3] Prior to becoming a BBC announcer in 1935, Frank Phillips had sung professionally. Nevertheless, his fame was in his announcing and he listed as some of his 'memorable broadcasts' the first news of the war, the death of Roosevelt, the dropping of the atom bomb on Hiroshima, the death of King George VI and the assassination of President Kennedy. (Information taken from an article by E. Vaughan Morris in the programme for the National Finals of 1970.)

in Glasgow, the bands including Clydebank and Scottish CWS. Parts of all of these concerts were broadcast, so the BBC was helping with costs. Many were organised by Harry Mortimer and Denis Wright. They brought prestige to brass bands, particularly through the use of guest conductors. Bantock and Boult have already been mentioned; other internationally-known orchestral conductors engaged included Sir Henry Wood, Sir Malcolm Sargent and Sir John Barbirolli. The last had this to say about a massed band concert he directed at Belle Vue in 1945: '[It was] One of the most stimulating events of my life: I cannot speak too highly of their virtuosity and sensitiveness. They rose to every effort and their diminuendos were superb.'[4] The use of leading orchestral conductors was no coincidence, as can be gleaned from this comment by Harry Mortimer:

> If asked what I considered to be my most important achievement in eighty years, I would like to be known as the man who brought the merits of brass bands to the notice of eminent players and orchestral conductors of my day. Not just brought them to their notice, but involved them in a way hitherto unheard of.[5]

Before the summer season of 1945 could get under way victory in Europe was achieved. The June *BBN* made the following announcement:

> This glorious and long awaited day in the history of our land brought many engagements for bands, and we congratulate all who kept their bands going during the war, and were thus able to take advantage of the opportunities the Day brought of taking part in the celebrations.

There were great celebrations, with hundreds of bands involved in parades, thanksgiving services, general rejoicing and efforts to raise funds for those soon to return from the war.

## Broadcasts

Many broadcasts were reported in *BBN* during 1936, though during the early part of the year there were complaints about the BBC's handling of bands. There was much criticism of programme content – mainly from older bandsmen who preferred the old operatic selections to music that would appeal to the ordinary listener. Reference was made during the year to over 80 broadcasts. However, enthusiasts felt that too few were allotted to the leading bands; broadcasts were a great shop window and fans were keen to have the best goods on display.

Bands located near London were given most of the nationally broadcast programmes as well as those for that region. Thus, a relatively few decent

---

4 Quoted in *BBN* from an unknown source.
5 Mortimer, 1981, pp. 88–9.

bands took the lion's share whilst the remainder – which included the best bands – were consigned mainly to their own regional programmes. Callender's was the band that benefited most from this policy. It was the best of the southern bands and, being within easy reach of London, commanded much airtime. However, even the Kent correspondent of *BBN* was concerned about this, writing:

> Callender's Cable Works' have given 126 broadcasts. This shows that Callender's are ranked as one of the finest bands in the country. But why is it Callender's get so many broadcasts? Surely we have other bands that could entertain listeners. No offence, Callender's, but I should suggest you alter your present name Senior Band to BBC Band or something to that effect.[6]

During the late 1920s Callender's had taken umbrage at some of their contest results, had ceased contesting and had commissioned a number of works for their own use. These were often featured in their broadcasts and, in Arthur Taylor's words, 'In the North, veteran brass band enthusiasts tended to turn off the radio in mid-concert – irritated by the new-fangled, modern sounds they heard.'[7] In February 1938 Callender's gave their 150th broadcast; up to this point Black Dyke had broadcast on only 28 occasions.

Denis Wright joined the BBC in July 1936. Though all bands did not share his views they did now have an ally in the Corporation. The number of broadcasts by the better bands rose and within a few years broadcasts were up to six or seven per week.

Broadcasts to the Empire were an interesting phenomenon. These, in the days before pre-recording, were made live, often in the middle of the night, sometimes with several announcers, each speaking in a different language. By January 1938 Enfield Central had completed three broadcasts to Canada and one each to Australasia, South America and South Africa. A correspondent in New Zealand reported that he had heard Hanwell and Morris Motors 'over the air'.

Early in 1938 representations were made to the BBC about the problems for bands (and their listeners) of daytime broadcasts. There were also complaints about waiting times between auditions and actual broadcasts. A correspondent claimed to know of two bands that had passed auditions 18 months previously but had not yet been offered a broadcast. The first was now defunct and the second reduced to 14 members. The most genuine complaint was that band broadcasts often started late due to the overrunning of earlier programmes and were then faded out during the final item.

---

6 *BBN* February 1936.
7 Taylor, 1979, p. 137.

On the outbreak of war, studios in London and several other centres were closed down and some programmes replaced by the playing of gramophone records. Though broadcasts restarted in October, regional stations remained closed, leaving just one national network – the 'Home Service'. Early in 1940 a second national network appeared, featuring programmes lighter in nature. This was called the 'Forces Programme'. One programme heard on the 'Forces' was *Music While You Work*. This was half an hour of non-stop, bright and cheerful music, broadcast each midweek morning and afternoon. There was usually at least one brass band per week in this series.

Denis Wright was relocated to Glasgow during 1940, but this did not affect the flow of band broadcasts. There were, in fact, 199 broadcasts during 1940.[8] Not that they were problem-free. On 20 December Black Dyke arrived at the BBC's Leeds studio but due to an air raid the members were ushered into a shelter and the broadcast abandoned.[9] This was not an isolated incident; there were regular complaints about broadcasts being curtailed or cancelled without explanation.

During 1941, in addition to routine broadcasts there were a number of special features. The first was a series of six programmes featuring brass soloists. Technically these were not band broadcasts because the soloists were accompanied by a pianist. But, with instrumentalists of the standing of Harry Mortimer, Jack Pinches and Bert Sullivan, the series created much interest. Another programme with special appeal consisted entirely of contest marches played by Bickershaw. This was also the year in which Denis Wright completed his *Concerto for Cornet*. Its first performance was broadcast from Glasgow in March; Harry Mortimer was the soloist with the BBC Military Band. Later in the year it was broadcast in its orchestral version, with the same soloist and the Scottish Orchestra, conducted by the composer. It was reported that in February 1942 Foden's and Mortimer gave the first broadcast of the brass band version of this concerto.[10]

A special series appeared in which the history of various bands was outlined in between musical items. Besses gave the first broadcast in this series, a former band member talking about its history. Black Dyke came next, with commentary by the bandmaster, followed by Foden's with Fred Mortimer, and Clydebank Burgh, whose history was retold by Denis Wright.

For Brighouse and Rastrick 1941 ended traumatically. The band had arrived for a broadcast in Leeds, but as the bus was entering the studio

---

[8] Newsome, 1995, p. 80; from Denis Wright's personal notes.

[9] Taken from a list of Black Dyke broadcasts in the writer's collection.

[10] Though this was reported in *BBN* of March 1942 (p. 3), Bram Gay assures me that it did not take place at that time.

car park a runaway tram hurtled into its rear, inflicting serious injuries on five bandsmen. They were rushed to hospital, and the broadcast went ahead with only 19 players.

Towards the end of 1942 Harry Mortimer succeeded Denis Wright at the BBC. He had been connected with brass bands since childhood and, having played with three major orchestras, knew many leading conductors. He was amongst the finest instrumentalists the brass band world had produced, was already creating a successful conducting career and was a member of one of the greatest banding families of all time. He was, therefore, able to become a powerful voice for bands in the BBC. The number and variety of bands 'on air' began to rise and both Mortimer and Wright became increasingly involved in 'broadcastable' events, particularly massed band concerts.

Nevertheless, the complaints persisted. Programme content was still not to the liking of the diehards and there were regular complaints about choice of bands, the times when they were featured and fade-outs during the final item.

An interesting letter to the *BBN* from Harry Mileman, a well-known conductor, attempted to stem the complaints, explaining some of the BBC's policies. Mileman had been involved in listener research for three years and in January 1944 he revealed some interesting statistics. The Corporation, he wrote, spent much money finding out what various types of people liked to hear and the times when they were available for listening. In view of shift work and the seven-day working week, programme times that may not suit some would be convenient for others. A cross-section of 800 people were interviewed daily. Those who liked brass bands had increased from 45 per cent to 55 per cent between 1941 and 1943, and those who disliked them had decreased from 30 per cent to 23 per cent in the same period.[11]

Mileman was later given a regular column in *BBN* called 'Radio Review'. It was basically a critical (some would say over-critical) résumé of programmes. Some broadcasts were now pre-recorded, not with universal success. Mileman told of one broadcast in which the overture 'Light Cavalry' had begun at the third bar! Nevertheless, the frequency of brass band broadcasts increased. In his review of May 1943, Mileman commented that there had been 32 during the previous month. His reviews came to an end when he took up the position of resident conductor with Scottish CWS.

In May 1943 Black Dyke gave its 100th broadcast. Included in the programme was its signature march *Queensbury* (Kaye), an arrangement

---

[11] The biggest 'like' was 60 per cent for cinema organs, whilst the biggest 'dislike', also 60 per cent, was for the symphony orchestra.

of Mozart's *Gloria in Excelsis* – the piece with which the band had won the 1860 Crystal Palace contest – and themes from Elgar's First Symphony.[12] Shortly after this Foden's also gave its hundredth broadcast.

In 1944 there was a dramatic decline in the number of band broadcasts and listeners were advised to bombard the BBC with complaints. These were numerous: broadcasts had slumped to two or three per week – some at inconvenient times, and there had been no bands on the Forces programme. Even Harry Mortimer came in for criticism especially when he wrote an article in *Radio Times* entitled 'The Future of Britain's Brass Bands', in which he defended the use of modern pieces, expressing the opinion that bands were currently going through a period of change. His most deadly 'sin', however, was to refer to bands of earlier periods as 'blow-hards'.

### Recordings

Commercial recordings during the 1930s were mostly made on ten-inch discs, played at 78 revolutions per minute (rpm). The late 1930s saw a decline in the number of releases – possibly a reflection of changing tastes, though Frank Andrews points out[13] that from 1926 electrical recordings were used extensively. These had an enhanced sound quality and enjoyed a long life in the catalogues of most major labels.

Most of the information in this section comes from *Brass Band Cylinder and Non-microgroove Disc Recordings 1903–1960* by Frank Andrews, a thorough and painstaking piece of research. He shows that in the years 1930 to 1935, 15 brass bands produced 99 recordings whereas, in the years 1936 to 1939 only nine bands featured, producing a mere 51 releases. St Hilda's, as both the colliery and the professional band, was the most recorded band in the earlier years, with 27 discs to its name. Foden's, Black Dyke and Creswell each made 13. However, from 1936 to 1939 Black Dyke came to the fore, but with a mere 14 discs to its credit.

The 1920s had been rich in brass band recordings, both in terms of the quantity made and quality of repertoire, which often included test pieces. The only such pieces recorded during the whole of the 1930s were *Severn Suite* (1930), *A Downland Suite* (1932) and *Kenilworth* (1936) – all made by Foden's. Other pieces of some substance issued in the years 1936–39 were the overture *Poet and Peasant* (recorded both by Foden's and Black Dyke), *The Three Bears* of Eric Coates (Foden's), the overture *Orpheus in*

---

[12] J.A. Greenwood had arranged abridged versions of both the Elgar symphonies. The great composer himself visited Queensbury in 1919 to hear the band play them.

[13] In a letter to the author.

*the Underworld* (Black Dyke) and Friedmann's *Slavonic Rhapsody* (Munn & Felton's). Black Dyke's remaining output consisted of marches, cornet solos, hymn tunes and novelty items, Foden's of marches, cornet solos, novelty items and medleys.

The growing popularity of massed band concerts is reflected in the appearance of live recordings. The first was of the Crystal Palace concert of 1932. HMV recorded these concerts each year until 1935, succeeded by Regal-Zonophone in 1936. In this year seven bands – Besses, Black Dyke, Foden's, Harton, Luton, Munn & Felton's and Wingates – were conducted by John Henry Iles and three discs were released. Repertoire, it must be said, was dated and unimaginative.

The other principal venue for massed band concerts during this period was the De Montfort Hall in Leicester where, from 1933, the annual contests ended with unnamed bands playing under the baton of the Festival's director, Charles A. Anderson.[14] These were recorded annually by Regal-Zonophone until 1940. Though they included nothing of real substance, the repertoire was more up to date than on the Crystal Palace discs. The remaining massed band recordings from the period included a 1936 studio recording by Foden's and Munn & Felton's – *Massed Brass Bands of the World Champions*, with Fred Mortimer conducting; a series recorded at Alexandra Palace in 1937 and 1939; Denis Wright conducting Luton Red Cross and two other local bands; and a 1938 recording of Baxendale's, Foden's and Wingates, under Fred Mortimer.

Inevitably, even fewer commercial recordings were released during the war years. The total number issued in 1940 was 31, falling to 20 in the following year. The principal recording band was Black Dyke. Many 1940 releases had been recorded in 1939 or earlier. Again, the choice of repertoire was not impressive.

Foden's was the principal recording band between 1942 and the end of the war, with 12 releases, including one to India and one to Eire. All the other Foden's wartime discs were recorded between August 1940 and August 1943, and released between January 1942 and June 1945. Items recorded include two overtures (*Raymond* and *Die Fledermaus*) made in 1943 but not released until 1945 and two Harry Mortimer solos (*Zelda* and *Hailstorm*), recorded in 1941 and released in 1942 and 1943 respectively. There was a Gilbert and Sullivan disc, and one containing Denis Wright's transcription of the *Introduction to Act 3, Lohengrin*, the remainder being made up of marches and other short items.

Black Dyke had a recording session with Regal-Zonophone in January 1942, resulting in two discs, released in September 1942 and November 1943. The band's signature march *Queensbury* is on the former and the

---

[14] This Anderson was uncle to Betty, mentioned earlier (and see 'Personalia').

overture *Impresario* (Cimarosa) on the latter. Fairey's also had a session, in 1941, producing four discs. One, released only in Australia, contained the Brahms *Academic Festival Overture*, with which the band had won the 'September'. The only other contesting band to record during these years was Ransome & Marles. They recorded for Decca in September 1943, producing four discs. Though again there was little of substance in this collection there was plenty to interest serious band listeners.

# Part Two
# Times of Change, 1945–80

# CHAPTER 4

# Introductory overview

## Social conditions

The end of World War II saw changes in all walks of life, not least in the world of brass bands. Thousands of bandsmen had been called to serve their country; hundreds did not return. Of those who did, many were no longer interested in banding or, after an absence of up to six years found it difficult to adapt to the ideas of a new generation of bandsmen and bandswomen. However, many bands were re-formed and there was an abundance of engagements and contests. Bandrooms that had been commandeered by the Civil Defence were now returned to their owners. Demobilisation proceeded slowly and as the call-up of bandsmen reaching 18 continued it was vital to continue training young players.

Nationalisation, introduced by the new Labour government, had a mixed effect on colliery bands. If the manager was pro-band all was well; if not, there could be problems. The biggest loss to the band movement was Bickershaw Colliery Band, which formerly had a pit owner who would almost have sold his soul for the band. As has been seen, it acquired a management that placed no value on it whatsoever, leading to its closure.

An important social change came about in the late 1940s with the introduction of the 'five-day working week'. Hitherto most employees worked until Saturday lunchtime. Now Saturdays were totally free for many workers.

The years 1952 and 1953 were marked by the death of King George VI (February 1952) and the Coronation of Queen Elizabeth II (June 1953). Like other major royal events both generated extra band engagements.

The later 1950s brought new difficulties, beginning in 1956 with the Suez crisis which led to petrol rationing and higher prices. In 1957 one correspondent wrote: 'In these days of high taxation and talk of bands struggling to keep going [there is] the depressing news of some being disbanded.' Petrol rationing was part of the reason for the closure of at least one band and the cause of many cancelled engagements.

Despite pressure for several years from the music industry, purchase tax on musical instruments remained at 60 per cent. After numerous petitions to the Chancellor of the Exchequer and much pressure on MPs, some relief was given in 1958, when it was halved.[1]

---

[1] *BB* 15 and 26 March 1958. See also *The Conductor*, April 1957, p. 10, and July 1957, p. 3.

Towards the end of the 1950s there were many advertisements in the band press placed by Antipodean bands seeking conductors and players, and there was a scheme through which Britons could emigrate to Australia, New Zealand or Canada. By 1957 some 2000 per week were so doing, many of them bandsmen or conductors. It could hardly be called an exodus, but it certainly reduced the number of bandsmen in this country.

*Developments and changes*

Nineteen-sixty was the start of a momentous period. It saw the end of National Service, the closure of over 2000 railway stations, the first man in space and the first man on the moon, and the introduction of colour television. The brass band movement had its own colourful history, with changes in the management of the National Brass Band Championships and damaging divisions within the movement. It was a time when the emphasis on engagements moved towards indoor events, when the lighter side of the repertoire underwent a minor revolution and when changes in the design of uniform took place. Old-fashioned tunics which buttoned up to the neck were replaced by those in a more casual 'mess-jacket' style. In keeping with The Beatles and George Best, many young bandsmen grew their hair long. Traditional peaked caps looked comical perched on top of a full head of hair, be the head male or female, and many bands dispensed with them.

There were a number of changes at the *British Bandsman*. Eric Ball (see page 131) had been editor since the death of Iles in 1951. First and foremost a musician, journalism was not his *forte*, but with help from colleagues he successfully ran the paper for 12 years. It often had a spiritual or even religious slant, but contained technical and historical features, and devoted space to news of bands in the top flight. News of the 'little' bands was not neglected, generally being found in the contributions of district correspondents. In March 1963 Ball was replaced by Alfred Mackler, a professional journalist with an encyclopaedic knowledge of bands. There was now more emphasis on technical articles and 'snippets' of news of local bands. Leading bands were not overlooked but they held a less prominent position. Mackler's term of office lasted only a year and by the end of March 1964 Ball was again in the editor's chair. However, in 1967 he took his final leave, being replaced by Geoffrey Brand (see page 134), who now became involved in the management of both the magazine and R. Smith & Co.

On the darker side, the coal industry was passing through difficult times due to the availability of alternative forms of energy – gas, electricity and nuclear power – along with competition from imported supplies of coal. Its labour force which, in earlier times, had been as high as 150 000 was down to a third of this by 1968, reflected in the smaller number of colliery bands. Again the North East was particularly badly hit, though some bands were saved through a change of sponsor. For example, Crookhall Colliery Band became Patchogue Plymouth, taking its name from an American company recently arriving in the locality; and Craghead Colliery became Ever Ready Craghead, through sponsorship by 'The Battery People'.

A sombre note was struck in 1970 as Arthur Butterworth[2] published an article in *Music in Education*, reprinted and spread over five editions of *BB* between 30 May and 27 June. Titled 'The Brass Band – A Cloth Cap Joke?', it was a hard hitting and critical appraisal of the route which he felt brass bands were taking. The preponderance of marches and novelty items and the reluctance to accept serious music into the repertoire were heavily criticised. Butterworth was also critical of bands' obsession with competition. His solution to the problem was to concentrate on educating young people coming into the movement, protecting them from traditional band policies. Though there was little immediate reaction, the article made people think and doubtless contributed to some changes in direction during later years.

In contrast to the Butterworth article, a two-part feature in *BB* early in 1971 entitled *The New Brass Age* highlighted the strengths of the movement, particularly in the area of youth. It also discussed the changing face of sponsorship – events rather than bands attracting much of it, the training of young players and conductors now taking place, a healthy widening of the scope of contests and vastly increased interest in the brass band in Europe.

The 1970s saw much political unrest in Britain, with regular confrontations between the unions and the Government, rising prices, rising unemployment, electricity rationing and for some, a three-day working week. Many brass band events were cancelled and a report that Bradford Council was to cease engaging bands for park concerts was symbolic of much that was happening.

Escalation of the violence in Northern Ireland created local hardships and there were more problems in the coal industry, with a total shutdown of all coal mines during 1972 as the miners went on strike. Edward Heath was the beleaguered Prime Minister; he was later to take an interest in brass bands. Amidst the financial problems value added tax (VAT) was introduced and purchase tax abolished. This was a blessing for company

---

[2] Butterworth was a former AOMF winner and holder of the BBCM diploma. After war service he became a professional trumpet player, first with the Scottish National Orchestra and later with the Hallé. He was also to become a noted and prolific composer, with several symphonies and concertos to his name. He composed several major brass band works, adjudicated at major contests and became music adviser of the National Youth Brass Band of Great Britain.

bands and those run by Education Committees, which could reclaim payments. Unsponsored bands, however, the very ones which needed relief, found none. In January 1973 the United Kingdom formally joined the European Economic Community. The 'Fanfare for Europe' that marked this event included concerts in York Minster and the Royal Albert Hall, London, given by Black Dyke and GUS (the former Munn & Felton's).

A new magazine, *Sounding Brass*, was launched in the spring of 1972. Published quarterly by Novello, its co-editors were Bram Gay (see page 160) and Edward Gregson (see page 123). Not restricted to brass band topics, it also catered for devotees of orchestral brass ensembles. It concentrated on technical, historical and biographical articles, with reviews of music and recordings. During 1979 the two founding editors resigned, finding that maintaining the high standard of the magazine was too big a drain on their time. Towards the end of 1980 (by which time it was owned by Rosehill Instruments) it closed down.

Another journal appeared called *Brass Band Review*. This was published monthly from January 1974 for about two years and was devoted to brass and military bands. Robert D. Alexander, at the time a relatively unknown businessman and former SA bandsman, was the publisher/editor-in-chief.

There were other positive sides to the development of brass bands during the 1970s, with better radio and television coverage and the introduction of several new competitions, including the European Championships, first held in 1978. This competition was symptomatic of the literal explosion of interest in British-style bands in Europe. European tours by bands had been almost everyday occurrences for a number of years but now, in the 'shrinking' world, bands were also visiting Canada, America, Australia and Japan. Conversely, bands from these places were coming to Britain.

Sponsorship now took on new dimensions. Though some works bands were still enjoying the patronage of their companies, sponsors were taking a greater interest in actual events. The mineral water company Britvic sponsored the Coal Industry Social Welfare Organisation (CISWO) contest in the late 1970s and Rothman's had its 'Brass in Concert' championships. From 1980 the National Bank of America sponsored the National Finals, increased prize-money being one of the benefits, with 1st prize in the championship section rising to £2000. The *Daily Mirror*, a leading newspaper, sponsored the British Open Championships. Perhaps more significantly, Boosey & Hawkes Musical Instruments recognised sponsorship possibilities with growing worldwide interest in brass bands. Seeing the highly successful Black Dyke as an important marketing tool, especially as it used Boosey & Hawkes instruments, they sponsored a number of its overseas tours. They also sponsored some of the New Zealand Championships, which meant not only financial assistance but also the presentation of new instruments. Yamaha did the same in Australia.

Both 1979 and 1980 witnessed the publication of a number of books about brass bands. No substantial history had appeared since the publication of Russell and Elliot's *The Brass Band Movement* in 1936. The first new publication was Arthur Taylor's *Brass Bands* (1979). Later in the same year Violet and Geoffrey Brand produced their *Brass Bands in the 20th Century*, a compilation of essays by leading authorities, including Geoffrey Brand himself, his wife Violet, Eric Ball and Edward Gregson. In 1980 Cyril Bainbridge, a feature writer on *The Times*, wrote a social history, *Brass Triumphant*. Towards the end of the year Wally Horwood produced his *Adolphe Sax 1814–1894 – His Life and Legacy*. Sax was the Belgian-born instrument maker who, through his family of saxhorns, contributed significantly to the development of brass bands. The same year also saw the publication of *Colour and Texture in the Brass Band Score* – an in-depth study of the subject by the highly respected SA composer Ray Steadman-Allen, and a useful reference book, *Music on Record I – Brass Bands*, one of the co-authors of which, Ray Horricks, produced many brass band recordings for Decca. For good measure, on the other side of the world, S.P. Newcomb, for seven years the editor of the *New Zealand Mouthpiece*, compiled his *Challenging Brass – 100 Years of Brass Band Contests in New Zealand 1880–1980*. A booklet called *The Magic of Black Dyke* was also published in 1980. This was by an avid fan of the band's, Frank Dean.

What might be called 'fringe' events were introduced during the late 1980s. Space forbids detailed discussion, but they included the BBC's annual 'Young Musician of the Year' competition, the first of which, in 1978, was won by Michael Hext (see page 84). The 'Euphonium Player of the Year' award was introduced in 1979, the first recipient being Barrie Perrins of the Hendon Band. There were Schools Proms in the Royal Albert Hall, National Festivals of Youth in Croydon and other events which, though not specifically for bands, created openings for them.

## Life for the bands

Civilian life was not easy in the post-war years. New instruments were still unavailable, there was little new music and uniforms could be purchased only through the sacrifice of personal clothing coupons.

New bands emerged and new personalities became established. Older leading figures had gone or were going (Halliwell died in 1946, Iles in 1951 and Fred Mortimer in 1953). The same was true of bands; some pre-war greats were still around but there were several new ones and the order of superiority had changed.

In 1951 the Festival of Britain helped create more engagements,[3] but the problem of bands being asked to give their services gratis caused resentment. In Wales three Welsh bands were booked for a massed band concert in connection with the celebrations. On requesting a fee they were replaced by two pianists!

There were regular criticisms of bands for their programmes and the sloppy way in which some presented themselves. *The Conductor* of January 1952 carried an article headed 'Whither Brass Bands?' that discussed the music played and the poor standards of some bands. Reports indicated that the popularity of brass bands was waning. For example, the Devon Education Authority had curtailed its Further Education music classes; at the Glasgow Charities Contest, of 17 bands that entered only 11 competed; and *BBN*'s Newcastle correspondent complained of fewer band broadcasts. In Leicester, park concerts were cut to an 'absolute minimum'. In the September *BBN* the Editor bemoaned the poor support, postponement and even cancellation of a number of events. But he also criticised bands for stagnation in their repertoire. The most scathing comment of the year appeared in the Huddersfield correspondent's column, quoting from the local press, 'our local bands [are] a contraption of wind and tin, disturbing the solitude of our Sabbath'. Strong words indeed from the heartland of brass bands.

Many bands were having difficulties remaining at full strength and the early 1950s saw the demise of several. Works bands became more common, however, though to what extent they were helped by their companies is not always clear. Whilst some provided employment for suitable players and appointed conductors and managers to act on the company's behalf, others simply provided rehearsal facilities, or perhaps paid a retaining fee to the conductor and some key players. Few of the new ones made it to the top and many were disbanded within a decade.

Negative comments abounded, reflecting further decline in interest. The Cumberland correspondent of *BBN* stated that there was not a single contest in his county during 1953. The High Peak correspondent expressed the opinion that bands were fast approaching a crossroads, with two problems in particular – increasing costs and prices which many bands could not afford, and the increasing problem of players being coaxed away from the 'little' bands with offers of retaining fees, paid engagements and expense allowances.

There was a scarcity of news from district correspondents throughout 1954 and 1955, though the demise of more bands was reported. There

---

[3] This festival, organised in 1951, commemorated the Great Exhibition of 1851 and demonstrated post-war developments in Britain. Special events were organised throughout the country, the principal site being on London's South Bank, where the Royal Festival Hall was built specially for the occasion.

were fewer new musical publications and there were frequent complaints of engagements being lost to 'canned' music. Despite a good summer and an upturn in the number of outdoor events the problems continued. Wingates were unable to attend the Area contest due to player shortage and Camborne had to miss the Finals through lack of money. Several contests were cancelled or suffered from poor attendance and it was observed that, for the first time in many years, there were empty seats in the King's Hall at the 'September'.

An abnormally large number of deaths occurred at this time. One of the most deeply-mourned was that of J.A. Greenwood, musical editor of Wright & Round, who died in December 1953 aged 77. He was described as 'the last link with the past' (see 'Personalia'). Deaths of local personalities revealed a shortage of suitable people to fill their places. A generation gap had been created by the war. Those in the age-range 20–30 in 1940 – many of whom were lost to the band movement – would, in 1955, have been 35–45 and well placed to take positions of responsibility.

Reports of band closures and cancelled contests were still common in the late 1950s, when additional problems were caused by the closure of mines, unemployment and movement of population. There were reports of poor crowds in Scottish parks and the reason given by one band for turning down offers of park engagements was that television had 'killed interest' in brass band programmes. This became a very real problem, reminiscent of that caused by cinemas 20 years earlier. By 1959 some parks were not providing seats for the listeners, and though this was a good summer and a successful season for some bands, others came in for criticism of poor deportment and presentation.

This was a bad period for works bands not in the top bracket. Several had their activities terminated by boardroom decisions. As Arthur Taylor put it: 'Management or workers decided that they [the bands] were uneconomic, and the money involved could be more profitably spent elsewhere.'[4] To quote just one example, in 1958 the highly successful Ferodo Works Band – winner of the 1955 Open – was closed 'for economic reasons'. Many subscription bands also disappeared around this time; 1960 witnessed the demise of the 96-year-old Irwell Springs, one of the great bands of the early years of the twentieth century. Amongst other problems, Clydebank Burgh withdrew from the Edinburgh Charities contest due to lack of finance, and it was announced that the famous Marine Parade Bandstand in Worthing was to be converted into a swimming pool. *Brass Band News* had closed two years earlier in 1958.

Conditions in banding in the 1950s were again reminiscent of the social conditions of the 'Hungry Thirties', many bands struggling but some

---

[4] Taylor, 1979, p. 163.

enjoying considerable affluence. Fairey's, Foden's, Munn & Felton's, Creswell and others were still regularly on tour, fulfilling engagements of a week or more. CWS (Manchester) (see page 88) was the busiest; in addition to its municipal engagements it participated in functions organised by the Co-op itself.

An interesting development in the presentation of park concerts was the so-called 'no sitting policy', introduced in the Victoria Embankment Gardens, London. There was, up to this time, no compèring in park concerts. When the band had finished a piece and the applause had been acknowledged, the conductor sat down whilst the bandsmen prepared to play the next item.[5] From 1955 in London's Embankment Gardens, conductors were provided with a microphone through which to talk to the audience and introduce subsequent items – but nothing to sit on between pieces. Leading conductors responded by developing their communications skills and concerts became both more enjoyable and more acceptable.

The term 'musical director' was now being used in preference to 'bandmaster'. More of these had undertaken some form of study and were therefore better qualified to deal with musical problems than were many of the bandmasters of earlier eras.

*British Bandsman* published its 3000th edition in September 1959. A series of editorials headed 'The Brass Band Scene, 1960', examined changes in the pattern of activities during the preceding decade. The park or seaside bandstand, it was pointed out, was now less of an attraction than in former times, when ordinary listeners had been fed selections from symphonic and operatic music such as they would have heard nowhere else. Now, at the touch of a switch, they could hear the finest artists performing these works in their original forms. Contests, formerly mainly a summertime activity, were now functioning all year round; new ones kept those bands which enjoyed contesting busy. The editor of *BB* pointed to differences between brass band contests and the wider competitive movement, where the main reason for competing was to receive criticism and advice from a professional adjudicator and to have the opportunity to measure standards. Brass band contests had, he felt, a sporting element, where the winning of prizes was all-important; he was not too happy about this. On a more positive note he praised those who worked 'for the benefit of young musicians . . . with their search for the meaning of musicianship as well as technical development'. Finally, he pointed to the continued importance of brass bands in the community – often required to participate in parades, fêtes, sports days, religious services and other events. These were important,

---

[5] It was not unusual for contracts to stipulate that conductors were not allowed to sit for more than three minutes in between items.

he said, requiring suitable music, well rehearsed, and with dress and deportment 'given due attention'.

During 1960 there were moves to form a Council of Brass Band Associations (COBBA). The prime movers were the North West Amateur Brass Bands Association and the Yorkshire Federation of Brass Bands. The idea was resisted in some quarters and did not come to immediate fruition. In late 1959 a new weekly journal, *British Mouthpiece*, had been launched. This replaced the now defunct *Brass Band News* as the 'alternative' to *British Bandsman* and gave its whole-hearted support to COBBA. The contesting scene became something of a hotbed during the 1960s, with what was virtually an attempted takeover of the Nationals. (This is all discussed in detail in Chapter 5.)

There was, nevertheless, from around the mid-1960s, an upturn in the fortunes of many bands and by the end of the decade new ones were being formed. There were also signs that the brass band was being recognised in other musical spheres. From 1968 both the Associated Board of the Royal Schools of Music and the Guildhall School of Music included brass band instruments such as the cornet, tenor horn and baritone in their syllabuses for grade and diploma examinations; and in the field of the competitive music festival there were classes for soloists playing brass band instruments, for brass band-type ensembles and even, in some instances, for full brass bands. An editorial in *BB* remarked on the healthy state of the brass band movement with so many young players entering, but warned of an urgent need for the training of conductors.[6]

Yet again, the years 1971–80 produced good times for some bands and disastrous ones for others. Bands which, during their respective heydays, had enjoyed the fullest of sponsorships were hit worst, with industry going through troubled times. Partnerships in engineering and mining faced the greatest dangers. Foden's and Creswell were amongst the hardest-hit of the major bands. Those such as Black Dyke and Yorkshire Imperial Metals, where sponsorship was less comprehensive, were safe for the time being. Non-sponsored bands such as Brighouse & Rastrick, Wingates Temperance, City of Coventry and Hanwell Silver enjoyed enhanced success as opposition from some of the former giants weakened.

## Instruments and instrumentation

Production of brass instruments ceased during the war as the factories undertook essential war work. Even in the months after the war it was impossible to acquire new instruments, as manufacturers were not allowed

---

[6] *BB* 5 July 1969, p. 1.

to make them without a licence. When production did begin, exports were the first priority and not until well into 1946 did supplies reach the home market.

Permission was now granted for the sale of a limited quantity of instruments, but they were subject to 100 per cent purchase tax. As late as 1949 this was still being levied at a prohibitive 66 per cent. In 1953, the matter was taken up with the Treasury and the Customs and Excise by the NBBC. A strong case was argued for its abolition, but not until 1957 was there a further reduction – to 30 per cent.

Converting to low pitch and increasing the bore size of the instruments were the two main changes to instruments during the second half of the twentieth century. During the 1930s all brass band instruments were made in high pitch and even in 1939, when the standard pitch of A = 440 vibrations per second was almost universally adopted worldwide, brass bands did not conform, remaining at a pitch almost a semitone higher than the rest of the musical world. In January 1944, Lockwood Home Guard Band gave a concert in a Huddersfield cinema. In order to combine satisfactorily with the cinema's organ, the band needed special tuning slides to put their instruments in tune with it. In due course bands were obliged to conform to the new pitch, but meanwhile some adopted this compromise, using tuning slides longer than those already fitted to the instruments.

From October 1945 there were a number of statements regarding the 'inconvenience' to Boosey & Hawkes, the principal manufacturers of brass band instruments, of having to make instruments in high pitch just for brass bands. Nevertheless, bands remained in high pitch for many more years, and on the rare occasions when they needed to they used low pitch slides. However, clearly the change had to be made. In *The Conductor* of April 1964 there was a report by Harry Mortimer of a meeting he had attended with representatives of the trade. According to him, the SA bands, worldwide, were already in low pitch, and for every instrument made in their own factory in high pitch for the home market many more were being made in low pitch for export. Boosey's then announced that they were to cease production of high-pitch instruments after 31 March 1965.

Black Dyke tried conversion early in 1965 but were disappointed and in July ordered a new set of low-pitch instruments. They were the first contesting band to do so, though a York SA band had bought a set in July 1964. Doubts were expressed when Black Dyke failed to secure a prize at the 1965 National Championships. The consensus was that lowering the pitch had deprived the band's sound of some of its brightness, but, as Myers points out, the increase in the bore size (to be discussed next) had also contributed to this.[7] Despite the doubts, both Crossley's Carpet

---

7  Myers in Herbert, 2000, p. 183.

Works (see Glossary) and Yorkshire Imperial Metals acquired low-pitch instruments early in 1966 and the move was given a boost when the latter won the 1966 Edinburgh contest. Next, CWS (Manchester) bought a set early in 1967 and when, at the Nationals in October, Black Dyke were winners and CWS runners-up, any remaining doubts were dispelled. Conversion by the whole brass band movement was then simply a matter of time.

The early 1950s saw a move to manufacture brass instruments with a wider bore, increasing the mellowness of their sound. Trombones were the first to be changed, the old narrow-bore instrument giving way to the modern medium-bore version. Whilst this was felt to be an improvement, the contrast between the tone of the trombone and that of the baritone was diminished, a fact which led to the redesign of all the lower brasses (baritones, euphoniums and basses). Once the medium-bore trombone was established, it was not long before a 'trigger' was attached to some models, enabling the instrument to be played either in B♭ or F.[8]

The bass trombone was problematical. The model used hitherto in bands was the G trombone – recognisable by its 'handle', attached to the slide to enable the player to reach the extreme positions. Though music for the bass trombone was written in concert pitch, its fundamental note was G; its slide positions were relative to the harmonic series of G and unrelated to those on other band instruments. So, whereas a tenor trombonist could transfer easily from the small-bore instrument to one with a larger bore, there was no such facility for the bass trombone player. As the G trombone did not balance up tonally to the medium-bore tenor, some players tried an instrument which had two triggers and could play in B♭, F or G. But the instrument was unwieldy and failed to provide a satisfactory solution. The answer was for players to relearn their reading and transfer to a large bore B♭ and F instrument. With the passage of time the double-trigger bass trombone became popular, extending the instrument's lower range even further.

\* \* \*

Even in pre-war times, for concert work there would always be some percussion, generally side drum, bass drum, cymbal and 'effects' – which could include triangle, castanets, wood block and various kinds of whistles. One player sufficed for these, though after the war some bands included a pair of timpani and possibly a xylophone, necessitating two.

---

[8] The trigger attached to trombone had the same effect as the fourth valve on the euphonium, enabling the instrument to play up to a fourth lower and also facilitating slide movements in certain passages.

Percussion was not allowed in contests for fear that it would conceal mistakes.[9]

Vaughan Williams's *Variations for Brass Band* (1958), unusually, had a part for celeste, but this merely doubled parts already being played. Its use was forbidden in the National Championships, for which the work was commissioned, and concert performances often relegate the part to the glockenspiel.

Scoring in most early original works means that performances lose little through the absence of percussion. With Gilbert Vinter, who revolutionised the 'original work' during the 1960s, it is different, and it is his writing which precipitated the introduction of percussion in contests. In his first contest piece, *Salute to Youth* (1962), as well as the percussion requirements of works by traditional brass band composers, Vinter also calls for wood block and tam tam. Though the work may be played without percussion, its absence is distinctly noticeable. By 1964 and *Variations on a Ninth*, Vinter's percussion demands are increasing, with band parts now for 'Percussion 1' and 'Percussion 2'. Vinter also requests temple blocks and xylophone, and the use of side drum both with and without snares. Different kinds of cymbals and beaters are also specified, and though the absence of these instruments does not leave any actual 'holes' in the music, their inclusion is becoming more critical. In Vinter's final work, *James Cook – Circumnavigator* (1969), vibraphones are needed and in the final bars there certainly is a hole unless timpani are played.

The non-use of percussion was now having a negative effect on contest performances and for Vinter's *Spectrum* (also 1969), the test piece for the British Open, the historic step was taken and the use of percussion allowed for the first time at one of the two leading contests. Though not making excessive percussion demands, *Spectrum* requires claves and bongos and a performance without percussion is lamentably incomplete.

It took several years for the National Championships to come to terms with the use of percussion. In 1973, championship-section bands were required to include percussion and it was introduced into the youth section in 1974. Following its acceptance by these bands, from 1975 bands in all sections included percussion.

Composers were now free to write integral percussion parts in their test pieces and they made increasing demands both in the range of instruments and in the abilities of the percussionists. The following shows some of the demands which were made:

---

[9] An exception to this was that percussion was allowed at the Edinburgh International Contest as early as 1952.

### Fireworks (Elgar Howarth, 1975)

| | | |
|---|---|---|
| 3 timpani | 3 wood blocks | Clashed cymbals |
| Tambourine | Xylophone | Triangle |
| Maracas | 4 suspended cymbals | Tam tam |
| 4 bongos | Snare drum | Glockenspiel |
| 4 temple blocks | Bass drum | Sizzle cymbal |

### Blitz (Derek Bourgeois, 1981)

| | | |
|---|---|---|
| 4 timpani | Clashed cymbals | Suspended cymbal |
| Snare drum | Tenor drum | Bass drum |
| Tam tam | Wood block | 5 temple blocks |

### Dances and Arias (Edward Gregson, 1984)

| *Timpani* | *Percussion 1* | *Percussion 2* |
|---|---|---|
| 30", 28", 25" | Snare drum | 5 Chinese temple blocks |
| and 23" | Bongos | Suspended cymbal |
| | 3 wood blocks | Tam tam |
| | Suspended cymbal | Bass drum |
| | Antique cymbal | Tambourine |
| | Bass drum (foot pedal) | 4 tom-toms |
| | Vibraphone (shared with perc. 2) | Xylophone |
| | Glockenspiel | Tubular bells |

On the premise of supply meeting demand, the standard of percussion playing in brass bands now moved forward by leaps and bounds.

The standard line-up for contesting bands remained at 24[10] throughout the 1930s, a period when there were virtually no changes to their instrumentation. The 24 maximum meant that most bands used only one 3rd cornet player. There were slight variations in the publication of band parts, as some village bands still included reed instruments. None of these were essential, cues being added to cornet parts. After the war, 25 players were allowed, which meant that bands could use two 3rd cornets as well as two euphoniums. In fact, modern scoring demanded the extra player. From time to time the issue of changing the instrumentation is raised. The fact is that the vast repertoire of music written for the specified instrumentation makes it increasingly difficult to contemplate change.

---

[10] The instruments normally used in a contest were: E♭ soprano cornet, eight or nine B♭ cornets, flügelhorn, three tenor horns, two baritones, one or two euphoniums, two tenor and one G bass trombones, two E♭ and two double B♭ basses.

## Organisations

### *The AOMF Scholarship*

The 1945 AOMF Scholarship winner was Bram Gay, second was Denzil Stephens, with Alan Stringer and Frank Bryce (see page 174), both of Besses Boys, taking the other places.[11] In 1946, the winner was Kenneth Dennison (trombone, Rothwell Temperance, and a future principal trombone and musical director of Fairey Aviation – see page 147). By 1951 National Service was creating problems: 16-year-olds were not entering, thinking that they would be competing against 18-year-olds, whereas most 18-year-olds, in fact, could not compete because they had been called up. It was therefore decided to reduce the age limit to 16. Elgar Howarth (see page 164) was the first winner under the new rule.

In 1960, the age limit of the AOMF Scholarship reverted to 18, but the examination was cancelled owing to insufficient entries, as indeed it was in several other years. It had obviously lost much of its appeal and was to lie dormant for a decade, the validity of its continuation in some doubt. Attempts made to revive the event in 1970 were frustrated by lack of entries. In 1971 Roy Newsome was appointed director of examinations and the Scholarship enjoyed something of a revival for a few years. Newsome was succeeded by Richard Evans (see pages 147–8).

### *The Bandsman's College of Music*

The Bandsman's College of Music attained considerable credibility in the post-war era and their diploma became a significant stepping stone in the education of brass band conductors. It was the movement's own diploma, though diplomas for brass band conducting were also offered by Trinity College and the Guildhall School of Music. The first BCM overseas examinations took place during 1956. These were in Australia and New Zealand.

In 1964 the College was in jeopardy, no examinations having been held for two and a half years. However, from 1965 they were revived and Sir John Barbirolli became president at the beginning of 1967. Following the death of Denis Wright in 1967, there followed another quiet period, but in 1975 George Thompson took over. This appointment led to the biggest entry for a number of years, with two successful candidates. Three were successful in 1978, two of them military bandmasters – a trend which was to continue.

---

[11] Stringer was to become principal trumpet with the Liverpool Philharmonic Orchestra.

*The National Brass Band Club*

Though dormant during the war, the NBBC re-emerged towards the end. In 1947, work began on fund-raising for what was to be known as the Bandsman's Empire Memorial Home and Shrine, an over-ambitious project, doomed to failure. However, a Bandsman's Empire Memorial Volume containing names of bandsmen killed in the war was compiled, lodged in St Sepulchre's Church, London, and dedicated in October 1953.[12] An Empire Memorial Fund was now set up to finance scholarships for promising bandsmen, but these were withdrawn in 1956 through lack of interest. Instead, grants were given to the National Youth Brass Band, the National Schools Brass Band Association and other organisations. In 1969, the Empire Fund became the Bandsman's Memorial and Educational Trust, funding various 'charities' within the band movement.

During 1951 the NBBC began awarding Honorary Life Membership to bandsmen with 50 years' service. By 1955 the Club had over 4000 members; facilities were provided for meeting colleagues at all Belle Vue contests and at some other events. A New Zealand branch was now established, holding its first meeting in Dunedin. Various other initiatives were instigated during the 1950s, including a database of band engagements and an index of bands, with times and venues of rehearsals.

By 1960 Sir Malcolm Sargent was President of the NBBC, whose current prosperity was, to a large extent, due to the enthusiasm and drive of the long-serving secretary, A.J. Molinari. Large numbers of new members were now enrolled but interest waned in the early 1970s. In 1974 there was a proposal to close down the Club but at a meeting in July the motion was defeated. In October, following the resignation of Bill England, who had succeeded Molinari, a new secretary was elected. She was Mrs Evelyn Bray – president of and the driving force behind Huddersfield Brass Band Association since 1958 and a former chairman of COBBA. Harry Mortimer became president and membership increased. There were regular reports during the next few years, with increases in the grants given to the various youth organisations and the organisation of a junior soloist competition. During 1979 Evelyn Bray was awarded the MBE in recognition of work for the NBBC but in 1980 concern was expressed over falling membership. The death of Evelyn Bray in 1983 was a severe blow, but the Club maintained its activities and in 1987 claimed that £7000 had been distributed by the Bandsmen's Memorial and Educational Trust since its inception – mainly to youth bands. However, interest once again waned and the Club gradually faded.

12 *The Conductor*, October 1953, p. 9.

## The National Association of Brass Band Conductors

Returning to the NABBC, 'No 1' was the most active Centre at first. The second issue of *The Conductor* detailed future plans, including lectures by Denis Wright and Eric Ball, a visit to a rehearsal of the Royal Artillery (Woolwich) Band, visits to BBC studios and the setting-up of a scheme whereby, for 10/-, student conductors could rehearse a band. Nineteen-fifty-six witnessed a project organised in collaboration with the London Symphony Orchestra Club. This was a 'Forum for Brass' – involving Sir Arthur Bliss and Harry Mortimer, with John White Footwear Band available for demonstrations.

Centres 2 and 3, trying to emulate No. 1, found themselves in trouble. The enthusiasm of the officers outweighed the availability of their members – too busy with their own bands to become over-involved in Association activities. However, in 1957 No. 3 Centre organised a competition for the Junior Quartet Championship of Great Britain – the equivalent of that which began in Oxford in 1945 (see page 109). This was to become an annual event, with a solo section added from 1959.

By 1950 Alfred Ashpole (see 'Personalia') was running an Adjudicators' Training Scheme. Trainees undertook ten 'Assignments', writing comments and giving unofficial adjudications. On their satisfactory completion, candidates were given a letter of recommendation.

Annual conventions alternated between London and the provinces. Speakers included distinguished guests such as Sir Adrian Boult and Antony Hopkins, a well-known writer and broadcaster on musical topics. The convention of 1953 was typical, taking place over a full weekend at the works of Hammonds Sauce Company, near Bradford. Following the Annual General Meeting (AGM), Tom F. Atkinson gave a lecture titled 'In the Adjudicating Box', Leonard Davies (see 'Personalia') talked about 'Scoring for the Brass Band' and Hammonds Sauce Works Band played the winning entries of a hymn tune competition. Sunday morning was devoted to a lecture-demonstration by three members of Fairey Aviation, whilst the afternoon saw Davies rehearsing a composite band prior to an evening concert.[13] The 1956 convention was perhaps the most ambitious of the period, being held at Kneller Hall, the Royal Military School of Music in Twickenham, with demonstrations involving both Morris Motors and Munn & Felton's bands.

From the 1960s the NABBC became actively involved in encouraging young conductors through workshops and competitions. The first competition was held in 1962, with the Finals in Bristol. Sir Adrian Boult

---

[13] *The Conductor*, April 1953, p. 2; and *BBN* January 1953, p. 3.

was a member of the assessing panel.[14] The winner was William Holding, who later emigrated to South Africa but is now back in England; other finalists included Peter Wilson and Betty Anderson. For the competition held in 1966, preliminary rounds were held in London, Stockport and Glasgow, with the Finals in Edinburgh as part of the annual Convention. Other winners include Frank Renton (1966) and Richard Evans (1967).

Conducting workshops have been organised by various Centres. No. 6 (Scotland) was the first, with events organised biennially from 1965. This Centre was, in fact, the most active of all at this time, largely through the initiatives of its secretary Peter Wilson and chairman Alex Thain.

In 1970 Geoffrey Brand directed a course for conductors on behalf of No. 1 Centre. This was to become an annual affair, replacing the Scottish event. The fourth course, held in Chelsea, attracted students not only from all over Britain, but also from the Channel Islands, Holland and Germany. These courses continued and, organised in London, were the most important regular activity of the NABBC during the late 1970s and were generally headed by army Directors of Music.

A National Brass Band Federation was formed in October 1954 to constitute an 'umbrella' organisation, linking the NABBC, the NBBC and the NLBBA. A former NABBC secretary became the Federation secretary and three members of the executive committees of each affiliated organisation formed the Federation, along with an independent chairman.[15] With the termination of the NLBBA in 1956, the Federation could no longer function and it was dissolved.

## The British Federation of Brass Bands

With its roots in COBBA, the British Federation of Brass Bands (BFBB) was established by the beginning of 1968. Sir John Barbirolli became President in 1969 and following his death a year later Harry Mortimer took over. This new body was seen by many as divisive and the work of 'selling' the Federation to the brass band world is still ongoing, as will be seen later.

During the AGM of 1970 the Director of the Music Department of the Arts Council of Great Britain, spoke about the functions of his department. He gave advice about approaching Regional Arts Councils when seeking funding and also advised about sponsorship. As a result, several concerts were arranged with sponsorship. The first took place in the Nottingham Playhouse, featuring GUS (the former Munn & Felton's) and being funded by the tobacco company of John Player. For its second concert,

---

[14] *The Conductor*, January 1962, p. 1.
[15] Ibid., July 1954, p. 4.

supported by the Northern Arts Association and a group of trades unions, the Federation brought together four Durham bands to perform in the city's cathedral. A third concert featured four bands from the Eastern Region of British Rail, along with a number of male voice choirs, performing in York Theatre Royal. Other concerts followed.

A highly commendable facet of the Federation's work during this period was the commissioning of new works. These were generally premiered in a Federation concert. With funds provided by the Arts Council the following works were commissioned and performed:

1971    Edward Gregson: *Concerto for French Horn and Brass Band*, premiered by Ifor James with Black Dyke, conductor Geoffrey Brand, Wigan, 13 March

1971    Gordon Jacob: *A York Symphony*, premiered by Men o' Brass, conductor Harry Mortimer, York Minster, 19 June

1971    Gordon Jacob: *Rhapsody for Three Hands and Brass Band*, premiered by Phyllis Sellick and Cyril Smith with Ever Ready Band, conductor Harry Mortimer, Middlesbrough, 13 February

1973    Gordon Jacob: *Psalm 103*, premiered by Black Dyke with York Celebrations Choir, conductor Geoffrey Brand, York Minster, 17 June

1973    Buxton Orr: *Concerto for Trombone and Brass Band*, premiered by Denis Wick (LSO) and Ever Ready Craghead, conductor Harry Mortimer, Durham Cathedral, 28 April

1974    Anthony Hedges: *Psalm 104* for Treble Voices and Brass Band, premiered by Hessle British Legion Band and a choir of 250 school children, conductor Harry Mortimer, Beverley Minster, 27 April

Other matters addressed by the Federation included brass band broadcasts. In an attempt to persuade the BBC to improve matters, the Federation met senior BBC officials to discuss a range of issues, including contracts. In the same year the Federation committed itself to setting up a National Grading System to run alongside the Belle Vue Registry. Plans were announced for a 'Brass Band Directory', the first edition of which appeared in 1976. With new editions appearing periodically, this has been one of the Federation's major successes.

In retrospect it may be seen that the Federation was trying to do too much too soon. Concerts and commissions were fine, as was the Directory.

Discussions with the BBC were all very well but, in fact, at that time hardly any of the regular broadcasting bands were connected with the Federation and many wanted to know on whose authority the Federation spoke to the BBC. The National Grading System and the Belle Vue Registry were both political hot potatoes and Federation involvement did nothing to bridge the gap between the two factions within the band movement.

### Junior and school bands: 1946–70

Fortunately, the lessons of the war years had not been forgotten and the continued development of young players helped the movement through further crises. Besses Boys was the most successful junior contesting band in the early post-war era, winning the title 'Junior Champion Brass Band of Great Britain' in 1945–46–47 (Figure 4.1). Not content with their achievements in these championships, they entered Class D in the Belle Vue May contest of 1947, winning 1st prize, and in the following May were placed third in Class B. After being barred from the Junior Championships for the statutory year, they returned in 1949 – and won again. The death of their conductor J.C. Wright early in 1950 was a serious blow but Fred Cowburn, secretary of the senior band and a major driving force, took over. William Haydock, formerly with Bickershaw Colliery, was engaged to take the band to the 1950 Junior Championships which it

Figure 4.1    Besses Boys' Band, British Junior Champions 1945, 1946, 1947, 1949 and 1950

won – for the fifth time. These championships then ceased but Besses Boys made several broadcasts and there were also prestige concerts, including a 1953 appearance at a massed band concert in Huddersfield Town Hall, along with Brighouse & Rastrick and CWS (Manchester), under guest conductor Denis Wright.

From 1955, in addition to functioning as Besses Boys' Band, several players were aiding the seniors. In 1958 they became members of Besses o' th' Barn Band, helping it to the runner-up position in the British Open Championships of that year. Nevertheless, the Boys' Band continued to function, doing stalwart work in producing promising young brass players.[16]

Another junior band was in the making in 1945 in the Yorkshire village of Grimethorpe. Here, the 'Schoolboys Band' was initially under the tutelage of George Thompson (see page 163). In 1948 they succeeded Besses Boys (barred because of their hat-trick) as Junior National Champions, winning at their first attempt. This band faded during the early 1950s but was re-formed in 1960 as Grimethorpe Juniors, specifically for sons and daughters of men employed at the colliery. Ken Johnson, soprano cornettist with the senior band, was appointed conductor in 1962, when the average age was 14. In the following year they took 2nd prize in the Area fourth section, qualifying for a place in the Finals and in 1964 they won the Junior Shield section in Belle Vue's Spring Festival. By 1965 Bill Lippeatt was conducting and the band was in the third section, winning its Area contest and also the Senior Trophy at Belle Vue. Through the Area win they were invited to play in the twin concerts following the National Championships in the Royal Albert Hall. They also made several broadcasts and television appearances, and produced a commercial recording.

Six of the boys became members of the senior band. These included Peter Roberts (soprano), Stan Lippeatt – the conductor's son – (flugelhorn) and David Moore (euphonium).[17] There were further changes of conductor with Barry Thompson,[18] himself a product of the earlier Grimethorpe Juniors, taking the band from 1969.[19]

Bradford became an important centre for school and youth bands. In addition to Bradford Boys' Band and the work being done in schools by

---

[16] Much of this information comes from the sleeve notes of a cassette released in 1993 to commemorate the band's 50th anniversary.

[17] See 'Personalia' for information about Roberts; page 291 for Lippeatt and for Moore.

[18] Thompson played with Carlton Main, Grimethorpe Colliery and Morris Motors prior to taking up conducting and, later, adjudicating.

[19] Much of this information comes from the programme of a concert celebrating the band's 25th anniversary, in 1985. See also the report in *BB* of 13 July 1985, p. 5.

Tom F. Atkinson, on the outskirts of the city (see page 18), Hall Royd Methodists Junior Band was regularly in the news, with 33 members, eight learners and its dynamic founder/conductor Ralph Nellist. There was also a band at Highfield Secondary School – conducted by the school's music teacher Miss Elizabeth Lumb. In the autumn of 1947 a massed junior band concert was mounted in which the three bands came together, some 80 boys playing under the baton of Denis Wright. A further massed boys' band concert was held in Leeds Town Hall during the autumn of 1950, organised by the NABBC.

In 1949 another junior band appeared in Lancashire – Wigan Boys' Club Band, tutored by William Haydock (the former Bickershaw conductor). It began with him teaching a group of beginners but it was not long before the band was established and attracting engagements. Over the next few years many fine players were produced. As there was not one particular band to feed, players dispersed over a wide field and the whole of the local banding community benefited from its work.[20] Gradually it ceased to be a boys' band and in 1973 became known as Wigan & District Brass Band.

A host of other junior bands were formed. London and Southern England became a hotbed of activity for school and youth bands in the late 1940s. Featherstone School Band, formed in 1948 in Southall, Middlesex, was just one which was regularly in the news. Kenneth Cook, composer, conductor, teacher and author, was music master at the school for some eight years and was a powerful influence. During 1964 this band embarked on a spectacular trans-Atlantic tour, playing in Boston, Detroit, Pittsburgh, Washington, Philadelphia and New York. They also crossed into Canada, returning there in 1967 for a three-week tour.[21]

Oakmead School Band, formed in 1958 by Courtney Bosanko,[22] was also widely travelled, visiting Switzerland, Norway, Denmark, Sweden and Italy between 1961 and 1968. During 1979, Oakmead's twenty-first anniversary year, the band undertook a tour of Iceland – probably the first British brass band to venture so far north.[23]

## The National School Brass Band Association

The National School Brass Band Association (NSBBA) was formed in 1952 to cater for the needs of a growing number of school brass bands. The

---

[20] This information is taken from an article by John Maines in *Brass Review*, Spring 2002.

[21] *BB* 15 July 1967, p. 4.

[22] Bosanko had an SA background and became a driving force in southern England's banding scene. He was awarded the MBE, and died in 1986, aged 75.

[23] *BB* 15 December 1979, p. 4 – with good history.

co-founders were Kenneth Cook and Lance Caisley – the latter was headmaster of Boscombe Secondary School and also became the first editor of the Association's quarterly magazine, *The Trumpeter*. An Advisory Council was formed, comprising musicians and teachers with a variety of backgrounds. By 1956 there were 30 bands in membership.

One of the first problems to be addressed was the provision of appropriate music; it was fortuitous that one member of the Advisory Council, Max Hinrichsen, was a music publisher. In collaboration with the Association he published a series of 'journals' which formed the basis of a repertoire for school brass bands. These were supplemented in 1954 with a handbook written jointly by Cook and Caisley, *Music Through the Brass Band*. This was targeted at teachers wishing not only to form a brass band, but literally to teach music through it. Lists of appropriate music from other publishers were also drawn up.

The Association organised courses – designed to help both music teachers who knew little about brass bands and band people who needed guidance in teaching methods. There were also regular festivals at both local and national levels. These were strictly non-competitive and provided opportunities for bands to play under musicians skilled both in teaching and band musicianship.

The NSBBA extended its activities during the 1970s, its first major venture being the commissioning of a new work, *Song of Freedom* – for brass band and treble voices – by the distinguished British composer Malcolm Arnold. Pupils submitted poems on the subject of 'Freedom' and extracts were chosen by Arnold as the text for the work. The first performance was given at a concert celebrating the Association's twenty-first anniversary in 1973, by a choir of 150 girls from Netteswell schools and the Netteswell Youth Band. The composer conducted. In 1975, the Association announced its first National Festival for primary school bands – reflecting the increase in brass band activity at this level. In May of the same year the Association launched a composers' competition. A group of well-known composers chaired by Sir Lennox Berkeley assessed the entries. Four selected works were performed at the 1976 National Festival, held in London, with a prize of £500 and guaranteed publication of the winning work. The results were:

| | | |
|---|---|---|
| 1st | *Concert Overture* | Philip Sparke[24] |
| 2nd | *A Spring Overture* | Philip Lane |
| 3rd | *Rhapsodic Prelude* | David Lyon |
| 4th | *Overture to Youth* | Eric Hughes |

---

[24] This work was later renamed *The Prizewinners*; Sparke was destined to become a leading composer of brass band music.

All four compositions were published and subsequently used in contests.

## National youth bands

Mention was made above of two concerts for massed junior bands. Denis Wright was the conductor on both occasions and the second one led to the founding of the National Youth Brass Band of Great Britain (NYBB). At some point Wright had discussed the idea with the founder of the National Youth Orchestra of Great Britain (NYO). A meeting of interested parties was held in Manchester in January 1951 at which the decision was taken to create a national youth brass band under Wright's direction. A council was formed, with representatives from many parts of England, Wales and Scotland. The first course took place in Bradford during the Easter week of 1952. It was a huge success, with 92 young brass instrumentalists receiving tuition from a group of experts and playing together under the baton of Wright. Since then, two courses per year have been held in various parts of the country, with specialist instrumental tutors and guest conductors from leading bands and orchestras, including Sir Adrian Boult who first conducted the NYBB in 1958. The upper age limit is normally 18 and the principal cornet player, using orchestral terminology, is known as the 'leader'. Many past leaders have distinguished themselves in their future musical careers.

Highlights for the NYBB in the 1960s included the return of Sir Adrian Boult as guest conductor at Easter 1962, when a BBC television film was made featuring Sir Adrian and comedian/trombonist George Chisolm. In 1964 the band made its first commercial recording – 'Youth Makes Music'. Denis Wright took his leave of the band at the conclusion of the Easter 1967 course, shortly after which he died (Figure 4.2).

Geoffrey Brand had already been appointed music adviser and on his first course the band cut another disc, *The National Youth Brass Band of Great Britain*. Guest conductors during the closing years of the decade included Gilbert Vinter, Sir Vivian Dunn of the Royal Marines and Herbert Møller (see page 310). In 1967 the music publishers Chappell gave a shield, to be awarded annually to a member 'for outstanding services'. A year later another trophy was presented, by PYE Records, for the winner of an inter-band solo competition. The summer course was held in Jersey and in this year a choir was formed. In 1971 the NYBB made its first overseas trip, holding a course in Denmark; it returned there in 1980. Girls were now becoming increasingly important. Under the headline of 'Women's Lib?', *BB* of 12 May 1973 showed a photograph of five girls, all in principal positions within the band – cornet, flugelhorn, tenor horn, trombone and euphonium.

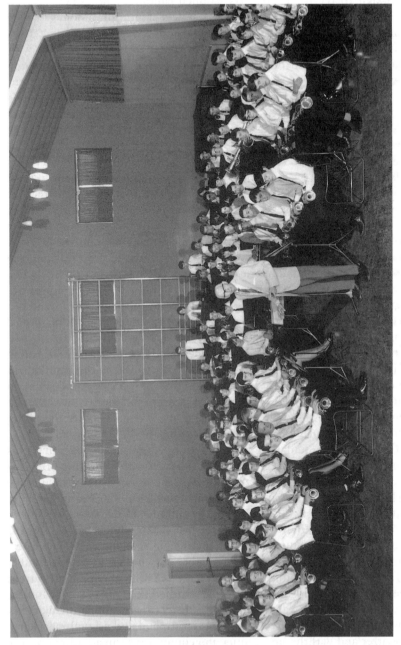

Figure 4.2    The NYBB and Dr Denis Wright on his final course, Easter 1967

Finance was a constant problem and the early 1970s saw a prolonged campaign to try to secure Arts Council funding. The NYO received considerable financial backing but, despite a significant amount of time being devoted to its discussion in Parliament, the Council was reluctant to change its policy towards the NYBB. It relented to a degree in 1974 with a rather miserly grant of £750. The Arts Council did, however, provide commissioning fees for several new works, the first of which was *Concerto for Band* by Wilfred Josephs, premiered during the summer of 1974. Geoffrey Brand resigned as music adviser early in 1975 and was replaced by Arthur Butterworth. In this same year the NYBB commissioned another new work, Paul Patterson's *Cataclysm*. A further commission came in 1976, *Tableaux of the Heraldic Animals*, by Richard Steinitz, a colleague of Butterworth's at the Huddersfield Polytechnic. Guest conductors during the later 1970s included Eric Ball, Harry Mortimer, Edward Gregson, James Scott and Roy Newsome.

Following the example of the NYBB, several other countries were to form national youth bands. The first to do so was Scotland and, rather wisely, the instigators took advice from Denis Wright. In 1957 he met officials from the Scottish Amateur Music Association to discuss the possibility of holding summer schools. The first was held the following year at St Andrews, and the National Youth Brass Band of Scotland (NYBBS) was born. The well-known Scottish brass band conductor and composer Drake Rimmer was general manager and for the first course tutors came from Kneller Hall. Amongst early conductors were Denis Wright and the Scottish composer Cedric Thorpe Davie; the first regular conductor was Bryden Thomson, the well-known orchestral conductor and a native of Scotland. He was succeeded in 1971 by Geoffrey Brand. Demand for places became so high that in 1978 a reserve section was formed to cater for those unable to gain admission to the main band.

Though run on similar lines to the NYBB, NYBBS meets only once per year and its upper age limit is 21. As has been the case with the NYBB in England, NYBBS has contributed greatly to the well-being of the brass band movement in Scotland. In 1962 it began its commissioning policy; by the end of the 1970s, 16 pieces had been added to the repertoire, including works by Malcolm Arnold, Gordon Jacob and Thea Musgrave. Courses continued annually in various venues in Scotland until 1969 when NYBBS made the first of several trips abroad, with a tour of Austria.

The next national youth band to be formed was in New Zealand; its first course was held in 1960. A major difference between this and its British counterparts was that all 50 students on the course, thanks to a government subsidy, were given free tuition, food and accommodation.

Switzerland was the first continental country to form a national youth brass band and the only one to organise regular, annual courses. The

National Jugend Brass Band (NJBB) was formed in 1976 by Markus Bach (see page 309). There is one course per year, always held in the village of Gwatt on the shores of Lake Thun. Prior to the course, prospective members are auditioned, given a seating place and later supplied with the appropriate band parts, so that players are not sight-reading when they meet for the first time. This is necessary, as the band gives it first concert on the Wednesday evening prior to going on tour, with three further concerts in various parts of Switzerland. There is also a 'B' band, which follows a similar pattern of events.

### Junior and school bands: the 1970s

School and youth bands continued to thrive though, with the inevitable turnover in membership, some enjoyed only a brief period of success before fading into the background. Many school bands developed into youth bands as their members grew older. Similarly, some youth bands became adult bands. Some school and youth bands entered the contest field, but many concentrated on concert work, often undertaking annual tours.

During the 1970s the education of young players moved on apace, not only through junior bands, but also through the development of the NSBBA, the NYBB and NYBBS, teaching in schools and the growth of O level and A level courses in music.[25] The raising of the normal school-leaving age to 16 and encouragement for more pupils to remain at school until they were 18 were significant developments. A greater number of school-leavers were now going to college or university – some to study music, many studying non-musical subjects. Though many bands suffered from the loss of their 18-year-olds, the formation of the City of London Band (see Glossary) was one benefit which came about as a direct result of these developments.

### *Area schools bands*

Where there were a number of school bands within close proximity, area bands and county bands appeared. The Yorkshire Schools Band, formed in 1961 when Denis Wright conducted the inaugural concert in Bradford, was one of the first of the area bands. There were regular concerts, with monthly rehearsals on Saturdays. By 1965 the band was 60-strong. Annual weekend courses were directed by Geoffrey Brand from 1969.

---

[25] These were study courses within the schools system. 'O' level meant Ordinary and led to an examination normally taken at the age of 16. For pupils who wished to study to a higher level, perhaps with university in mind, the 'A' (Advanced) level was available, normally taken at 18.

Wakefield Schools Band was formed in 1970 and quickly established a healthy contest record. Though never becoming National Youth Champions, they regularly won the regional contest. There were also primary and intermediate groups within the system and, quite separately, a Wakefield Youth Band was formed, which won the 1973 British Youth Championships in Liverpool (see page 118). A new Wakefield Metropolitan Schools Band was formed in 1977, meeting monthly under conductor Les Hepplestone, a former member of Brighouse & Rastrick, Yorkshire Imperial and Grimethorpe.

## Youth bands

A number of county youth bands now appeared. Though not having the prestige of a national band they were able to draw on good players from a large area and expose them to higher standards than were possible in their individual bands. They could hold shorter sessions at regular intervals as well as periodical residential courses.

### *The first county youth band*

The first county youth band was formed in Cornwall. A half-day course was held in Truro in October 1954 under the direction of Fred Roberts, conductor of Camborne Town, and former principal cornet player of Brighouse & Rastrick and bandmaster of CWS (Manchester). In the following year a committee was convened to oversee the formation of a county youth brass band. It received financial support from the County Education Authority and the band gave two concerts in Truro, the second one conducted by Denis Wright. Though there were regular, short courses, the formation of the Cornwall County Youth Brass Band did not take place until 1959, following an amalgamation of the youth band committee and the Cornwall Brass Bands Association. The outcome was a full four-day course near St Austell, again with Wright conducting. The second annual course took place during the Easter holidays of 1960.

Annual courses continued, weekend rehearsals being held under local tutors during the early part of each year and an intensive four-day course over the Easter period, with sectional rehearsals under local tutors, a guest conductor for the full band and a final concert. Guest conductors during the 1960s included Eric Ball, Geoffrey Brand, Malcolm Arnold and Arthur Butterworth. Ball composed his *Fowey River* for the 1964 course, whilst Arnold penned *Little Suite No. 2* for that of 1967, conducting the first performance himself. Eric Ball then composed *St Michael's Mount* for the band, which was given its first performance on the 1969 course.

Roy Newsome directed courses in 1972–73–74 whilst Albert Chappell (see page 176) officiated in 1975–76–77. Eric Ball returned for the band's twentieth course in 1978 but Chappell, now residing in Cornwall, directed that of 1979. Eddie Williams (see below), who had been the band's musical adviser for a number of years, now resigned owing to other commitments and was succeeded by Chappell. At the latter's invitation, Harry Mortimer directed the 1980 course.

*Other youth bands*

The youth brass band movement developed rapidly during the 1960s and 1970s as school music programmes produced more players. One band active during this period was Crewkerne Youth Band (Somerset), formed in 1960. Each Whitsuntide from 1962 this band undertook a four-day tour of Cornwall. During 1967 it gave no fewer than 76 performances over a wide geographical area and in 1970 visited Holland.

In Cornwall, St Dennis Youth Band, formed in 1962, regularly featured in the prize lists of local contests. In 1968, it played in the Youth Championship Finals in London for the first time, gaining 2nd prize. This was followed by wins in 1972 and 1973. There was a hat-trick of Area contest wins in 1974–75–76 and in the Association contests, held annually, St Dennis Youth was undefeated in over 20 years. These successes were all under the leadership of Eddie Williams, a former horn player with Camborne, Brighouse & Rastrick (1942–46) and Fairey's (1954–58), who founded the band.[26]

The newly formed Netteswell School Band competed in the fourth section in the London Area contest of 1964 and created such an impression that it was invited to appear in the twin concerts in the Royal Albert Hall in October. A few months later it became known as the Harlow (Netteswell) Youth Band. Later still, members formed the nucleus of Netteswell Youth Band, which made the first of several appearances in the Finals of the National Youth Band Championships, in 1969. The band visited Germany and Holland in 1970, participating in various festivals. In 1971, it broadcast in the series 'Youth Orchestras of the World' and during the Christmas periods of 1972 and 1973 performed in Westminster Abbey. Overseas tours continued, one of the more unusual ones being a seven-day visit to Israel in 1980. Other exceptional tours included visits to Czechoslovakia in 1989 and East Slovakia two years later.

Mere Manor Youth Band (Wiltshire), formed in 1966 and frequently in the news, toured Holland in 1968, as did the City of Oxford Youth Band

---

[26] Trethewey, 1988, pp. 33, 34, 53 and 54.

whose tour was organised by Frank Wolff, a Dutch expatriate who settled in Oxford after the war. This band also was formed in 1966 and made annual continental tours from the very beginning, courtesy of Wolff. The ninth, in 1975, encompassed parts of France and Germany but in the following year the band spent 23 days in Canada and the USA, 1976 being the latter country's bi-centennial year.

The London Borough of Redbridge held its first youth brass band course in 1967. The 43-strong band was conducted by Geoffrey Brand and amongst the organisers was John Ridgeon, the borough's brass supervisor. This led to the formation of the Redbridge Youth Band, which won the London Area Youth section in 1969 and in the following year won the National Youth Championships. In 1971 it entered the third section, winning at both the Area contest and the Finals. In 1975 the name was changed to Redbridge Brass Ensemble. Ridgeon had been the principal driving force but he left in 1977, being replaced by Ray Farr (see page 166).

Huntingdon and Peterborough Youth Brass Band, formed in 1969, won the London and Southern Counties Regional contest in 1973, 1978 and 1979, each win leading to an appearance at the Royal Albert Hall in the Butlins Finals.

Loughborough Juniors was formed in 1972 by Bud Fisher from younger members of the senior band, of which he was a member. He very quickly moulded them into a fine band, in 1974 winning the Midlands Youth Championships and qualifying for the Butlins Championships in the Royal Albert Hall. At this time the average age was 13½ and the youngest member a mere seven years old. It was renamed Loughborough Youth Band in 1976 and in 1978 became the Butlins Youth Band Champions.

Further south, Solent Youth Band was founded in 1974 from the former Southsea Junior Band. It won the Southern Television Award as the best young band in southern England, the reward for which was sharing a television programme with the well-known composer and conductor, Ron Goodwin. In 1975 the band won the second section of the Area contest, but in 1977 became the Solent Concert Band. Wesley Garner was its principal driving force.

Most school and youth bands had members of both sexes within their ranks. Perhaps the most illustrious exception was Trinity Girls Silver Band, founded in 1969 and attached to Holy Trinity Church, North Ashton (Lancashire). They were conducted for many years by John Newbiggin, head of brass for the Wigan Authority. He was succeeded in 1976 by Jack Withington, solo horn player with Wingates. His twin daughters played in Trinity Girls and were each to become fine cornet players – members of Foden's and other top-class bands.

*More county youth bands*

Several counties now followed the example of Cornwall. Mid-Hants
Schools Band, formed in 1965 by a local brass instructor, John Knight,
became National Youth Champions of Great Britain at its first attempt, in
1968. There was a broadcast in the following year and in 1970 the band
went to Holland to participate in an international youth festival. There
were now regular overseas tours. In 1973 the band changed its name to
Hampshire Youth Concert Band. A three-day course was held in 1979,
with 141 players participating in three graded bands. Later in the year the
band visited Vienna.

The Northampton Youth Band was formed in 1968. It visited Germany
in both 1973 and 1974. In later years, under the baton of John Berryman
(see page 153), it indulged in some contesting, and became National Youth
Brass Band Champions in 1992.

Cheshire Youth Band, founded in 1970, regularly visited the USA from
around 1980, when they began their bi-annual trips to Chester County,
Pennsylvania. Their chief mentor was Peter Room, county music adviser
and senior housemaster with the NYBB. During the late 1980s there were
also tours in Denmark and Portugal.

*Youth bands in South Wales*

South Wales was quite a hotbed for youth bands. Being a mining and
heavy engineering area, brass bands were very much a part of local culture.
Treorchy Secondary Modern School Band was so named in 1957.
Developing from Parc & Dare Juniors it was highly successful and by
1962 had progressed to the championship section in the National
Championships, conducted by Ieuan Morgan (see page 177). By taking
2nd prize in the Welsh Area contest it qualified to take part in the Finals
at the Royal Albert Hall – the first junior band to reach this level. It had
also won the Youth Brass Band Championships of Wales four years in
succession and was attracting prestigious engagements.[27]

In 1965 several boys moved into the senior band. This performed
wonders for the latter but the school band, understandably, lost some of
its momentum. However, as Upper Rhondda Secondary School Band it
again won the Finals of the National Youth Band Championships in 1976,
1977 and 1979. In 1984 it was renamed Treorchy Comprehensive School
Band.

---

[27] *BB* 17 February 1962, p. 1; 19 May, p. 2; 20 October, p. 2; 16 February 1963, p. 1;
30 March, p. 7; and National Fuels Distributors (Parc & Dare) centenary booklet, p. 17.

Further east the county of Monmouthshire had a thriving scheme for school and youth bands of which, as early as 1955, there were 11. Despite this, the first course of the Monmouth Youth Band was not held until 1968, when 70 students were selected from the county's 16 bands. This became an annual event, held during the Easter holidays. After local government reorganisation in 1974 the band was renamed Gwent County Youth Band. Holding monthly rehearsals and the annual course and concert, its primary objective was the improvement of young players in the district. Nevertheless, it entered the national contests in later years, and in 1994 and 1999 became National Youth Brass Band Champions. Further major awards included winning the European Youth Championships in 1998 and Outstanding Performance Award in the 1999 National Festival of Music for Youth.

East Glamorgan Youth Band was founded in 1962 and gave concerts annually. Taking part in the 1967 concert were 100 boys and girls aged between 10 and 19. By 1970 it had become the Glamorgan County Youth Band, its residential course this year attracting 152 players, aged 11–18. There were also West Glamorgan and South Glamorgan youth bands, the former founded in 1975 and the latter founded a year earlier and bound for the USA in 1979. West Glamorgan Youth Band won the Boosey & Hawkes Youth Championships in 1984, 1986 and 1989.

Amongst later developments in Wales was the founding of Tredegar Junior Band in 1970.[28] Initially there were about 20 members, aged 9–18. During their first five years they won every contest entered, crowning this by becoming the first Butlins Youth Band Champions in 1974, and winning again in 1975. Tredegar Juniors then went through a relatively quiet period though there were plenty of local successes and regular concerts. The 1990s saw further highlights, with wins in the European Youth Championships of 1993 and 1994.

## Individual players

With the proliferation of junior bands and improvements in teaching methods it was inevitable that good young players would emerge, some of them entering the music profession. It is, however, remarkable that four of the early ones were female. The first was Gracie Cole (see page 38), who not only made history when she won the AOMF Scholarship in 1942,

---

[28] The Childs family played a significant part in the early development of Tredegar Juniors. John Childs, a former euphonium player with Tredegar Town Band now became conductor of both bands. His two sons, Robert and Nicholas (see pages 248 and 257) progressed through the Juniors and the town band, and several other family members were also involved.

but made further history by appearing as guest soloist in two concerts given by Besses o' th' Barn, at one of which she played principal cornet in the finale. Later she appeared regularly as a guest soloist with other bands and also fulfilled several engagements for the BBC. By June 1945 she was touring with Gloria Gaye's professional dance band. A month later she was fully professional, playing with the renowned Ivy Benson's Girls' Band.[29] The second young lady, Joan Hinde, was from the Sheffield area. During 1946 she was offered contracts with both Ivy Benson and Gloria Gaye, but her teacher felt that she was too young at 12! She made numerous guest appearances on radio and television, and in February 1949 embarked on a six-month tour with radio stars Elsie and Doris Waters, after which she became a professional trumpet player. There was also now another up-and-coming girl soloist, seven-year-old Betty Woodcock, already winning prizes in solo competitions. Also from the Sheffield area, she achieved some fame as a child prodigy and won the Juvenile section in the 1946 All-England Solo Championships (see page 104). However, in 1949, along with her family, she emigrated to Australia. The fourth member of this group, Marie Fawbert, came from a well-known Midlands banding family. She was taught by her father from the age of three and by her ninth year was regularly winning prizes in solo contests. At 15 she joined Ivy Benson's band. However, in the late 1960s Marie returned to her roots – Shirland Miners Welfare Band – and since then has taught countless children to play.

These were just some of the early post-war examples of young brass banders going into the music profession. Moving into a later generation, in 1971 at the age of 13, Nicholas Thompson played a solo in the Royal Albert Hall massed bands concert. He was already a member of the NYBB and was its leader on both 1972 courses. Later playing with City of Coventry in the BBC's 'Best of Brass' competition (see page 197), he was voted 'Bandsman of the Future'. An outstanding euphonium player at this time, Andrew Fawbert (brother of Marie) was also a member of the NYBB and its principal euphonium player on several courses. He won the Junior Solo Championships in 1973. Both of these players were to enter the professional musical world, Thompson as a trumpet player and Fawbert as a trombonist.

In 1978, aged 17, Michael Hext, a young Bedfordshire trombonist and son of Terry Hext, principal trombonist with GUS, won the first BBC 'Young Musician of the Year' award, worth £1000 and offering virtually an open invitation to enter the music profession. However, the greatest discovery was Ian Bousfield, the 15-year-old solo trombone player of

---

[29] There is a lengthy article about Gracie Cole in *BB* of 20 December 1986, pp. 6–7.

Yorkshire Imperial, who won the highly prestigious Shell-LSO Music Scholarship, worth £3000.[30]

A year later Wendy Picton, a young Lancashire lady, became the first female to win the Butlins solo title. In 1985 she stepped aside from brass bands and, launching her own group, Brass Beaux, within two more years was a featured soloist with the New Squadronaires dance orchestra. Indicative of her versatility, she commissioned a Euphonium Concerto by Derek Bourgeois and premiered it in both its orchestral and brass band versions. She did much to promote brass in schools and undertook several overseas tours.

It was still relatively rare for young brass players to turn professional, despite success in the amateur field. Bill Millar was one of many who did not. As a 14-year-old he enjoyed a string of successes in 1978. A member of Wingates, he won the Butlins Solo Championships, the AOMF and to crown an exceptional year, collected the prize for the best soloist in Rothman's 'Brass in Concert' championships. He was also the Butlins winner in the following year. Later he developed into one of the finest euphonium players of his generation (see page 291).

## Courses

Educational courses for bandsmen were rare pre-1939. Amongst the earliest was a series of classes in bandmastership, held in London from 1936, that were directed by Harold Hind, then a professor and examiner for Guildhall School of Music. He was assisted by Denis Wright and Eric Ball. Even after the war it was some time before courses appeared with any regularity, bandsmen generally learning either through individual lessons or correspondence courses. Alfred Ashpole was active with these, but a big step was taken in 1948 when Leonard Davies became principal of the Parr School of Music in Manchester. Here, again through correspondence courses, students could undertake studies for a range of examinations, with tuition offered in bandmastership, conducting, scoring, harmony and theory.

### Short courses

Several one-day or week-end courses were organised in different parts of the country during the 1950s and 1960s – some for players but most for conductors. Lancashire County Education Authority sponsored several.

---

[30] Bousfield later left Yorkshire Imperial to become a professional trombonist, playing principal trombone with the Hallé Orchestra, the LSO and now with the Vienna Philharmonic.

One of the first was held in Preston during November 1953, under the direction of Leonard Davies and the County Music Organiser. These courses continued on a regular basis and included a 20-week series 'for bandmasters and senior bandsmen'.

A course advertised by the University of London in 1973 was rather more specialised, with 24 classes in 'The music of the brass band and the problems of conducting it'. Geoffrey Brand was the tutor.

Short courses were run throughout the 1970s, often directed by a leading figure from the brass band world. The Lancaster University Brass Band Summer School of 1975, directed by Elgar Howarth, was the most comprehensive. In addition to Howarth himself, Harry Mortimer and Roy Newsome were conductors and conducting tutors, James Shepherd (see page 138), John Ridgeon and Bram Gay supervised private lessons and ensemble work. Members of the Philip Jones Brass Ensemble (PJBE) were in residence for three days, advising and performing late-night concerts and Besses o' th' Barn gave a mid-week concert. The 100 or so delegates formed two bands which rehearsed under each conductor. The bands presented one concert each, both combining on the final evening under the direction of the Summer School's President, Sir Charles Groves. Eleven delegates were conducting students, working under the supervision of the conducting tutors. The final 'icing on the cake' was provided by a camera crew from Granada Television which was present for most of the week, preparing a documentary programme and giving student conductors the opportunity to be filmed 'in action'.[31]

*Annual summer schools*

The above are just a few of the short courses offered. The first of many annual 'Summer Holiday Schools' took place in 1950 in the form of a week's study for brass band conductors. As part of the Workers' Music Association's Summer School, it was held in Shrewsbury and directed by Denis Wright. Later courses were held at Wortley Hall near Barnsley. Approximately a third of the students attended through scholarships awarded by the trade unions, CISWO or the Co-operative Society.

The Parr School ran the first of several Brass Band Summer Schools at Grange-over-Sands in September 1955, primarily for conductors. About 70 delegates attended. With the death of one of the principal tutors, Edith Alston (Mrs Leonard Davies), in 1962 and the deteriorating health of Davies himself, this series seems to have been abandoned.

---

[31] There is a preview by Sally Groves in *Sounding Brass* of January 1975, pp. 119ff. and a review by Bram Gay in the following October, pp. 88ff.

*Full-time courses*

A number of professional courses for bandsmen were begun during the 1970s. The first sign of this development was the formation of a brass band in 1971 at the Guildhall School of Music and also its graduate course offering places to a small number of brass band instrumentalists. From September 1975 the Birmingham School of Music incorporated a specialist option in Brass Band Studies and Techniques in its graduate course.

However, the first full-time course specifically for brass band players was a two-year residential course at the Isle of Ely College of Further Education, founded in 1974. It survived for only a few years, coming under the shadow of a course instituted in 1976 at Salford College of Technology. This was also a two-year course, but led to a Diploma in Band Musicianship that was recognised for entry into teacher training. Though also catering for wind band and popular music, the course was initially targeted mainly at the brass band. Roy Newsome, composer and jazz pianist Goff Richards, and David Loukes, a brass band conductor and former trombonist with the Hallé Orchestra, were appointed full-time lecturers and the part-time staff included several leading players and conductors from the brass band movement.[32]

The Salford courses put brass bands fairly and squarely on the academic map and paved the way for other institutions to forge links with the brass band movement. Across the Pennines a course at Huddersfield Technical College catered for bandsmen at 'foundation' level, with individual instrumental lessons and a brass band, the Tecol Band, later to become Sellers Engineering Band (see Glossary). At Huddersfield Polytechnic an optional module in Brass Band Studies was introduced into the Bachelor of Arts (BA) course in 1980, with brass band instruments now acceptable for first study.

## Conclusion

This concludes a momentous 45-year period in which the fortunes of bands changed, time and time again. A number of organisations thrived for much of the period, but several seemed to have fulfilled their purpose by its end. The adoption of standard pitch and the general acceptance of percussion as a legitimate part of the band were significant developments which added to the maturity of bands and to their acceptance in the wider musical world.

---

[32] See the article by David Loukes in *Sounding Brass*, May 1976, p. 10.

However, the overriding consideration for bands was the education of the younger generation and the continuation of that education in adult life through the various courses. As a follow-up to the schools system, a youth band movement emerged, becoming nationwide and eroding the working-class bias of earlier generations of bands as children of professional parents now played alongside those with working-class backgrounds.

Many bands have already been mentioned, some of which will be met again in later chapters. One which has not yet been discussed is the CWS (Manchester) Band.[33] Formed in 1901 as the CWS Tobacco Factory Band, it took its modern title in 1937. From the late 1940s onwards, as will be seen in Chapter 7, it quickly rose into the upper echelons of bands and commands quite a lot of space during the next few chapters.

---

[33] CWS are the initials of the Co-operative Wholesale Society, a large retail chain which was one of the first companies to give dividends to its customers proportionate to the amount which they spent. Linked to the Labour movement, it has sponsored several brass bands and is generally known as 'The Co-op'.

# CHAPTER 5

# Contest developments

There were fewer local contests during the war and rules regarding borrowed players were generally relaxed. This dearth of contests was soon over once peace was re-established. *BBN*, during 1946, either advertised or reported 48 full band contests. Twenty-eight took place in the months June to September, indicating that the majority were still held outside. Whit Friday march contests were also held this year, most of them for the first time since 1939. The number of contests gradually increased, peaking in 1948.[1] The number of winter events was on the increase from this year, confirming that there were now more indoor contests. With the passage of time other important contests were established but the two most important groups remained the Belle Vue contests and the National Championships.

### The National Brass Band Championships: 1945–70

In September 1944 a patriotic display was held at Belle Vue. Titled 'March to Freedom', it featured 10 bands, a 1000-voice choir and various other ensembles. John Henry Iles was the director and a national newspaper, the *Daily Herald*, sponsored the event. Around 20 000 spectators attended. On the rebound of this success Iles broached sponsorship of the National Championships to the newspaper and in January 1945 the following announcement appeared:

> The 'Daily Herald' has decided to organise and sponsor a series of area contests in which every part of Britain will participate. Handsome cash prizes and trophies will be provided for contests in each district and any profits therefrom will be donated to charity.[2]

Iles was delighted. Regional qualifying contests was a concept he had tried unsuccessfully to introduce early in the century.

The Clydeside Correspondent, in *BBN* of October 1945, quoted part of a letter dated 24 February 1945 which had been sent to the Scottish Amateur Bands Association and, presumably, to committees in all regions. In addition to the sponsorship news disclosed above, it stated:

---

[1] The 38 advertised contests of 1946 increased to 60 in the following year and to 85 in 1948. The figures for 1949 and 1950 were 74 and 78 respectively.
[2] See Hailstone, 1987, pp. 222–3; and Mortimer, 1981, p. 139.

> The 'Daily Herald' [will provide] trophies, Judges' fees, printing and all other expenses in connection with the contests, the first three bands in the 1st section to be invited to compete at the Championship Contest to be held in London.

Iles's successor as administrator of the National Brass Band Championships of Great Britain was Edwin Vaughan Morris MBE (1901–97) – generally known as Vaughan Morris. He spent much of his life in journalism, starting as a reporter, but during the war he held a number of senior positions in the Ministry of Labour and National Service. He was a forceful person who would stand no nonsense. Taylor described him as 'the highly efficient, much respected autocrat',[3] whilst Harry Mortimer wrote:

> although we did not always agree, I have nothing but praise for the way in which Vaughan Morris tightened the rules concerning registrations . . . platform discipline and in general added more prestige and dignity to the whole structure than even his worthy predecessors.[4]

In 1945, Vaughan Morris took over the running of the Nationals as part of his work for the *Daily Herald*. There were to be eight Area qualifying contests during the spring followed by the Finals which, for the championship section, would take place in October in the Royal Albert Hall, London. Other sections would be held at Belle Vue in late September.

The first series of the new Nationals was a huge success. Qualifying contests took place as follows:

*Midlands Area*, 2 April, De Montfort Hall, Leicester; three sections (including juniors), 41 bands

*North West and North Wales*, 9 June, Belle Vue, Manchester; three sections, 13 bands, plus junior section of four bands

*Scottish Area*, 16 June, Heart of Midlothian football ground, Edinburgh; four sections, 19 bands

*North Eastern Area*, 23 June, Bradford, Lister Park; three sections, 34 bands

*Northern Area*, 7 July, Newcastle, City Hall and Durante Hall; three sections, 12 bands

*South Wales*, 7 July, Neath, Gnoll Football Field; three sections, 30 bands

*London & Southern Counties*, 11 August (no location or venue named); three sections, 18 bands, plus Junior section of three bands

*West of England*, 25 August, Bristol (no venue named); two sections, 11 bands

---

3 Taylor, 1979, p. 160.
4 Mortimer, 1981, p. 142.

The Midlands contest actually took place before the end of the war. Held on Easter Monday, it was combined with the already well-established Leicester Brass Band Festival. Harry Mortimer conducted a massed band concert in the evening and the hall was full all day.

The nationwide picture was highly satisfactory. Some things needed addressing however, in particular the disparity in conditions in different Areas. The majority of events, but not all, took place in halls; Scotland had four senior sections whilst most other areas had three; the West of England mounted second and third sections only. The North West and London had junior sections whilst the third section in the Midlands was, in reality, for juniors. The number of bands invited to the Finals of the championship section also lacked uniformity with four from the North East (virtually Yorkshire), three from South Wales and two from each other Area (except the West of England).

The Finals were eminently successful. The main event was the championship section contest, held in the Royal Albert Hall, London. There was a specially designed adjudicators' box, and every ticket was sold. However, the new test piece, Denis Wright's *Overture for an Epic Occasion*, was felt not to be sufficiently difficult to 'sort out' the prizewinners. Some Area winners may have concurred, because none appeared in the top four places, which were:

| | | |
|---|---|---|
| 1st | Fairey Aviation | 2nd in the North West |
| 2nd | Horden Colliery | 2nd in the Northern Area |
| 3rd | Parc & Dare | 2nd in South Wales |
| 4th | Brighouse & Rastrick | 3rd in the North East |

Fairey Aviation received 200 guineas and held the *Daily Herald* National Championship Trophy for a year. This was, and still is, proudly displayed by its recipient at concerts. There was also a blue sash, worn by each band member; however, the real attraction was the title 'National Champion Brass Band of Great Britain'.

The London contest was followed by a spectacular evening gala concert. That of 1946 featured eight bands – Fairey Aviation as the 1945 National Champions, and the winning band from each of the other seven areas. Soloists were the distinguished pianist Eileen Joyce, leading soprano Gwen Catley and Harry Mortimer, and the conductor was Dr Malcolm Sargent (to be knighted in 1947). Each half of the concert opened with a fanfare played by the trumpeters of the Royal Military School of Music. This was the style and format set by Vaughan Morris for the gala concerts. The hall was filled to overflowing for both contest and concert.

The lower section Finals were held at Belle Vue a week earlier. Here, the junior Finals were thrown open, not all Areas having provided a junior preliminary.

The pattern for the Nationals was now set. Eight Areas were established, in each of which there would be three senior sections and a class for juniors. Two bands from each section in each Area would be invited to their respective Finals. Additionally, the winner of the championship section Finals would receive an invitation to the following year's Finals, being given a 'bye' in its Area.

From 1947 a fourth section was added. In the West of England, Camborne, the previous year's second-section Finals winner was promoted, but given a bye because there were no other contenders. Black Dyke were winners at the Finals. They were conducted by Harry Mortimer, as were the runners-up – Fairey Aviation.

In 1948, for the first time, the West of England had a championship section, won by Camborne. In Wales the winners were Parc & Dare. Cory's came second but caused a surprise at the Finals, being runner-up to Black Dyke. In 1949 Black Dyke completed a hat-trick. Eighteen bands competed in the Royal Albert Hall in the 1950 Finals, with three from Cornwall due to a Camborne Area hat-trick creating a bye.

An announcement in 1950 that caused concern was that the *Daily Herald* was withdrawing its financial support of Area contests. Through the Association network each region was required to look after its own qualifying contest. In a letter to *BBN* in July 1951, Tom F. Atkinson paid tribute to the *Daily Herald* for having supported Area contests since 1945. Financial responsibility for the 1951 series was undertaken by local committees with varying degrees of success. In January 1952 representatives from each committee met Jerome Chester and Vaughan Morris from the *Daily Herald*. The meeting resulted in the formation of the National Brass Band Contesting Council (NBBCC), with Chester as president, Vaughan Morris as honorary general secretary and Atkinson as secretary. The Council worked quietly in the background, fine-tuning various aspects of the Nationals to ensure their smooth running. Its chief objectives were to discuss, review and improve standards of contesting, to advise on test pieces and to draw up a list of approved adjudicators.[5] A National Registry of Bandsmen was also compiled, in which some 27000 individuals were registered.[6] Unethical borrowing of players for contests was problematical, even with the help of the Registry and the co-operation of most players. However, gradually a greater number of contests adopted the new rules regarding registration and borrowing, and the situation improved.

---

5 Brand, 1979, p. 60.
6 Hailstone, 1987, p. 229.

An indication of the current popularity of the Royal Albert Hall event was reflected in a report complaining of the 'black market' in tickets, one pound (20s.) being regularly offered for tickets priced at 7s. 6d. Indeed, the Finals became so popular that the 7000 capacity of the Royal Albert Hall was felt to be inadequate and in 1952 the event was taken to the even larger Empress Hall at Earl's Court.[7]

In March 1954 it was announced that the Finals of all four sections would be held in London, with the Championship section in the Empress Hall and the other three in various nearby halls. In fact, the police intervened and in order to avoid unmanageable traffic congestion in parts of the city insisted that the championship section should return to the Albert Hall.[8] This aggravated the problem of demand for tickets as, in all, 60 bands from 30 counties competed. As was now customary, BBC sound radio and television were present at the event, which one commentator aptly described as 'the brass band cup final'.

In 1955, for the first time, Her Majesty the Queen accepted patronage of the Nationals. In this year, the NBBCC ruled that 3rd prize-winners at Area contests would, if the adjudicator considered their performance to be 'of exceptional merit', be invited to the Finals. In fact, Foden's and Creswell were invited in the championship section, resulting in a record 20 bands playing in the Albert Hall. Four others were invited in the lower sections. Another important decision was that in future new test pieces would be set for lower section finalists, which, hitherto, had played the same music in the Finals as in the Areas.

Harry Mortimer was absent from the 1956 Nationals on BBC duties. Therefore his bands had to find alternative conductors. Black Dyke played under its bandmaster, Jack Emmott, Rex Mortimer took Foden's and Stanley Boddington took both Munn & Felton's and Morris Motors. The most dramatic change was that Major G.H. Willcocks took Fairey's – and won (see page 146). Another innovation this year was the first annual presentation of a Baton of Honour to the conductor of the winning band in the championship section. It was presented during the eight o'clock concert by the composer Ralph Vaughan Williams, there to hear the first performance of Frank Wright's arrangement of his *English Folk Song Suite*.

In 1958 Vaughan Morris introduced the 'Spotlight on Service' ceremony, in which, each year, a person who had given distinguished service to the brass band movement was presented with a Baton of Honour. Up to 1970 these were presented as follows:

---

[7] The seating capacity at the Empress Hall was 10 000 – 3000 greater than that at the Royal Albert Hall – but was still unable to satisfy the demand for tickets.

[8] Brand, 1979, p. 61.

| 1958 | Denis Wright | 1965 | Gershom Collison |
| 1959 | Eric Ball | 1966 | Stanley Boddington |
| 1960 | Frank Wright | 1967 | Drake Rimmer |
| 1961 | W.B. Hargreaves | 1968 | John Baldwin |
| 1962 | Harry Heyes | 1969 | Alex Thain |
| 1963 | Alex Mortimer | 1970 | Jack Atherton |
| 1964 | William Wood | | |

The *Daily Herald* ceased publication in September 1964 and there was much concern for the future of the Nationals until it was established that sponsorship was being undertaken by *The People*, a Sunday paper with a circulation of five and a half million. There was now to be more accent on youth and from 1965 there were once again National Youth Band Championships, for the first time since 1950. Vaughan Morris continued as administrator.

Things did not go well during the 1965 Area contests under the tenancy of *The People*. Following their conclusion, a change of plans for 1966 was announced in the following terms:

> Contests have mushroomed to such an extent – with neither cohesiveness, nor objective purpose as a basis for their inaugurations – that well managed and well presented contests are being drained of support to the extent that it is no longer practical to continue their presentation. Withdrawals of Bands entered in the current year's Area Finals[9] reached the high proportion of over one in five and most of these failed to notify their intention not to be present on the day.[10]

This was unacceptable and it was stated that there were to be no more Area contests. Further, the National Registry of Bandsmen and the NBBCC would cease to operate after the 1965 Finals. The Finals would continue, bands appearing by invitation. This was greeted with dismay. The Registry had brought the borrowed player situation under control and the loss of Area contests was devastating.

The problem of the Registry was partially solved by the intervention of the management of Belle Vue. In November the company announced that it would administer the Registry for a two-year experimental period, commencing in January 1966. To cover costs previously borne by the National Championships, four shillings per bandsman would be charged.

The abolition of Area contests was more complex, but the North East Area Committee took the lead. Renaming itself the Yorkshire Brass Band Festival Committee, it declared its intention to organise a Yorkshire Championships in 1966 with the expectation that the highest-placed

---

[9] Area contests were frequently, if not logically, referred to as 'Area Finals'.

[10] *BB* 29 May 1965, p. 3.

bands would be invited to the Finals. Vaughan Morris not only accepted, he offered the use of the Area trophies. At around the same time the West of England Committee stated that it would organise its Area contest and by the end of October most Area committees had agreed to do likewise.

In fact, the NBBCC continued to function. However, it refused to accept certain conditions laid down by Belle Vue's management, in particular the imposition of registration fees. It planned to retain its own Registry, running alongside separate registries already established in Wales, Scotland and the West of England. The confusion now developing was further fuelled by an announcement that Vaughan Morris was to retire on account of his age. In fact, though he did retire from *The People*, from 1967 he assumed sole charge of the Nationals.

From the early 1960s the NBBCC adopted a more belligerent stance than hitherto and a number of causes of discontent were highlighted. There was, for example, concern that bands could choose in which section they would compete. Inevitably some stayed in lower sections so that they could almost guarantee winning prizes. From 1961 the NBBCC instructed the Areas to form grading committees to ensure that bands competed at appropriate levels. It was also concerned that the Finals of the CISWO contest were held so close in time to the National Finals and was unhappy that this contest, as well as some others, took advantage of the Council's choice of test pieces, in some cases even using them before the dates on which they were used in the Nationals. The Council was also critical of contests held in holiday camps, maintaining that they could not be taken seriously and suggesting that bands were being exploited by the camp owners. Thus, the NBBCC was attempting to exert its influence beyond the boundaries of the National Championships.

In 1967 came a ruling that it would henceforth be compulsory for the winners of the Finals in Sections 2, 3 and 4 to move into the next section higher in the following year, though they would be given a bye to the Finals. A further change was moving the championship section adjudicators from their box in the auditorium to one in the Grand Tier – further away from the stage and well off-centre. There was concern that they would not hear a well-balanced sound; however, tests had been carried out and the results seemed to be acceptable. The reason for the change was that locating the box in the arena effectively made all the seats behind it redundant by obscuring their view of the stage.

A change to the Royal Albert Hall itself now took place. Owing to its vastness it had a notorious echo which had been a problem since the hall opened in 1871. A canopy had been placed over the stage in 1945 but to little effect. In 1969 this was replaced with a much larger one and, at the same time, sound diffusers, looking like huge plastic mushrooms, were hung from the roof. Though this did not totally solve the problem there was a considerable improvement.

In 1968 and 1969 the championship section winners took the title 'World and National Champions'. Any overseas brass band with an acceptable instrumentation and being National Champions in its own country could also compete for the title 'World Champion'. However, the only one to do so was Excelsior from Holland.

This proved to be but a stepping stone to the revolutionary changes of 1970. The NBBCC now ruled that any British band which had been National Champions on two or more occasions since 1945 would compete for the single title 'World Champions'. The bands were Black Dyke, Brighouse & Rastrick, CWS (Manchester), Fairey's, Foden's and GUS (the former Munn & Felton's). They would not compete in the Area contests but would automatically qualify for the World Championships. Interest was expressed by a number of overseas bands but the only one to accept the challenge was Concord Brass Band from Copenhagen, which competed in 1970. Two bands from each Area championship section would still qualify in the normal way and would compete for the title 'National Champion Band of Great Britain'. Despite the dubious titles, both contests ran for two years.

There was a significant increase in the number of overseas visitors at this time; walking round the corridors of the hall one could meet enthusiasts not only from the major European countries but also many Americans and Japanese, as well as Australians and New Zealanders who had arranged their holidays or business trips to coincide with the Championships.

In August 1971 it was announced that R. Smith & Co were to become owners of the National Championships, with *BB* (its sister company) as sponsor. Peter Wilson, a leading figure in the Scottish band scene, was to become organising secretary. He had much experience both as player and conductor, and particularly as an administrator. The retirement of Vaughan Morris was confirmed and, following the 1971 Finals, the World Championships were suspended by the new management, with the Nationals reinstated as before.[11]

## Divisions within the brass band movement

For some time there had been fears of divided loyalties within the movement. COBBA (see page 61) was now established and on many issues

---

[11] Vaughan Morris was awarded the MBE in 1968. Following his retirement in 1971 he linked up with the Decca recording company, producing 58 LPs. In December 1987 he moved to Australia to be with his daughter and her family; he died there in 1997, aged 96. (There is a good article about him in *BB* of 5 December 1987, p. 5.)

took an opposite stance to that of the NBBCC. For example, COBBA offered support to a contest run by Butlins at its Skegness holiday camp, even suggesting that the company might consider running band contests at all of its venues. This was patently against the wishes of the NBBCC. COBBA also supported the Belle Vue Registry and proposed to organise its own grading committee. Ted Buttress was chairman and it soon became apparent that many of the differences of opinion between the two councils were due to the mutual mistrust which existed between him and Vaughan Morris. In truth, both organisations were capable of doing good work.

Buttress explained the objectives of COBBA, stressing that members were democratically elected, representing 11 out of the 17 brass band associations in existence and covering, he maintained, 85 per cent of bands in England and Northern Ireland. His letter stated:

> The Council was formed to extend the activities of associations to a national level and to carry out national projects which local groups could not, but would benefit bands everywhere . . . All the member Associations believe that it is essential that the movement should have a National body because they realise their own scope is limited.[12]

Harry Mortimer had been elected president, but in the same edition as the above letter appeared he resigned, referring to 'recent correspondence in the band papers' and stating: 'it seems quite possible that there may be developments with the Council which will conflict with the position I hold here at the BBC and this could cause me great embarrassment.' One letter obviously referred to was a lengthy one written by the Chairman of the Gloucester Brass Bands Association who expressed the view that: 'After a stormy meeting . . . several bands left our . . . Association because we declined to affiliate with the said "Council", which appears to be showing efforts to "take over" or split the band movement.'[13]

In October 1963 there were discussions regarding COBBA adopting the *British Mouthpiece*, by then in financial difficulties. From mid-1964 it sponsored the magazine, now designated 'The Official Organ of the Council of Brass Band Associations'. Harry Mortimer, having retired from the BBC, returned to COBBA as music adviser.

Attempts to form a National Brass Band Federation had been tried unsuccessfully in 1954 (see page 69) but in 1965 a more far-reaching idea was put to the test. At the instigation of COBBA a meeting was called to discuss unity within the movement. Representatives of associations and other interested organisations were invited and a working committee was selected to plan the formation of a British Federation of Brass Bands (BFBB – see page 69). The group met in December under the chairmanship of

---

Mortimer to formulate aims and objectives and to consider finance and methods of administration. The Federation's objectives included: widening the repertoire by encouraging new works, forging further ties with Local Education Authorities, and seeking recognition by Government of the national status of brass bands. A full-time salaried secretary would eventually be needed. Meanwhile, an executive committee of 15 was elected, charged with drawing up contest rules and appointing a grading panel.

This development was seen as divisive in many quarters; detractors felt that most of these matters were already being taken care of by the NBBCC. By early 1967 'Comment' in *BB* was talking of controversy clouding the brass band horizon. The North West Area Contest was cancelled and the committee disbanded. The contest went ahead, organised by the NBBCC, but there was talk of a boycott and a 12-month ban from the Association for bands that participated. This, however, was denied.

Separate to all of this there had been a dispute between the North East Area committee and Vaughan Morris. Encouraged by the success of the 1966 Yorkshire Championships the committee arranged a follow-up event in 1967. Following discussions with the bands, adjudicators were appointed and test pieces selected. Vaughan Morris refused to accept these and ruled that the NBBCC would organise the North East Area Contest, with the result that there were both a Yorkshire Championships and the official Area contest.

There was a spate of letters in *BB* – mainly against the Federation – and a full-page advertisement placed by the NBBCC declaring that it would, after all, organise the 1968 Area contests.

Fred Bradbury, a former secretary of the Yorkshire Federation of Brass Bands and a tireless worker, was now secretary of BFBB. In an article in *BB* he appealed for support, declaring his intention to meet individuals and national organisations as part of a recruitment drive. The Federation, now established, was seeking charitable status and holding meetings with other national organisations within the movement.

Meanwhile, the NBBCC reiterated its intention to continue operating the National Registry as a free service. It was now obvious that the two bodies were on a collision course. This was intensified with the billing of the 1969 Championships as 'World and National Championships'. Predictably, this precipitated a critical letter from Bradbury and a characteristically verbose reply from Vaughan Morris. Further controversy arose when, in the years 1970 and 1971, the National and World Championships were separated from each other.

So, the arguments continued and there were now two distinct camps within the movement. This is exemplified in part of a report of the meeting of the Executive Committee of the South West Brass Band Association which took place on 5 July 1970:

> It was agreed that no action be taken to become a member of this organisation [the Federation]; and that this Association would not support the proposed National Grading System as outlined by this Federation; it was agreed that the National Contesting Council had for so many years brought the Brass Band Movement up to the high standard it was today, and this Association would continue to give its 100% support to the National Contesting Council and its Officers.

## The W.D. & H.O. Wills Contest

Meanwhile, further fuel was added to the flames when, in mid-1969, it was announced that a new national contest was to be organised, sponsored by W.D. & H.O. Wills, staged in association with COBBA, administered by Ted Buttress and beginning in the autumn with four regional contests. The Finals were to take place in the Midlands during the following spring. It differed in several ways from the existing Nationals: bands were able to choose in which region they would compete, the same adjudicators would officiate at all regional contests and every band achieving 180 or more points would be invited to the Finals. Adjudication would be 'open' – that is, adjudicators would not be screened – and percussion would be required. Bandsmen would be allowed into the halls free (at the Nationals they needed to buy a ticket if they wished to sit in the auditorium) and in addition to prize monies paid, profits would be distributed to competing bands to help defray expenses. Following the Finals, winning bands from the championship section in each region would mass to give a concert, conducted by Harry Mortimer.

Though regarded by some as an attempt to depose the existing National Championships this formula was seen by others as just what bands were wanting.

The first series of regional contests took place during autumn 1969 and spring 1970. The Finals were held in Leicester's De Montfort Hall in March, all sections being provided with a new test piece:

| | | |
|---|---|---|
| Championship | *Suite – Embassy* | Allan Street |
| 2nd section | *Overture – Promenade* | Frank Bryce |
| 3rd section | *Overture – The Pacemakers* | Edward Gregson |
| 4th section | *Overture – Fancy Free* | John Carr |

Morris Concert Band (formerly Morris Motors) were winners of the Championship section and the evening Festival Concert featured them, Camborne, Ransome & Marles and Yorkshire Imperial. The total number of bands participating in the regionals was well below the anticipated 250 and no leading bands appeared. Nevertheless, the project was seen as a success and plans were formulated for a second series.

In the second year a higher quality of band was attracted through the introduction of a 'Champion of Champions' section, to which selected bands were invited without having to qualify – a further snipe at the Nationals which insisted on having a cross-section of bands from all over the country rather than just the very best. The Champion of Champions and the Championship sections were both held in the Royal Albert Hall. The event attracted a BBC broadcast and there was an LP of highlights from both contest and concert – given this year by GUS, Yorkshire Imperial, City of Coventry and Ransomes.

It came as a shock to learn late in 1973 that Wills had withdrawn their sponsorship. It was planned, however, that the main event would continue in London, with the premier section being known as the 'British and European Championships'. But even this was cancelled. The economic climate of the country – three-day working week, political unrest and so on – were blamed, but withdrawals by several bands seemed to indicate that the band world had concluded that a further round of national championships was unnecessary.

## The National Brass Band Championships: 1970s onwards

The Championships had gone through a series of changes of ownership and there were to be more. To clarify these, here is a chronological list of the principal changes:

1945    *Daily Herald* takes over from J.H. Iles; E. Vaughan Morris becomes administrator as part of his work for the newspaper
1964    *Daily Herald* closes down; Nationals taken over by *The People* but Vaughan Morris continues as administrator
1967    Vaughan Morris retires from *The People* but remains as sole administrator for the Nationals
1971    Vaughan Morris retires; R. Smith & Co., music publishers, become owners; Peter Wilson becomes organising secretary

Following the final retirement of Vaughan Morris and the takeover of the Nationals by R. Smith & Co., Geoffrey Brand, as managing director, was now effectively in charge. As was seen earlier, no time was lost in dispensing with the World Championships and restoring the Nationals. There was a further increase in prize monies and all seven competitors in the 1971 World event were given byes to the 1972 Nationals. The absence of leading bands from Area contests created a dilemma for Area committees as some of the Area contests were now less attractive. In 1973 there was a compromise: only bands which had held the top title in the previous four years were given byes. This involved Brighouse (twice winners), Black Dyke and GUS. From 1976, all bands except the reigning champions were required to qualify.

The managements of the Nationals and the British Open Championships, were responsible for two joint initiatives during 1973. In future years the members of any band winning both competitions in the same year would receive special 'Double Championship' medals, and in the event of the British Open being won by a band which had not qualified for the National Finals that band would receive an invitation to the Finals.

Percussion was introduced in the 1973 Championship section. Further, there was to be a full weekend of activities, with a Festival Dinner on the Friday evening and then, following the contest and gala concert on the Saturday, a concert of contemporary music on the Sunday, performed by the City of London Band. A change in the lower section rules meant that from this year Finals winners would move up a section in the following year but would not now be given a bye to the Finals.

The 1974 Finals were marked with a win by the Cory Band, the first time the title National Champion Brass Band of Great Britain had gone out of England.

In 1969 a new award had been inaugurated, the 'Insignia of Honour', awarded to an instrumentalist for 'conspicuous service to brass bands'. The first award went to Derek Garside and the second, in 1970, to Lyndon Baglin, both of CWS (Manchester). With changes in the management of the championships these awards and those of the Baton of Honour (see above) were phased out and discontinued after 1976, as the following shows:

|      | *Insignia*       | *Baton of Honour* |
|------|------------------|-------------------|
| 1971 | James Shepherd   | William Scholes   |
| 1972 | Norman Ashcroft  |                   |
| 1973 | Bert Sullivan    | George Thompson   |
| 1974 | Edward Gray      |                   |
| 1976 | Barrie Perrins   |                   |

Following several weeks of speculation it was announced that, from 26 August 1975, 'ownership and editorial responsibility' of *British Bandsman* would pass to Robert D. Alexander. A later announcement confirmed that from the end of October the National Brass Band Championships would also become his property. *BB* would still present the National Championships but would no longer be the sponsor. Peter Wilson remained as organising secretary.

In 1976 the NBBCC was replaced by the National Brass Band Championship Advisory Committee. Amongst its first tasks was clarification of the use of various registries that now existed. Henceforth, any accredited registry was acceptable at Area level, but at the National Finals only the National Registry could be used.

Further changes took place during 1977 as, once again, links between *BB* and the Nationals were severed. From 3 September *BB* was owned and published by Austin Catelinet Ltd, of Beaconsfield. Peter Wilson left his position with the Nationals in order to become managing editor of *BB* and Robert Alexander now had sole charge.

During 1978 the Advisory Committee attempted to regularise the problem of promotion and relegation, based on the results of three years of Area contests. A storm arose in the Welsh region which had its own system, based on six specified contests within one year. When the Welsh Area committee refused to change, the contest management decided that it would run the contest from London but the Welsh bands refused to support them. The result was that in 1980 there was no Welsh Area contest and the previous year's prizewinners were invited to the Finals. The year 1980 was also marked by tributes to Fred Mortimer, in honour of the centenary of his birth. At the close of the Royal Albert Hall contest Foden's took centre stage; Harry Mortimer conducted *Severn Suite* (Elgar) and Rex Mortimer directed 'Heroic March' from *An Epic Symphony* (Fletcher), each having been part of the success story of Foden's in the 1930s.

## Gala concerts

The evening concert was an important feature of the Nationals. The 1946 event was described in detail above and the concerts continued on this lavish scale. In 1950, Princess Elizabeth (later, Queen Elizabeth II) attended.

By 1951 Sir Malcolm Sargent had become a regular guest conductor and nine bands was the 'norm'. Guest soloists at this time ranged from the renowned french horn virtuoso Dennis Brain to jazz trumpeter Kenny Baker. An innovation in 1952 was that the massed bands performed the test piece, conducted by its arranger Frank Wright. This procedure was followed for a few years but never met with universal approval as, with Wright often adjudicating, it was felt that those bands that had rehearsed under him were at an advantage. In 1953, for the first time, part of the concert was shown live on television.

To alleviate the problem of demand for concert tickets, twin concerts were instituted in 1954. The music played was identical at both and

Sir Adrian Boult was the guest conductor in this first year. There was a new conductor for the 1956 concert, Karl Rankl.[14]

The twin concerts, commencing respectively at 5 pm and 8 pm, continued up to 1973 after which, to the relief of the bandsmen, the earlier concert was replaced by the Butlins National Youth Brass Band Championships (see page 104). The eight o'clock concerts continued, with a variety of guest conductors and soloists, and with occasional changes in the number of participating bands. Three important new instrumental solos were commissioned by the Nationals and premiered in the concerts whilst in the hands of Brand and Wilson – *Euphonium Concerto* by Joseph Horovitz (1972), *Cornet Concerto* by Ernest Tomlinson (1974) and *Rhapsody for Trombone* by Gordon Langford (1976).

With regular appearances by the trumpeters of either the Life Guards or the Royal Military School of Music, the concerts maintained their quality, with top-line international artists, varied programmes and often an element of the spectacular.

## National Youth Band Championships

Youth Band Championships were commenced in 1945, along with the revival of the Nationals. They ran for only six years, Besses Boys' Band winning in five of them.

The so-called 'accent on youth', a policy change at the instigation of *The People*, meant that the Youth Band Championships were to be revived. As a preliminary step the band of Netteswell School from Harlow appeared in the twin concerts of 1964.

For the Youth Championships of 1965, the age limit was 16 and bands could have between 22 and 25 players. No percussion was allowed and players registered with a senior band were ineligible. The winners of the 1st and 2nd prize in each Area contest were invited to the Finals. Area contests and Finals were held on the same days as other sections, and the winner of the Finals was featured in the twin concerts that same evening. The Area test piece was Eric Ball's *The Young in Heart* and contests were held in most regions. Ten bands competed in the Finals, held in Chelsea Town Hall, the winners duly appearing in the evening concerts, playing the test piece.

There were no Youth Band Championships during 1966 or 1967, but in the latter year a group of boys from a local band played in the Albert Hall before the announcement of results and Grimethorpe Juniors, winners

---

[14] Rankl had been music director at Covent Garden from 1946 to 1951, after which he became principal conductor of the Scottish National Orchestra. Austrian-born, he settled in England in 1939.

of the Yorkshire Area third section, appeared in the twin concerts playing the test piece which had brought them success.

The Youth Championships returned in 1968, but only at Finals level. Chelsea Town Hall now became the regular venue and this series continued until 1973, in which year the winners were taken to a television studio for a live appearance.

There were radical changes in 1974, with sponsorship by Butlins Holiday Camps. The Finals were now held in the Royal Albert Hall following the National Championships. Bands were allowed between 20 and 50 players, including percussion. Members of participating youth bands were also allowed to play with a senior band. One band only from each Area qualified for the Finals and all adjudication was open. Regional winners were given an engagement at their nearest Butlins camp and the Finals winner was offered a contract to record for Decca. In 1979, prize monies were doubled and a £50 travel grant awarded to all qualifying bands. From 1978 Butlins introduced a Solo Championship, with junior and senior sections, preliminaries and finals. These were organised separately from the band competitions and ran for a few years. Table 5.1 shows the venues, test pieces and winning bands for the Youth Championships from 1945 to 1982.

*All-England Solo Championships*

An adjunct to the National Championships, the All-England Solo Championships were organised in 1946 and 1947, with six preliminary rounds and a Grand Final to determine the various All-England solo champions. There were senior classes for cornet, euphonium and trombone, with a single class for juniors and another for juveniles. The results of the 1946 Finals (which took place at Belle Vue) are shown below:

| Seniors | Cornet | 1st | Charles (Charlie) Rushworth (Nutgrove) |
| | | 2nd | Eric Bravington (Hanwell) |
| | Euphonium | 1st | Arthur Doyle (Luton) |
| | Trombone | 1st | Frank Wesson (Hickleton Main) |
| Juniors | | 1st | Denzil Stephens (euphonium, Black Dyke) |
| Juveniles | | 1st | Betty Woodcock (cornet, Stocksbridge) |

Rushworth was a regular winner in solo contests and a one-time member of Bickershaw Colliery Band. The senior euphonium winner, Arthur Doyle, had a fine reputation as a recitalist. A member of the Luton Band at the time, he had previously played with Munn & Felton's and was later to join the Philharmonia, on tuba. The senior trombone winner,

*Table 5.1    The National Youth Band Championships 1945–82*

(a) *National Youth Band Championships*

| 1945 | Belle Vue | Poetic Fancies (Laurent) | Besses Boys |
|------|-----------|--------------------------|-------------|
| 1946 | Belle Vue | The Forest Chief (E le Duc) | Besses Boys |
| 1947 | Belle Vue | Homage to Pharaoh (Rimmer) | Besses Boys |
| 1948 | Belle Vue | Knights of Old (Greenwood) | Grimethorpe Juniors |
| 1949 | Belle Vue | Mignonne (Thomas) | Besses Boys |
| 1950 | Belle Vue | Runnymede (Ashpole) | Besses Boys |
| 1965 | Chelsea | Impromptu (Ball) | Gwaun-cae-Gurwen Youth |
| 1968 | Chelsea | Three Songs Without Words (Ball) | Mid-Hants Schools |
| 1969 | Chelsea | In Switzerland (Ball) | Queensbury Music Centre |
| 1970 | Chelsea | Youth Salutes a Master (Ball) | Redbridge Youth |
| 1971 | Chelsea | English Country Scenes (Ball) | Queensbury Music Centre |
| 1972 | Chelsea | A Dales Suite (Butterworth) | St Dennis Youth |
| 1973 | Chelsea | Partita (Gregson) | St Dennis Youth |

(b) *Butlins National Youth Band Championships*

| 1974 | RAH* | Torch of Freedom (Ball) and Patterns (Gregson) | Tredegar Juniors |
|------|------|-----------------------------------------------|------------------|
| 1975 | RAH | Countdown (Patterson) | Tredegar Juniors |
| 1976 | RAH | Andalucia (Kelly) | Upper Rhondda Comp. Sch. |
| 1977 | RAH | Coliseum (Wood) | Upper Rhondda Comp. Sch. |
| 1978 | RAH | Metropolis (Langford) | Loughborough Youth |
| 1979 | RAH | Three Brass Band Sketches (Catelinet) | Upper Rhondda Comp. Sch. |
| 1980 | RAH | A Circus Suite (Johnson) | Kilmarnock Area Schools |
| 1981 | RAH | Margam Stones (Wood) | Kilmarnock Area Schools |
| 1982 | RAH | Sinfonietta (Horovitz) | Kilmarnock Area Schools |

* Royal Albert Hall

Frank Wesson, later became a member of Carlton Main.[15] The name Denzil Stephens appears regularly throughout the book and the Juvenile winner, Betty Woodcock, was discussed on page 84.

The exercise was repeated in 1947. Willie Lang of Black Dyke won the senior cornet championship, whilst in the Juniors Tom Atkinson was winner and Stephens runner-up, reversing the previous year's results. Maurice Murphy (see page 137) became Juvenile Champion.

---

[15] At one time there were four members of the Wesson family at Carlton Main, all playing trombone. The bass trombonist was Jack Wesson senior, brother of Frank – the 1946 Champion. Jack had two sons, Jack Junior and Billy, both of whom also played at Carlton Main.

## Belle Vue

*The Spring Festival*

There were more than 100 entries for the first post-war May contest but due to limitations of time and accommodation only 80 were accepted. From 1947 the five-class format was reinstated. Large entries in 1946–47–48 persuaded the Belle Vue management to revive the July contest in 1949, but a mere 14 bands appeared in the two-section contest.

From 1952 the May and July contests were combined and renamed the 'Spring Brass Band Festival'. There were six sections, named after the trophies competed for: Grand Shield, Senior Cup and Senior Trophy; Junior Shield, Junior Cup and Junior Trophy.[16] In 1955 and 1956 there were seven sections, a Primary Cup section being added.

By the late 1950s the grounds of Belle Vue were becoming somewhat run down and its popularity waned. Even a change of ownership and considerable cash injections failed to stem the decline. Nevertheless, improvements during the early 1960s gave the showground a new lease of life. From around 1964 Harry Mortimer became more involved in the running of the contests,[17] having a say in the appointment of adjudicators, the selection of test pieces and choice of bands. Despite this, by 1970 attendances had fallen dramatically and investments had been curtailed.[18]

In 1972 Concordia Brass Band from Holland became the first overseas band to compete for the Grand Shield. Bad news followed, with the announcement that the 1975 Festival was to be reduced to three sections. The 1976 event went ahead in conjunction with the Granada Television 'Band of the Year' competition (see pages 111–12). There was a slight upturn in the following year with four sections in the Spring Festival, again combined with 'Band of the Year'.

*The British Open Championships*

After the war the Belle Vue September contest continued, but once again it faced competition from the Nationals, reinstated in 1945. In this year Kenneth Wright's 1935 Crystal Palace test piece, *Pride of Race*, was the test piece. The competition then provided a new work each year until 1962. All except that of 1960 were original and included seven by Eric Ball, two by Denis Wright and one each by two Salvation Army composers – Dean Goffin of New Zealand and Erik Leidzen of Sweden. There was

---

16  The trophies had formerly been used at Crystal Palace.
17  See Mortimer, 1981, Chapter 10 – 'Belle Vue: Hail and Farewell'.
18  Nicholls, 1989, pp. 57–9.

also, in 1957, the first test piece by a lady composer, *Carnival* by Helen Perkin, who also composed the 1962 September test, *Island Heritage*. Fairey Aviation dominated during the 1940s, achieving seven wins and three 2nd prizes in the ten years 1941–50.

In 1951 only 14 bands competed, with many of the elites absent. This could have been due partly to the heavy concert season during Festival of Britain year, but there were mutterings about poor prize-money. As far back as 1918 the 1st prize had been £100; now it was only £75. For the Centenary Contest in 1952 this was doubled. All leading bands were present and the test piece was *Scena Sinfonica* (Henry Geehl) – an original work composed in the style of an operatic selection in deference to the past.

Hitherto the contest had been known as the Belle Vue September Contest. In 1952 it became the 'September Open' but since 1955 has been called the 'British Open Championships'.[19] In addition to cash prizes and 'specials' – awarded by instrument makers, music publishers or uniform manufacturers – the 'Open' winner holds the £2000 Gold Trophy for a year. This is a shield that has been presented annually since 1924 and on which winning bands have their names engraved.

The National Band of New Zealand took the title in 1953, whilst Munn & Felton's achieved its only Belle Vue win in 1954. Fairey's and Foden's withdrew this year owing to the fact that, on doctor's orders, Harry Mortimer was unable to conduct.

In 1958 an adjudicating system not used at brass band contests for many years was tried. When every band had completed its initial performance the adjudicators nominated six to play again. The final results were based on the performances heard in the play-off. The winner was Carlton Main – not totally unexpected, as they had won 3rd and 2nd prizes in the two previous years. One quirk was that Foden's, playing last, drew to play first in the play-off and therefore had to return to the platform immediately.

Fairey's began the 1960s in fine style with a hat-trick (1961–62–63). They were barred in the following year and Foden's won – for the first time in 38 years. Fairey's returned in 1965 to triumph again. Additional excitement was created during the band's 'exile' year when they opened the proceedings with a performance of their hat-trick test piece, *Life Divine* (Jenkins).

In 1966 the event was made into a full weekend's festival, with a 'Cavalcade of Marching' on the Sunday afternoon following the 'Open' and a massed band concert in the evening. The Cavalcade was organised by the North West Association and an audience of some 5000 watched

---

[19] Littlemore, 1999, p. 92.

17 local bands. The evening concert featured Black Dyke, CWS (Manchester) and Fairey's, with Harry Mortimer and comedian Jimmy Edwards conducting. The exercise was repeated in 1967, with the 'Marching Cavalcade' sponsored by W.D. & H.O. Wills and incorporating a competition.

An important change made in 1970 was to bring the adjudicators' box closer to the bands. The King's Hall, which housed the 'Open', was a multi-purpose building, circular in shape and used as a circus or a concert hall, and for boxing or wrestling. For band contests the boxing ring served as the platform. This was in the centre, surrounded with tiered seating from which the audience looked down towards the performers. However, the location of the adjudicators was poor; they were placed behind a curtain high up at the back of the hall – a position not conducive to critical listening. To alleviate this the boxing ring was now placed off-centre and an adjudicators' box erected close to it, giving the adjudicators a more accurate sound. There was now another hat-trick, Black Dyke winning in 1972–73–74.

Elgar Howarth composed his somewhat controversial *Fireworks* as the test piece for the 1975 British Open. It was a kind of 'Young Person's Guide to the Brass Band', complete with narration. The narration was left unspoken during the contest, creating confusion for the audience which, to say the least, was not enthusiastic. However, on the following day Grimethorpe and Black Dyke performed *Fireworks* in the concert, complete with narrator and with Howarth conducting. Suddenly the piece made sense and was hailed as a success.[20]

In 1976 there was no massed band concert, but the winning band recorded a half-hour programme for the BBC in the King's Hall following the announcement of the results – a policy adopted for several years. The concert was reinstated in 1978, the bands taking part being the NYBB, Besses and City of Coventry, with all proceeds donated to the NYBB.

## The European Championships

Reflecting the growing interest in British-style brass bands on mainland Europe, the European Brass Band Championships were begun in 1978, initially taking place in the Royal Albert Hall on the day following the National Championships. The 1st prize was £1000, there was a special prize for the highest placed continental band and all unplaced such bands received a new instrument. There was no limit on the number of players

---

[20] Having completed a hat-trick in the previous year, Black Dyke were barred from competing and Grimethorpe were asked not to compete, as their musical adviser had composed the test piece and would, in fact, be adjudicating.

at first, many European bands being quite large. Some used trumpets and french horns. From 1980, however, brass band instruments only were permitted, with an upper limit of 35 players plus percussion. As a general rule, the champion band of each country was eligible to participate, plus one extra from the host country. Each band played two pieces – a set test piece and another of its own choice.

### Other contests of national significance

Gradually more contests appeared which were of interest to some leading bands. These are looked at briefly, in the order in which they appeared. Some are still ongoing whilst others have ceased. Latitude has been used with dates, some of the contests being reviewed up to their closing date, possibly well beyond 1980, whilst consideration of some others which began pre-1980 is deferred until Chapter 10.

### *Quartet and solo championships*

The earliest contest of national significance to be run outside of Belle Vue and the National Championships was not for full band but, initially, for brass quartets.[21] Many such contests were already taking place and one organised in Oxford in 1944 by Morris Motors Band attracted 17 'parties'. Later in the year it was announced that this competition would in future carry the title 'Brass Quartet Championship of Great Britain'. Between 1955 and 1958 there was also an 'A' section, for quartets of a slightly lower standard.

In 1959 a Cornet Air Varié Championship was introduced to which was added, in 1960, a class for the euphonium. From 1961 entries were accepted for all brass band instruments except percussion. A trophy was awarded to the highest-placed competitor in each class of instrument and the six competitors placed highest in the preliminary round competed in the Finals, along with the previous year's winner, for the title 'Champion Soloist of Great Britain'. From 1965 the champion soloists of Scotland and Wales also competed in the Finals.

There were two noteworthy achievements by young cornet players during the 1960s. The first was a hat-trick for James Shepherd in 1962–63–64[22]

---

[21] The standard brass quartet comprises two cornets, a tenor horn and a euphonium. Other combinations are also used, including the trombone quartet and the tuba quartet.

[22] In fact, 1964 was a very special year for Shepherd. He had recently left Carlton Main to join Black Dyke, and at Oxford he not only completed his personal hat-trick, but helped Black Dyke to win the Quartet Championships and also became the first recipient of an award for the best instrumentalist in the quartets.

and the second a unique double for James Watson who, at the age of 14, became Junior and Senior Solo Champion in 1966.

Most quartets played traditional music dating from the pre-war years, but in 1966 the GUS quartet played a new composition by Gilbert Vinter. This was revolutionary by the standards of the time and helped GUS to a convincing win. Vinter produced two more such works for the following two years, each again won by GUS, giving them a hat-trick (see page 153). A list of winning quartets and soloists is given in Appendix E.

## *The Edinburgh International Contest*

A contest was instituted in Edinburgh in August 1949, taking place on the Saturday before the start of the city's International Music Festival. To give it an international flavour, five English and five Scottish bands were invited. CWS (Manchester) were winners of the event, which attracted an audience of some 6000, with an estimated 15 000 attending the evening massed band concert. This became a major event in the brass band calendar.

English bands dominated in the contest's early years, but later top English bands did not attend. The contest was held in Princess Street Gardens, an attractive setting visually, though its close proximity to one of Scotland's busiest railway stations made it less attractive aurally. The last contest took place in 1992, after which it closed down through lack of finance. Winners are shown below:

| | | |
|---|---|---|
| 1949 CWS (Manchester) | 1964 Kinneil Colliery | 1979 CWS (Glasgow) |
| 1950 CWS (Manchester) | 1965 City of Coventry | 1980 Bo'ness & Carriden |
| 1951 Scottish CWS | 1966 Yorkshire Imperial | 1981 Whitburn |
| 1952 Clayton Aniline | 1967 Carlton Main | 1982 CWS (Glasgow) |
| 1953 National Band of NZ | 1968 Kinneil Colliery | 1983 Ever Ready |
| 1954 CWS (Manchester) | 1969 Broxburn Public | 1984 Whitburn |
| 1955 CWS (Manchester) | 1970 Whitburn | 1985 Whitburn |
| 1956 Ferodo Works | 1971 Dalmellington | 1986 Whitburn |
| 1957 Carlton Main | 1972 Stanshawe | 1987 CWS (Glasgow) |
| 1958 Scottish CWS | 1973 Lochgelly Public | 1988 Wm Davis Constr. |
| 1959 Carlton Main | 1974 Lochgelly Public | 1989 CWS (Glasgow) |
| 1960 Carlton Main | 1975 Skellerup Woolston | 1990 Whitburn |
| 1961 CWS (Glasgow) | 1976 Burton Construction | 1991 Newtongrange |
| 1962 National Band of NZ | 1977 Rochdale | 1992 Whitburn |
| 1963 Grimethorpe | 1978 Web Ivory Newhall | |

## *CISWO (Coal Industry Social Welfare Organisation)*

Another event begun in 1949 was the CISWO contest, organised by the North Eastern Divisional Welfare Committee and held in Sheffield City Hall. There were three sections in the contest, which was followed by a concert with massed colliery bands and male voice choirs. The contest was restricted to bands within the boundaries of the North East Division of CISWO, but it led to the founding of a national competition whilst continuing as a festival in its own right.

The first Mineworkers' National Brass Band Championships, with four sections, took place in the Winter Gardens, Blackpool, on 13 October 1962. Bands from each Coal Board Division appeared, by invitation. There was no massed band concert following the Finals, but it became traditional for the reigning champions to perform a short concert before the announcement of results. The Sheffield event was now a qualifying round and gradually other Coal Board Divisions set up similar events.

In 1972, CISWO introduced open adjudication, with adjudicators sitting and marking separately. There was also a pre-draw.[23] In 1974, the two adjudicators each chose a different winner, with the result that there was a tie for first place with Cory's and Grimethorpe being awarded the same total of marks. On this occasion the result was allowed to stand, but in future years one adjudicator was given the role of 'tie-breaker'.

With sponsorship from Britvic from 1979, the event was expanded to form a full weekend Festival, beginning with a massed band concert on the Friday evening, the contest on Saturday and with Sunday devoted to a solo competition. This format continued for a number of years.

The following shows a list of winning bands in the championship section from the inception of the national contest:

| | | | | | |
|------|----------------|------|------------------|------|----------------|
| 1962 | Carlton Main | 1970 | Cory | 1978 | Carlton Main |
| 1963 | Carlton Main | 1971 | Cory | 1979 | Grimethorpe |
| 1964 | Markham Main | 1972 | Cory | 1980 | Grimethorpe |
| 1965 | Markham Main | 1973 | Grimethorpe | 1981 | Carlton Main |
| 1966 | Carlton Main | 1974 | Cory/Grimethorpe | 1982 | Brodsworth |
| 1967 | Grimethorpe | 1975 | Grimethorpe | 1983 | Grimethorpe |
| 1968 | Grimethorpe | 1976 | Grimethorpe | 1984 | Cancelled |
| 1969 | Grimethorpe | 1977 | Desford | | |

Grimethorpe were winners every year from 1985 to 2000.

## Granada Band of the Year

The first Granada Band of the Year contest took place in the King's Hall, Belle Vue, in November 1971. The men behind it were Bram Gay and

---

[23] Traditionally, immediately before the start of the contest, band representatives draw lots to determine the order of play. This aids anonymity when adjudication is closed but is totally unnecessary when it is open. To avoid the necessity of every band having to be there for the start of the contest the CISWO draw was made some weeks before the date of the competition, to enable the bands to make appropriate travel arrangements.

Arthur Taylor, a Granada Television producer. Ten bands participated, the winner taking £500 and a presentation cornet. A rerun of its performance was filmed after the announcement of results and subsequently screened by Granada and four other ITV companies. Adjudication was by a panel of three, two assessing musical standards and the third – Arthur Taylor, the producer of the television programme – giving an assessment based on programme content, presentation and suitability for screening. Cory's were the first winners.

The 1972 contest was held on the day after the British Open Championships. It was the first entertainment contest for Grimethorpe's new conductor, Elgar Howarth, and the band's win was in no small measure due to his witty and effective arrangements. In the following year the event was held in May, on the day following Belle Vue's Spring Festival, partly to help salvage this struggling contest. In 1975 each band was required to include a set test piece in its programme – part of Elgar's *Introduction and Allegro for String Quartet and String Orchestra*, specially arranged by Arthur Butterworth.

Amongst the adjudicators during these early years were Sir Charles Groves, Maurice Handford and Colin Davis (knighted in 1980), all well-known orchestral conductors.

The contest was run in conjunction with Belle Vue's Spring Festival until 1981 when, following the closure of Belle Vue, 'Granada' found a new home – at the Spectrum Arena, near Warrington (Figures 5.1 and 5.2).

A conflict with the Musicians' Union (MU) arose in 1977 (see page 195). The programme was screened only on Granada but the 1st prize was doubled, to £1000. There was no television involvement in 1978 or 1979 because of MU objections. Television returned in 1980. Not all the bandsmen in the ten competing bands were MU members, but those who were not agreed to enrol in the event of their band winning.

Back on course, there were several more memorable occasions, none more so than in the year 1985 when Grimethorpe, five-times previous winners and determined to stop Desford's hat-trick from going any further, played the whole programme without conductor or announcements. Their conductor, David James, suddenly appeared in order to direct the final bar of the final piece.[24]

Due to the closure of the Spectrum the competition was taken to the Isle of Man in 1987 when Soli Deo Gloria, from Holland, was amongst the eight competitors. Unfortunately, this proved to be the last Granada competition. Here is a list of winners:

---

[24] In the following year Desford did a similar thing, beginning its programme with *Anything you can do, I can do better!*

Figure 5.1    Besses o' th' Barn with Roy Newsome in the King's Hall, Belle Vue, c. 1980

113

Figure 5.2    Desford and Howard Snell acknowledge the applause at a Granada contest, c. 1982

114

| 1971 | Cory | 1980 | Fairey's |
|------|------|------|----------|
| 1972 | Grimethorpe | 1981 | Grimethorpe |
| 1973 | Grimethorpe | 1982 | Desford |
| 1974 | Stanshawe | 1983 | Desford |
| 1975 | Brighouse & Rastrick | 1984 | Desford |
| 1976 | Grimethorpe | 1985 | Grimethorpe |
| 1977 | Grimethorpe | 1986 | Desford |
| 1978 | Carlton Main | 1987 | Desford |
| 1979 | Fairey's | | |

*Pontin's Championships*

On a weekend in April 1974 Pontin's hosted a four-section contest at its Southport campus, organised by the Prescot Band. More than 1000 supporters spent the weekend on site.

Not only did this become an annual event, from 1976 there were preliminary rounds, held at Easter in three different camps – Southport, Brean Sands (Somerset) and Hemsby (Norfolk) – with the Finals in Prestatyn, North Wales, in November. A total of 140 bands participated, 45 qualifying for the Finals. Eric Ball composed his *Holiday Overture* as test piece for the Finals, though new commissions were not to be a feature of Pontin's contests. A Youth Section was introduced in 1977.

## Other contests of some importance before and during World War II

In 1936, the number of contests advertised and/or reported in *BBN* was 146. Approximately a third were organised by Associations whilst the rest were privately run, many having no restrictions on band membership. Most were outdoor events, held during the summer. Few attracted leading bands, which were too busy with engagements to be concerned with many contests. Of the 146, 31 were solo or quartet contests.

A handful of contests attracted some top bands, generally by offering high prize-money. One of these was held at Southport in April 1936, as part of its week-long Musical Festival. The prizewinners were Foden's, Besses, Brighouse and Black Dyke.

Butlins Holiday Camp, Skegness, was the location of another contest, in July 1937. This had four sections, with trophies and £250 in cash prizes. It attracted a good entry, the prizes all going to colliery bands – Grimethorpe, Creswell and Bickershaw. This competition ran for a further two years, the 1939 event being followed on the Sunday by a massed band concert conducted by Denis Wright. Four bands were engaged, part of the programme was broadcast, and it was here that a new seating formation was adopted (see pages 37–8).

The Leicester Brass Band Festival was inaugurated in 1923. In 1936, its four sections attracted 68 bands. Prizes in the championship section went to Munn & Felton's and Hanwell. During the years 1936–39 there was an evening massed bands concert.

One more English contest warrants a mention and that is the West of England Bandsman's Festival, still held annually in the aptly named Cornish village of Bugle. Though primarily for Cornish bands, the contest sometimes attracts bands from further afield, occasionally one of the 'cracks'. The day begins and ends with bands marching through the village to and from the contest field. In 1936 Munn & Felton's, the reigning national champions, competed. To the delight of the locals they were beaten into second place by Camborne. In the following year Black Dyke entered and it must have given the event a tremendous boost when this famous band appeared – and won.

The Scottish Amateur Band Association (SABA), formed in 1895, has always maintained a tight grip on banding activities within its borders. In the immediate pre-war years there were few contests in Scotland other than those run by SABA, which included the Edinburgh, Glasgow and Fife Charities events as well as the Scottish Championships.

In Wales, the majority of brass bands were in the south where two very active associations controlled most contests – the South Wales & Monmouthshire Association and the West Wales Association. Bands had the benefit, also, of the Welsh National Eisteddfod where there were classes for brass bands. This alternated annually between South and North Wales.

* * *

Despite a huge drop in contesting activities following the outbreak of war in 1939, efforts were made to maintain some momentum. Many contests had sections for boys and girls; it was seen as essential to give these 'bandsmen of tomorrow' every possible incentive. In 1942, there was an upturn in full band contests in England. News from Scotland was also optimistic. The Edinburgh Charities contest was a resounding success. Held in Princes Street Gardens, bands played an own-choice test piece, a march and a hymn tune. It took the form of a single section contest, but to encourage lower-section bands there were special awards for those from sections three and four placed highest – a formula adopted in many future contests.

A number of contests were again held in 1943, despite problems with travel. In Scotland, the Edinburgh Charities contest this year coincided with the start of the capital's 'Wings for Victory' week so there were huge crowds in the city. There were no cash prizes but £50 was donated to charity. Another important contest took place in Edinburgh in October in the Usher Hall, the city's main concert venue. Though there were no actual Scottish Championships during the war, this was obviously a preparation for post-war years. A substantial audience attended and using this hall helped raise the profile of bands.

The 1944 Edinburgh Charities contest was won, for the third time in succession, by Clydebank Burgh. This proved to be an exceptionally successful year for this band. Having completed its hat-trick in Edinburgh it went on to win the Glasgow Charities, becoming the first band to achieve seven wins there and also completing the unusual 'double' of winning both the Edinburgh and Glasgow contests in the same year.

## *Other significant contests post 1945*

Contests returned in great numbers after the war, more associations becoming active and new ones being formed. Some had kept going during the war, organising contests for member bands. More were now so doing. But there were also privately run contests, many of which were a part of some other event such as a carnival or flower show. Whit Friday contests also returned. In 1946 there were eight of these in villages in the Saddleworth area.

However, poor attendances at several contests in England were reported during 1951. York's Festival of Britain contest, one of the worst hit, was cancelled due to insufficient entries. Conversely, a similar event in Forfar (Scotland) was highly successful. In fact, in contrast to reports from England, Scottish contests seem to have had a good year. The Edinburgh Charities celebrated its Golden Jubilee in 1955, and an 'All-Star' band was formed to give an evening concert following the competition.

At Bugle, Camborne Town, the most successful West of England band of the time, won for the third time in succession in 1952; special medals were struck for the bandsmen. Munn & Felton's returned to win in 1954 and 1955, their visits coinciding with concert tours in the South West.

Possibly reflecting the success of the Edinburgh International Contest, a new competition took place in Leeds Town Hall in November 1949. This was billed as an 'Inter-County' contest, with bands from Yorkshire and Durham. In addition to the normal prizes there was a trophy for the county whose bands attained the highest aggregate of marks. Yorkshire emerged as winners and this became an annual event. A Yorkshire versus Lancashire contest was held in 1954, in Huddersfield Town Hall. Equally successful, it was held in reverse the following year at Belle Vue, as Lancashire v. Yorkshire. Inter-county rivalry was keen and the contest became known as 'The Battle of the Roses'. The idea caught on and there were a number of other Inter-County and even Inter-Association contests.

In 1964 the Luton Band ran a contest to find the Champion Subscription Band. Feeling is always high that the dice is so heavily loaded in favour of sponsored bands that there ought to be separate categories for them and for unsponsored bands. This was, therefore, an interesting experiment – but somewhat nullified by the fact that not all the better subscription bands participated. City of Coventry were winners, with East Ham second and Hanwell third.

Concern was expressed in Wales in 1964 when it was announced that the brass band section in the National Eisteddfod was to be open to all comers, with one prize only – of £500. It was felt that this would be a gift to some 'marauding' English band. No such band appeared and the prize went to Ystalefera Public. The same conditions applied in 1965 but, though Brighouse & Rastrick competed, the £500 prize once again went to Ystalefera. The 'open' idea was dropped in 1967, though the £500 prize was retained for the Class 'A' winner.

A new system of finding the 'Champion Band of Wales' was begun in 1966, based on the results of six specified local contests. This system created complications with regard to qualification for the Nationals and the European Championships. Qualification for English bands was based on the results of the National Championships and in Scotland the winner of the Area contest (which was also the Scottish Championships) represented Scotland in the following year's European Championships. The situation in Wales now meant that its 'Champion Band' would represent Wales in Europe but would not necessarily qualify for the National Brass Band Championships, as this was determined at the Area contest.

What were described as the first 'British Youth Band Championships' were held from 1969, organised by Liverpool Youth Music Committee as part of the Liverpool Show, an annual event lasting three days and attracting more than 100 000 visitors. With the arrival of the Butlins Championships in 1974, however, this contest was discontinued.

Other contests, which arrived or thrived during the 1970s included the Reading Guild Contest, founded in 1946; Leamington Spa, dating from 1969; and Lansing Bagnall Open Challenge, founded in 1977. There was also the Milton Keynes Brass Band Festival, an entertainment contest supported by the local Development Corporation and founded in 1975. From 1978 there was also an entertainment contest in Yeovil and a 'Northern Open Championship' was also established that year. Though not attracting the very best bands, the latter was a flourishing event and well supported by bands in all sections. It was sponsored for 20 years by Pilkington's, the glass manufacturers of St Helens, after which, in 1999, sponsorship was offered by Wilkinson's, a chain of general stores.

Several of the above-mentioned events – and many others – survived to the end of the century and beyond.

## Conclusion

Contesting continued to be regarded by many as the lifeblood of brass banding. The Belle Vue contests and the National Championships remained the pacemakers but there were also many other events that provided incentives and opportunities. Nevertheless, by the early 1950s it was apparent that enthusiasm was not as widespread as it had been. *BBN* appealed to bands not to concentrate on the Area contests at the expense of those at local level.

In contrast, the late 1970s saw almost frenetic contesting activities throughout Britain. By 1980, however, some contests had already gone out of existence. Though no one could say that the contest was actually in decline, it had probably peaked in the late 1970s. Paradoxically, however, many of the leading bands were now more involved in contest work than they had been through most of the post-war years.

# CHAPTER 6

# Composers and repertoire

## Introduction

The repertoire of early brass bands comprised original marches and dances, arrangements of extracts from opera and oratorio, and hymn tunes. Early test pieces were generally choruses from opera or oratorio and towards the end of the nineteenth century the contest march appeared. From quite early times there were also selections – initially from opera, oratorio or from the works of a particular composer. These were, in effect, collections of contrasting tunes, linked by cadenzas or short transitory passages. There were also pieces designated 'fantasia' or 'overture' but these were stylistically akin to the early selection and though they could loosely be described as original there was no recognisable form or structure and therefore they could not reasonably be regarded as 'works'.

The first acknowledged original brass band work was Percy Fletcher's tone poem *Labour and Love*, test piece for the 1913 Crystal Palace contest. Like the early fantasias it is operatic in style; however, its themes are interrelated and therefore, despite having the structural freedom of the tone poem there are strong unifying features, justifying the use of the term 'work'. The score carries a detailed synopsis of the piece, which was the first of many examples of 'programme music' composed for band.

It opened the door for more original works; they came slowly at first but then, after World War II, at an ever-increasing rate. Most were composed by minor composers, some of whom specialised in the genre. Until *circa* 1960 virtually all original works were composed with the contest in mind, a handful of them being by major British composers. From the early 1960s there was a steady stream of works commissioned by various arts bodies. These were not composed specifically for contests, though some were used later as test pieces.

This chapter aims to place the principal works and transcriptions into some kind of perspective. Appendix G gives a selected list of them and the chapter, which of necessity is little more than a thumbnail sketch, should be read with frequent reference to this. It is possible to mention but a few of those that are listed. For convenience, works for solo instruments and choral works are classified separately. There is also a brief look at the non-serious repertoire.

## Original works

*1921–60*

The most durable works from the inter-war years were *Life Divine, An Epic Symphony, Lorenzo* (the most successful of a series of works composed for the Belle Vue contests by Thomas Keighley) and the oft-quoted group of pieces which appeared between 1928 and 1936 by major composers – Holst, Elgar, Ireland, Bantock, Howells and Bliss.

The early post-war years saw the emergence of two brass band specialist composers, Dr Denis Wright and Eric Ball, each of whom composed works suitable for bands of all abilities – a significant development. Wright had been composing for brass band since 1925 but his only early work to achieve lasting success was *Tintagel* which, although composed in 1930, did not come to the fore until 1956, when its publication was taken over by R. Smith & Co. Wright had the distinction of composing the test piece for the first post-war National Championships, *Overture for an Epic Occasion* (see page 91). Other works included *Glastonbury* and *Tam o' Shanter's Ride*, the former a good example of a worthwhile piece for a lower-section band and the latter introducing a number of techniques new to brass bands at the time. Wright also composed the first concerto for a brass band instrument, his *Cornet Concerto* of 1941 (see page 46). His principal contribution, however, was through his transcriptions and arrangements.

Eric Ball became the most prolific composer of brass band music, writing a vast amount both for the SA and for contesting bands. A small selection of these is shown in Appendix G. Almost all had some kind of spiritual message, *Resurgam* being possibly the most profound of all brass band works. It was dedicated to the composer's sister-in-law, Elsie Dorsett, whom he affectionately called 'Elsa'. She died of tuberculosis when only 25, in 1942 and the score bears the following quotation, from the Book of Wisdom:

> The souls of the righteous are in the hand of God,
> And no torment shall touch them.
> In the eyes of the foolish they seemed to have died;
> Their departure was accounted to be their hurt,
> And their journeyings away from us to be their ruin:
> But they are in peace.

Other composers from this era included Henry Geehl, a pianist, composer and conductor who worked mainly in the theatre, Dean Goffin and George Hespe (see page 172).

The years 1957–60 saw another flurry of pieces by leading composers – Vaughan Williams, Rubbra and Howells. The Vaughan Williams work was the first of several sets of variations written for brass band. Other mainstream composers to write for band included Gordon Jacob, William Alwyn and Peter Yorke.

## 1961–70

These years were dominated by Eric Ball and Gilbert Vinter. Ball reached his compositional maturity, particularly in the National Championship test pieces of 1967 and 1969. Meanwhile, Vinter breathed new life into a repertoire still largely nineteenth-century in style. He guided the brass band gently forward with works such as *Symphony of Marches*, *Triumphant Rhapsody* and *Spectrum*. In addition to test pieces composed between 1962 and his untimely death in 1969 (more of which are shown in Appendix G), he also composed a cantata, *The Trumpets* (see page 190), and breathed new life into the repertoire of the brass quartet with *Elegy and Rondo* (1966), *Fancy's Knell* (1967) and *Alla Burlesca* (1968). Sir Arthur Bliss made a welcome return to the band scene when he composed *Belmont Variations* for the Nationals of 1963.

It was during this period that band pieces commissioned by sources other than contests were appearing. The BBC commissioned a number of such works, as did the Scottish Amateur Music Association – specifically for the NYBBS. These included works by Malcolm Arnold and the Scottish-born composer Thea Musgrave. Melodically and harmonically, the Musgrave work was the most modern-sounding band piece to date. Several other bodies commissioned brass band works. These included the much-admired *Three Impressions for Brass* by Arthur Butterworth and Phyllis Tate's *Illustrations*. Bryan Kelly, a prolific mainstream composer, wrote the first of several brass band works during this period, whilst Allan Street, a college-of-education lecturer in Nottingham, was also producing test pieces for lower-section bands.

## 1971–80

During this decade there was a phenomenal escalation both in the amount of band music composed and in the number and range of composers. Malcolm Arnold (knighted in 1992) had already written his two attractive *Little Suites* in the 1960s. His *Fantasy for Brass Band* was commissioned for the 1974 Nationals. There were two more test pieces by Eric Ball, whose *Kensington Concerto* (1972) was intended to be his swan song. However, he continued writing for several more years and the 1976 Nationals test piece was part of the fruits of his extra labours.

The two composers who, between them, now brought about something of a revolution in serious band music were Edward Gregson and Elgar Howarth. Though not specifically brass band composers, each wrote sufficient band music for them to be considered as specialists.

Gregson was born in 1945 into a Salvation Army family but though weaned on SA music, all of which at the time was in conservative musical idioms, it was he who began the revolution. He studied at the Royal Academy of Music and was much influenced by the music of Bartók, Hindemith and Stravinsky. He was a reader in music at Goldsmith's College, University of London, and in 1996 became principal of the Royal Northern College of Music (RNCM). In his band works he did much to free their rhythms, introducing frequently-changing and irregular time-signatures such as 5/8 and 7/8. His harmonic language was also firmly based in the twentieth century, relying more on intervals of the 2nd, 4th and 7th than those of the 3rd, 5th and 6th which pervade earlier styles. He also indulged in such contemporary devices as chord clusters (chords built on adjacent notes), mirror harmony (a chord sequence which appears the right way up and, concurrently, upside down) and polytonality (the simultaneous use of more than one key). Gregson often called for increased use of mutes and an enlarged percussion section. *Connotations*, the *Concerto for French Horn* and the *Concerto for Tuba* were his principal brass band works during this decade. As Appendix G shows, like Wright and Ball, Gregson composed for bands of all technical levels.

The musical language of Elgar Howarth was not dissimilar to that of Gregson. His most celebrated brass band work was *Fireworks* (see page 108). He also wrote instrumental concertos. However, by introducing other composers of note to the genre – including Harrison Birtwistle, Hans Werner Henze and Derek Bourgeois – he helped 'modernise' brass band repertoire. Like Gregson, Bourgeois (b. 1941) conducted and adjudicated, and composed for bands of various standards. He had a great facility for contrapuntal writing, often made exceptional technical demands and introduced highly complex rhythms. He also portrayed extremes of emotions. A Cambridge Doctor of Music, he was a prolific composer who had played tuba in his student days. His early band pieces were concertos for band, the first being an adaptation of an earlier flute concerto.

Birtwistle (b. 1934) was a fellow student of Howarth's in Manchester in the 1950s and became one of the leading British contemporary composers of the 1960s. His *Grimethorpe Aria*, bleak and dissonant in style, introduced new scoring techniques – with a separate part for each instrument and so-called *senza misura* – sections in free time without barlines, introducing an element of aleatory into the music. Paul Patterson (b. 1947), another contemporary composer, also used this technique extensively in his *Cataclysm*, commissioned by the NYBB. The German composer, Henze (b. 1926), was one of the most prolific twentieth-century composers. His one brass band work, *Ragtimes and Habaneras*, comprised 11 short movements, alternating between the idioms of Scott Joplin and the Cuban dance. This was premiered by Grimethorpe and Black Dyke in a Promenade Concert, conducted by Howarth.

Meanwhile, symphonist Robert Simpson (1921–97) composed two works for the National Championships as well as other works, commissioned by Desford Colliery Band. Wilfred Heaton (1919–2000), initially an SA composer but one-time resident conductor of Black Dyke, composed his *Contest Music* for the 1973 Nationals. Though receiving a number of concert performances it was rejected at first as a test piece, being considered to be ahead of its time for this purpose. It was eventually selected for the 1983 championships and became one of the best-loved of all test pieces.[1] Philip Sparke (b. 1951) studied at the Royal College of Music and, as was seen on page 74, won a composer's competition with his overture *The Prizewinners*. He was to become one of the most prolific writers of test pieces in the 1980s, but his first major work arrived in 1979, commissioned as the test piece for the New Zealand Championships of that year.

Thomas Wilson, a Scottish contemporary composer, followed his 1967 *Sinfonietta* with a much more substantial work in 1973. The Lancastrian John Golland (1942–93) wrote a number of brass band pieces, the most substantial of which was his *Sounds*. Though composed in 1974 it did not achieve recognition for several years. It was selected as the set test piece in the European Championships of 1993. Sadly, Golland died a few days before the contest. Amongst his other notable works were two Euphonium Concertos and a Concerto for Band.

The BFBB also began to commission works about this time (see page 70) and several other mainstream composers began to make their marks, including Joseph Horovitz, in particular with his *Euphonium Concerto*; Robert Farnon, with the 1975 Nationals test piece; and John McCabe, whose 1977 essay *Images* was commissioned by Besses. George Benjamin composed his one brass band work *Altitude* in 1977 and two years later *Vivat Regina* by William Mathias was first heard in a massed band concert in the Royal Albert Hall.

## Transcriptions

The word 'transcription' implies a more or less faithful reproduction of a work in a new format – that is, in the present context, scored for brass

---

[1] Since his death in 2000, Heaton has been given much greater recognition as a composer. Several high-profile recordings of his major works are now available.

band. However, transcriptions are often called 'arrangements'. They have always formed an important part of brass band repertoire, but as original works have multiplied there has been less call for them, particularly on the contest platform. An overture was almost a statutory ingredient in band programmes until relatively recently. The first 'modern' such transcription was that made by Denis Wright of the Brahms *Academic Festival Overture*, used as the test piece for the 1937 Belle Vue September contest.

Movements or extracts from symphonies were also popular for a time and, here again, Wright set the tone with his *Themes from Symphony No. 5* (Beethoven), fashionable during the war years. This was followed by extracts from other Beethoven symphonies and also from symphonies by Schubert and Tchaikovsky – Eric Ball, Frank Wright and J.A. Greenwood all contributing. Shortly after the war Denis Wright transcribed the orchestral accompaniments to Handel's *Messiah* and also to a number of works for piano and orchestra. These were part of his bridge-building policy of trying to persuade musicians with other enthusiasms to listen to brass bands.

From 1952 Frank Wright became the main architect in the transcription of overtures. His contribution included *The Frogs of Aristophanes* (Bantock), *Le roi d'Ys* (Lalo), *Les francs juges*, *Le carnaval romain* and *Benvenuto Cellini* (all by Berlioz), *La Forza del Destino* (Verdi) and *Die Meistersinger* (Wagner). All were used as test pieces in the National Championships. Several other overtures were transcribed – most used as contest pieces as well as being played in concert.

Other transcriptions included *Four Dances from Checkmate* (Bliss/Eric Ball), a symphonic poem, *The Accursed Huntsman* (Franck/Siebert), and a highly successful working by Eric Ball of Boëllmann's popular organ work, *Suite Gothique*.

During the 1970s there was a spate of transcriptions of Tudor music, mainly by Elgar Howarth. However, Howarth's masterly rendition of Mussorgsky's *Pictures at an Exhibition* (1979) dwarfed all previous transcriptions.

## Middle-of-the-road music

What today might be labelled 'popular classics' appeared during the 1930s, mostly transcribed by Denis Wright. His contributions included such pieces as Strauss's overture *Die Fledermaus*, Tchaikovsky's *Capriccio Italien* and the overture *1812*, and a suite from Bizet's *Carmen*. There were also pieces by Elgar, Grainger, Rossini and Wagner. Frank Wright transcribed many pieces, including the overture *Orpheus in the Underworld* (Offenbach) and Vaughan Williams's *English Folk Song Suite*.

The BBC competitions referred to on page 188 produced a range of pieces that might be described as 'middle-of-the-road'. Though none became best-sellers, they provided a platform for unknown composers.

Transcriptions of several light orchestral pieces appeared in the 1960s, the most successful being Geoffrey Brand's arrangement of *Pineapple Poll*, a ballet using music of Sullivan's, reassembled by Charles Mackerras in 1951 when the Sullivan copyright ran out. There were also solos and instrumental features, including Godard's popular *Berceuse* arranged as a trombone solo by Eric Ball, and Ball's own witty double trio *Quid pro quo*, featuring cornets and trombones. Allan Street helped popularise the flugelhorn with his arrangement of Mozart's 'Say Ye Who Borrow' (from *Magic Flute*), whilst three pieces – *Rhapsody for Soprano Cornet*, *Introduction and Burlesque for Bass Trombone* and *Cornet Roundabout* were composed by Gregson under his pseudonym Robert Eaves.

Other pieces popularised in the 1960s included Frank Wright's transcription of Walton's majestic Coronation March, *Crown Imperial*, and Malcolm Arnold's riotous *Padstow Lifeboat*. Pieces from the 1970s included Gregson's *Prelude for an Occasion* and three original marches.

### Popular music

This heading covers an even larger area of music than the other categories. Pre-war popular music for bands ranged from selections – mainly from musical comedy – to some of the tunes featured by dance bands. There was a vast amount of it and it was usually scored with the average band in mind, so the market was extensive. Many early selections were arranged by Denis Wright and published by Chappell. Using the pseudonym Frank Denham, Wright also arranged popular tunes of the day.

Band music was but a small part of the output of Chappell's as, indeed, it was with many other publishers. Feldman's published medleys such as *Communityland* and standard hits such as *Tiger Rag* and *Alexander's Ragtime Band*. These were also in their general catalogue and throughout the 1930s they issued, on average, two brass band items per month. The publisher Lawrence Wright (not connected with Wright & Round) came into the brass band market just before the war, publishing a series of 'Savoy medleys', popularised by Debroy Somers and his Savoy Orpheans. The tango *Jealousy* was amongst the 'singles' published by this company. Other pre-war publishers of popular band music included Keith Prowse, Peter Maurice, and Francis, Day & Hunter.

Music publishing almost ceased during the war, though a few pieces filtered through, mostly arranged by Denis Wright and including tunes such as *The Bells of St Mary's* and *Soldiers in the Park*, along with a selection from the 1943 show *Oklahoma*. Some marches also appeared, including *Pennine Way* and *Beaufighters*, adopted respectively by Bickershaw Colliery and Fairey Aviation as their signature tunes, played whenever they broadcast. Both were composed by Maurice Johnstone of the BBC. There was also the rousing march-medley, *Sousa on Parade*.

After the war, selections from musical shows became very popular, amongst them: *South Pacific*, *The King and I* and *The Sound of Music* – all by Richard Rodgers; *West Side Story* by Leonard Bernstein; and Cole Porter's *Can-Can*. Other frequently played medleys included *Jolson Memories* and *Ancliffe in the Ballroom*. From 1951 new versions of selections from the more popular Gilbert and Sullivan operettas were published – all arranged by Denis Wright. Arrangements of pieces by Johann Strauss, Leroy Anderson and Eric Coates also began to appear in the 1950s, along with instrumental solos. Trios now became popular, usually for cornets or trombones.

Surprisingly, there were fewer arrangements of dance band numbers. Nevertheless, by 1960 there was a great deal of up-to-date popular music. A lull in the appearance of shows was compensated for with composer-based selections and miscellaneous medleys such as *Mancini Magic*, *Souvenir de France* and *The Black & White Minstrels*.

From the late 1960s Edrich Siebert[2] became the most prolific arranger of popular band music. Working for a range of publishers, he produced arrangements of hits such as *When You're Smiling*, *Moonlight Serenade* and *Congratulations*. He also wrote a series of popular original pieces with catchy titles such as *Brass Tacks*, *Marching Sergeants* and *Over the Sticks*. Gilbert Vinter, Denzil Stephens and Ron Hanmer also wrote original popular music. Other arrangers from this period include Allan Street and Frank Bryce. Selections continued to appear during the 1970s with titles such as *Robert Farnon for Brass*, *Great Film Themes*, *Beatles Medley* and *Christmas Swingalong*.

These were now supplemented by the fantasias of Gordon Langford, a professional pianist, composer and arranger of light music, including his *Fantasy on British Sea Songs* and *A West Country Fantasy*. Langford revolutionised the style of popular band music with these and also with his arrangements of traditional tunes such as *Men of Harlech*, *All Through the Night* and *When the Saints Go Marching In*.

More names were added to the list of arrangers in the 1970s, including Derek Broadbent, Derek Ashmore and Elgar Howarth – the latter particularly under his pseudonym W. Hogarth Lear.[3] Broadbent (see page 159) continued to arrange both modern and traditional songs,

---

2 Siebert's real name was Stanley Smith-Masters.
3 W. Hogarth Lear is an anagram of Elgar Howarth.

Ashmore arranged and published popular songs under licence from the original publishers and was able to release these within weeks of them having entered the charts. Amongst the early arrangements by Hogarth Lear were *Hogarth's Hoe-Down*, *Cops and Robbers* and an elegant setting of *Jeannie with the Light Brown Hair* as a euphonium solo, accompanied by the lower part of the band. Goff Richards, a highly skilled pianist and big band arranger was also building a reputation for popular band pieces, one of the first being *The Elvira Madigan Theme*, a tenor horn feature based on a theme from a Mozart piano concerto, featured in the 1967 film of that name. There was also his lively version of Strauss's *Tritsch Tratsch Polka*, written in the style of James Last.

**Conclusion**

There is so much which sits comfortably under the heading of 'popular music' that it is impossible to do full justice to it. Items mentioned above literally just skim the surface. As in other branches of music, in the later years discussed, writers could not be 'pigeon-holed'. Thus, we find Howarth and Howard Snell (see page 163) writing both serious and lighter music; the same applies to Goff Richards, but perhaps the other way round; Derek Bourgeois wrote in all three genres. Other versatile composers in the later years of the century included Ron Hanmer, Darrol Barry and Alan Fernie. Hanmer was a professional arranger/composer specialising in popular music, Barry was a product of the early Salford courses in band musicianship and Fernie, hailing from the Scottish brass band scene, was a professional trombonist, teacher, composer and arranger. A growing number of overseas writers included Bruce Broughton, James Curnow and William Himes – all from America.

# CHAPTER 7

# Personalities and bands

## The end of an era

### Harry Mortimer

By 1945 Harry Mortimer OBE (1902–90) had become the most prominent musical figure in banding. In the post-war years he supervised hundreds of brass and military band broadcasts – vetting programmes, monitoring standards, creating new programme formats and auditioning. He was awarded the OBE in the Queen's Birthday Honours list in 1950. Mortimer was not doing much playing now, but as a conductor was in demand by the finest bands, having succeeded William Halliwell as the most successful contest conductor. During the 12 years from 1945 to 1956 he conducted 15 winning performances in the two major contests. The wins were with the following bands:

|                      |   |
|----------------------|---|
| Fairey               | 8 |
| Black Dyke           | 3 |
| Foden's              | 2 |
| Munn & Felton's      | 1 |
| Bickershaw Colliery  | 1 |

He regularly conducted two or three bands in one contest and on his last appearance on the London contest platform (1955) took five, winning with Munn & Felton's, and leading Black Dyke and Morris Motors to fifth and sixth places respectively. In the following September he became a 'one-band man', winning the British Open with Fairey's. During the latter part of 1956, as part of his work for the BBC, Mortimer went to Canada and Australia. Whilst in Australia he was chief adjudicator at the Australian National Championships.[1] This trip meant he had to miss the National Championships of Great Britain and effectively terminated his career as a contest conductor, though he remained attached to both Fairey's and Foden's in an advisory capacity.

Contesting was not the only path down which Mortimer trod. On the concert platform he was highly successful, appearing regularly with all his bands. Following the success of a series of wartime massed band concerts,

---

[1] He had previously adjudicated at the New Zealand Nationals, in 1953.

he decided to form a massed band of a more permanent nature. His first initiative was to assemble a large band of about 50. This group, formed in 1951 and called 'Harry Mortimer's All-star Band', met from time to time. It was made up of players from many of the finest bands.[2] In addition to giving concerts, the All-Star Band made 18 ten-inch LP recordings. It was short-lived, however, because of the logistics of getting players together. A more realistic approach, Mortimer found, was to use three complete bands.

Men o' Brass – the ensemble which was to succeed the All-Star Band – initially included Fairey's, Foden's and Morris Motors. Formed in 1952, the group 'blossomed' in the 1960s, beginning with an engagement at the Canadian National Exhibition (CNE) in Toronto during 1961 and making its London debut in the BBC's Light Music Festival of 1962. During 1965 Men o' Brass gave the première, in the Royal Festival Hall, of Gilbert Vinter's cantata, *The Trumpets*. Later in the same year Sir Malcolm Sargent recorded several of his own transcriptions with Men o' Brass as part of his seventieth-birthday celebrations. Demand for concerts escalated and Men o' Brass appeared in many parts of the country. Their performances included one in aid of Sargent's Cancer Fund for Children and another to celebrate Harry Mortimer's 'Sixty Years in Banding'. The former was held in the Royal Albert Hall, London, with Harry Mortimer and Sir Vivian Dunn conducting; the latter was at Belle Vue. Men o' Brass produced a sonority and depth characteristic of what Mortimer liked to call his 'brass orchestra'.

Problems with the inclusion of the Morris Concert Band in Men o' Brass during the early 1970s led to their replacement by City of Coventry, in 1972. This was a prelude to further changes. Foden's were also experiencing difficulties at this time and Mortimer's connection with Fairey's was less strong than it had been. Having established the group name, he was loath to let it go, so began using different combinations of bands. For example, a Men o' Brass concert in Bristol during 1974 featured City of Coventry, Morris Concert and Wingates. Gradually the name Men o' Brass appeared less frequently.

In 1964, Harry Mortimer retired from the BBC. This enabled him to become more involved in the politics of the movement. As president of COBBA he was heavily involved in many of the disputes which arose from the late 1960s. He also travelled more, and was still in demand as conductor and adjudicator, but as he became less involved with individual bands he became more immersed in administration. He was a key figure in the Wills Contest and became increasingly involved with running the Belle Vue contests.

---

[2] Bands from which players were drawn included Black Dyke, Callender's, Creswell, Fairey's, Ferodo, Foden's, John White Footwear, Luton, Morris, Munn & Felton's, Ransome & Marles, and Rushden Temperance.

To celebrate his 75th year, in 1977 there were several special events, including an appearance as guest conductor at the gala concert following the National Championships – his first appearance there since 1955. There were many tributes and in the following year he received the prestigious Ivor Novello Award 'for outstanding services to British music'.

## Denis Wright

There have already been several references to Denis Wright OBE (1895–1967). During the later 1940s Wright's conducting engagements became rather spasmodic though he continued to appear at massed band concerts and also, until 1955, in BBC programmes. He was actively involved with the NABBC from its inception and published a book called *The Brass Band Conductor* in 1948. He was also in demand as an adjudicator.

A regular traveller, Wright first visited Holland in 1949. Two years later he made the first of four visits to the Antipodes, primarily to adjudicate at the New Zealand Championships.

Having been awarded the OBE in the New Year's Honours of 1959, he entered his 65th year in 1960 as busy as ever. Another book, *The Complete Bandmaster*, appeared in 1964. In 1965, Wright became one of the first recipients of a new award bestowed by the Royal Academy of Music, the Hon.ARAM. A year later he received an even higher award, the Hon.RAM.[3] He continued with his travels, making a number of visits to Denmark and Sweden, and in 1966 undertook a tour of the Far East.

In 1952 he founded the NYBB. Always alert to the possibilities of educating the brass band fraternity, he continued to direct many other courses. He died shortly after the NYBB's 1967 Easter course. Tributes poured in to the band press recognising his immense contribution over 40 years. Through his work at the BBC, his compositions, arrangements and transcriptions 'Doctor Denis', as he was affectionately known, had done much to bring musical credibility to the brass band movement. He had helped pioneer the brass band overseas, particularly in Denmark and Sweden and had stimulated its development in the Antipodes.[4]

## Eric Ball

The career of Eric Ball OBE (1903–89), born in Kingswood, Bristol, on 31 October 1903 into an SA family, was inextricably linked with the 'Army'. At the age of 18 he joined its Editorial Department and in 1926

---

[3] The Hon.ARAM was bestowed on outstanding ex-students of the Academy and the Hon.RAM was awarded in recognition of outstanding services to music.

[4] Roy Newsome's *Doctor Denis* (1995) is a comprehensive biography of Denis Wright.

became an officer. Two years later he formed the Salvationist Publishing & Supplies (SP&S) Band, remaining as conductor until its disbandment soon after the outbreak of World War II. He then became 'Instructor' to the Rosehill Band before taking on the SA's most senior musical post – bandmaster of the International Staff Band (ISB). He was, however, becoming increasingly interested in spiritualism, studying extra sensory perception and becoming involved in faith healing. Faced with the choice of renouncing these activities or relinquishing his officership, he chose the latter, resigning in April 1944. He then worked for ENSA for a time, during which Harry Mortimer recommended him for the post of professional conductor with Brighouse & Rastrick.[5]

His appointment at Brighouse in 1944 brought immediate rewards both for himself and the band. Within months he had also become an adviser to *BB* and was elected to a vice-presidency in the newly formed NABBC. Before the end of 1945 he was adjudicating and was also examining for the Guildhall School of Music's diploma in brass band conducting (LGSM). In 1946 he became musical editor for R. Smith & Co.

Some of Ball's compositions and arrangements were discussed above on pages 121 and 122. Test pieces literally flowed from his pen during 1945–46. One of these, *Salute to Freedom*, was the test for the 1946 Belle Vue contest at which he conducted Brighouse. There was consternation amongst rival bands which felt that, with the composer conducting, the band had an unfair advantage. In the event Brighouse had what is loosely called a 'bad day' and finished seventh! However, a month later their fortunes changed when, competing at the Royal Albert Hall, Brighouse became National Champions. This enhanced Ball's status and placed him in great demand.

In 1947 he became professional conductor of CWS (Manchester) and in the following year also took on Carlton Main. At the 1948 'September' he led CWS into first place and Carlton into third.

The 1950 'September' test piece was one that many still regard as Ball's finest work, *Resurgam*. Harry Mortimer had this to say:

> Whilst I won the contest with the Fairey Band, Eric only managed fourth place [with CWS (Manchester)]. The first to offer his sincere congratulations, he did something which confirmed, if such confirmation was needed, my opinion that he was the most noble of friends and the least conceited of musicians, avowing that I understood the piece better than he did, and found more depth in it than he had imagined.[6]

Ball had one further success with CWS, winning the 1952 'September'. He left Carlton Main in 1950, Brighouse in 1953 and CWS a year later.

---

[5] Much of the information comes from *Eric Ball, the Man and his Music* (Cooke, 1991).

[6] Mortimer, 1981, p. 150.

Meanwhile, in 1949 he had added Ransome & Marles to his list of bands, helping them to a 2nd prize at Belle Vue in 1949 and a win two years later, and remaining with them until 1958. During 1958 and 1959, acting as guest conductor, he led Fairey's to qualification for the Finals in both years.

Despite his successes, contesting was not Eric Ball's favourite pastime and he now stepped down in order to concentrate on his other activities – composing, his work for R. Smith & Co and appearances as a public speaker, guest conductor and adjudicator.

In 1951, he became the editor of *BB*, and so occupied one of the most influential positions in the brass band world. He was also back in favour with the SA and, though never again wearing the uniform, was regularly involved in its activities. He visited Australia and New Zealand in 1952 and 1955, ostensibly as an adjudicator and lecturer, but also linking up with Salvationists.

Ball retained the editorship of *BB* until 1963, returning in 1964 and staying in office for three more years. He had by now severed his connections with individual bands, though he accepted guest-conducting appointments and also did some adjudicating. He became a great traveller, visiting Canada and the USA, the Antipodes and several European countries. In 1969, Eric Ball was awarded the OBE 'for services to brass band music'.

On his seventy-fifth birthday he was reported to be very busy, and compositions were still appearing. Ball's last major test piece was his *Sinfonietta 'The Wayfarer'*, composed for the 1976 Nationals, though an earlier transcription of *Dances from Checkmate* (Bliss) was set as Nationals test piece in 1978.

As time went on he increasingly focused on his SA work and became less involved with contesting. A great champion of youth, Ball was involved in the early activities of the NYBB and the NSBBA. He retained his interest in both organisations, occasionally directing their courses or festivals.

*Frank Wright*

The last of the leading personalities of the period spanning the war years, Frank Wright MBE (1901–70), was born in Smeaton, Victoria, Australia, in 1901. After becoming the Australian cornet champion, he took up conducting and adjudicating, officiating at the Australian Championships in 1932, those of New Zealand in 1933, and in England at the Crystal Palace Championships of 1934. During this year, his first in England, he conducted St Hilda's professional band and in January 1935 was appointed Music Director to London County Council's Parks Department.

During the post-war years Wright became a highly influential figure in the brass band movement. In June 1945 he was appointed Professor of Brass and Military Band Scoring at the Guildhall School of Music and also became an examiner for the GSM diploma in Brass Band Conducting. He was editor of *The Conductor*, the official magazine of the NABBC, from its first issue in July 1946, and also edited the book, *Brass Today*, a compilation of essays about bands and the playing of brass instruments, published in 1957. He became a key figure in the National Brass Band Championships, adjudicating regularly, frequently being an associate conductor in the gala concerts, and composing or transcribing several test pieces.

As an adjudicator he was immensely proud of the fact that he had adjudicated at every Kerkrade World Music Festival (WMC; see page 306) from its inception in 1950. In 1965, he was awarded an Hon.FTCL and in the New Year Honours list of 1966 received the MBE.

In 1970 Frank Wright had to withdraw from his adjudicating appointment at the National Finals due to ill health. Shortly after this he was elected Master of the Worshipful Company of Musicians,[7] but died within days of the announcement of this honour and what was to have been his installation ceremony became, in effect, a memorial service.[8] Though Mortimer and Ball were still reasonably active, the passing of Frank Wright on 16 November 1970 may be seen as the end of an era.

### Into a later generation – Geoffrey Brand

Geoffrey Brand was one of the most important brass band figures to emerge during the 1960s. Like Eric Ball's, his musical career began in the SA. Following studies at the Royal Academy of Music and military service, he joined the Royal Philharmonic Orchestra, touring America. He was then a member of the orchestra of the Royal Opera House before becoming, in 1955, a BBC Producer. In 1965, he was given responsibility for all band broadcasts emanating from the London region, filling a gap which had existed since Harry Mortimer's retirement in 1964. Brand was made an Associate of the Royal Academy of Music in 1962 and was already a regular visitor to the continent, in particular working with bands in Denmark and Sweden. During the early 1960s he was engaged by a number of bands and enjoyed several contesting successes.

---

[7] The Worshipful Company of Musicians is an ancient London guild, founded by Royal charter in 1604. It awards prizes and scholarships. The Iles Medal is one such award.

[8] *BB* 21 November 1970, p. 1; tributes appear 28 November, pp. 1 and 8. There is an excellent profile of Frank Wright in *The Conductor* of January 1971, along with further tributes.

Geoffrey Brand left the BBC in 1967 in order to become more actively involved in the music business. This proved to be a momentous year: he became chairman of the NSBBA, succeeded Denis Wright as music advisor of the NYBB and also became editor of *BB* and professional conductor of Black Dyke. His eight years here were very fruitful. In addition to many contest successes he was instrumental in acquiring prestigious engagements, recording contracts and television appearances. Owing to his involvement with *BB* and the Nationals (see page 100), he withdrew from contesting for a time and in 1975 resigned from Black Dyke. Due to pressure of other work, he then resigned from the position of music adviser to the NYBB. His eight years here had also been highly successful, with the commissioning of new works, commercial recordings and the introduction of several high-profile guest conductors.

Brand continued travelling abroad, visiting Australia in 1971 and New Zealand a year later. In 1973 he was in Oslo, planting the seeds of the British brass band through broadcasts and conducting engagements. In 1975 he returned to Australia, adjudicating at the National Championships and directing a series of training sessions for conductors. He was now a frequent trans-globe traveller, making several more visits to Australia before the end of the 1970s – adjudicating, conducting and teaching. He also became a regular visitor to Japan. In 1977 he spent a month in New Zealand and was there again during the following two years. In addition, there were regular visits to Europe and in 1979 he became the first English conductor to direct the course of Switzerland's NJBB.

'GB' was also in demand as an adjudicator and had several arrangements and transcriptions published. Throughout much of this period he was editor of *BB*, though he credits his wife Violet with assuming responsibility for much of the work involved. Together they produced the 1979 book *Brass Bands in the 20th Century*.

Having left *BB*, Geoffrey Brand returned to the contest scene, accepting in 1975 the position of musical director with GUS. Though he had limited success here, he led Brighouse & Rastrick to a win at the British Open in 1978. In the same year he also conducted Ever Ready at both the Open and the Nationals. He resigned from GUS in 1978 but remained with Brighouse until 1980.

## The 'Top Ten' bands – 1946–80

As in Chapter 2 (see page 27), in this extended period of 35 years the criterion for selecting the top ten bands has been to assemble a 'league table' indicating bands' successes in the National Championships (incorporating the titles of 'World Champions' between 1968 and 1971) and the British Open Championships (Table 7.1). Again, three points were awarded for a win, two for a second place and one for a third.

*Table 7.1 The 'Top Ten' bands 1946–80*

|  |  | Prizes won | | | Points |
|---|---|---|---|---|---|
|  |  | 1st | 2nd | 3rd |  |
| 1 | Black Dyke Mills | 20 | 7 | 8 | 82 |
| 2 | Fairey Aviation | 13 | 9 | 4 | 61 |
| 3 | CWS (Manchester) | 6 | 7 | 7 | 39 |
| 4 | Munn & Felton's / GUS | 7 | 2 | 10 | 35 |
| 5 | Brighouse & Rastrick | 6 | 3 | 7 | 31 |
| 6 | Foden's Motor Works | 4 | 5 | 4 | 26 |
| 7 | Grimethorpe Colliery | 2 | 3 | 7 | 19* |
| 8 | Yorkshire Imperial | 4 | 2 | 3 | 19 |
| 9 | Carlton Main Frickley Colliery | 1 | 6 | 4 | 19 |
| 10 | Wingates Temperance | 1 | 3 | 2 | 11** |

\* Also won 1st prize in 'Nationals' of 1970
\*\* Also won 1st prize in 'Nationals' of 1971

## Black Dyke Mills

Though winning its 1945 Area contest, Black Dyke Mills Band was unplaced at the Finals. Following two relatively unsuccessful years, Harry Mortimer conducted at the 1947 Area contest, helping to win 1st prize there and leading the band to a hat-trick at the Nationals in 1947–48–49. Arthur O. Pearce retired as bandmaster in December 1948 after having served for 37 years, earning the sobriquet 'Prime Minister of Brass Bands'.[9] Following a short period when ex-solo horn player Joe Wood took over, Alex Mortimer was appointed bandmaster and, later, musical director. It was he who steered the band to its next success, in the 1951 Nationals (Figure 7.1). In 1954 Alex Mortimer left Black Dyke for CWS (Manchester) and Edmund Hoole became bandmaster. However, following the death of a daughter, he moved away from the district and Jack Emmott, a former Black Dyke euphonium player and an ex-army bandmaster, succeeded him in 1956.

Now Maurice Murphy became principal cornet player and Geoffrey Whitham played solo euphonium. These two inspirational players, ably

[9] This was Arthur Oakes Pearce – always referred to as Arthur O. Pearce. He died on 13 January 1951, aged 79.

Figure 7.1 Black Dyke – National Champions 1947, 1948, 1949 and 1951 – with Alex Mortimer

supported by other soloists, gave the band a real fillip, propelling it once again to the top. Murphy had won the Juvenile class in the All-England Solo Championships in 1947, when aged 11. Born in Hammersmith but moving to the North East whilst still quite young, he played with Crookhall and Harton before moving into Yorkshire in 1951 to play with Yewco (see Glossary). After its demise in 1956 he moved to Fairey's as assistant principal cornet player but in March 1957 became principal cornet of Black Dyke.

Geoffrey Whitham joined Black Dyke as its second baritone player in June 1947, aged 15, but by September 1950 was playing solo euphonium. In 1959 he achieved legendary status through his performance of the euphonium solo in *Le roi d'Ys* (Lalo) during Black Dyke's title-winning performance at the Nationals. Whitham also played tuba with the Liverpool Philharmonic and Hallé orchestras, and the City of Birmingham Symphony Orchestra (CBSO), but remained as solo euphonium at Black Dyke until his appointment as bandmaster in 1963.

However, Black Dyke did not take another title until 1957 when George Willcocks led them to victory at the 1957 British Open. Major G.H. Willcocks, MVO, MBE (1899–1962)[10] had a short but spectacular career in brass bands, his first involvement being in 1952 when he became a vice-president of, and an examiner for, the Bandsman's College of Music.

---

[10] Major Willcocks had previously had a distinguished career in the army, being Director of Music the Band of the Irish Guards and Senior Director of Music the Brigade of Guards.

Harry Mortimer knew him through broadcasting and when Mortimer found that, owing to BBC commitments, he could not conduct in the 1956 Nationals he invited Willcocks to conduct Fairey's. Willcocks was an excellent conductor and could bring the best out of his players. With his dignified military bearing and at times spectacular gestures he was a joy to watch. Almost inevitably he led Fairey's to 1st prize, in his first brass band contest.

Black Dyke was at the time in need of a professional conductor and for the next five years Willcocks and Black Dyke produced brass band magic, first with a beautifully refined performance at the British Open in 1957, followed by exciting performances at the Nationals of 1959 and 1961.[11] Willcocks also had successes with other bands, including Luton. He had enjoyed a meteoric rise to the top as a brass band conductor and his untimely death in January 1962 left the band world in general, and Black Dyke in particular, stunned. At the relatively early age of 63 he had appeared to be fit and full of vitality.[12] 'The Major', as he was affectionately known, left a small legacy of compositions and arrangements for Black Dyke, some of which were subsequently published. Shortly after the death of Willcocks, Maurice Murphy moved on to become principal trumpet player of the BBC Northern Orchestra.[13] It took Black Dyke several years to recover from these twin blows.

It was announced in July 1962 that James Shepherd, the reigning Champion Soloist of Great Britain was to replace Murphy as principal cornet player, but within a month he had decided to remain at Carlton Main. However, early in 1963 he agreed to occupy what was generally regarded as the 'hottest seat' in brass bands. Aged 26, Shepherd was to serve as principal cornet at Black Dyke for a decade, playing a leading role in the band's return to the top. Like Murphy, he was brought up in the North East. During National Service he played in the Royal Army Medical Corps staff band. He was widely recognised as one of the leading cornet players of his generation and achieved a hat-trick in the Solo Championships of Great Britain. Shepherd was employed as an instrumental teacher for the West Riding and Bradford Education Authorities and in these roles formed and conducted the highly successful

---

[11] The winning performances were of Helen Perkin's *Carnival* at Belle Vue in 1957 and the overtures *Le roi d'Ys* (Lalo) and *Les francs juges* (Berlioz) at the Nationals.

[12] *BB* 20 January 1962, p. 6. For further article and tributes, see also *The Conductor*, April 1962, pp. 3 and 6–9.

[13] Murphy has spent the remainder of his career as a professional trumpet player, in 1977 becoming principal trumpet with the LSO, playing alongside Willie Lang and developing into one of the world's finest orchestral trumpet players. He has kept in touch with the brass band world and regularly returns as guest soloist. There is a good article about him in *BB* 11 July 1987, p. 9.

Queensbury Music Centre Band (see page 213). During the early 1970s he formed his James Shepherd Versatile Brass (JSVB), a hand-picked ten-piece ensemble. He resigned from Black Dyke in 1973 in order to concentrate on promoting this group.[14]

During 1963 Jack Emmott resigned from the post of bandmaster, later emigrating to New Zealand. His successor was the band's euphonium player, Geoffrey Whitham, who first conducted Black Dyke in the Whit Friday contests of 1963, was appointed bandmaster later in the year and helped the band gain 3rd prize in the September contest. He left at the end of 1965 to begin a new career, taking over from Gersham Collison as musical director of Hammonds' Sauce Works Band.

In 1964 Major (later Colonel) C.H. Jaeger, Director of Music of the Irish Guards, became Black Dyke's professional conductor, whilst John Clough became solo euphonium player in succession to Whitham.[15] Under Jaeger the band won the 1964 Area contest and were runners-up at the Finals. A hat-trick at the Area contests (1964–65–66) and a further 2nd prize in the Nationals of 1966 were also achieved under him.[16] He resigned in January 1967 and was succeeded later in the year by Geoffrey Brand, who led the band to a win at the Nationals in his first year. Brand took Black Dyke through its most successful period for some time by also winning the British Open Championships of 1968, taking 2nd prizes in the Nationals of 1968 and 1969, in 1970 becoming World Champions and in 1972 achieving the rare 'double' of winning both the Open and the Nationals in the same year (Figure 7.2).

Meanwhile, Roy Newsome succeeded Whitham as bandmaster. Under Newsome, Black Dyke became the 1966 Yorkshire Champions and the first 'BBC Band of the Year' (see page 191). Like many other budding conductors, Newsome had played in a number of bands before taking an interest in conducting. His first success was leading his local band, Elland Silver, to first place in the 4th section National Finals of 1958. Following a successful period conducting Slaithwaite (1961–65), he became bandmaster of Black Dyke.

---

[14] Shepherd remained with his JSVB until 1989 when, though retiring, he allowed the group to continue under the same name. He continued to appear as guest soloist and conducted a number of bands, including the various Jayess bands in Queensbury. There is a good biography in *BB* 17 June 1978, p. 1.

[15] Clough was a former principal cornet player of Bradford Victoria. In Black Dyke he held various seats in the cornet section before moving to baritone, from whence he moved to solo euphonium.

[16] Jaeger was promoted to Lieut. Col. during 1966 and in 1968 became Director of Music at Kneller Hall. He died on 27 September 1970. There is a good biography in *The Conductor* of July 1965, p. 3.

Figure 7.2    Geoffrey Brand conducting Black Dyke in a packed Royal Albert Hall in 1972

In 1969 Black Dyke went abroad for the first time since its Canadian tour of 1906 to assist in a town-twinning ceremony in Roubaix, France, on behalf of the City of Bradford. Amongst the band's more special engagements during 1970 were a weekend in Belfast and five days in Holland.

Towards the end of 1970 Newsome resigned. He was succeeded in January 1971 by Denis Carr, though with a change of title from bandmaster to resident conductor. Son of John R. Carr, a well-known conductor and adjudicator in the North East, Denis had made his contest debut as a cornet player at the age of eight at the 1946 Area contest in Newcastle. He was featured in the 1948 gala concert at the Royal Albert Hall, playing a duet with Willie Lang, but later switched to the euphonium. After National Service he became a music teacher and in 1965 was appointed Senior Lecturer in Music at the City of Leeds College of Education. He joined the BBC as a producer in 1975 and in 1979 became the BBC's Education Officer for the North of England. For a time he presented a weekly brass band programme on local radio. During the late 1960s Carr was with Yorkshire Imperial Metals Band, playing solo euphonium and becoming assistant conductor. For many years he was a tutor with the NYBB and in 1975 directed the first course of the Belgian National Youth Band. In 1977 he returned to Yorkshire Imperial Metals as musical director, conducting their winning performance at the Nationals in 1978.[17]

Due to ill-health Carr resigned within a few weeks of becoming Black Dyke's resident conductor, to be followed in June by Wilfred Heaton (see page 124). During this year Black Dyke undertook the first of several Swiss tours. Heaton remained only until the end of the year and at the beginning of 1972 Newsome was back, as resident conductor.

In May 1972, along with Fairey's, CWS (Manchester) and GUS, Black Dyke crossed the Atlantic to participate in a Canadian Brass Band Festival (see page 304).

Geoffrey Brand was by now the editor and a director of *BB*, which had become the main sponsor of the Nationals. In January 1973 he relinquished his contesting commitments, but his association with Black Dyke continued for a further two years, during which Roy Newsome conducted the band in contests.

During his two periods with Black Dyke Newsome worked alongside three professional conductors – Colonel Jaeger, Geoffrey Brand and Major Peter Parkes. This was a highly successful decade and the success helped bring Newsome to the fore. He did, in fact, conduct two winning performances at the British Open (1973 and 1974). Whilst still at Black

---

[17] There is a biography of Carr in the British Open Championships programme of 1982 in connection with the award of the Iles Medal.

Dyke he undertook several freelance appointments, including a week with Cory's in the USA, adjudicating the Australian Championships, being guest conductor with the NYBB and directing summer schools in Switzerland.

James Shepherd resigned as principal cornet player in May 1973 and was succeeded by Phillip McCann, who had spent his formative years in his native Scotland as a member of Kinneil Colliery Band (see Glossary). During this period he became Junior and Senior Champion Soloist of East Scotland on three occasions. He was a member of the NYBB and its leader on eight courses and in 1963 became principal cornet player with Yorkshire Imperial Metals. In 1967 he took up a similar position with Fairey's, also becoming leader of Men o' Brass. A year later he became the Champion Soloist of Great Britain.

McCann took up his appointment as principal cornet player of Black Dyke in June 1973, holding it with distinction for 16 years. Full-time employment was found for him at Yorkshire Imperial, Fairey's and, initially, at Black Dyke. However, in 1980 he became a full time lecturer at Huddersfield Technical College, where he formed the Tecol Band (see page 87).[18]

Later in 1973 Black Dyke became British Open Champions for the second year in succession, giving Newsome his first major championship win as conductor. The band now brought about an incredible sequence of contest successes, first of all, in 1974, completing its hat-trick at the British Open (Figure 7.3).

Major Peter Parkes succeeded Geoffrey Brand in 1975. He was Director of Music of the Band of the Grenadier Guards. Following a short spell with the Band of the Royal Army Medical Corps he left the army in 1979, becoming free to accept additional conducting appointments within the brass band movement. Over the ensuing years he took on many other bands, meeting with much success. In 1980 he took Whitburn to the Scottish Area and Yorkshire Imperial to the Yorkshire Area, winning both events. Within months he was also conducting Loughborough Youth Band and City of Coventry.

Under his direction Black Dyke continued its winning ways. Barred from the 1975 Open, it went on to win the National Championships – the start of a further hat-trick – and, along with two more wins on returning to the Open, a 'double-double' in 1976–77. With further wins in the Nationals of 1979 and at the first two European Championships (in 1978 and 1979) Black Dyke were dominating the contest scene (Figure 7.4).

These successes were reflected in the large number of commercial recordings made and the demand for concert engagements. Amongst the highlights of the second half of the 1970s was a television programme

---

18 There is a good article about McCann in *BB* 25 July 1987, p. 9.

Figure 7.3    Roy Newsome conducts Black Dyke as it completes its British Open hat-trick in 1974

Figure 7.4   Peter Parkes in full flight winning the Nationals with Black Dyke, *c.* 1976

144

*Previn meets Brass Bands*, in which the famous orchestral maestro attended a rehearsal and a pseudo concert in Queensbury. He was so impressed that he immediately set wheels in motion for Black Dyke to appear with the London Symphony Orchestra (LSO), of which he was principal conductor. The concert, in the Royal Albert Hall, was televised live.

On one of the many recordings made by the band, former Prime Minister Edward Heath appeared as guest conductor and at another session they made a single on the Apple label for Paul McCartney (of Beatles fame). Perhaps the greatest honour was when the Freedom of the City of Bradford[19] was bestowed on the band during 1977 – the year of the London hat-trick and the second 'double'. Following Newsome's final departure at the end of 1977, Michael Antrobus, a professional trumpet player and conductor of several local bands, became resident conductor, to be succeeded in 1979 by David Loukes, who had earlier conducted Wingates and JSVB, had helped pioneer the Salford Band Musicianship courses, and subsequently moved to Cornwall.

The highlights of 1979 were a Norwegian tour sponsored by Boosey & Hawkes, the recording of a track for Wings made in the famous Abbey Road studios under the supervision of Paul McCartney and yet another win at the Nationals. In 1980 the band undertook a further Boosey-sponsored tour, this time in Southern Germany, Luxembourg and Belgium.

The band was sponsored by the company of John Foster & Son Ltd, owners of a worsted mill in the hill-top village of Queensbury, near Bradford. Its premises were known as Black Dyke Mills, hence the band's name. However, the company received little in return for its sponsorship, its products being marketed under the name John Foster and whilst publicity concerned with the band generally used the full title of 'John Foster & Son Ltd, Black Dyke Mills Band' it was known worldwide simply as 'Black Dyke'. The company was, nevertheless, immensely proud of its band. In due course the mills went into liquidation, but the band played on.

## Fairey Aviation

The domination of the war-time contesting scene by Fairey Aviation continued during the early post-war years, with five wins and four 2nd prizes in the twelve major contests of 1945–50. The 'double' was achieved in 1945. Results between 1951 and 1960 were less impressive, partly

---

[19] This is an honour bestowed by a City Council on an individual or group for outstanding service to the community. In the case of Black Dyke it was a recognition of recent successes and the reflected honour brought to the city. The home of Black Dyke is in the town of Queensbury which is within the precincts of the City of Bradford.

because peace had brought prosperity to more bands. With a more level playing-field than was the case during the war, more leading bands shared the prizes at major contests. There was, however, a Nationals win in 1954 and a further 'double' in 1956.

Fairey's were heavily involved in concert engagements and broadcasts, and undertook several tours, including one for ENSA in 1945, in which they toured Holland.[20] They returned there in 1948 and 1949, in each year winning 1st prizes at music festivals.

Although served by a number of bandmasters Harry Mortimer, as musical director, conducted Fairey's on many engagements and in all contests up to September 1956. Frank Smith (see page 31) was the first bandmaster, with Elgar Clayton, who as well as being principal cornet player also became bandmaster later, taking rehearsals which Mortimer could not attend and conducting on the more routine engagements. Elgar Clayton MBE won the AOMF Scholarship in 1926 and first came into prominence as a solo cornet player with Wingates. In 1933 he became principal cornet player with the newly formed Munn & Felton's and in the early 1940s moved to Fairey Aviation. In these positions he came under the influence of both William Halliwell and Harry Mortimer. He remained with Fairey's until 1950, by which time he was taking a serious interest in conducting, working with several bands and becoming professional conductor of Forfar Instrumental (Scotland), with which he took 2nd prize in the 1947 Scottish Championships. During the early 1950s Clayton emigrated to New Zealand. The move was temporary, however, as he was back in Britain, conducting both Forfar (winning the Scottish Championships in 1954) and Scottish CWS. In 1958, he moved permanently to New Zealand. He was awarded the MBE in 1984.

In 1951 Jack Atherton (see also page 148) became bandmaster of Fairey's, to be followed in 1952 by Robert Mulholland[21] who was, in turn, succeeded by Leonard Lamb, a former cornet player with Fairey's and a successful conductor of several local bands. In 1956 Lamb became bandmaster and from 1959 conducted Fairey's in all major contests under the guidance of Harry Mortimer. He was also professional conductor of Lindley Band (near Huddersfield) for a time, leading them to second place in the British Open of 1964, when Fairey's were barred because of their hat-trick. In the following year he led Fairey's to their 'double'.

As was seen above, Mortimer was unable to take his bands to the Nationals in 1956 and Fairey's were conducted by Major Willcocks. By

---

[20] Strictly speaking, Holland is a small part of The Netherlands, but because in Britain the whole of The Netherlands is often referred to as 'Holland', this name is used during the early part of the book when discussing activities in The Netherlands.

[21] This was Robert Mulholland senior, father of the founder of *BBW*.

winning, they completed an astounding year, becoming National Champions under Willcocks and British Open Champions under Mortimer whilst their quartet, under Leonard Lamb, had become Quartet Champions of Great Britain.

In 1960, owing to a change in the parent company's name the band became 'The Fairey Band'. They began the 1960s with a hat-trick at the Open (1961–62–63) and a 'double' in 1965, but then passed through a less successful contesting period, Lamb having a prolonged illness in the late 1960s. His name appeared in the record books for the last time in 1967, with 2nd prize at the Open. After five years of serious illness, Leonard Lamb died in 1973 aged 63.

Elgar Clayton was succeeded as principal cornet player by Norman Ashcroft (b. 1919). Having played with various brass bands in the North East, including Harton Colliery, Ashcroft had then spent two years playing trumpet with the Carl Rosa Opera Company before returning to Harton as principal cornet player. In 1950 he took a similar position with Fairey's, holding it for 17 years. The New Zealander Ken Smith was Ashcroft's assistant for some time during the 1950s. Whilst in England Smith made a number of solo recordings and regularly appeared as a guest soloist. On his return to New Zealand he became a leading figure in bands, education and the wider world of classical music.

Euphonium soloists during this period included Wilf Mountain, Harry Cheshire and Marcus Cutts. Kenneth Dennison, the long-serving trombone soloist and the 1946 AOMF winner, became musical director in 1969, collecting 3rd prize in the Open that year followed by 2nd prizes in the World Championships of 1970 and 1971, and at the Open in 1975. He left in 1976 and almost immediately took up a similar appointment with City of Coventry, where he remained until late 1979. He was also regularly in demand as an adjudicator.

Ashcroft stood down from the position of principal cornet in 1967, being succeeded by Phillip McCann. Cutts was succeeded by Lyndon Baglin in 1977 (see page 149). There were also three extraordinary soprano players – Bert Howarth,[22] Roy Roe and Brian Evans (see 'Personalia').

Fairey's were one of the bands which took part in the Canadian Brass Band Festival of 1972. During the summer of 1976 Dennison was replaced by Richard Evans.

In 1975, after a spell conducting local bands Evans, a former member of both the NYBB and Black Dyke, had been invited to become musical director of Wingates. One of his first projects was to prepare the band for the British Open Championships, playing Elgar Howarth's *Fireworks*. The

---

[22] Howarth gave sterling service playing soprano with both Foden's and Fairey's, and later conducted several bands.

band won 1st prize in what was Evans's first appearance as a conductor at the Open, and being Wingates' first Open win since 1939. In 1976 he moved to Fairey's. Here he achieved a 3rd prize in the Nationals in 1977 before being offered a rare full-time salaried position as musical director of Leyland Motors Band.

During 1976 Fairey's underwent another name change, now becoming known as Fairey Engineering Works Band. As such, the band gave a Royal Command Performance in Manchester in 1977. At the end of the year Evans was succeeded by W.B. Hargreaves (see page 156), who led Fairey's to victory in the Area contest of that year. Brian Broadbent, a former euphonium player with Black Dyke, was appointed bandmaster in the spring of 1979. This was Fairey's best year for some time. Under Hargreaves they won the British Open Championships and two television competitions, and 1980 saw the band on a week's tour in Holland.

### CWS (Manchester)

In 1947 Fred Roberts became bandmaster of the CWS (Manchester) Band after 17 years at Brighouse & Rastrick as principal cornet. His protégé Derek Garside, also of Brighouse, accompanied him, later becoming principal cornet at CWS. Garside had begun playing in 1941, aged ten, taught by Roberts. In January 1944, having won several prizes in solo contests, he joined Brighouse & Rastrick.

As principal cornet player with CWS (Manchester) Garside developed into one of the world's foremost cornet soloists. In 1948 he commenced his National Service, during which he played solo cornet in the RAF College Band at Cranwell. On demobilisation he returned to CWS. In 1951 Garside appeared as a guest soloist in Switzerland, sowing the early seeds of a Swiss brass band movement.

By August 1948 Eric Ball was making regular visits to CWS and results came quickly: CWS won its first major title at the 'September' of that year and gained prizes at both major contests in 1950.

In 1952 Jack Atherton succeeded Roberts as bandmaster, Eric Ball remaining as professional conductor. Whilst still a boy Jack Atherton (1909–83) had joined Harton Colliery Band as a tenor horn player, being taught by George Hawkins (see 'Personalia'). In 1931 he moved to London and joined Hanwell, returning to Harton in 1939 as musical director and remaining there until 1950, after which he took a number of more prestigious bandmasterships before settling down as musical director at Carlton Main from 1954.

There was another Belle Vue win for CWS (Manchester) in 1952 and again in Eric Ball's final year, 1953, when CWS claimed prizes at both contests. Following Garside's earlier success, there was a tour of Switzerland, CWS being the first leading brass band to tour there.

Alex Mortimer (1905–76), the middle one of the three brothers, then became the band's musical director, superseding both Ball and Atherton. He was born in Hebden Bridge, Yorkshire. When the family moved to Luton in 1910 he joined Luton Red Cross Band, which was conducted by his father Fred. Becoming one of the finest euphonium players of all time he moved north and played solo euphonium at Foden's from 1924, leaving in 1944 to become Liverpool Philharmonic Orchestra's principal tuba player. In 1949 he resigned in order to take over the conductorship of Scottish CWS. However, during October of this year he was appointed as Black Dyke's bandmaster, leading them to victory at the 1951 Nationals. In 1954 he moved to CWS (Manchester), here making his most significant mark. Individualistic and unpredictable, he moulded CWS into what many regarded as the finest band of the era. He was also associated with many other bands, including Brighouse & Rastrick, but most notably with Scottish CWS which he led to victory in the Scottish Championships of 1957, 1959 and 1960.

During the first few years under Mortimer's leadership, despite its high standing, CWS (Manchester) acquired a reputation as being 'always the bridesmaid, never the bride' with a run of lower prizes.[23] Though a prolific recording band, giving many fine broadcasts, and on tour for long periods each summer, the combination of CWS and Alex Mortimer did not reach its peak in contests until the 1960s, when there were four major titles (National Champions in 1962 and 1963 and British Open Champions in 1960 and 1966). For the 1962 Nationals bid there was doubt about Mortimer's fitness to conduct and the performance was highly charged emotionally. He was suffering from chronic bronchitis and the bandmaster was standing by to conduct if necessary. In the event, Mortimer managed to reach a stool provided for him and directed the band in an inspired winning performance, generally regarded as one of the finest of all times.[24] Mortimer continued as musical director throughout the 1960s, whilst Derek Garside remained as principal cornet.

Lyndon Baglin, after playing with several local bands in his native Gloucestershire, came to the fore when he became solo euphonium player with CWS in 1961, the year in which he also became the Solo Champion of Great Britain. He played in the two winning performances at the Royal

---

[23] Between 1954 and 1959 CWS (Manchester) was placed fifth (1954), third (1955) and second (1956) at Belle Vue, and second (1954, 1956 and 1957) and third (1955 and 1958) at the Royal Albert Hall.

[24] The test piece was Frank Wright's transcription of Verdi's overture to the opera, *The Force of Destiny*.

Albert Hall. However, his work demanded that he move periodically to different parts of the country and in late 1963 he was back in Gloucestershire. Moving to Bradford in 1966, he played briefly with Black Dyke but in 1967 became solo euphonium player with Brighouse & Rastrick, playing in a number of title-winning performances and for a time undertaking the duties of secretary. Through his work Baglin was on the move again in 1970 and had to leave Brighouse. After a spell with Stanshawe (see page 270) he returned north in 1977 and joined Fairey's, contributing to their successes in the latter part of the period.

Meanwhile, on the concert platform CWS was in greater demand than any of its rivals. In addition to normal engagements, the Co-op required its bands to play at exhibitions and other functions. In its centenary year of 1963 concerts were arranged in several major cities, the CWS (Manchester) band playing on three successive evenings in each of eight venues,[25] plus a six-day engagement in Piccadilly Gardens, Manchester. In addition to other commitments, which included full weeks in Eastbourne and London, this was a massive strain on a group of 'amateur' musicians and quite a number left at the end of this hectic season.

Alex Mortimer's poor health persisted throughout the 1960s and in 1970 he retired after 16 successful years. Having brought much distinction to the band, with polished performances the likes of which had rarely been heard, it made sense for him to be retained in an advisory capacity. He survived for a few more years despite deteriorating health, but died on 14 January 1976.

Mortimer was succeeded by Tommy White, who had been bandmaster since 1960. In March 1972, however, Derek Garside laid down his cornet and became musical director. This obviously created an opening for another star cornettist and in July a promising young player called Tom Paulin left Scotland's Dalmellington Band to take up the challenge. However, late in 1973 he left CWS.[26] Following this John Hudson (see page 257), who had played assistant principal cornet for some time, was promoted to principal, remaining in this position until the end of 1977.

The 1970s were not good years for CWS. A 2nd prize in the 1973 Nationals under Garside was the band's only success at national level. In 1974 the bandroom burned down, damaging instruments and uniforms, and destroying the music library which contained many irreplaceable items. Garside retired following the 1976 Finals, after which he conducted Foden's for a time. Trevor Walmsley (see page 156) succeeded him as musical

---

[25] These were Plymouth, Cardiff, Newcastle, Leeds, Bristol, Swansea, Birmingham and Bournemouth.

[26] After brief spells with GUS, Grimethorpe and William Davis, Paulin emigrated to Australia.

director. Failure to qualify at the 1977 Area contest ended a run of 24 successive appearances in the Finals. Following Walmsley's departure in 1979, Maurice Handford became music adviser. A former assistant conductor to Sir John Barbirolli at the Hallé Orchestra, his stay at CWS was short and fruitless and later in the year Frank Renton (see page 255) was engaged to conduct the band in the British Open Championships. By now, however, CWS (Manchester) was but a shadow of its former self.

## Munn & Felton's / GUS

Munn & Felton's suffered considerably throughout the war and was unable to participate in the 1945 contests. The band came some way back to form in 1946, however, winning the Midlands Area contest and several lower prizes at national level between then and 1952, before taking 1st prize at the British Open Championships in 1954 from the No. 1 draw.[27] Stanley Boddington conducted on this occasion but for the Nationals win of 1955 Harry Mortimer was in charge as professional conductor.

Coming from a Salvation Army background in Kettering, Stanley Boddington MBE (1905–86) made his mark in the contesting band world as bandmaster and musical director of Munn & Felton's from its inception in 1933. A modest man and a fine band trainer, he adhered mainly to his work with that band, though, after Harry Mortimer withdrew from contesting in 1956, he directed Morris Motors in some contest performances. During 1973 Boddington celebrated 60 years in banding and in 1975, on reaching his seventieth birthday, retired from what had now become GUS, after 42 years continuous service (Figure 7.5). Following this he undertook some teaching in local colleges and also helped Desford Colliery Band (see page 252). His last major assignment was conducting Grimethorpe in its bid for the National and European Championships of 1978, leading them to third place in the former and second in the latter. Boddington had several arrangements published and in 1982 was awarded the MBE.[28]

Munn & Felton's toured Holland during the summer of 1955. They had acquired some fine players and had a concert reputation second to none, with some 130 broadcasts to their credit. Boddington led the band

---

[27] Bands draw lots to decide the order of play. Statistics suggest that bands which play early in a major contest with a large entry are at a disadvantage compared with those which play later. The 'No. 1 draw' is possibly the worst of all, not least because it has a depressing effect on the members of the band concerned.

[28] Following his death in December 1986, a Stanley Boddington Memorial Cup was presented to the winning conductor in the National Championships. There is a good biography in the 1987 Nationals programme. See also Boddington's obituary in *BB*, 10 January 1987, p. 1.

Figure 7.5   Stanley Boddington with GUS in the King's Hall, Belle Vue, in 1974

to wins in the Nationals of 1957 and 1960. In 1958 the band underwent the first of several name-changes, becoming Munn & Felton's (Footwear) Band.

James Scott joined in 1957, initially as assistant principal cornet, later becoming principal. Scott had something of a brass band pedigree, his father having been a member of Besses o' th' Barn. James was playing principal cornet with City of Coventry by the time he was 16, being a pupil of its then conductor, George Thompson. He followed Thompson to Grimethorpe when the latter became its musical director, but it was as principal cornet player with Munn & Felton's that he built his reputation as one of the finest players of his generation. During this time he twice became the Champion Soloist of Great Britain.

In 1960 he was appointed musical director of the newly formed Cammell Laird Band in Liverpool and also played the trumpet professionally. Scott's next important conducting appointment was with Brighouse & Rastrick, with whom he had considerable success between 1973 and 1975, before moving to Foden's where he remained until 1979. He had several successes with Grimethorpe between 1978 and 1980, and in 1979 fulfilled some engagements with Yorkshire Imperial. During the late 1970s he worked as an instrumental teacher on the Wirral and was becoming one of the most sought-after adjudicators.

In 1953, at the age of 13, Scott's successor at Munn & Felton's, John Berryman was the youngest member of Camborne Town Band and also a member of the NYBB, being its leader on eight courses. He was a prizewinner in the first Solo Championships of Great Britain in 1959, joining Munn & Felton's shortly afterwards and becoming principal cornet player in 1960. In 1969 he returned to Cornwall as a conductor, but in 1973 became resident conductor of Grimethorpe. From 1976 he was musical director of William Davis Construction Group Band (see Glossary), some years later returning to Kettering as resident conductor of his former band – under its new name.

Munn & Felton's faced another change of name in 1962 when the parent company became part of Great Universal Stores. Now GUS (Footwear), it retained a high profile as a concert band, made quality broadcasts and recordings, and achieved two major wins at the Nationals in 1964 and 1966.

By the mid-1960s the link with Harry Mortimer was broken and the band was generally conducted by Stanley Boddington. The loss was compensated for to a degree by a good working relationship with Gilbert Vinter, a staff conductor with the BBC and destined to become a leading brass band composer. Vintner conducted GUS from time to time and in the late 1960s composed the three brass quartets which helped the GUS Quartet to its hat-trick at the Oxford Quartet Championships of 1967–68–69 (see page 122).

Following John Berryman's departure, David Read, hitherto Berryman's assistant, became principal cornet player. Read was the subject of a scathing letter which had appeared in *BBN* in August 1949. It was from the secretary of Askern Colliery Band and highlighted the dilemma facing promising young players. The letter accused neighbours Carlton Main of 'baiting' its young cornet player, who had left Askern to join the undoubtedly superior Carlton Main. It is quite possible that had Read remained with Askern he would not have gone on to the distinguished career which the move precipitated. From Carlton Main he went on to become a member of the Welsh Guards Band and whilst with them also played with Morris Motors and the All-Star Band. He then joined Munn & Felton's. On three occasions he became the British Cornet Champion, and in 1973 achieved the highest accolade by becoming the Champion Soloist of Great Britain. His most important conducting appointment was with the Cambridge Band.[29] Read became a Senior Peripatetic Music Teacher for the Cambridge area education authority and a much sought-after adjudicator.

The long-serving solo euphonium player Bert Sullivan was a founder member of Munn & Felton's. He had previously played with several other bands, both in his native Scotland and in Wales and England. He had several times been a guest player with Besses, touring Canada with them in 1932. He remained with Munn & Felton's until he retired in 1968, for most of this time playing solo euphonium,[30] but being replaced in 1967 by Trevor Groom, a former SA player, who held the position for some ten years.

The 1970s began well for GUS with a win at the World Championships of 1971. GUS was also amongst the four bands which travelled to Canada in 1972. Stanley Boddington was now approaching his seventies. Later in the year David Read relinquished the principal cornet seat, reverting to the position of assistant principal and also taking on the role of bandmaster in order to reduce the pressure on Boddington. He was replaced as principal by Tom Paulin (see page 150 n. 26).

Geoffrey Brand was engaged during 1975 on Boddington's retirement. This same year brought a further name-change – to GUS (Kettering) Band. Several key players had now left, company support was not what it had been during the Munn & Felton years and, though the new partnership secured a win at the Area contest of 1978, there was no reward in the major contests. Shortly after the 1978 Nationals Geoffrey Brand resigned and Keith Wilkinson, who had been Brand's assistant, became musical director. He held a PhD in mathematics and was a lecturer at the University of Nottingham.

---

[29] From 1978 this band was known as Cambridge Co-operative Band.

[30] Sullivan died on 6 June 1993, aged 91. His obituary may be found in *BB*, 3 July 1993, p. 10.

The band was now known as The Great Universal Band but from the beginning of 1980 became simply The GUS Band. This proved to be a good year, the band winning not only the Area contest, but a BBC television competition and 2nd prize at the British Open.

### Brighouse & Rastrick

Brighouse & Rastrick Band retained a high profile during the war years and in 1944 engaged Eric Ball as its professional conductor, a position he held until 1953. After the war Brighouse was in demand for concerts and Ball became heavily involved in these. Fourth prize in the first *Daily Herald* National Finals in London in 1945 augured well, and was followed by a win in 1946.

As National Brass Band Champion Band of Great Britain for the first time in its history, Brighouse was even busier during 1947, touring in the Channel Islands, Southern England and Scotland. At around this time the band instigated a series of twice-yearly massed band concerts in Huddersfield Town Hall. For these, they engaged two other bands and all played together under a leading guest conductor. Though remaining at the forefront in concert work Brighouse was less successful in contests during the late 1940s and early 1950s, its best achievements being the 3rd prizes at the Nationals of 1948 and 1951.

Fred Berry, the long-serving bandmaster, retired in 1949,[31] being succeeded by a number of conductors, including John Harrison. A cornet player in his younger days, Harrison was bandmaster at Brighouse & Rastrick during the early 1950s before moving to the newly-formed Crossley's Carpet Works Band in nearby Halifax (see Glossary). He then moved to Cornwall, becoming musical director of St Dennis in 1955.[32] Within two years he had moved north again – to Harton Colliery – but early in 1958 he was back with Crossley's. Harrison was a two-band man during the 1960s. His main appointment was at Crossley's until its closure in 1970, but he was also professional conductor of Cory's for several years from 1964, commuting from Halifax. During the early 1970s he worked as a freelance professional conductor and adjudicator. Early in 1974 he helped Whitburn Burgh to a Scottish Area contest win but had already accepted the position of resident conductor at Wingates, with whom he secured another Area win in the same season. In 1975 he became resident

---

[31] Fred Berry, a former euphonium soloist with Besses o' th' Barn, whom he accompanied on their first World Tour (1906–08), became a noted conductor, particularly with Brighouse & Rastrick. He died on 20 May 1953. (For further information see Newsome, 1998, n. 29, p. 134, and 'Profile' in *BBN*, December 1909, p. 4.)

[32] *BB* 14 May 1955, p. 6, and the St Dennis Band 150th Anniversary booklet, Trethewey, 1988, p. 27.

conductor of Lindley, following which he retired from top-class banding, devoting himself to teaching and conducting in the lower sections.[33]

Eric Ball was succeeded as professional conductor at Brighouse by Alex Mortimer (1953–55) and Willie Wood (1956 – see 'Personalia'). Trevor Walmsley then took over both roles, as musical director. During the early 1950s Walmsley[34] conducted Croydon Borough Band and in 1955 became musical director of Irwell Springs in Lancashire. A year later he took up a similar post with Brighouse & Rastrick. He next conducted Wingates for a time prior to returning to Brighouse. In 1965 he moved to Yorkshire Imperial Metals, remaining there for 12 years and taking them into the upper echelons of bands. He was appointed musical director of the failing CWS (Manchester) in 1976, serving for three years before accepting a similar appointment with Ever Ready, which he held until the end of 1980.

Walmsley resigned from the post of musical director of Brighouse & Rastrick in 1962. Though the band was now passing through an unsettled period, stability returned in 1963 with the appointment of W.B. Hargreaves as professional conductor. Within weeks he had lifted the band, taking 3rd prize in the Area contest and 2nd in the Finals. A number of resident conductors were tried, but in 1964 Walmsley returned.

Walter B. Hargreaves (1907–98) was born in Glasgow and first played the cornet at the age of four. After attending the Royal Scottish Academy of Music he embarked on a professional career as a trumpet player, but returned to his roots in 1944 as musical director of the City of Edinburgh Band. In February 1948 Cory's appointed him as their conductor on the recommendation of Harry Mortimer. He helped them towards their biggest contest success up to that time – 2nd prize in the 1948 Nationals. Following a similar result at the 1950 British Open, Hargreaves left Wales to become professor of trumpet and cornet at the Royal Marines School of Music at Deal, in Kent. Of diminutive proportions but with boundless energy, it was here that 'W.B.' earned the affectionate title 'The Wee Professor' (Figure 7.6).

The most sought-after contest conductor of the 1960s, Hargreaves enjoyed successes with Crookhall in Durham, Kibworth in the Midlands, Cory's, Parc & Dare and Tredegar in South Wales, and Markham Main and, in particular, Brighouse & Rastrick – both in Yorkshire. Though a full-time professor at the Royal Marines School of Music, he worked tirelessly with these bands as well as taking on adjudicating appointments and transcribing music. As a conductor he reached the first of several pinnacles in 1968, steering Brighouse to the title World & National Brass

---

[33] Harrison died on 11 January 1999, aged 86.

[34] Walmsley earned the DFC during World War II, when he served as a pilot in the RAF. There is a good biography in *BB* of 11 December 1976, p. 1.

Figure 7.6   Walter B. Hargreaves – 'The Wee Professor'

Band Champions, successfully defending this in 1969. Jimmy Hickman was bandmaster at the time.[35] Successes at the Royal Welsh National Eisteddfod included leading the then almost unheard-of Tredegar Town Workmen's Silver Band into first place in 1968. Hargreaves visited Australia

[35] Hickman was one of the old school of bandmasters. He had been connected with Carlton Main and also with Slaithwaite in its hey-day. See *BB* of 25 April 1970, p. 3, for a good biography.

in 1972 and Holland in 1973. Towards the end of this year he entered hospital to undergo an operation that, at the time, would have put an end to the active life of many. Not so Walter Hargreaves; he bounced back and continued with his hectic schedule.

The Wee Professor was professional conductor of Brighouse & Rastrick from 1963 to 1973 but even before his departure he was throwing himself wholeheartedly into building the fledgling Stanshawe Band into a first-class combination (see page 270). 'W.B.' spent his seventieth birthday in hospital but was soon in action again, becoming professional conductor of Ever Ready – based in County Durham, a considerable distance from Deal. His stay here was brief, however, because early in 1978 he was engaged to take Fairey's to the Area contest. After collecting the almost inevitable 1st prize he accepted the position of professional conductor.[36]

The soloists featured in a Brighouse & Rastrick broadcast during 1964 included Ken Aitken-Jones, David Horsfield and Denis Carr. The quality of these players is reflected in the fact that they earned a number of prizes in the Quartet Championships of Great Britain in Oxford, including a win in 1962. As a 15-year-old, Ken Aitken-Jones had played with Creswell Colliery then later, during military service, for six years with the band of RAF Fighter Command. In 1951 he joined Yewco as principal cornet. From the mid-1950s he was with Carlton Main, helping them win the British Open Championships in 1958. In the early 1960s he joined Brighouse as principal cornet and bandmaster but in 1967 emigrated to New Zealand, where he conducted a number of bands with some success. He returned to England in the 1970s, but did not again become involved in top-class banding.

David Horsfield subsequently played principal cornet with Brighouse and became a member of Black Dyke and of JSVB. He also did some conducting at a local level, and formed his own publishing and recording company. Denis Carr's career was outlined above on page 141. In 1967 Lyndon Baglin succeeded Carr on solo euphonium.

Following Brighouse's successes of the late 1960s, the next decade began quietly. Hickman left at the end of 1971 and Hargreaves indicated that he also was on the point of leaving. He was still on the staff of the Royal Marines School of Music at Deal in Kent and the journey to and from Brighouse was becoming exhausting. However, he remained for a while longer, making his final appearance at a concert in September 1973. His successor, James Scott, was already making his presence felt. Taking over early in the year, Scott led the band to third place in the British Open and to a win in the Nationals. The following year proved to be one of travel for Brighouse, with two visits to Holland and eight days in Switzerland.

---

36   For a detailed biography of Hargreaves, see *Sounding Brass*, October 1976, pp. 83–5.

The band had hit another quiet period and was again experimenting with different conductors. Scott led Brighouse to third place in the Nationals of 1975 and in the following year Maurice Handford steered them into a similar placing at the Open. From late in 1973 Derek Broadbent was resident conductor and took them to some of the 1977 contests, earning 2nd prize in the Open. Amongst Broadbent's early brass band conducting appointments was one with Slaithwaite Band, where he succeeded Roy Newsome as conductor. From here he moved to take up the residency at Brighouse and was also now building a reputation as an adjudicator and composer.

Moving away from contests, Brighouse and its new resident conductor achieved fame in an unexpected direction. Broadbent had begun his career as a cornet player in a local band and then spent nine years as an army musician, following which he was employed as musical director of a holiday camp, involved in all forms of popular musical entertainment and developing a facility for making arrangements in the 'pop' idiom. As conductor of Brighouse & Rastrick Band he made several such arrangements; one was an up-beat version of the well-known *Floral Dance*. This was played regularly in concerts, creating a strong reaction with audiences, with feet tapping, hands clapping and even dancing in the aisles. It was recorded by the band in 1975 but had little immediate impact outside of the brass band world. In due course it was featured by the BBC on some early morning programmes hosted by the popular disc jockey Terry Wogan. Record sales began to increase and by early 1977 the disc was amongst the 200 best-selling records in Britain. Within a short time it was in the pop charts at No. 50 and amidst all the publicity came an enquiry from the television programme *Top of the Pops*. Brighouse appeared on the show and, incredibly, the record climbed to No. 2. In the nature of things this kind of phenomenon is transitory and the era of *Floral Dance* ended quickly, but as Broadbent himself wrote: 'we always believed that we were doing something for all the Brass Band Movement. We were making people listen, making people aware, and all bands, not just those with big names, were getting better concert attendances.'[37] The band was awarded silver and gold discs for, respectively, quarter- and half-million sales and there is no doubt that they helped raise the profile of bands at the time. The name Brighouse & Rastrick and the sound of a brass band both became known and admired by millions of people worldwide.

It was a shock to the band movement to learn that, due to pressure of work, Brighouse would not compete in the Area contest of 1978. However, later in the year Geoffrey Brand was engaged as music adviser. Now freed

---

[37] This information comes from an article by Derek Broadbent in Littlemore, 1987, pp. 29–31. See also *Floral Dance 25th Anniversary 1977–2002 – Souvenir Brochure*.

from the shackles of the *BB* and its sponsorship complications, he led Brighouse to victory in the British Open Championships and in so doing deprived his old band Black Dyke of a double hat-trick at the Open. The partnership of Brand and Brighouse continued, but the only further reward was an Area contest win, along with a tour of Denmark sponsored by Boosey & Hawkes.

Brand left Brighouse at the beginning of 1980 and W.B. Hargreaves stepped in to take the band to the Area contest. However, it was resident conductor Derek Broadbent who conducted the band in the National Finals, band and conductor being rewarded with another win. Thus, Brighouse & Rastrick ended the decade on a high note and could look back on ten years which had brought three major titles and worldwide fame (Figure 7.7).

### Foden's Motor Works

Though Foden's Motor Works Band chose not to attend contests during the war they remained one of the foremost concert bands and were the first brass band to be taken abroad by ENSA. On 3 May 1945 – five days before VE Day – the bandsmen were taken to Calais by landing craft. Their intention was to entertain the troops, but Foden's were soon playing to a liberated nation and on VE night gave a concert in Brussels. They travelled over 2000 miles through Belgium, Holland and France, playing in hospitals and convalescent camps, and to freed prisoners of war.

However, this was not the Foden's of the 1930s. Fred Mortimer was 65 years old, Harry was not playing regularly with the band and several former players had either retired or were growing old. Mortimer senior would still not allow Foden's to compete at Belle Vue (see page 29) and having won the three previous Nationals (1936–37–38), they were – incredibly! – barred from the first post-war event.

The replacement of Harry Mortimer was achieved with the appointment of Bram Gay as principal cornet. Though still in his teens he was already playing with Foden's. He succeeded Mortimer as principal cornet player and won the AOMF Scholarship in 1945. During National Service he was in the Band of the Scots Guards following which, at the age of 23, he became principal trumpet with CBSO. From there, in 1960, he went to Manchester to a similar position with the Hallé. Moving to London he became first of all a trumpet player and then, from 1970, Orchestral Director at the Royal Opera House. Despite a busy professional career, he conducted a number of bands and also became involved in music publishing. He was joint-editor of *Sounding Brass*, the quarterly magazine which appeared in 1972. Travelling to his native Wales, he conducted Cory's with some success (1976–78) but found it difficult to combine this with his work at Covent Garden.

Figure 7.7   Brighouse & Rastrick at Castle Howard in 2000

161

In 1948, when Gay began his national service, Teddy Gray took over as principal cornet player with Foden's, having played with both Wingates and Bickershaw in his early career. He also became principal cornet player in the All-Star Band and Men o' Brass. Resigning from Foden's in 1971 after 23 years' service, he worked as an instrumental teacher in schools. His most significant later appointment, dating from 1974, was as musical director of Royal Doulton Band in Staffordshire. This became a very busy band, appearing on television, broadcasting and making an LP, fulfilling a week's engagement in Folkestone and winning the 2nd section of the Area contest – all in Gray's first year. Royal Doulton was never to become a top-class band but it remained busy and attracted good engagements.

Mortimer senior was in poor health during his later years and it was Harry who led Foden's to its first two post-war titles, at the Nationals of 1950 and 1953. Fred died in June of that year. Following this, Rex, the youngest of his sons, became bandmaster and Harry the professional conductor. Rex Mortimer was born shortly after the family settled in Luton. Though overshadowed by his elder brothers he held his place as a player both at Luton and Foden's. He also conducted other bands, being professional conductor with two Yorkshire bands – Markham Main and Crossley's Carpet Works – and becoming musical director of the newly formed Cammell Laird's in Liverpool in 1959.

On Harry Mortimer's retirement from active participation in major contests in 1956, Rex became musical director at Foden's whilst Harry remained as musical adviser. The only other Foden's championship win during the 1950s was at the 1958 Nationals when Rex achieved his first major title as a conductor. Though not regaining the supremacy it enjoyed during the 1930s, Foden's was still a powerful force, in constant demand for concerts, broadcasts and recordings. However, during the 1960s the band again managed only one win at the highest level – the 1964 British Open. The 1970s were also problematical and its greatest achievements were 2nd prizes in three Area contests.

When sponsors of bands which benefit from their benevolence run into difficulties the bands concerned face problems which seem not to beset unsponsored bands. They have come to rely on financial backing; when that crumbles they are in trouble and many do not survive. Foden's certainly struggled during the 1970s. It was one of the last of the genuine works bands, with virtually all band members employed by the company. When redundancy strikes in these circumstances it is inevitable that some bandsmen will be forced to leave the district, and the band, in search of fresh employment. This happened at Foden's, though the first major problem (which had nothing to do with redundancy) came in 1971 when principal cornet player Teddy Gray retired. Perhaps even more devastating was the fact that, at the age of 63, Rex Mortimer took early retirement in

1975. This ended a family association with Foden's that had lasted over half a century. Rex Mortimer had conducted the band for 22 years and had been involved in over 500 broadcasts.

His immediate successor was a 32-year-old composer, John Golland, some of whose music the band had recently recorded. However, Golland's experience with the baton was limited and his stay short-lived. Rex Mortimer returned briefly, but on 26 October 1975 he conducted Foden's for the last time.[38]

James Scott now became musical director but the band was not in very good shape. He remained for four years and had the satisfaction of winning 2nd prizes in the Area contests of 1977 and 1978.

Meanwhile, in 1976, the band's quartet won the Oxford Quartet Championships. Two years later Colin Cranson, the band's solo euphonium player, was appointed bandmaster to work alongside Scott; however, both left in mid-1979. Derek Garside, the former CWS star, accompanied Foden's on a Swiss tour and conducted at the British Open, after which he became resident conductor.

In July 1980 the company of Foden went into liquidation. Fortunately, the American company which bought the remnants of the business allowed the band to continue. Towards the end of 1980 a new musical director, Howard Snell, was appointed. Though having played in an SA band, his early musical career had been entirely that of an orchestral trumpet player. In particular, he was principal trumpet with the LSO for many years and was the founder and conductor of the Wren Orchestra. He made his debut as a brass band conductor with Grimethorpe, in 1973. Prior to 1977 he was musical director of Desford Colliery. Through his own highly specialised arrangements he had quickly made them into one of the leading concert bands and also had some notable successes in contests. From 1980 he was set to make a substantial mark with Foden's.[39]

## Grimethorpe Colliery

Grimethorpe Colliery Band was one of the many talented Yorkshire bands unable to break into the top flight in the early post-war years. A 2nd prize at the 1945 'September' under George Thompson was its only success at the highest level during this period.

Initially learning to play the euphonium in an SA junior band, George Thompson (1907–84) joined Callender's Cable Works Band in 1929. Studying with Denis Wright, amongst others, he became the first recipient of the LGSM (Brass Bandmastership) diploma, in 1933. Thompson

---

[38] Rex Mortimer died on 18 August 1999, aged 88.
[39] Much of this information is taken from Littlemore, 1999, pp. 115–30.

conducted Grimethorpe from 1942 to 1947, then returned south. Here he conducted a number of bands, including Hanwell, winning the Southern Area Championships of 1950 and 2nd prize in the National Finals with them. He left in 1953. Moving around, he led Markham Main to 3rd prize in the North East Area and earned two Belle Vue September prizes with the short-lived John White Footwear Band (see Glossary). He also conducted City of Coventry, Creswell and St Dennis.

There were several changes of conductor at Grimethorpe after Thompson left but in 1957 he returned and the band began making its mark. Third prize in the 1960 British Open heralded a move towards the top. Grimethorpe came to the fore during the 1960s when, for the first time in its history, it became one of the top ten most successful contesting bands. Two outstanding performances under Thompson's baton during this decade were of the overture *Rienzi* (Wagner) in the 1963 Area contest and *Spectrum* (Vinter) at the 1969 British Open Championships. Prizes at national level included wins at the 1967 Open and 1970 Nationals. Very much an individualist, Thompson was a fine band trainer. He spent a great deal of time arranging music specially for Grimethorpe, little of which is published. He was also co-author (with Kenneth Cook) of a publication for young players, *Learning to Play*, published in the late 1940s.

Reaching the age of 65 in 1972, Thompson retired after 15 years' service. Freed from the ties of Grimethorpe, he now worked with several lower-section bands, but suffered a heart attack later that year. During 1975 he became Director of Examinations for the Bandsman's College of Music and also returned to Grimethorpe for a time to train and conduct them at contests. In 1977 George Thompson was awarded the MBE.[40] He was replaced by two conductors, local man Derek Ashmore taking on the role of resident conductor and Elgar Howarth becoming musical adviser.

The influence of Elgar Howarth has been enormous. To start at the beginning of his musical career, he won the AOMF Scholarship in 1951 at the age of 16. At this time he was playing solo cornet with Barton Hall Works Band near Manchester, conducted by his father. He studied at Manchester University and the Royal Manchester College of Music, and during National Service played in the Central Band of the Royal Air Force. As a professional trumpet player he made his mark initially in the orchestra of the Royal Opera House and then, from 1963 to 1969, as principal trumpet in the Royal Philharmonic Orchestra. He was also an occasional guest conductor of the London Sinfonietta – a chamber orchestra specialising in contemporary music. From 1965 he was a key member of

---

[40] George Thompson died in August 1984, aged 77. His death is reported in *BB* of 18 August 1984.

the PJBE as player, composer, arranger, and conductor. This group became world famous, pioneering new music for brass ensemble.

Howarth became musical adviser to Grimethorpe Colliery Band in 1972. In addition to his work as conductor he composed several important brass band works himself and, using the anagrammatical pseudonym 'W. Hogarth Lear', wrote short, witty pieces with picturesque titles such as *Pop Goes the Posthorn* and *Pel Mel* (see also page 128). Many of these had a visual element and greatly enhanced Grimethorpe's lighter repertoire, opening new doors in television. So great was Howarth's influence that *Brass Band Review* wrote:

> It has been said that Elgar Howarth, who is to present six brass band programmes for Granada from July 1 to August 5, will do for the brass band movement what André Previn has done and is doing for the symphony orchestra.[41]

Howarth's first contest was the Granada Band of the Year competition in 1972 which, thanks largely to his individual approach to programming and his own arrangements, Grimethorpe won. Shortly after this Ashmore resigned, being replaced as resident conductor by professional trumpet player Dennis Wilby (see 'Personalia').

Grimethorpe also won the next television contest under Howarth, but their highest placing in the two major contests were 2nd prizes in the 1973 Open and the 1974 Nationals. Nevertheless, Grimethorpe Colliery Band was now established as a leading band.

The 'procession' of conductors continued with the appointment of John Berryman in 1973. Snell was brought back in 1974, George Thompson returned in 1975 specifically to take Grimethorpe to contests, whilst yet another conductor, Ernest Woodhouse (see 'Personalia'), took them in 1976. The orchestral conductor Bryden Thomson conducted at the Open of 1976 and Howarth at the Nationals. Woodhouse left in 1977 and the American trumpet player and orchestral conductor Gerard Schwarz[42] took Grimethorpe into second place in the 1977 Nationals. James Scott led them to victory in the 1978 Area contest and a professional french horn player, Anthony Randall, conducted at the British Open. Stanley Boddington then came out of retirement to steer them into third place in the Nationals and second in the European Championships. Snell again conducted Grimethorpe, in the 1977 British Open. James Scott returned

---

[41] *Brass Band Review* June 1975, p. 22.

[42] Schwarz, then the principal trumpet player of the New York Philharmonic Orchestra, was known to bandsmen through a recording called *Cornet Favourites*, featuring solos familiar to English bandsmen. He later became a conductor and, following appointments with a number of American orchestras, was appointed music director of the Royal Liverpool Philharmonic Orchestra in 2001.

to conduct at contests in 1980, Ray Farr having already become resident conductor, in 1979.

Farr had been a professional trumpet player, playing mainly with the BBC Radio Orchestra. He had an SA background and was to become an important brass band figure, both as conductor and arranger. For a time he combined his professional career with brass band conducting. Based in London, it was inevitable that he would initially conduct southern-based bands. These included City of Coventry, Redbridge Youth and Newham.

Despite all the to-ing and fro-ing of conductors, Howarth remained as musical adviser. He was not particularly attracted to contesting but had an astounding effect on the band's concert work (Figure 7.8). Engagements which came Grimethorpe's way through his influence were many and varied. In 1974 and 1975, for example, Grimethorpe and Black Dyke appeared in the Henry Wood Promenade Concerts in the Royal Albert Hall (the first brass bands to ever perform in this series); then in 1976, the year of the bi-centennial celebration of American Independence, the British Council sent two British brass bands – Grimethorpe Colliery and Cory's – to tour in the United States as part of the festivities. Grimethorpe remained in the USA for three weeks. The band also made a number of appearances at the Queen Elizabeth Hall (QEH) in London, one of which, in November 1977, was shared with the internationally famous classical guitarist John Williams and the London Sinfonietta, Howarth conducting throughout. In a 1978 QEH concert Grimethorpe shared the stage with the PJBE and the Yugoslavian trombonist and avant-garde composer Vinko Globokar; whilst at around the same time, in Scotland Bo'ness & Carriden Band joined forces with Grimethorpe, under Howarth, for a concert in the Scottish National Orchestra's Promenade Concert season.

Through Howarth, Grimethorpe now began to achieve international recognition, with appearances at the Fourth International Art Workshop in Montepulciano, Tuscany and a Twentieth-century Music Festival in Zagreb, Yugoslavia – both in 1979. The Montepulciano event was organised by the German composer Hans Werner Henze, whose *Ragtimes and Habaneras* was one of the works which 'sold' these concerts. Grimethorpe also provided the music for a local opera and played a concert of English music in the cathedral. A crew from Granada Television accompanied the band and filmed a programme called *Arrividerci Grimethorpe*. In 1980 there were concerts in Vienna and Innsbruck; in Vienna there were also radio and television appearances and a performance of Globokar's *La Tromba e Mobile* for trombone and brass band.

On the entertainment side, Grimethorpe now began its association with the singer/pianist Peter Skellern. Skellern, from Bury in Lancashire, had played in brass bands, being first of all a member of Besses Boys' and later a member of the NYBB. However, he was known to the public primarily

Figure 7.8   Elgar Howarth – an enormous influence

as an entertainer. The first collaboration was the making of a record of *You and I*, following which Skellern and the band were featured in a television series called *The Entertainers*. Later in the year they appeared at the London Palladium and later again on Michael Parkinson's television chat show.

Thus, despite a somewhat inconsistent record in competition, Grimethorpe had become the biggest name in the brass band world for its concert presentations, both serious and light, and this was almost entirely due to Howarth's programming and commissioning policy.

### Yorkshire Imperial

Yorkshire Imperial Band (formerly Yorkshire Copper Works; see page 35) took some time in fulfilling its early promise. In 1959, in line with the name of the parent company the band took the new name and began to make its presence felt, with a win in a BBC knock-out competition in 1961. It had a succession of conductors and its first notable success came in 1962 when it won 3rd prize in the British Open Championships. Trevor Walmsley took the band to the Open in 1965, leading it to fifth place. He then became musical director, his first important successes being a win at the 1966 Edinburgh International Contest and 2nd prize at the British Open.

In 1963 Phillip McCann became principal cornet, staying until 1967. Walmsley continued as musical director, but as his business interests took him away from the district from time to time Denis Carr, now playing solo euphonium, also became assistant conductor. An influx of quality players during 1969 gave the band a boost. With their help in 1970, the band won the first of two successive British Open Championships.

After the 1971 British Open win there were no further spectacular results for a few years. Trevor Walmsley remained until 1976, steering the band into three Area contest wins, a 3rd prize in the Open (1975) and a 2nd in the Nationals (1976) before his departure. Denis Carr then became musical director. His first year in the role was reasonably productive, with an Area contest win and third place in the Nationals. In the following year, Yorkshire Imperial became the National Champion Band of Great Britain; but Carr left at the end of 1979.

Peter Parkes was engaged to take the band to the 1980 Area contest, which they duly won. A further name-change took place – to the Yorkshire Imperial Metals Band – shortly after which a school music teacher and former player and conductor of Brighouse, Peter Kitson, became resident conductor. The orchestral conductor John Pryce-Jones then became involved. He was a Cambridge organ scholar who in 1970 became a conductor/repetiteur with Welsh National Opera and then, in 1978, joined English National Opera as a staff conductor. His early connection with brass bands was in South Wales and in 1978 he took Cory's to the Granada 'Band of the Year' competition, winning 2nd prize. However, it was in 1980 that he really came to the fore in bands, taking Yorkshire Imperial Metals to a win in the British Open – on his first attempt. Shortly afterwards he was appointed their musical adviser. His professional career has been such that brass bands have of necessity been a sideline activity for him.

With three major titles and four Area contest wins in the decade, 'Yorkshire Imps' had become a major force in the contest field.

### Carlton Main Frickley Colliery

Carlton Main Frickley Colliery Band, formerly known as South Elmsall, was conducted by Noel Thorpe from 1919 to 1938. He was succeeded by Albert E. Badrick, a former member of Callender's who held the position until 1947. The band's most successful periods came later: first under Eric Ball, who became professional conductor in 1948 and later under Jack Atherton, who took over in 1954. 'Frickley' toured Holland three times – in 1949, 1950 and 1952. Emulating the successes of Fairey Aviation in earlier years, it also won prizes in international competitions. The band was at its peak between 1956 and 1960 when it was the most successful contesting band overall, its high point being as winner of the 1958 British Open Championships.

Amongst Carlton Main's principal cornet players were Ken Aitken-Jones in the late 1950s, and James Shepherd who joined in 1960. An innovation during 1958 was the appointment of Andrew Owenson as the official 'arranger'. This resulted in the band acquiring much of its own unique repertoire.

After the successes of the late 1950s it is surprising to learn that Carlton Main was not in the first three places at any Area contest during the 1960s and that it had but limited success at the Open, with just a 4th prize in 1963 and a 2nd in 1969. One theory for the cause of this slump is that several key players defected to near neighbours Grimethorpe. Despite these relatively poor results, however, Carlton Main remained one of the leading concert and broadcasting bands. Atherton remained musical director until 1969.[43]

---

[43] From 1968 Jack Atherton's name was associated with Mirlees Works Band and in 1970 he became its professional conductor. Following a period of poor health, he retired in 1974, aged 65. Shortly after this he suffered a stroke which left him severely debilitated. He died on 17 March 1983, aged 74. There is an informative obituary in *BB* of 23 April 1983, p. 2.

Bill Lippeatt, who had played cornet with a number of bands including Grimethorpe and Ransome's, conducted for a time early in 1970, before the appointment as musical director of Robert Oughton (1920–95). Oughton was a leading cornet player in the post-war years, playing with Munn & Felton's and Grimethorpe and serving in the Scots Guards before becoming principal cornet player and bandmaster of Ransome & Marles. He was resident conductor of Scottish CWS for much of the 1960s, though he spent two years (1961–63) pioneering brass banding in the Faroe Islands (see page 320). He acted as professional conductor to several other Scottish bands before moving to Yorkshire in 1970 to become musical director of Carlton Main. On leaving here he returned to Scotland where he conducted a number of bands and continued periodically visiting the Faroes. He died in 1995.

After winning the Area contest in 1971 and taking 2nd prize at the British Open in the following year, Carlton Main had little further success, with just one 2nd prize and two 3rds at Area contests during the remainder of the decade. Conductors after Oughton included Major Arthur Kenney (1975), Denzil Stephens (1977) and David James (1978–80). (Kenney's career is outlined below on page 173.)

Kevin Bolton was principal cornet player at Carlton Main during the early 1970s, later becoming resident conductor, and then the 'professional'. Carlton Main's most notable achievement during the late 1970s was winning a television competition in 1978 under Denzil Stephens.

### Wingates Temperance

Wingates Temperance Band, second only to Brighouse & Rastrick amongst the most successful unsponsored bands of the time, maintained its status and continued to attract good engagements despite being located in a depressed area. Though winning the North West Area championships in 1945 and 1948 it was unable to consolidate with prizes in the Finals and the only reward for its regular appearances in the British Open during the 1940s was a 2nd prize in 1947. With no financial support, the band was able to use only local conductors including, from 1954, Hugh Parry, who battled against enormous odds to keep them in the top flight. At regional level, Wingates had to face the might of Fairey's, CWS and Foden's; nevertheless they achieved 3rd prizes in 1957 and 1959, and a 2nd in 1960. There were further successes during the 1960s, particularly at the British Open, with a 2nd prize in 1961 and further rewards in 1966–67–68. Wingates also earned further Area contest prizes but the end of the decade brought another unsettled period, despite a highly successful tour of Holland during 1969. The 1970s began well as Wingates, conducted by Dennis Smith (see 'Personalia') won the 1971 Area contest and followed this by becoming National Champions, in the final year of the experiment with the World Championships. Other conductors during the 1970s included Trevor Walmsley, John Harrison and Malcolm Brownbill – who was also the musical director of the Liverpool City Police Band and conductor of several other bands.

In 1975 Wingates engaged a promising young local conductor, Richard Evans, who was to become a leading figure in the brass band world and who, as was mentioned earlier, led Wingates to victory at his first British Open as a conductor.

In 1976 Wingates took 2nd prize at the Area contest and first in the following year. Conductors engaged towards the end of this period included Frank Renton, James Scott and Dennis Wilby. Wilby remained until late 1980, during which time the band won a 2nd prize in the 1979 Area contest, made an LP for Decca and toured Norway. After proudly bearing the name Wingates Temperance for over a century it was announced in 1980 that the band would in future be known as The Wingates Band. There was much speculation that this was in readiness for sponsorship.

\* \* \*

That concludes this survey of the ten most successful bands in the period 1946–80. Much could be written about the many bands which were outside the 'Top Ten'. Space forbids even a mention of most of them. Brief comments will be found on some of them in the 'Glossary of Bands' beginning on page 326. However, several more bands secured a major title during this period. They are discussed briefly below and their discussion is followed by further comment about bands which have been mentioned earlier in the book.

### Other prizewinning bands

As was mentioned on page 36, Ransome & Marles Works Band was formed in Newark-on-Trent in 1937. It leaped to fame in 1949, with 2nd prize at the 'September', followed two years later with its only major win, at the same contest. Both performances were conducted by Eric Ball. Throughout this period David Aspinall was musical director and business manager. He was a former playing member of Wingates and Besses, and a former musical director of Creswell Colliery and Friary Brewery (see Glossary). Though finding it difficult to keep a permanent foothold in the top echelons of banding, Ransome's was a force to reckon with in the Midlands, winning the Area contest three years in succession in 1950–51–52 and representing the Midlands at the Finals on ten occasions between 1945 and 1960. It was a very successful concert band, and broadcast regularly.

In 1953 Robert Oughton became principal cornet player and bandmaster. Following the sudden death of David Aspinall early in 1957 Oughton took over as the regular conductor. Eric Ball continued to visit, however, directing broadcasts and some of the band's more important engagements. In 1958 George Hespe became professional conductor but during the following year Oughton resigned and Hespe assumed all conducting responsibilities.

George Hespe (1900–79) enlisted in the army as a band boy. After studying at Kneller Hall, he became bandmaster of the 1st Battalion the Seaforth Highlanders, an appointment he held from 1928 until his retirement from the army in 1933. Following this he conducted bands in the Sheffield area. He was a fine tuba player and for a time played professionally with the BBC Northern Orchestra. Between 1945 and 1950 Hespe had two spells conducting the short-lived St Hilda's/Yewco Band and during 1947 he conducted Grimethorpe. He became professional conductor of both Carlton Main and Creswell Colliery in the early 1950s, and of Ferodo (see page 175) from 1953 until its demise in 1958, helping it win the 'September' in 1954. He was a cultured musician and composed a number of pieces, including the 1953 Belle Vue test piece, *The Three Musketeers*.

The partnership of Hespe and Ransome & Marles enjoyed some success, including 2nd prize at the 1962 British Open Championships. Hespe also conducted Yorkshire Imperial and Luton bands during 1959 and 1960, and he took Black Dyke to the 1963 Area contest. After this last performance he suffered a heart attack which, though he survived it, ended his conducting career.

Various conductors then helped out at Ransome's until, early in 1964, Dennis Masters (see 'Personalia') was appointed musical director. Ransome's appeared in the prizes at Area contests six times between 1961 and 1970, with one win. By 1970 they were called Ransome Hoffman Pollard Works Band. Stanley Boddington took them to the Area contest in this year, but Masters led them into second place at the Nationals. The 1970s brought mixed fortunes, with several more changes of conductor and further name changes; in 1972 the band became the RHP (Newark) Band. There were two Area contest wins – in 1971 under Masters and in 1977 with Stephen Shimwell, another local conductor. Shimwell conducted for the last four years of the decade, helping the band to its 3rd prize at the 1978 British Open Championships. In 1979 sponsorship was withdrawn and the band continued as The Ransome Band.

In South Wales, Cory Workmen's Silver Band made regular broadcasts in the post-war years and was in greater demand for concerts than any other Welsh band. In 1947 W.B. Hargreaves became its professional conductor and the band had a flurry of successes at the top level under his dynamic leadership, including 2nd prizes in the Nationals in 1948 and in the 'September' of 1950. Hargreaves then took up his appointment at the Royal Marines School of Music and Cory's became rather quiet. In 1959 the most important figure in Welsh banding at the time, T.J. (Tom) Powell became musical director (see Personalia).

Cory's were well to the fore in Wales during the 1960s, with five Area wins. Their 1961 win was directed by Powell but, because of his ill-health, Hargreaves returned to direct the band's winning performance a year later. Tragically, Powell collapsed and died in 1965 whilst directing Cory's in the BBC studios. They then tried a number of conductors, eventually engaging John Harrison of Halifax (see page 155) who steered them to wins in the Area contests of 1964, 1965 and 1967.[44] In 1966 the Welsh Associations introduced a new system of determining the Champion Band of Wales (see page 118) that was designed to encourage bands to attend local contests. The title went to the band in each of the four sections with the best record in six specified events. Cory's were the first winners of the title in the championship section, repeating the feat in the following two years.

Under the permanent direction of Major Arthur Kenney from the early 1970s, Cory's again dominated Welsh banding and, with a series of successes at national level, were becoming one of Britain's elite bands. Major Kenney had had a distinguished career as an army musician, his final appointment being as Director of Music of the Band of the Welsh Guards. Whilst still serving, he conducted Yorkshire Imperial Metals at the Yorkshire Area contest of 1965. On leaving the Guards he became musical director of Cory's and immediately found a winning formula. The Cory/Kenney partnership was hugely fruitful. He remained with the band until the end of 1975, by which time it had been in the top five places in the British Open on three occasions, had taken third place in the Nationals in 1971 and made history in 1974 when it became the first non-English band to earn the title of National Champion Band of Great Britain. Towards the end of the following year Kenney moved north to take over at Carlton Main. This was an unsettled period for him; he resigned in mid-1977 and in the following April left Britain to take up a military appointment in Tripoli, establishing a school for military musicians. However, by 1980 he was back in Wales.

Kenney was succeeded by Bram Gay who helped the band qualify for the Finals again in each of the next three years, earning 3rd prize in the

---

[44] There was no Welsh Area contest in 1966, but Cory's received an invitation to the Finals.

Nationals of 1976. This year was the bi-centennial year of American Independence and, along with Grimethorpe, Cory's toured America. They were there for two weeks, the first under Bram Gay and the second with guest conductor Roy Newsome.

Gay was succeeded in 1978 by Denzil Stephens. Under him the band enjoyed considerable success, benefiting from his skills as composer and arranger. They won the Area contest of 1979, went on to take second place in the Finals and had a good year in other contests, being the first band to win all six qualifying contests as well as becoming Welsh Champions. They also became 'Radio Band of Wales'. The year was crowned when the band became runner-up in the 1979 European Championships. In concert, Cory's took a leaf out of Grimethorpe's book, representing brass bands at a British Music Week in Italy in 1978 and a year later presenting a programme of modern music at the QEH.

Besses o' th' Barn undertook an ENSA tour during late 1945. During the early 1950s it benefited greatly from an influx of players from Besses Boys Band. It lived on its reputation for concert work, but reappeared in the British Open prize-lists of 1957 and 1958, winning in 1959. Willie Wood (see 'Personalia'), first connected with Besses in 1920, continued as musical director until his retirement in 1963, when Frank Bryce was appointed.[45] Besses had no success at Area level during this decade, but earned sixth places at the British Open Championships of 1964 and 1966. Bryce's strength showed in popular concerts, where his flair for arranging came to the fore. Besses regained a little of their former glory in the 1970s, Bryce leading them to an Area win in 1972. He then asked to be relieved of some of his responsibilities, resulting in the internationally renowned french horn player Ifor James becoming professional conductor.

Though having only limited success in contests, James increased the scope of the band's concert work; he obtained Arts Council grants for commissioning new works and, through his contacts, secured prestigious concert bookings in arts festivals where they could be performed. Besses gave a number of premières, including *Chromoscope* (Patterson, 1974), *Concerto for Tuba and Brass Band* (Gregson, 1976) and *Images* (McCabe, 1977). In his concerts James used colleagues from the professional world and in fact made a recording of Mendelssohn's *Capriccio Brillante*, transcribed for piano and band and played by the distinguished pianist-composer John McCabe.

In 1978 Roy Newsome became musical director. Taking third place in the Area contest this year, Besses attracted an invitation to the Finals where they

---

[45] A product of Besses Boys, Bryce had also played in Besses o' th' Barn Band. He was a member of the 4th/7th Royal Dragoon Guards Band for five years, during which time he studied at Kneller Hall (*BB* 6 April 1963, p. 2).

earned 2nd prize. Alec Evans, well known locally, became associate conductor in 1979. Under Newsome and Evans, Besses made several interesting recordings. In 1980 they made an LP and gave a concert commemorating the sixtieth anniversary of the death of their former legendary conductor Alexander Owen. Elgar Howarth and Arthur Butterworth, both former winners of the AOMF Scholarship, were guest conductors.

Based at Chapel-en-le-Frith in Derbyshire, Ferodo Works Band existed only from 1951 to 1958. By offering generous retaining fees it attracted good players, including two former Black Dyke principal cornet players, Willie Lang (see page 30) and Bernard Bygraves (see 'Personalia'). Ferodo made its contest debut in Nottingham under Fred Mortimer in 1952, but at the Leicester Band Festival, on Easter Monday 1953, won 1st prize under George Hespe, who was musical director for the remainder of the band's existence. Ferodo reached its peak in 1954 when it won the 'September'. Despite this it is often cited as a prime example of the impossibility of 'buying' a band. As if to emphasise the point, it was closed down by the company 'for economic reasons', giving its final concert in New Brighton in July 1958.

The National Band of New Zealand is a composite band made up of some of the best players in that country. The New Zealand Brass Band Association forms the band about once every four years for the purpose of a world tour. Famed for its marching as well as its concerts, the band first visited England during its inaugural tour of 1953 – it competed at the Edinburgh International Contest and the British Open, winning both. It was on tour again in 1962, conducted by Ken Smith (senior), father of the cornet player who was with Fairey's for a time. The band spent a fortnight in England, playing in Cornwall and London prior to going to Kerkrade to compete in and win the WMC. Following this the band returned to Britain to participate in the Edinburgh International Contest which, once again, it won. This contest had its problems, however, as, in view of rules regarding registration, the NBBCC was uncomfortable about the New Zealanders competing. The problem was overcome when the Council agreed to issue 'one day' cards – normally used by deputy bandsmen – to the whole band. The New Zealanders then toured Canada and the USA. The next tour was in 1970, when a marketing expert accompanied the band so that New Zealand as a country could exploit the goodwill generated by the band. Further tours took place in 1974 and 1978. The latter, 14 weeks long, took in London, Kerkrade, the USA and Canada. There were, in total, over 80 concerts and marching displays. A Maori group travelled with the band and the tour coincided with the twenty-fifth anniversary of the formation of the first National Band of New Zealand.

\* \* \*

Scottish CWS Band won the Scottish Championships nine times between 1946 and 1971, including a hat-trick in 1946–47–48. Conductors included Fred and Alex Mortimer, Geoffrey Whitham, Gregor J. Grant (see 'Personalia'), Enoch Jackson (see 'Personalia') and Elgar Clayton. In 1959 Robert Oughton took over. Not regular competitors at the great English contests, Scottish CWS nevertheless won 2nd prize at the Nationals in 1958 and several other lesser prizes during this period. Willie Barr served as principal cornet for most of the period under review and Peter Wilson played solo euphonium during the late 1950s. Known from the early 1960s as CWS (Glasgow), the band passed through their least successful period in contests during the latter part of that decade. Their only Area prize-winning performances (second in 1962, and first in 1964 and 1965) were directed by Alex Mortimer. They commenced the 1970s well with an Area win in 1971 under Geoffrey Whitham, but were not successful again until 1979, when Nigel Boddice led them to second place. Boddice (see 'Personalia'), conducted the band regularly from 1977.

During the early post-war years City of Coventry Band lived in the shadow of the leading Midlands bands, but in 1948 achieved a win in the Area championships and 4th prize in the Finals. It then faded for a time. Albert Chappell was amongst the early bandmasters at Coventry and Eric Ball was professional conductor for a while. Chappell's roots were in the SA and in the late 1930s, at the age of 16, he was playing solo trombone in the Coventry SA Band. During the war he served in the Royal Artillery and from 1942 to 1947 was the solo trombone player in its Woolwich band. He became bandmaster at City of Coventry in 1948 but remained there for only a short time and during the 1950s conducted other Midlands bands. Cyril I. Yorath (see 'Personalia') took over from 1957 to 1959 but then Chappell returned as musical director, linking this work with his teaching career. He brought City of Coventry to the fore during the 1960s. Though its highest placing at the top level was 4th prize at the Nationals, in 1968, it made the top three at seven of the decade's Area contests, winning in 1966, 1967 and 1970. Chappell remained until 1975 and during the first half of the 1970s led City of Coventry to three wins and two 2nd prizes in Area contests, and 2nd prize in the 1971 Nationals.[46] The next conductor was Ray Farr. He was there for only a year (1975–76) before Kenneth Dennison took over, remaining until 1979. During 1980 City of Coventry engaged Peter Parkes as professional conductor.

Following the difficulties of the 1930s and the war years, Parc & Dare quickly established itself as a leading Welsh band in the post-war era. Though not making a mark at national level, it dominated the Area contests between 1945 and 1960, with hat-tricks in 1945–46–47 and

---

[46] Albert Chappell died in 1999, aged 82.

1953–54–55, and further wins in 1957 and 1958, and appearing in the National Finals 12 times between 1945 and 1960. The band slipped into the background during the early 1960s but in 1965 Ieuan Morgan, its former euphonium player, and the founder/conductor of Treorchy Secondary School Band, was appointed conductor.[47] A number of players from the school band were imported into the senior band, which returned to its former status in style to win a £500 prize at the National Eisteddfod of 1966. With an influx of good players and the engagement of W.B. Hargreaves as professional conductor, a new era was predicted. The new combination brought immediate results with a win in the 1970 Welsh Area contest. Parc & Dare became Area champions in 1975, 1976 and 1978, Welsh Champions in 1976–77–78 and also achieved a hat-trick in the Eisteddfod in the same period.[48]

Hanwell Silver Band, in earlier times the foremost London band, took a back seat for a time after the war, winning the Area contest only in 1946 and 1950. On the appointment of George Thompson as musical director, the band achieved its greatest success – 2nd prize in the 1950 National Finals. In 1953 Hanwell qualified for the Finals for the fifth time but Thompson resigned a few weeks before the contest. They were conducted on the day by Eric Bravington.

Bravington was the 2nd prize winner in the 1946 All-England Solo Championships (see page 104). In his youth he had played principal cornet with Hanwell and from 1957 to 1967 was its musical director, combining this with a career in music. He played trumpet in the London Philharmonic Orchestra (LPO) from 1939, served in the Welsh Guards from 1941 to 1948, then returned to the orchestra as principal trumpet, becoming the orchestra's managing director in 1959. In 1957 Bravington was appointed musical director of Hanwell, leading the band in three Area wins and three 2nd prizes between 1961 and 1970, and also in 1970, the first year of the World Championships, taking 3rd prize in the Nationals. Unfortunately, his work as managing director of the LPO kept him away from the band at certain times and eventually his heavy schedule compelled him to relinquish his position at Hanwell. A leading brass band adjudicator, regularly officiating at major contests, Eric Bravington was awarded the OBE in 1974.

Several very interesting programmes came the band's way during the 1970s. The first was a live appearance on television's *Top of the Pops*, pre-dating Brighouse & Rastrick's *Floral Dance* show by five years. Two

---

[47] Ieuan Morgan was awarded the MBE in 1985 for services to brass bands in Wales. He had also become a noted adjudicator.

[48] *BB* 7 February 1976, p. 7, and 19 February 1977, p. 4; and Parc & Dare Centenary booklet, p. 17.

appearances were made as the backing group to Peter Skellern, singing *You're a Lady*, which reached No. 3 in the charts. Another interesting 'date' was recording the signature tune for the popular television programme, Esther Rantzen's *That's Life*. The band also undertook two highly successful tours of Switzerland during the 1970s.[49] In 1974 Hanwell appointed Bramwell Tovey as its professional conductor (see page 258). Five years later in 1979 the band accepted sponsorship, becoming Roneo Vickers Band, and in 1980, having retired from his position as managing director of the LPO, Bravington returned as musical director.[50]

Morris Motors Band engaged Harry Mortimer as professional conductor in 1945 – a certain prescription for success. They soon became the premier Southern band, regularly broadcasting and attracting important engagements. At national level they took fifth place at the Nationals of 1952, sixth in 1955 and 1957, and in 1958 secured prizes at both the Nationals and the Open. Morris Motors won the London & Southern Counties Area contest nine times and appeared in the Finals on 12 occasions between 1945 and 1960. From 1963, when they became Morris Motors (BMC), the band made a further small mark at national level, with lower-order prizes at each British Open between then and 1966. From 1957 to 1963 Stanley Boddington directed Morris's contest performances. From then on, the long-serving resident conductor Cliff Edmunds took over, helping the band to a 3rd prize at the Open of 1965.

Another name change came in 1970, this time to Morris Concert Band, but the band lost its sponsorship during this year and struggled for survival. Tommy Morcombe, its major driving force, retired as band manager at the end of 1971. He had joined in 1930, became band manager in 1943 and founded the Quartet Championships of Great Britain in 1945. During his managership the band had visited Holland, Belgium, Sweden, Norway and Denmark. Morris Motors was one of the original bands in Men o' Brass – of which Morcombe became secretary.

Harry Mortimer and several more players left Morris's early in 1972. For the Area contest – the band's first appearance there for some years – W.B. Hargreaves was engaged and the contest duly won. There were further changes of conductor and the band won the Area contests in 1974 and 1975. Thereafter its name ceased to appear in prize-lists and in fact the band was not invited to the British Open after 1975. The band had earned no less than 15 lower-order prizes at the highest level. Other bands began to appear in Oxford in the later 1970s; gradually Morris's players drifted away and the band ceased to exist.

---

[49] Much of this information comes from Brighton, 1983, pp. 11–16. See also *BB* 27 January 1979, p. 1.

[50] Eric Bravington died in August 1982.

Conducted until the end of 1935 by David Aspinall and after 1936 by Harold Moss (see 'Personalia'), Creswell Colliery Band earned a succession of 3rd and 4th prizes in the major contests and remained a popular concert and broadcasting band. Moss stayed with the band until 1948. In 1954 Ernest Woodhouse (see 'Personalia') became musical director, and for a time during the early 1950s George Hespe was professional conductor – succeeded by Willie Wood and then George Thompson. In 1956 the band celebrated its 300th broadcast, Harold Moss returning as guest conductor in a programme shared with Woodhouse. Creswell won the Midland Area contest four times and appeared in the Finals on ten occasions during the first 15 post-war years. During the 1960s, suffering as a result of problems within the coal industry, Creswell lost much of its momentum. Area contest successes during the period were limited to a win and a 3rd prize. Woodhouse resigned at the end of 1966 and was succeeded by Dennis Smith (see 'Personalia'). By 1971 the band had lost its championship status.

The Luton Band maintained its status during the early post-war years, winning the London & Southern Counties Area Championships in 1945 and 1947. In 1959, after a quiet period, Major G.H. Willcocks took the band to the Area contest, securing 3rd prize and an invitation to the Finals. He then directed an Area win in 1960. Between 1961 and 1970 the band had two further Area wins, was in the top three eight times and was placed sixth in the Nationals of 1960. Luton's musical director, Albert Coupe, had been with the band since the Mortimer days of the 1920s and remained there until 1975. Awarded the MBE in 1970, he continued as musical director until 1974.[51] He was succeeded by the band's euphonium player, Lyn Morgan,[52] who took over in 1976, with W.B. Hargreaves as musical adviser. Luton did consistently well again at the Area contests between 1971 and 1980, winning on three occasions and being out of the top three only three times. There were also a number of overseas tours.

Harton Colliery was the North East's most successful band over a long period of time. It won the Area contest in 1947–48–49 and again in 1956, and at national level gained sixth prizes in the Finals of 1947 and 1948. By 1950 it had over 150 broadcasts to its credit. Jack Atherton conducted from 1939 to 1950, after which the position became rather unsettled. Harton had a succession of distinguished principal cornet players, including Jack Mackintosh who left in 1930 to become principal trumpet with the BBC Symphony Orchestra. Later holders of the position included Norman Ashcroft and Maurice Murphy.

The premier Scottish band in pre-war times, Clydebank Burgh was less prominent after 1945. Nevertheless, with two wins in the Scottish

---

[51] Mortimer, 1981, p. 55; Coupe died in 1984, aged 79.
[52] Lyn Morgan was a former principal horn player in the RAF Central Band.

Championships (1955 and 1956) and runner-up position four times it was still at the forefront of Scottish banding. It rarely competed either at Belle Vue or the Nationals. Conductors during the late 1950s included Alex Mortimer, who led Clydebank to victory in the 1955 Scottish Championships (taking them to a record 16 wins overall) and Rex Mortimer, who conducted the band's title-winning performance in the following year. Clydebank was a regular broadcasting band and, as has been seen, made several trips to London to play in the parks.

Slaithwaite Band which had done so well just before the war, though making several serious bids, never regained its former status. Like thousands of other bands it functioned at a local level, playing an important part in the life of the community.

## Conclusion

There were undoubtedly more knowledgeable conductors about now than in earlier periods and though some of them were connected to a number of bands – not necessarily at the same time – the days when leading conductors took several bands to the same contest were over. Many of those who acted as professional conductors had experience of music in other genres, be it in the orchestra or in military bands. Even the bandmasters/resident conductors had more musical experience than their counterparts in pre-war years. There was also an increasing use of the term 'musical director' – freely used to denote any conducting post.

These were times of change. Perhaps not all the changes were for the better, but the band movement had become more professional in its outlook in the years after 1945. Changes are not particularly obvious in the names of leading bands – those at or near the top stayed there by and large, though some changed their titles through switching sponsorship. To try to ease the confusion over all the name changes, Appendix H lists some of them, along with approximate dates.

Many works bands came and went – for example, Ferodo Works, the new St Hilda's, John White Footwear, Crossley's Carpet Works and Cammell Laird's. These and others are referred to above or in the Glossary of Bands. From the 1960s there were also wholesale changes in the leading figures, a new generation superseding a diminishing earlier one. There was also an influx of conductors from other musical spheres.

Changes in the social structure of the nation also affected brass bands. Though bands were benefiting from their younger members being taught in schools, on reaching 18 far more were leaving their roots to study in other places than was the case earlier. Some continued to play with bands in the vicinity of their studies but a good many did not. A sizeable proportion of these never returned to banding.

Though firm statistics do not exist, it is generally felt that there were far fewer bands in 1980 than there had been in, say 1950. Further, largely through the school and youth band movements, the brass band was no longer what it used to be called – 'the working man's orchestra'. Many who had begun their musical life in the school brass band had gone on to build careers in a wide range of professions, keeping their banding as a hobby and for relaxation. There were also more females taking to banding, many of them keeping it up whilst bringing up a young family.

# CHAPTER 8

# Engagements, broadcasts, television and recordings

## Engagements

There were many park engagements during 1946, along with Whitsuntide festivities. Even the South West Lancashire correspondent declared this was a 'boom year'. Birmingham also reported a high standard of park concerts. In the South West, Cornish bands were busy, one claiming a record number of engagements. In the Midlands Ransome & Marles and in Lancashire Wingates were both fully occupied. There were also plenty of carnivals, galas, fêtes and shows, and bands were once more playing at football matches. Some processions were back in place and many bands were again taking up Christmas playing. They would be out 'carolling' throughout the night of Christmas Eve, often continuing during Christmas Day.

In the immediate post-war years there were a number of tours and extended engagements slightly reminiscent of pre-war tours. ENSA organised overseas tours by Foden's, Besses and Fairey's. There were also several home-based tours. During May 1945 Brighouse & Rastrick toured the West Country and week-long engagements came the way of a few bands during 1946. Brighouse and Clydebank took such engagements in London, whilst the latter and Scottish CWS each played for a week in Aberdeen. During 1947 Brighouse enjoyed two weeks in Scotland, one week in Eastbourne, another in Guernsey, and a fortnight in London. It seems odd that this non-works band undertook the longest tour recorded; no doubt many deputies were recruited.

In 1948 Foden's fulfilled a week's engagement at an exhibition in Birmingham, Harton spent a week in Southport and one in Morecambe, whilst Fairey's played for a week in Scarborough. Parc & Dare had a weekend in Cornwall and Scottish CWS reported such a busy season that they had had to turn down a week's engagement in Aberdeen. Black Dyke, Foden's and Munn & Felton's all played again in Scottish parks, the main centres being Edinburgh, Glasgow, Aberdeen and Dunfermline. Most leading bands were again busy in 1949.

In 1950 CWS (Manchester) played at a week-long exhibition in Morecambe visited by 100 000 people. They also toured Scotland and then played for a week in London's Embankment Gardens. Foden's also did the London engagement. Munn & Felton's spent three weeks in Scarborough and undertook a short tour of South Wales. Thus, the better bands were again on the crest of a wave.

Band engagements were given a further boost in 1951 due to extra functions taking place in connection with the Festival of Britain.[1] For example, both Foden's and Fairey's undertook full week engagements in Liverpool as part of the celebrations. In London, which proved to be a major venue for the better bands, Ransome and Marles played for a week in Hyde Park during May, Cory's were to be heard in the Embankment Gardens, whilst Morris Motors played at the horse show at Earls Court. The most substantial appearance in the capital, however, was by CWS (Manchester) which entertained large crowds for three weeks during July in various London parks.

There were fewer engagements of note in the years immediately following the Festival of Britain. One worthy of a special mention, however, concerns Clydebank which, in 1953, provided music at the launch of the Royal Yacht *Britannia*, appearing on both television and radio. Two engagements that attracted attention for a different reason both involved Fairey's. The first was a local concert to 'open' a new bandstand; the other was providing music at an Agricultural Show. Were these minor engagements an indication that even a band of Fairey's standing had to take on small-scale invitations in order to fill its diary?

Normal summer engagements were regularly undertaken by many bands and one item of good news during 1954 was that Thorne Council was to engage ten bands – eight of which were top-named ones – for Sunday afternoon and evening concerts during the summer season.[2] This was to become a regular venue for one of the best series of Sunday band concerts until well into the 1960s.

A concert that took place in Scotland in September 1954 started a new trend, with Scottish CWS and Govan Burgh bands participating in a concert with the Scottish National Orchestra. The bands combined for a 15-minute interlude in each half of the concert under their respective conductors and performed with the orchestra in *Finlandia* (Sibelius) and *1812* (Tchaikovsky). A similar concert took place in 1955 in Manchester, when Clayton Aniline (see Glossary) appeared with the Hallé.

Concerts of note during the later 1950s included a series held at the Free Trade Hall, Manchester, in aid of the Printers' Pension, Almshouses & Orphan Asylum Corporation. That in 1957 featured Fairey's and CWS

---

[1] The Festival of Britain was organised in 1951 to commemorate the centenary of the Great Exhibition of 1851 and to demonstrate post-war developments in Britain. Special events were organised throughout the country, the principal site being on London's South Bank, where the Royal Festival Hall was built specially for the occasion.

[2] Thorne is a small town near Doncaster.

(Manchester), with solo pianist Eileen Joyce, whilst three years later Fairey's were joined by Brighouse & Rastrick and Owen Brannigan, the famous bass singer. George Weldon, assistant conductor of the Hallé Orchestra, regularly conducted at these events.

There were still plenty of massed band concerts but fewer of the high-profile events of the war years. They could be heard in the well-tried venues in Hanley, Sheffield and Huddersfield, as well as in St Andrew's Hall Glasgow, the Victoria Hall Bolton, the Albert Hall Nottingham and in Liverpool's Philharmonic Hall – all fine halls, ideally suited to this type of concert.

The years 1952 and 1953 saw leading bands still taking on some extended engagements. In 1954, however, there was a further reduction in these, though CWS (Manchester) and Clayton Aniline each spent a week in Scotland, whilst Munn & Felton's had a few days in Cornwall, giving concerts in Falmouth and Camborne.

Unexpectedly, these engagements escalated in 1955: Clayton Aniline undertook two weeks in Scotland, whilst Foden's and Clydebank each spent a week in London. Munn & Felton's had one week in London and two in Scarborough. Then, after a fortnight at home they spent a week in Jersey. This had become a hot-spot for brass bands; in addition to the Munn & Felton's visit, Fairey's had already played there for a week and had also played for a week in Eastbourne, one in London and another in Southend-on-Sea. CWS (Manchester) had a particularly busy summer, visiting Switzerland, then Plymouth and Swansea for a week each, and two weeks at a Co-op Exhibition in Newcastle.[3] These figures reduced gradually over the next few years and by 1960 five bands shared a mere eight week-long engagements in just six venues. The brass band was now suffering increasingly from the effects of competition from other forms of entertainment, the younger generation supporting pop music such as rock and roll, while older people were becoming addicted to their favourite television programmes.

The emphasis for most bands was still on outdoor performances and, though a new style of programme music was becoming available with a greater range of rhythms and harmonies and more imaginative scoring, many bands stuck to out-dated pieces, losing the support of an increasingly critical audience. An article in *The Conductor* of April 1959 sounded a strong warning with the following comments:

> The Edinburgh Music Festival Committee has excluded bands. Certain seaside resorts are not engaging bands this year. The B.B.C., we are told, is contemplating the exclusion of brass bands from peak hour

---

[3] These Exhibitions were concerned with promoting the image of the company and advertising its goods.

broadcasting, after 6.30 p.m. Does all this mean we are losing our patrons? Are we less popular than formerly with the authorities whose business it is to provide entertainment for the public? Perhaps the word 'entertainment' gives the clue to the situation.

During the first half of the 1960s normal engagements were still relatively plentiful for the better bands, though there were progressively fewer long-term ones. London continued to offer two or three week-long engagements per year, CWS (Manchester), GUS and Carlton Main being the 'regulars'. However, in 1967 and 1968 CWS was the only band engaged for a week and in 1969 there was no full week for any brass band.

From the mid-1960s there was a change in emphasis towards single concert bookings. Several municipal authorities now held regular series of indoor concerts during the winter months. Leading bands took on most of these, accepting fewer summer engagements. The Fairey Band, for example, gave only 17 open-air concerts in 1965 and from 1968 Black Dyke ceased accepting park engagements. This pruning by leading bands created opportunities for other bands.

Engagements of special note during this period included a massed band concert in 1964 sponsored by the Scottish Industrial Exhibition and featuring four leading Scottish bands conducted by Gilbert Vinter. Also in 1964, Tullis Russell Mills Band joined forces with a French orchestra in a performance of the Berlioz *Messe solennelle* as part of the Edinburgh Festival. The Yorkshire Summer Festival held an annual contest and massed band concert; the 1964 event took place in Harrogate with Arts Council support, the massed band being conducted by Maurice Handford. The International Eisteddfod, held annually at Llangollen, promoted a concert in 1965 in which Denis Wright conducted Black Dyke, Brighouse & Rastrick and Foden's before an audience of 11 000. Foden's played in Westminster Abbey during the Abbey's 900th-anniversary celebrations in 1966, providing music before and after a service which was called 'One People at Work'.

In 1969 Black Dyke appeared in a Royal Command Performance concert in Bradford before the Duke of Edinburgh, who was presented to the members of the band following the concert. A number of Welsh bands were involved in events connected with the Investiture of Charles as Prince of Wales. At around the same time the famous jazz trombonist Don Lusher appeared with GUS (Footwear) Band in a concert in Kettering. He had commenced his playing career in the SA, had climbed to fame and was to become a regular guest in band concerts.

Massed band concerts continued to be popular during the second half of the decade. These included 'A Festival of Brass' in Sheffield's City Hall with Malcolm Arnold conducting three leading Yorkshire bands, four Scottish bands combining in the final concert of the 1968 Edinburgh

Festival and four bands performing in York Minster playing under Pierino Gamba.[4] A later concert in the Minster involved Yorkshire Imperial Metals and Carlton Main conducted by Geoffrey Brand. The 400-voice York Celebrations Choir was formed for this concert. It was to take part in several major band concerts. A unique situation arose at a concert during 1970 in the Free Trade Hall, Manchester – 'A Festival of Brass and Voices' featured Fairey's (Harry Mortimer), Foden's (Rex Mortimer) and CWS (Manchester) (Alex Mortimer), and this was said to be the only occasion that all three brothers appeared as conductors in a single concert.

In 1970 Harry Mortimer devised a new concert format. Under the title 'Champion Brass' he brought together the reigning British Open and National champions. Each played a short programme under its own conductor before combining under Mortimer's baton. The first in this series took place in Wolverhampton and featured Grimethorpe and Brighouse.

Following his appointment, in 1972, as music adviser to Grimethorpe Colliery Band, Elgar Howarth introduced modern pieces into the banding repertoire, gaining access for bands into university music programmes and music festivals, most of which had hitherto ignored them. Performing, in particular, Harrison Birtwistle's *Grimethorpe Aria*, commissioned for and first performed in the 1973 Harrogate Festival, Howarth and Grimethorpe also appeared at Lancaster and Warwick universities and in the Leeds Festival. A climax was reached in 1974 when Grimethorpe and Black Dyke played in a Henry Wood Promenade Concert in the Royal Albert Hall. The Birtwistle piece was undoubtedly the principal attraction for the Prom organisers, but *Severn Suite* (Elgar) and *A Moorside Suite* (Holst) were also performed. The same two bands returned to the Proms in 1975 with another new work, Henze's *Ragtimes and Habaneras*. On this occasion Harry Mortimer shared the conducting with Howarth.

Besses o' th' Barn had by now engaged as its professional conductor Ifor James, a colleague of Howarth's in the PJBE. Following Howarth's lead, James also commissioned modern pieces for his band (see page 174) and, though not having quite the same aura as Grimethorpe and Howarth, Besses and James made a significant impact in serious musical events.

Other bands also benefited from this type of venture. Black Dyke under Geoffrey Brand gave a concert as part of the 1974 Cheltenham Festival. Further north, Dalmellington Silver Band gave a late-night concert in the Scottish National Orchestra's Proms. In the following year GUS appeared

---

4 Gamba was born in Rome in 1937. Hailed as a child prodigy, he conducted a performance of Beethoven's 1st Symphony at the age of eight. He had been guest conductor at the Nationals Gala Concert in 1965 and was guest conductor at a number of other massed band concerts.

in the prestigious Three Choirs Festival, held that year in Worcester, and in 1976 played in Gloucester Cathedral in connection with the Cheltenham Festival.

Thus, in the 1970s brass bands were gaining acceptance in the wider field of classical music whilst a new generation of composers and conductors built on the foundations laid in earlier years. This progression was due largely to an influx of musicians who had begun their musical careers in brass bands, gone into the music profession and then returned to their roots armed with the skill, experience and contacts to take brass bands into new arenas. It was also partly thanks to a new generation of instrumentalists undertaking professional training at colleges and universities who were willing to perform new music – much of which did not appeal to many of the older generation of players.

However, although the outlook for bands was positive in many ways, there were concerns during the second half of the 1970s. Park engagements were said to be 'drying up', with warnings of a further decline in the popularity of the music which many bands were still offering. In fact, bands were in danger at both ends of the musical spectrum. The general public was increasingly unimpressed with the fare being offered by local bands unwilling to use the more modern programme music which was available. On the other hand, many brass band supporters were unhappy with the avant-garde music being offered by some of the top bands.

## Broadcasting

In the early post-war years an average of seven dedicated brass band programmes per week were broadcast on radio, together with a few by military bands. Most went out on the light music channel. Occasionally a band or a soloist would be heard in a more general programme; *Children's Hour* provided one such outlet.

Towards the end of 1946 a new series appeared – *Brass Bandstand*. Broadcast at the peak audience time of 6.30 p.m. on Sunday evening, it featured some of the best bands, including Black Dyke, Creswell Colliery, Parc & Dare and Bickershaw. The series was brought to a close with excerpts from a Belle Vue massed band concert. Programmes in this series were generally produced on location. All were organised by Harry Mortimer through the BBC and were a means of taking high-quality bands into the community.

Two further programme formats were introduced during 1946 – *Sounding Brass and Voices* and *Listen to the Band*. By 1950 other new programmes included *Welsh Bandstand, Village Bandstand, Brass Band Parade* and *Up and Coming* – a series specifically for bands giving their first broadcast. The success of many of the regular programmes was in part due to Harry Mortimer's policy of finding imaginative titles. More new programmes appeared with titles such as *Lift up the Banner* – a Salvation Army series, *Saturday Bandstand, Marching with the Band* and – perhaps the *coup de grâce* – *Tea and Trumpets.*

From 1956 bands started appearing in *Friday Night is Music Night*, along with one of the BBC's orchestras and star singers. This series attracted higher listening figures than dedicated band broadcasts and provided a welcome platform. Another idea aimed at widening the audience was to give bands a place in programmes featuring various types of music, broadcast continuously from seven to nine o'clock each weekday morning.

The declining standards of some bands – often due to player shortage or a lack of dedication – had an effect on broadcasting from 1957. The BBC stated that there would henceforth be fewer band broadcasts and that higher standards were expected. There would be increased fees for bands offered engagements but many bands would be required to reaudition. New staff with specific brass band interests were now enlisted. The first of these was Geoffrey Brand, who worked alongside Harry Mortimer in London. Later, William Relton took charge of band broadcasts in the North Region.[5]

More new ideas were introduced during the late 1950s. Amongst these was a 'Let the People Sing' programme from the Royal Albert Hall, featuring massed bands of the Boys' Brigade; a half-hour broadcast from the British Open Championships; and, from 1958, a broadcast by the winners of those Championships. *Saturday Bandstand* continued; along with the band there were now soloists, often a singer, but sometimes instrumentalists – perhaps pianists or even a harmonica player.

In 1959, for the first time, brass bands were featured in the Third Programme – forerunner of Radio 3 and dedicated mainly to serious art music. Three original brass band compositions were played in each programme and the first bands featured were Fairey's and Foden's.

Band broadcasts reached a peak in the mid-1950s. An analysis, based on those billed in *BB*, reveals that in 1955 there were over 300 broadcasts, shared between 82 bands. A similar analysis of 1960 broadcasts shows them down to 230, with the number of bands broadcasting now only 67. This was a further reflection of changing public tastes and the deteriorating standards of some brass bands.

From 1954 the BBC gave the brass band movement a fillip with a series of competitions called 'New Music for Brass', offering prizes for the

---

[5] William Relton, as a teenager, played flugelhorn with Brighouse & Rastrick, and for a short time was the band's principal cornet player. After military service in the RAF, he joined the CBSO. He later played with a number of London orchestras prior to joining the BBC as a producer in 1957.

winning compositions. Encouraging a new style of light music, they organised prestige concerts, parts of which were broadcast. The first, the 'Fred Mortimer Memorial Competition', commemorated the death in the previous year of the famous conductor. There were two categories, one for a ceremonial march and the other for a three-movement suite. Three entries for each were selected for the Finals and performed in a concert in Manchester, the adjudicators being Sir Arthur Bliss, Maurice Johnstone and Frank Wright. A 1955 competition offered three prizes for 'New and Original Compositions for Brass Band'. The adjudicators for the Finals, which took place in Hanley, included Sir Adrian Boult, Eric Coates, Stanley Boddington, Harry Heyes (a well-known Midlands brass band conductor) and Harold Moss, along with a 'jury' drawn from the audience. In 1956 the title was 'New Music for Brass', with the competition taken to Edinburgh. Featuring Foden's, the All-Star Band and Scottish CWS, it was hailed as one of the finest brass band occasions ever witnessed in Scotland. In a lengthy report, *BB*'s correspondent 'Glenside' commented thus:

> The 1956 highlight in Scottish brass band circles . . . took place in the famous Usher Hall, Edinburgh, last Saturday, an event that had been eagerly anticipated by keen band enthusiasts . . . The B.B.C. are doing our movement a great service with this annual competition, and their organisation of this spectacular event left nothing to be desired.[6]

In 1957 the competition moved to the Royal Festival Hall in London where, from 1958, it became part of a BBC Light Music Festival. During the next three years the featured bands were the reigning National Champions.[7] The BBC also commissioned some special piece or feature each year. In 1955 Gordon Jacob's *Suite in B♭* appeared and in the following year *The Moor of Venice* (William Alwyn) was commissioned. A totally new concept was introduced in 1957 with a work for orchestra and band by Denis Wright entitled *Cornish Holiday*. This idea was repeated in 1958 with the same composer's *Casino Carnival*. The BBC Concert Orchestra was involved on both occasions, the performances being conducted by the composer.

Subsequent festivals were for brass band and a soloist only. The 1959 feature was a performance of Denis Wright's transcription of the attractive Litolff *Scherzo*, with Semprini at the piano, whilst George Thalben-Ball was the organist in 1960 in Wright's working of Handel's Organ Concerto in B♭ (*The Hallelujah*). Peter Yorke's suite *The Shipbuilders* was commissioned for the same occasion.

---

[6] *BB* 2 June 1956, p. 5.
[7] These were Munn & Felton's in 1958, Foden's in 1959 and Black Dyke in 1960.

The 1965 event was exceptional, its centrepiece being the first performance of Gilbert Vinter's cantata *The Trumpets*, commissioned by the BBC. With six choirs, Men o' Brass, organ, a large array of percussion and the bass soloist Owen Brannigan, Vinter himself conducted the performance, which formed the second half of the concert. Men o' Brass had provided the first half. For the 1966 Light Music Festival Pierino Gamba was guest conductor, with GUS and Fairey's, plus a choir and a solo singer. In 1967 Black Dyke (as BBC Band of the Year) and Morris Motors Band took part in an International Festival of Light Music in which Malcolm Arnold and Harry Mortimer were the conductors. Several new pieces were premiered, including Arnold's renowned *Padstow Lifeboat*, with its famous imitation of the lighthouse's foghorn.

A major innovation introduced by the BBC during the 1960s was a series of knockout competitions, beginning in 1961 as *Northern Brass*, masterminded by William Relton. Restricted to bands from the North Region, the Midlands and Northern Ireland, it was transmitted only in those regions. Sixteen bands were invited – not from the top level; each week two of them played a short programme, broadcast live, and one was knocked out. There were two adjudicators, seated in a remote studio and assessing the performances in a true broadcasting situation. Following the Final, the four semi-finalists combined in a massed band concert. In the 1962 series each semi-finalist played a specially composed piece as part of its programme. Yet another refinement was introduced in the following year, one piece being selected each week for both bands to include in their programmes. Following this the series was redesigned to incorporate a higher level of band and renamed *Challenging Brass*.

Further changes came in 1967: 27 leading bands were invited and three appeared in each broadcast. The Finals, also with three bands, took place in Huddersfield Town Hall, Black Dyke being declared 'BBC Band of the Year'. Following this series, the Head of BBC Light Music attacked brass bands saying that some broadcasts were 'not good enough'. He stated that 16 leading bands had been selected for the 1968 series, with the Final again leading to the title 'BBC Band of the Year'. In the event, five bands declined the invitation. The series nevertheless went ahead, the winner being Brighouse & Rastrick.

Yet another new formula was introduced from 1970. Each of the 16 chosen bands pre-recorded the music for the preliminary rounds and the semi-final. In 1972 City of Coventry were winners and Desford Colliery runners-up. These were the only two bands taking part in the concert, but this included a rare performance of Gordon Jacob's *Rhapsody for Three Hands and Brass Band*, commissioned in 1971 by the British Federation and, as in its premiere, featuring Phyllis Sellick and Cyril Smith (see page 70).[8]

*Table 8.1   The winners of the BBC knockout competitions 1961–74*

**Northern Brass**

| | | |
|---|---|---|
| 1961 Yorkshire Imperial Metals | Leeds Town Hall | |
| 1962 Markham Main | Huddersfield Town Hall | St Nicholas Eve (D. Wright) |
| 1963 Cammell Laird | Free Trade Hall, Manchester | Anthem for Brass (Johnstone) |

**Challenging Brass**

| | | |
|---|---|---|
| 1964 Ransome & Marles | City Hall, Sheffield | Challenging Brass (Vinter) |
| 1965 Rushden Temperance | Town Hall, Leeds | Three Miniatures (Powell) |
| 1966 Hanwell | St George's Hall, Bradford | The Overseer (Yorke) |

**BBC Band of the Year**

| | |
|---|---|
| 1967 Black Dyke | Town Hall, Huddersfield |
| 1968 Brighouse & Rastrick | Royal Festival Hall, London |
| 1969 Hammonds' Sauce Works | Royal Festival Hall, London |
| 1970 Black Dyke | Royal Festival Hall, London |
| 1971 Cory | Royal Festival Hall, London |
| 1972 City of Coventry | Royal Festival Hall, London |
| 1973 City of Coventry | Royal Festival Hall, London |
| 1974 Ever Ready | Royal Festival Hall, London |

Table 8.1 indicates winners of these competitions between 1961 and 1974, along with venues of the Finals, and semi-final test pieces – where they existed.

In 1975 a radical change was announced. The actual competition was dispensed with and the award based on all performances during the year on Radio 3's *Bandstand* programme. The band adjudged by a panel of BBC producers to have given the year's best programme, was awarded the title 'BBC Band of the Year'.

From 1971 a competition called *Fanfare* appeared on Scottish Radio which ran on similar lines to *Challenging Brass*, Scotland's best eight bands being invited to compete. From 1979 there was also a 'Radio Wales Band of the Year' competition, the first winner of which was Cory.

---

[8] Smith and Sellick were man and wife, both well known as piano soloists and also as a duo. In 1956 Smith had a stroke which paralysed one arm. The couple continued playing duets, but 'for three hands'. A number of works were specially composed for them, including the one by Gordon Jacob.

Moving back in time, by 1963 the number of band broadcasts had slumped. Even Harry Mortimer bemoaned the fact that in one particular week there were just two brass and two military bands on air. In the comparable week 16 years earlier, there had been broadcasts by eight brass and nine military bands. However, though never again reaching these figures, by 1965 it was noted that band broadcasts were on the increase and that a greater proportion of programmes were devoted to serious band music. Admittedly, during the middle years of the decade there seemed to be more military bands than brass bands broadcasting and, alas, during 1967 more programmes were axed.

A short but interesting series was broadcast during early 1964 featuring three brass bands and three famous personalities from the fields of jazz and the big band. Trumpeters Kenny Baker and Eddie Calvert appeared with Hanwell and Foden's respectively, whilst the Luton Band was joined by bandleader Ted Heath. All three had begun their playing careers in brass bands, and the series was called *Brass Roots*.

Further staff changes at the BBC now affected band programmes. Harry Mortimer retired in April 1964. For a time each region was responsible for its own band broadcasts until, in 1965, Geoffrey Brand was given responsibility for broadcasts either originating in or sponsored by the London region. For some of these he was able to import bands from the North and the Midlands to broadcast from various London venues. From early 1967 William Relton, who had been in charge of band broadcasts from the North, moved away to take charge of some orchestral broadcasts. However, when Brand left the Corporation later in the year Relton was given responsibility for brass and military band broadcasts.

*Bandstand* returned during 1968 and there was also a short series entitled *Vintage Years of the Crystal Palace*. Towards the end of 1969 a series called *Junior Bandstand* appeared, one of the programmes being played by the Cornwall County Youth Brass Band, conducted by Malcolm Arnold.

In 1970 band broadcasts suffered another setback as Relton moved on to become Manager of the BBC Symphony Orchestra. It was a fact that unless someone with specialist knowledge of and a vested interest in bands was in a position of influence, band broadcasts suffered. The popular radio programme *Marching and Waltzing* was now axed and there were complaints from many listeners about the poor coverage of brass bands and also of the fact that the majority of pieces now broadcast were marches.

An innovation that to some extent alleviated the growing dearth of band broadcasts was the development of local radio. Stations that made use of (mainly local) bands quite early on included Radio Merseyside, Radio Sheffield, Radio Durham, Radio Nottingham and Radio Stoke-on-Trent. Brass bands were being heard on all of these stations by the end of 1970, some featuring knockout competitions similar to *Challenging Brass*. Other stations followed. Radios Blackburn and Solent featured bands from 1971 and Radios Bristol, Leeds, Birmingham, Oxford and Newcastle from 1972. Radio Clyde joined these in 1974. This increased brass band coverage on radio in many regions, though the standard of performance was generally well below that heard on national radio.

Two new programmes which appeared during 1972 were *Brass, Strings and Other Things* and *Breakfast Special*, a long, early-morning programme featuring a range of music of differing genres. The next year saw a four-programme historical series, *A Century of Brass*, but throughout the year there were rarely more than two brass band broadcasts per week.

Special programmes in 1975 included another *Brass Roots* series, dedicated entirely to particular bands and their respective histories. There was also, in 1975, a rare appearance of a brass band in the BBC's International Light Music Festival – William Davis Construction Group Band. The first half of the concert was shared with the BBC Midland Light Orchestra and the second with the BBC Concert Orchestra in *Friday Night is Music Night*. In 1976 another shared programme format appeared – *Among Your Souvenirs*; whilst other new programmes included *As Prescribed*, *Bryden's Bandbox* and *Sam on Sunday*.

By 1978 there were more broadcasts, though fewer by the better bands, with just two by Black Dyke and one by Grimethorpe. However, there was now more variety in the music broadcast, with original works, transcriptions of light orchestral pieces, overtures, songs from the shows and a wider selection of lighter band pieces, a welcome change from the steady stream of marches that had dominated a few years earlier.

## Television

Prior to 1953 television was a luxury enjoyed by only a small percentage of the British population and there were just two channels, the BBC and Independent Television (ITV – the commercial channel). The Coronation of Queen Elizabeth II in that year was the signal for the mass popularisation of television as a broadcasting medium.

There were occasional reports of bands appearing on television during 1951 and 1952, and from 1953 the National Finals were visited by BBC television crews, with extracts from both the contest and the concert screened live. In 1955 Black Dyke celebrated its centenary and to mark this appeared on television. In the same year CWS (Manchester) appeared in a *Brass and Voices* programme. Munn & Felton's had a programme of their own in 1958 and appeared in *Concert Time* a year later with the BBC Midland Light Orchestra, whilst Brighouse & Rastrick were given a serious slot on *Panorama* in 'An inquiry into the work done by the amateur brass band movement'. However, this represents an average of little more than one band programme per year.

Other television appearances by brass bands in the 1950s were as part of other programmes – for example *Top Town* and *Opening Night at the Radio Show*. Programmes such as *Wish You Were Here*, *This is Your Life* and *People and Places* also occasionally featured a brass band and there were a few appearances by youth bands in children's programmes.

A 1960 documentary film about the Northumberland Miners' Picnic on the BBC's *Monitor* caused much upset in the band world. It was considered to be high-handed and even derisive. Comment in *BB* the week after the showing of the programme remarked: 'one felt the film was made rather to entertain than to inform – something strange for this valuable series – and was not without its technical faults.' The Northern correspondent of *BB* was more blunt, commenting: 'I watched this in the company of two friends totally unconnected with brass bands and it was a merciful relief to me when it ended.'

Brass bands had not been well-served by television. They did rather better from the mid-1960s with more dedicated programmes. BBC 2 was launched during 1964, so there were now three channels. Antony Hopkins, the famous writer and broadcaster on musical topics, and Morris Motors collaborated in a *Let's Make Music* programme during January 1964. In Wales, ITV presented a knockout competition for Welsh bands, Cory's being the first winners, in 1965. Several youth brass bands appeared on BBC 1 in *Youth Makes Music*, whilst in 1966 Crookhall featured in *These Happy Sounds*.

Two special programmes appeared in 1967. One, about Frank Wright and his work as Music Director for the Greater London Council, featured a number of brass bands whilst the other, *Top Brass*, traced the fortunes of three as they prepared for the National Championships. They were GUS (reigning champions), Black Dyke and Woodfalls Silver, making its first appearance at the Royal Albert Hall.

In 1968 Grimethorpe participated in the first episode of a series starring Thora Hird – *The First Lady*, Trinity Girls appeared in *Nice Time*, the Yorkshire Schools Brass Band played specially arranged carols in a Yorkshire Television (YTV) Christmas Day programme, and Cornwall County Youth Brass Band was featured in *Songs of Praise*. This last programme proved to be a good outlet, regularly using brass bands to accompany hymn-singing.

In *Where There's Brass* (a clever *double entendre*), Michael Parkinson, host to one of Britain's most successful 'chat' shows, looked at the social side of banding, aided by musical extracts played by Black Dyke and Brighouse & Rastrick. Black Dyke were also filmed 'In Concert' for ITV and Fairey's featured in a programme called *A Blow-in*. Several bands appeared on television during 1969, including Netteswell Youth Band, declared winner in an edition of *Opportunity Knocks*.

Bands were now getting more televised coverage and 1970 proved to be another good year. St Dennis appeared in a programme about china clay, the region's principal industry and, still in Cornwall, the NSBBA welcomed cameras to its festival in Truro; a band appeared in a documentary about the opening of part of the M62 motorway whilst another was seen playing at an international rugby match. Following its success at the World Championships in 1970, Black Dyke was featured on the children's programme *Blue Peter*.

The fact that bands were now regularly entering peoples' living rooms via their television sets and being seen by vast audiences was obviously an excellent profile-raiser, perhaps compensating for the poor representation on radio. The incidental appearances on programmes such as *Songs of Praise* continued, but there were also more dedicated band programmes. For example, during 1971 Dobcross Silver Band (Yorkshire) was featured in a documentary introduced by the nationally known, local playwright, Henry Livings. Even more significant was a 1972 series using an earlier title, *Where There's Brass*. The organisers of the National Championships had negotiated this series. Now on colour TV, each band played a 25-minute programme in peak-viewing time. Programmes were built around local concerts and featured bands from different regions – Black Dyke, GUS, City of Coventry, Patchogue-Plymouth, Dalmellington and St Dennis. Disc jockey Brian Matthews presented the programmes, which attracted an audience estimated at 12 million.

The ITV Granada company, based in the North West, took an interest in brass bands from 1971 when it began its annual 'Granada Band of the Year' competition, which resulted in the later screening of a 50-minute programme (see page 111).

### Television and the Musicians' Union

An unpleasant situation arose concerning brass bands and television, stemming largely from the success of the Granada competitions. The programme makers put up proposals for a series of regional competitions in 1977; these were to be screened locally throughout the ITV network, with successful bands going through to the Granada Band of the Year. Unbeknown to bands, there was an agreement between ITV and the Musicians' Union (MU) which stated that no programme using musicians who were not Union members (in effect, most amateur musicians) could be screened without MU approval. Hitherto, this had been given for Band of the Year programmes. However, some union members were complaining on the grounds that brass band television programmes were depriving them of lucrative engagements. The television companies argued that brass band programmes were highly specialised and that removing them would not create openings for professional musicians. Nevertheless, the MU refused to sanction regional competitions and, in fact, demanded that members of bands performing in 'Band of the Year' should join the Union. Bands generally were against this, fearing that MU rules would later be applied to other band events and that bands would be priced out of their normal engagements.

However, two bands (Grimethorpe and Brighouse & Rastrick) had *en bloc* become members of the MU, though 16 others refused to join. The Granada contest continued but without television for the next two years, depriving the event of much of its attraction. A direct result of this was the formation of 'Top Brass', an association of 16 leading bands, convened to look after their particular interests; however, it had little impact and existed for only a short time.

A further problem occurred during 1980 stemming from a dispute between the MU and the BBC over pay and threatened closures. It coincided with some of the recording sessions for a BBC knockout competition called 'Best of Brass' (discussed on page 197).

* * *

In the wake of *Where There's Brass* (see above), Granada Television screened a series called *Sounding Brass* during 1974. This featured four established northern bands – Foden's, Besses, Black Dyke and Grimethorpe – plus two up-and-coming bands – Stanshawe from Bristol and Solna Brass from Sweden. Elgar Howarth was the presenter and Arthur Taylor, the man behind 'Granada Band of the Year', the producer. In a further series of *Sounding Brass* in 1975, the 11 programmes included documentaries of the New Zealand Championships and Lancaster University's Brass Band Summer School (see page 86).

Other television features during the early 1970s included a visit to the contest at Bugle in Cornwall in 1973, a brass band playing the theme from Dvořák's *New World Symphony* for a commercial advertisement, regular appearances on Yorkshire Television's *Choirs on Sunday* and its sequel, *Stars on Sunday*, an appearance on *Blue Peter* by Grimethorpe Juniors and an oft-repeated clip of the Two Ronnies augmenting the percussion section of a brass band.[9]

---

[9] In this clip the band, Aldershot Brass, was joined by the diminutive Ronnie Corbett playing an outsize bass drum and Ronnie Barker brandishing a pair of cymbals. Marching briskly, the band played a medley of marches to which the two comedians sang humorous words.

In 1976 BBC Television North West introduced a knockout competition in which eight leading bands from the region met, two by two (as in *Challenging Brass*), in a series called *Champion Brass*. Its success was the springboard for a range of programmes that now appeared on BBC television nationally. The first was a documentary based on the National Brass Band Championships, including the Butlin's Youth Band Championships and the gala concert. This was followed by a four-programme series, each one featuring Area contest winners at championship and youth levels, and a distinguished soloist. Those appearing were:

Parc & Dare, Upper Rhondda Secondary School Band and Don Lusher (trombone)
Fodens, Rochdale Metropolitan Youth Band and John Fletcher (LSO tubist)
Yorkshire Imperial, Wakefield Schools Band and George Chisolm (trombone)
Hendon, St Dennis Youth Band and Ifor James (french horn)

A great coup for brass bands came in 1977 when the television series *Omnibus* filmed two programmes featuring the famous orchestral conductor, André Previn, called 'Previn Meets Brass Bands'. Besses o' th' Barn made the first programme and Black Dyke the second.

In 1978 Harry Mortimer and Men o' Brass were featured in a 50-minute programme called *My World of Music*. Later in the year came word of a new series – *Best of Brass*. This was produced by Ken Griffin, an ex-military band musician who had produced the four-programme series mentioned above, and who took a great interest in bands on television. He now produced this national competition on the lines of BBC North West's *Champion Brass*. Rules stated that programmes must entertain and should contain no pieces lasting longer than four minutes. The first series began in August 1978; the 1st prize was £1000 and there was a new instrument for the winning soloist. Eight bands were chosen for the seven programmes (four first rounds, two semi-finals and the Finals). Fairey's were the winners of the first series and Philip Morgan of Parc & Dare won the soloist prize. There were many comments in the band press about the programme, mostly critical. Under the heading 'Best of Brass under fire', *BB* wrote:

> The brass band world is buzzing with animated discussion on the current BBC television series 'Best of Brass', now in its third week . . . Few of the viewers who have expressed opinions think highly of the mock-up bandstand in which players are caged . . . Many feel embarrassed for the judges as they strive to criticise without causing

offence, in full view of the competitors . . . But the over-riding dismay is with the choice of music (for which the bands are not entirely blameless) and, above all, for the incredibly poor sound reproduction that they and the viewers are having to suffer.[10]

There were more *Champion Brass* and *Best of Brass* programmes in 1979, but the 1980 *Best of Brass* series was hit hard by the Musicians' Union strike mentioned above. Bands were asked not to cross picket lines, the outcome of which was that, after winning their respective first rounds, Yorkshire Imperial and Fairey's withdrew from the competition, which was eventually won by GUS.

Another 1978 television initiative came in the form of a series filmed in Northern Ireland with the title *Star Brass*. It featured well-known Irish bands and an Irish singer, along with brass soloists from the mainland. After several repeat showings of this series, a second series, on similar lines, but with different soloists, was screened in 1980.

Other programmes of interest to band people during 1979 were *Test Pieces* – a programme shown on Scottish television, based on the Scottish Area championships and a programme with Michael Parkinson that featured interviews with Harry Mortimer and André Previn, with music provided by Black Dyke.

Meanwhile, ITV extended brass band presentations beyond its 'Granada Band of the Year' competition. First, Granada itself sent a film crew to Italy with Grimethorpe, on its visit to the 1979 Montepulciano Art Workshop (see page 166), resulting in a 40-minute documentary, *Arrividerci Grimethorpe*. Later in the year YTV produced the first of a six-band series with the title *Brass in Concert*. The format of this series, whose music adviser was Roy Newsome, was that three of the programmes featured a leading band and a promising young soloist, whilst the other three featured a leading youth band and an established soloist. Bands taking part in the first series were Grimethorpe, Brighouse & Rastrick and JSVB, and Trinity Girls, Warren Youth and Upper Rhondda Comprehensive School; soloists included Bill Millar (see page 85), Phillip McCann and Don Lusher.

Thus, brass bands were gaining recognition by the television authorities during this era. Programmes of varying types were screened and brass bands enjoyed a popularity in excess of anything witnessed since before World War I.

### Recordings

The years 1945–60 were poor years for fully commercial 78 rpm discs of brass band music, though these were supplemented by what are described

---

[10] *BB* 19 August 1978, p. 1.

here as 'semi-commercial' recordings. Fully commercial discs were those issued on recognised labels, generally the product of professional recording sessions, with contracts agreed between band and company. The following table gives a break-down of commercial discs recorded by leading bands in the years shown:

| | 1945–50 | 1951–55 | 1956–60 | Total |
|---|---|---|---|---|
| All-Star Band | – | 14 | 3 | 17 |
| Fairey Aviation | 3 | 7 | – | 10 |
| Munn & Felton's | – | 2 | 5 | 7 |
| CWS (Manchester) | – | 2 | 4 | 6 |
| St Hilda's | 4 | – | – | 4 |
| National Band of New Zealand | – | 4 | – | 4 |
| Foden's | – | 2 | – | 2 |
| Ferodo | – | 2 | – | 2 |
| Brighouse & Rastrick | 1 | – | – | 1 |

This represents a total of 53 recordings at an average of just over three per year. Of these, 33 were made by Paxton, eight by Columbia, three by Parlophone, four by HMV and four issued by Boosey & Hawkes. Additionally, five recordings were released during 1945 that had actually been recorded during the war.[11] Repertoire was generally up to date and included several test pieces, recorded as follows:

| | | | |
|---|---|---|---|
| 1946 | Fairey Aviation | *Overture for an Epic Occasion* (Wright) | Columbia |
| 1947 | Brighouse & Rastrick | *Oliver Cromwell* (Geehl) | Columbia |
| 1952 | Fairey Aviation | *The Frogs of Aristophanes* (Bantock) | Paxton |
| 1952 | CWS (Manchester) | *Scena Sinfonica* (Geehl) | Columbia |
| 1953 | Foden's | *Diadem of Gold* (Bailey) | Paxton |
| 1954 | Fairey Aviation | *Sovereign Heritage* (Beaver) | Paxton |
| 1955 | Munn & Felton's | *Tournament for Brass* (Ball) | Paxton |
| 1955 | Munn & Felton's | *Resurgam* (Ball) | Paxton |
| 1956 | Ferodo Works | *Sinfonietta* (Leidzen) | Columbia |
| 1956 | Munn & Felton's | *Blackfriars* (Cundell) | Paxton |

All except one were title-winning pieces for the bands concerned. There was a handful of other recordings that could loosely be described as serious. These included *Introduction to Act 3* of *Lohengrin* (Wagner), *The Explorers* (a concert overture by Peter Yorke), two movements from *L'Arlesienne* (Bizet), a selection from the ballet *Robert the Devil* (Meyerbeer) and Dvořák's *Slavonic Dance No. 8* – all recorded by the All-Star Band; and *Music for the Royal Fireworks* (Handel) recorded by Fairey's. All were

---

[11] These figures are gleaned from Andrews, 1997.

conducted by Harry Mortimer and recorded by Paxton. The remainder of the pieces recorded were either marches or other light material, but were relatively up to date. So, whilst the quantity of recordings had receded, quality of repertoire was an improvement on most of that of the previous 25 years.

*Semi-commercial recordings*

Semi-commercial discs, made mostly in the years 1949–51, were, in the main, recordings of concert or contest performances or, in some cases, recordings made in the band's own rehearsal room. Most of them were recorded by a Wigan-based company called William Grimes & Sons. Bill Gaskell, secretary of Wingates, worked for this company and organised recordings at contests, concerts and in bandrooms. In *BBN* of November 1949 Gaskell reported that 80 discs were available. In the following March an advertisement for Grimes Gramophone Records stated that a new company had been formed – JAMCO Records, Wigan. Many recordings were issued on the Grimes label and many others, including some re-releases of the Grimes issues, on JAMCO. Though most were made by leading bands, many were made by more modest ones, particularly at contests, with sales generated by the bands concerned. Through this scheme some test pieces were recorded which otherwise would not have been, but as copies were made only to order they are now quite rare. The following numbers of recordings made by the better bands gives an idea of the extent of the project:

| Fairey Aviation | 19 | Ransome & Marles | 7 |
|---|---|---|---|
| CWS (Manchester) | 16 | St Hilda's/Yewco | 6 |
| Foden's | 14 | Carlton Main | 6 |
| Black Dyke | 14 | Creswell Colliery | 3 |
| Wingates Temperance | 14 | Grimethorpe Colliery | 3 |
| Brighouse & Rastrick | 7 | Munn & Felton's | 2 |
| Cory's | 7 | Massed bands | 3 |

This total of 121, which includes a small number of privately-made recordings and is by no means complete, represents a considerable input to the recording market. Repertoire covered a wide range, with a generous quantity of test pieces. It provided a substantial outlet for band music at a time when major recording companies were showing reduced interest.

*Microgroove recordings*

During the late 1950s microgroove recordings superseded 78 rpm discs. On these there was less needle-noise and consequently a higher sound quality. Because of the smallness of the grooves and slower speeds much longer recordings could be made. A 12-inch LP recording running at 33 rpm could hold up to 30 minutes' music per side and therefore longer pieces, especially test pieces, could be recorded complete and without a break.

The earliest microgroove recordings were made in 'mono' – that is to say, the complete sound was relayed through a single speaker. By 1960 'stereophonic' recording was becoming popular. Here, by separating the sound of the two halves of the band or orchestra and feeding it to different speakers placed some distance apart, a truer sound could be achieved.

Much of the information given below is gleaned from the book *Brass Band Recordings* (1991). Subtitled *A complete guide to brass band recordings since 1957*, this has been meticulously compiled by enthusiast Tim Mutum.

The amount of music recorded on EPs and LPs in the years 1957–60 was considerable. In fact, 24 × 7-inch EPs, 6 × 10-inch LPs and 10 × 12-inch LPs were issued. Men o' Brass made 12 (of various sizes), all recorded by Decca, whilst the eight All-Star Band recordings were 7-inch EPs, released by Paxton. Munn & Felton's produced six in various formats, all except one released by EMI – the exception being on Paxton. All six CWS discs were on the Fontana label; Foden's and Black Dyke made three each for Paxton, whilst Fairey Aviation's two discs were on Qualiton.

Thus Paxton was the leading brass band recording company, followed by Decca. Repertoire was again wide-ranging, including test pieces, overtures and selections, popular classics, instrumental features and good quality light music.

An analysis of recordings made by leading bands and those issued by leading brass band recording companies reveals a dramatic increase from 1966, the output more than doubling. Paxton's remained a major producer but their releases were all either 7-inch or 10-inch. Keepoint, a minor recording company, also issued some 10-inch discs but most other releases were standard 12-inch LPs.

The increased output coincided with the entry of PYE Records to the brass band market. This company had a major impact, its 36 releases coming in the same time-span as 30 from EMI and 16 from Paxton. There was also one disc each from RCA and Decca, both of which were to feature heavily in brass band recording in the future, and a unique 7-inch EP on the Apple label, featuring two Paul McCartney numbers, recorded by Black Dyke in 1968.

CWS continued to record for Fontana and GUS mainly for EMI, however, Black Dyke had releases on Paxton, EMI and PYE labels as well as the Apple EP. Recordings made by Fairey's were mainly on Paxton, whilst the All-Star/Men o' Brass recordings were generally on EMI.

Harry Mortimer remained the predominant conductor, appearing not only with the All-Star Band, Men o' Brass, the Fairey Band and Morris Motors, but also on some of the discs made by GUS and Foden's.

Many other bands made recordings during the period. There were also recordings, all made by PYE, of highlights from the gala concerts of the National Brass Band Championships from 1967; and recordings of some Mineworkers' Festivals held in Sheffield – in 1961 on Fontana, and in 1969 and 1970, when Polydor issued double albums. EMI recorded the Festival Concert following the first Wills Championships in 1970. Recorded repertoire was now a truer reflection of contemporary band programmes.

The expansion noted above continued during the 1970s, though there were changes in leading recording bands. Black Dyke remained at the forefront, with both Grimethorpe and Brighouse & Rastrick making more recordings than in the 1960s. Whilst Cory's, Yorkshire Imperial Metals and Besses moved into the top ten recording bands, GUS, CWS, Foden's and Morris moved out. The other band that appeared there for the first and only time was the Virtuosi Brass Band of Great Britain (see Glossary). This had its own company, which appeared briefly as Virtuosi, its function being to record the Virtuosi Band.

There were further changes amongst leading brass band recording companies during the 1970s. With the introduction of its 'Sounds of Brass' series Decca became the leader, followed by PYE, EMI and RCA. Polydor maintained its connection with bands and was joined by Grosvenor. Three other companies appeared late in the decade – Chandos, Polyphonic and Two-Ten – each being attached to a music publishing house. Chandos Records was a subsidiary of Chandos Music Ltd; Polyphonic a sister company to Studio Music; and Two-Ten part of R. Smith & Co., the name being derived from the '210' in the company's address.[12] Two-Ten produced some interesting LPs but did not continue for long, whereas Chandos and Polyphonic became major brass band recording companies. The managing director of Chandos, Brian Couzens, had worked for both RCA and Polydor, but with an eye on the decline in brass band recording by PYE, RCA and EMI, he founded his new company. Stan Kitchen of Studio Music likewise built up his Polyphonic label at around the same time.

Thus, the brass band recording business was flying high by 1980. Bands were generally paid fees for making the recordings and were able to buy copies at discounted rates to sell privately and in their concerts. Record-making, therefore, became a profitable part of the activities of many bands.

---

12 The address was 210 Strand, London.

## Conclusion

The above reveals fluctuations in the popularity of brass bands in the various types of media and it is difficult to find logical reasons for its unsynchronised rise and fall on radio, television and in the recording business. The writer has concluded that this popularity or lack of it is largely dependent on the enthusiasm of just one or two people who happened to be in the right places at the right time. Mortimer, Brand and Relton obviously had an impact on broadcasting, Arthur Taylor and Ken Griffin likewise in television, and it would be relatively simple to pinpoint certain people in the recording business who have had an influence there – not least, of course, Brian Couzens of Chandos and Stan Kitchen of Polyphonic. Vaughan Morris and record producer Ray Horricks were the principal driving forces behind Decca at this time.

# Part Three
# The Years of Maturity,
# 1981–2000

# CHAPTER 9

# Introductory overview

## Social conditions – the state of the nation

Following success in the 1979 general election, Margaret Thatcher became Prime Minister and was to dominate the political scene in Britain throughout the 1980s. She followed a turbulent decade in which successive governments had faced inflation, rising unemployment, a miners' strike, electricity rationing and an enforced three-day working week. After an all-out stoppage by miners, Edward Heath had called an election on 'Who governs Britain?' – and lost. During the early Thatcher years manufacturing output decreased as unemployment rose and many textile and engineering firms closed. A recession between 1979 and 1982 aggravated the old North–South divide – closures affecting mainly the traditional industries located in the North and Midlands whilst the service industries of the South suffered less. Reminiscent of the 1930s, this was yet another period during which many people lived in poverty as others became better off.

The miners' strike of 1984, with ugly confrontations between miners and the police, caused serious divisions throughout Britain – often within families. Further, a new system of collecting local taxes was introduced. What was dubbed the 'poll tax' led to violence, riots, and, eventually, to Thatcher's downfall. In 1990 John Major took over as Prime Minister and the Poll Tax was revised. Then 1992 was the year of the so-called 'Black Wednesday', a massive devaluation of the pound bringing further hardships.[1] Of even more significance for brass bands was the fact that the greater part of the coal industry was closed down, to the total devastation of many small communities.

### Improved funding

A brighter side to banding emerged during the second half of the period with the setting-up, in 1991, of the Foundation for Sport and the Arts. Linked financially with the football pools,[2] it provided capital funding for many bands, primarily for the purchase of new instruments or rehearsal

---

[1] Tiratsoo, 1997, pp. 201–6.

[2] The football pools is a system of gambling based on the results of football matches. The Foundation for Sports and the Arts, set up by the pools promoters, is currently distributing some £60 million annually to a wide range of projects.

premises. Bands regularly received four- or even five-figure sums and from 1995 there were also grants from the National Lottery. In 1997 a further scheme was introduced called 'Arts for Everyone' (A4E). Grants were now given in abundance to brass bands, dozens of them benefiting from the various schemes.

## Organisations

Despite new initiatives being introduced into the AOMF syllabus, there was now virtually no call for the Scholarship and it was wound up, the final award being made in 1990. (A full list of AOMF winners is shown in Appendix B.) A similar fate awaited the Bandsman's College of Music. In 1981 George Thompson retired from the post of Director of Examinations and was replaced by Ernest Woodhouse, who in turn was succeeded in 1985 by Denzil Stephens. However, in 1995 the BCM was closed down, with the declaration that its original aim, 'to encourage the serious study of the brass band and its music', had been achieved. There were by now many opportunities for such study to be undertaken in a number of colleges and universities.

The NBBC had already gone and with the departure of the AOMF Scholarship and the BCM, brass band organisations were passing through a shaky period. Had they outlived their usefulness?

The NABBC survived the crisis though not without difficulty. The Adjudicators' Training Scheme had been withdrawn but in 1985 a new programme was drawn up in conjunction with the Guildhall School of Music. However, this was an examination, not a training scheme. There were written and oral examinations, instrumental performance and a *viva voce*. On completion, candidates undertook six mock adjudicating assignments. Despite over 80 enquiries, only two candidates actually entered. Both passed and were awarded the diploma of LGSM in Brass Band Adjudicating. There were no further examinations and the scheme was withdrawn in 1990. Finally, in 1997, the NABBC, in conjunction with the University of Salford, offered a Licentiate Diploma in Brass Band Adjudication. Again there was an examination and assignments. The first award of the new diploma was made in 1999.

From 1953 *The Conductor* was sponsored by the publishers W. Paxton & Co. Ltd and put on general sale – not, as hitherto, restricted to members of the NABBC. Following the death of Frank Wright in 1970, Wesley Johnstone became editor.[3] Novello, who agreed to look after the magazine, now absorbed Paxton. From spring 1972 *The Conductor* was incorporated

---

[3] Johnstone was Head of Music for Portsmouth Education Authority.

in *Sounding Brass*, Novello's new quarterly magazine (see page 56), but when this closed down during 1981 *The Conductor* took the form of a news-sheet. From 1982 it was restored to magazine form, funded by the Association. Owing to financial problems the magazine was not published during 1987 nor the early part of 1988, but was then reinstated, supported by a small publishing company, Mostyn Music, that was owned by an NABBC member, Tony Cresswell. From May 1974 *The Conductor* was edited by Bram Wiggins, a former professional trumpet player, now a composer and adjudicator. He was succeeded in 1978 by Philip Catelinet (see 'Personalia'), who officiated until 1991 when the present incumbent, Jeffrey Turner, took over.

In 1981 Sydney Swancott became the Association's chairman, a position he held until the end of the century and beyond, and in 1983 André Previn became patron. Relative stability returned and the usual round of national conventions and regional events continued. The death of Harry Mortimer in 1992 robbed the NABBC of the last of its founding members and its president since 1959. In 1993 Roy Newsome became the third president in the Association's history.

Amongst those giving masterclasses during the 1990s were Kevin Bolton, Frank Renton, Geoffrey Brand and Kenneth Dennison. The most successful regional activities were workshops based on the study of Area test pieces. During the early part of the decade the flagging No. 6 Area (Scotland) was relaunched, Nigel Boddice becoming its chairman in 1998. The NABBC was thus quite buoyant during the closing years of the century.

Though an Association of Brass Band Adjudicators (ABBA) had been under consideration for decades, it was not until 1999 that one was actually formed. Its initial members were those on an approved list of adjudicators for the National Championships, but as time went on other names were added. The Association's aims were: 'To maintain and improve a professional level; and to protect and enhance the status of Brass Band Adjudicators.' David Read became its first chairman.

## The Federation

The 1980s saw an upturn in the fortunes of the British Federation of Brass Bands (BFBB). In 1984 Harry Mortimer became patron and Peter Parkes became president. By 1986 there were 19 associations in membership out of a total of 26. The Federation had taken over the management of the PRS's control of brass band performances and was offering training in band administration. There was a two-day conference in 1990, by which time there were regular newsletters highlighting the BFBB's work.

In 1992 a new chairman was elected who was to breathe life into an organisation which, despite its vision, had had but little success. His name was David Stanley. Under his leadership, plans were made to take over the National Registry, to open a national office, to appoint at least one salaried officer and to establish a policy for youth.

However, proposals for increasing membership fees caused antagonism in certain quarters and it became increasingly obvious that outside financial help was needed if the Federation was to be effective. This came in 1994 with a grant of £17 000 from the Foundation for Sport and the Arts. Here was the springboard for future progress. The Registry was taken over, as was management of Boosey & Hawkes' list of recognised adjudicators, and schemes were introduced to 'Train the Trainers'. A part-time national officer was appointed and a delegate elected to represent British bands in the newly formed European Brass Band Association (EBBA). From 1996 separate bands and even individuals could become Federation members.

Another organisation had been formed in 1993, the Brass Band Heritage Trust (BBHT). Led by BBC producer Paul Hindmarsh and supported by leading figures from the movement, its initial aims were 'to preserve the past, secure the present and plan for the future'. The practical manifestation of this was an attempt to establish an information centre which, ostensibly, would serve both past and present, and the creation of a network for youth – with an eye on the future. Happily, BFBB and BBHT were able to collaborate and through their combined efforts funding was acquired and a National Centre opened in Dean Clough Mills, Halifax.[4]

Weekly subscriptions were now raised from a few pounds per band to a still very modest £50 per band. This caused bad feeling and the Federation initially lost many of its members. A conference was called at the National Centre, attracting a good attendance and a good response to the case for the Federation presented by David Stanley. A small practical benefit to member bands at this time was the offer of an insurance package, Fedsure, with reduced rates being negotiated for member bands.

Peter Parkes, already president of the BFBB, now also became chairman of BBHT. With a £15 000 Arts Council grant and the promise of a further £18 000 over three years from various charitable trusts, the two organisations were able to appoint a full-time development officer in 1998. The BFBB now looked after the National Centre and employed the development officer, whilst the BBHT signed a four-year contract with Boosey's for the management of the Youth Band Championships. In 1999 the Arts Council grant was extended by three years and the Federation moved into purpose-built accommodation in Barnsley.

---

[4] Dean Clough was formerly the home of Crossley Carpets, whose works' band is discussed in the Glossary.

A further accolade came the Federation's way when it was invited by EBBA to manage the European Championships held in the year 2000 in Symphony Hall, Birmingham. This was aided by a £24 000 grant from the Millennium Festival Fund. Outside of the competition itself the accent was very much on youth. There was a Young Conductors' Competition (won by a Spanish conductor) and the formation of the first-ever European Youth Brass Band. The first half of the Festival concert was performed by the NYBB.

Within the space of four years, the combined BFBB and BBHT had made progress which in earlier times could only have been dreamed of.

## Youth – widening horizons

### *Junior and school bands*

Let us return first of all to some of the groups mentioned in Chapter 4. In the 1960s and 1970s Besses Boys' Band was still functioning, conducted by a former soprano player of the senior band. However, it was seldom in the news until the announcement during 1978 that Barrie Chappell, another former member of Besses o' th' Barn, had become the conductor. In 1983 Besses Boys' Band celebrated its fortieth anniversary with a concert in which Harry Mortimer was guest conductor; a special commemorative cover was produced by the local post office. Chappell was so successful that 1986 heralded the band's seventh successive win in the Area Youth Championships. For good measure, the 1987 fourth section Finals were won and in the following year there was a memorable four-week engagement in Australia – part of the bicentennial celebrations. In 1991, after 12 consecutive appearances in the Finals of the National Youth Band Championships, Barrie Chappell stood down and once again the band went out of the limelight. By the time of its fiftieth anniversary, in 1993, there were girls in membership. For constitutional reasons, however, the name remained Besses Boys' Band.

Grimethorpe Juniors went out of existence for a time but was reformed in 1984 by Stan Lippeatt and another former member of the Juniors, both now in the senior band. There were 33 members, with ages ranging from seven to 17. In 1990 the Junior Band was again re-formed, but on account of the members' ages it was now called Grimethorpe Colliery B Band, later being renamed Grimethorpe & District.

Oakmead School band's travels continued but in 1984 there was threat of closure as, formerly a boys' school, it was to merge with a girls' school. However, it survived and soon had girls within its ranks. To celebrate its fortieth anniversary in 1999, the band visited Canada.

Of course, many new school, junior and youth bands were being formed. In Derbyshire, the Glossop School Band was founded *circa* 1975 by the school's woodwork master, trombonist Jack Fletcher, who rehearsed the band each lunchtime in the school's joinery workshop. Showmanship was this band's speciality and it acquired an impressive record in junior entertainment competitions alongside its highly successful concerts in the school and surrounding districts. Other laurels came its way during the 1980s. It regularly won the Imperial Youth Championships in Blackpool, knockout competitions on Radios Manchester and Stoke, and also won the first Action Research Entertainment Contest, held in Oldham in 1984. There were also regular appearances on television. During the later 1980s the band suffered due to school reorganisation, the opening of a sixth-form college leading to the loss of older members. Though the band continued, it enjoyed less success and eventually amalgamated with another local school band. Jack Fletcher retired in 1988.

Wardle High School, located near Rochdale, was also to achieve fame and to an extent took over from Glossop. It was a newly opened comprehensive school when its first band was formed in 1982. By the end of the year there was a first-year band, a second-year band, a School Band and even a Youth Band. The School Band met with immediate success, both in contest and concert, and enjoyed periodical television appearances. The music master, Garry Walczak, was the principal driving force but he received vigorous support from the headmaster. Sadly, he died in 1996, but a new, supportive head encouraged further progress. By 1995 there were five school bands with a total membership of 250 pupils, plus the Youth Band, specifically for ex-members of the school bands. The various Wardle bands competed in many contests and had regular successes, particularly in the Action Research contest (later held annually in Blackpool), and becoming recognised as the Youth Entertainments Championships of Great Britain.

A few miles to the west Smithills School Band, located in Bolton, was another band with a remarkable success story. From a mere handful of instruments in the school's music storeroom in 1990, by 1992 the Senior Brass Band had already produced a CD and within another year there was a 70-piece concert band. The driving force behind the bands was the school's head of music, Christopher Wormald, a former member of the NYBB and Besses Boys' Band and now a french horn player, who had been a member of JSVB. By the year 2000, mainly through his inspiration, the Senior Brass Band had won several awards in connection with both the National Federation of Music for Youth and the Child of Achievement in the Community. It had also won a 1st prize in the WMC (Kerkrade) competition, had undertaken successful tours in Norway, Japan and America and had appeared twice on the television programme *Blue Peter*.

Probably the only multi-ethnic brass band in Britain at the time, it gave numerous concerts and made several CDs.

In the case of each of the above bands – and indeed, many others – one person was the musical driving force behind the band. Of course, they needed co-operation from their respective head teachers but in return they brought status to their schools, just as a successful sports team could do.

## Area school bands

Queensbury Music Centre had an area band with roots going back to 1969. It was formed as a direct result of the disbanding of Black Dyke Juniors. The company, John Foster & Son Ltd, loaned its instruments to the West Riding of Yorkshire Education Department which in turn put them into two Queensbury schools. Pupils were taught by James Shepherd, Black Dyke's principal cornet player, but in his capacity as a schools brass instructor. He then formed the Music Centre Band which, in 1969, appeared on television and in its first-ever contest qualified for the National Youth Championships in London, winning 1st prize and becoming National Youth Brass Band Champions of Great Britain. Renamed The Queensbury Band in 1982, it had reached championship status by 1988.

Meanwhile, in 1981, as more players became available an offshoot appeared, named Jayess (JS – after its founder). As yet more arrived, a Jayess Junior Band was formed. Both bands were successful and later the 'Jayess '87 Beginners Band' appeared. In 1995 the senior band, which had achieved championship status and was no longer a youth band, became known as the Yorkshire Co-operative (Jayess) Band.

New area bands also appeared from time to time, Scotland being particularly vibrant. Kilmarnock Area Schools Band was formed *circa* 1978, winning the Area contest of the Butlin's Youth Championships in 1979 under Andrew Keatchie, head of brass in the region. Senior members formed Kilmarnock Concert Brass, which won the Area championship section contest in the same year, becoming the youngest-ever Scottish Champions and achieving a remarkable 'double'. In 1980–81–82 the Schools Band became Butlin's National Youth Band Champions, completing a brilliant hat-trick. In 1985, on religious grounds, Keatchie refused to take the band to the Finals, which now took place on a Sunday.

Another young band that appeared in Scotland during the 1970s was West Lothian Schools. However, it was not until after its first residential course in 1984, when Nigel Boddice became the band's musical director, that the band really developed – at such a speed that it won the Finals of the 1985 National Youth Championships. Following another win in 1990, there were regular appearances both on radio and television and then further wins in the restyled Championships of 1995, 1996 and 1998. The band regularly became Scottish Youth Champions and was twice European Youth Band Champions. It was also well-travelled, the most extensive trip being to Australia, in 1996.

Another recent arrival on the school band scene was the Stockport Schools Band. The speciality of this band was 'entertainment'. It was a regular competitor and several times winner of the Action Research Competition in Blackpool. Through success in this competition the band appeared on *Blue Peter*.

There were many other area schools bands but the above is a fairly representative selection.

School bands continued to thrive, though with the inevitable turnover in membership some enjoyed a period of success and then faded into the background. Many school bands developed into youth bands as their members grew older and, similarly, youth bands became adult bands. Some school and youth bands entered the contest field but many concentrated on concert work, often undertaking tours.

*The National Schools Band Association*

The NSBBA continued along similar lines to those outlined in Chapter 4 though, in order to incorporate mixed brass and wind bands, it changed its name during 1980 to the National School Band Association (NSBA). The Association received major boosts during the 1990s – a sponsorship deal which enabled it to improve and upgrade the presentation of its magazine and festivals, and a grant of £25 000 from the Foundation for Sport and the Arts.[5]

*Youth bands*

Moving into the area of youth, Youth Brass 2000 was formed in 1990 as a junior wing of Rigid Containers Group (the former GUS Band). Under the leadership of trombonist Chris Jeans, 'entertainment' became the band's speciality. It enjoyed a particularly good year in 1996, becoming both Entertainment Champions of Great Britain and also Radio 2's 'Youth Band of the Year'.

A late-comer to the youth band competitive movement was St Helens Youth, the outcome of one of several private music-teaching practices set up to combat the reduction in school instrumental teaching. Lynda Nicholson (see 'Personalia'), one of several teachers in the St Helens district,

---

[5] For further information about the NSBBA/NSBA, see Brand, 1979, ch. 10; and quarterly publications of *The Trumpeter*.

was the driving force behind the band, which had the distinction of becoming National Youth Band Champions in the year 2000.

Other youth bands active at this time are too numerous to mention. As with school bands, some concentrated on contests whilst others were more concerned with concerts and tours. All contributed to the well-being of brass bands as a whole. Teaching was now generally more formal than for previous generations and the band movement was again to move forward as players of this generation matured.

## National youth bands

In the NYBB, Roy Newsome succeeded Arthur Butterworth in 1984 but with the title changed from music adviser to music director. In 1989 a new series of solo competition was introduced. The 'Katie Ogden Awards'[6] were made during the Easter course to the winners of events for individual sections, who then proceeded to the Finals in the summer, competing for the 'Harry Mortimer Award'. The same year saw the NYBB featured in a Henry Wood Promenade Concert, with Sir Charles Groves conducting.

In 1988 a further LP was made. It took its title, *Hammer of the North*, from a commissioned work by Michael Ball, and was followed in 1992 by the band's first CD – *40 Years Young*, recorded as part of their fortieth-anniversary celebrations with Harry Mortimer as guest conductor and Maurice Murphy, the band's first leader, as soloist. A gala concert in the Barbican formed the highlight of these celebrations. Besides soloists Phillip McCann and Evelyn Glennie, the internationally renowned percussionist, 16 former NYBB leaders performed special features.

In 1994 the Arts Council offered commission fees for works which entailed collaboration with some other medium. The NYBB took advantage of this, commissioning a work by composer and educationalist Philip Wilby for brass band, organ and electronic percussion instruments. Called *Dance Before the Lord*, this was premiered in Gloucester Cathedral. Also in 1994, Wilby became the first of a number of NYBB composers-in-residence. A year later the young Scottish composer Peter Graham was commissioned under the same scheme to compose a ballet, *Dancing in the Park*. This was performed in the RNCM Opera Theatre, Richard Evans conducting, with dancers from the Northern Ballet School.

In 1995 the NYBB received a welcome three-year sponsorship from British Gas which was followed in 1997 by a two-year association with the Mobil Oil Company. From the mid-1990s, grants from the Arts Council also began to appear, enabling the band to do more forward-planning in

---

6 The 'Katie Ogden Awards' were founded in memory a girl of that name who had died young after a life of illness and suffering. They were funded by her grandfather.

terms of booking concert halls and guest conductors, and commissioning new works.

Nineteen-ninety-six saw another concert in the Barbican and a tour in the Smoky Mountain region of North Carolina in America. LSO Brass were the NYBB's guests at the Barbican and for the finale the NYBB was joined by this distinguished group, playing under the orchestra's principal conductor, the American Michael Tilson Thomas. Martin Ellerby was now composer-in-residence, responding to two further commissions.

In 1997 long-serving secretary Bill England retired and was replaced as administrator by Philip Biggs.[7] He quickly acquired a grant under the A4E scheme for a three-year programme of regional auditions.

In the year 2000 the band mourned the death of Mrs Maud Wright, widow of the band's founder. She had been actively involved in the running of the band almost up to her death.

Of the several thousand players who have been members of the NYBB many have become leading figures in the brass band world, some have graced professional orchestras and military bands, whilst others have done important work in teaching or with community bands. The NYBB has given concerts in some of the finest concert halls in England, including the Barbican and the Royal Albert Hall in London, Symphony Hall in Birmingham and the Bridgewater Hall in Manchester. It has been involved in two Henry Wood Promenade Concerts, has regularly broadcast, appeared on television, has made several commercial recordings and commissioned many new works.[8]

There was much excitement in 1981 for two other national youth bands, as the NYBBS travelled to Switzerland for a joint course and concerts with its opposite number, the NJBB. In the following year the NJBB came to Scotland on a return visit. NYBBS visited Denmark in 1984 and in the following year there was a commission from the distinguished composer Peter Maxwell Davies (knighted in 1987) for a work for choir and band. The fruits of this was *The Peatcutters – a reflection on a disastrous fire on the Orkney island of Hoy*, where Maxwell Davies lived. The work was premiered in the 1985 Edinburgh International Festival.

---

[7] Philip Biggs, a former member of Cambridge Co-op, has become an important figure within the brass band movement. He first came into prominence as a co-founder of the All England Masters Championships. In the early 1990s he became administrator to both the NYBB and the BBSS, and was also organising concerts locally. He was now establishing links with bands, professional brass groups and soloists, and by the late 1990s was promoting prestigious concerts and festivals.

[8] For further information about the NYBB see 'The NYBB – A Lasting Tribute', chapter 26 in Newsome, 1995; 'The National Youth Brass Band of Great Britain – A brief history', compiled by Roy Newsome, in the Souvenir Programme for the NYBB's 50th-anniversary concert, held in St George's Hall, Bradford, on 30 March 2002; and 'The National Youth Brass Band of Great Britain', by Maud Wright, chapter 8 in Brand, 1979.

In 1992 Geoffrey Brand retired from the conductorship of NYBBS, having served for 21 years. He was replaced by Richard Evans.

The Young Ambassadors was a band formed by Frank Wolff of Oxford in 1978, primarily for the purpose of making overseas tours. Many of its members were formerly in the NYBB. By 1983 it had already completed ten tours and plans were in hand to visit America in the following year. In 1987 the band made an LP but touring remained its *raison d'être*. During Easter 2000 the band undertook its sixty-fourth overseas tour, eight of them having been trans-Atlantic. Elaine Wolff (see 'Personalia') was a major driving force from the outset. She was a daughter of Frank, and the band's principal cornet player.

Not until 1983 did Wales have its National Youth Brass Band. It was administered by the Welsh Amateur Music Federation and Edward Gregson was the first music director. Like NYBBS, the NYBBW holds one course per year. In 1996 James Watson was appointed music director in succession to Gregson, who then became the band's president. There have been several guest conductors and a liberal number of commissions, especially by Welsh composers. By the year 1999, 20 major works had been commissioned and premiered. The band has performed in a wide range of venues in Wales, has been featured at the Welsh National Eisteddfod and has travelled abroad.

## County youth bands

These bands continued to flourish. In Cornwall, home of the first, course directors in the 1980s included Peter Parkes, Richard Evans, Ray Farr, John Berryman and Derek Broadbent, as well as Albert Chappell, now the band's music advisor. The twenty-fifth anniversary was celebrated in 1983 and during this year the band won the County Youth Band section in the National Festival of Music for Youth held in the Royal Festival Hall. It also opened the final night of the Schools Proms in the Royal Albert Hall. From 1989 courses were moved from Easter to the period between Christmas and New Year. It was now becoming difficult to attract members and during the 1990s there was something of a lull in activities.

In Hampshire, John Knight was succeeded as music director by Maurice Arnold in the early 1980s and during 1983 Hampshire Youth won the renamed Boosey & Hawkes National Youth Brass Band Championships. Concert and competition successes continued, 1986 being a particularly eventful year.

Before 1986 a maximum of 50 players had been allowed in the Youth Championships but this was now reduced to 35; rather than disappoint 15 members, Hampshire Youth did not attend. Maurice Arnold retired for health reasons and was replaced by Leighton Rich, a former euphonium player with Parc & Dare and the Coldstream Guards. Rich brought a new dimension to the band's activities with a policy of commissioning works of special interest. Within a period of eight months during 1989 there were 17 concerts, including the premieres of three new works. The concerts also served as fund-raising events to keep down the cost of touring. The next three years saw visits to Canada, Germany, Czechoslovakia and California. Tours were now a regular thing, a particularly impressive one taking place in 1997 in the USA.

Another county youth band with a good record was that of Northamptonshire, conducted by John Berryman – it became National Youth Band Champions in 1992.

The tradition of youth bands in Wales continued. West Glamorgan Youth Band carried the title Boosey & Hawkes Youth Champions in 1984 and 1989 whilst Gwent County Youth Band – the former Monmouth Youth – also carried the title twice, in 1994 and 1999.

Thus, the brass band movement was being well served by its youth and all augured well for its future.

### Conferences and education

In 1989 there was a travelling exhibition called 'Brass Roots'. It addressed '150 years of Brass Bands' and was housed in suitable venues in Bradford, Edinburgh, Llangollen, Manchester, Salford and London. As well as exhibitions of old photographs and programmes there were workshops, and concerts featuring old instruments and old band music. The principal driving forces were Professor Trevor Herbert of the Open University and Arnold Myers, curator of Edinburgh University's collection of rare instruments. A decade later Elgar Howarth and Grimethorpe gave a series of concerts in York University in the form of a 'History of Brass Band Music', accompanied by lectures and talks from Professor Herbert and Bram Gay.

Howard Snell organised Brass Band Conferences at the RNCM in 1993 and 1994. The first was a huge success. Snell was so encouraged that he expanded the event from a single day into two days for the following year, incorporating a concert in the Free Trade Hall that featured Black Dyke, Britannia Building Society (the former Foden's) and the NYBB. Another important part of the weekend was an open forum for championship section bands. Though 19 of them agreed to form an 'English Brass Band Forum', with the promise of early expansion to include lower-section bands, the idea did not materialise, partly due to adverse comments made about the British Federation. This drew an angry response from supporters of the Federation and planted a fear in the minds of some band representatives that the new organisation would reopen old divisions. Within weeks the Forum was suspended and the projected 1995 Conference replaced by a 'Brass Day'.

An important aspect of banding in the 1990s was the spread of workshops, seminars and masterclasses. These, often sponsored by an instrument firm, were directed by leading instrumentalists and were additional to the growing number of courses.

Parallel with these trends, a number of bands became attached to centres of learning – Black Dyke and Grimethorpe became bands-in-residence at, respectively, the Royal Academy of Music and the Royal College of Music, whilst Foden's became ensemble-in-residence of the University of Leeds. Additionally, brass bands were formed at the Welsh College of Music and Drama and at the Royal College of Music. Though not forming brass bands as such, brass students at the Royal Academy and Guildhall periodically performed original brass band music.

Youth of the brass band world regularly entered open competitions such as the BBC Young Musician of the Year and the Shell LSO Scholarship. To win even the Brass Semi-finals and compete in the Finals of the BBC event – against strings, woodwind, pianists and percussionists – is an honour to be coveted. Elaine Wolff was the next brass bander to achieve this – in 1980. Others followed in her footsteps including, in 2000, David Childs. This followed the banning of the euphonium from the competition in that year by the BBC. Subsequent to a successful campaign, led by Steven Mead (see page 252) and Robert Childs (father of David), the BBC reversed its decision. The winning of the 2000 Brass Semi-final by David, playing euphonium, thus had extra significance. For the Finals, Wilby's *Euphonium Concerto* was scored for orchestra and performed with the BBC Philharmonic Orchestra.

## Courses

### Short courses

Several one-off short courses were mentioned on pages 85–6 and the North Regional Trust began an annual series of week-end courses in 1984. Leading figures were engaged to direct workshops covering a variety of topics. In 1990 nine tutors looked after a total of 100 instrumentalists and 19 trainee conductors.

By now, summer schools were also becoming popular. The Wessex Summer School, begun in 1970, was possibly the first of the modern schools. It was organised by John Grinnell, then a sixth-form student. Courtney Bosanko was course director and the first course attracted 44 young people.

By 1981 there were 150. It was non-residential but many of the players (and their families) camped out or came with caravans. The age range was from ten to 21 and the 1985 course attracted 200 instrumentalists from 52 different bands. There was also a large contingent of tutors, headed by Derek Broadbent as course director, who produced several compositions for the 'Wessex'. Students were now being attracted from overseas and numbers escalated even further, with 299 attending in 1990 and a staggering 325 by 1993. This was the largest of all the summer schools.

Another summer school was founded in 1978 with Edward Gregson as course director. This was part of a much larger project covering many different activities organised at Marlborough College in Wiltshire. It was a one-week course initially but in 1980 was expanded to two, though few delegates attended both. Gregson now directed the first week and Roy Newsome the second. The course was called 'Sounding Brass' (Gregson was a co-editor of the magazine of that name) and ran until 1985, after which it ceased, largely because of a new course, sponsored by Boosey's.

This new course was part of a venture known as the Boosey & Hawkes Open College. A number of weekend study courses were organised but the main event was a one-week residential summer school at Trent Park College of Education, London. It was given extensive publicity and the emphasis was on brass – both brass band and orchestral. There was a large array of tutors, Sir David Willcocks was president and Harry Mortimer headed the brass band team.

Out of the Open College grew the Harry Mortimer Summer School, first held at Goldsmith's College in London in 1986, then moving to Oxford in the following year, where it remained until 1998. Roy Newsome was course director and the administrator was Gordon Higginbottom. Both they and the original tutors had been involved with the Boosey summer school and decided that, though Boosey's had chosen not to pursue the idea, there was call for such an event. They therefore founded the highly successful Brass Band Summer School. Mortimer was president until his death in 1992 and was succeeded by Philip Jones; Higginbottom was administrator until 1998, after which Philip Biggs took over. From 1999 the course was held in Bromsgrove.

The International Brass Band Summer School was founded in 1990. Its first three courses were held in Brecon, Wales. Geoffrey Brand was musical director and Alan Lewis, head of brass in a local college, was course director. The format was to have intensive morning and evening rehearsals, with time for recreational activities or relaxation after lunch. A public concert at the end of the course featured one or more of the tutors as soloists. In 1993 Lewis took up an appointment in Sedbergh, North Yorkshire, and the course was rehoused there. This course was also very successful, attracting a large number of overseas delegates.

There was obviously a market for brass band summer schools and each one developed its own character. Another appeared in 1994 as part of the famous Canford Summer Music School which catered for a range of activities, mainly in the sphere of classical music. James Watson and selected players from Black Dyke were enlisted to organise a brass band course. In keeping with most Canford courses and in contrast to other brass band summer schools, this was specifically 'for the accomplished brass player'. Numbers were restricted and the music studied was of an advanced nature. There was no brass band course at Canford during 1999, but in 2000 Fairey's and James Gourlay followed along the lines laid down by Black Dyke and Watson.

*Full-time courses*

The Salford course in band studies was given graduate status in 1986. A year later a degree was validated, becoming the first BA in Band Studies in Europe. Elgar Howarth became composer-in-residence in 1986, was succeeded by Michael Ball in 1988 and Philip Sparke in 1990. David King (see page 248), having been a student at Salford, became a lecturer there in 1987, to be joined by composer Peter Graham in 1991. Newsome retired in 1989 and was succeeded by King as Head of Band Studies. In 1991 Salford College of Technology became University College Salford, prior to becoming part of the University of Salford two years later.

Harry Mortimer had been associated with the Salford courses in an advisory capacity since their inception and in 1988 was awarded an Honorary PhD. Other future recipients of honorary Salford awards included Sir Malcolm Arnold, Sir Harrison Birtwistle, Elgar Howarth, Philip Jones, George Lloyd and Roy Newsome. The University bands achieved worldwide recognition through tours and broadcasts. The brass band visited Holland, Belgium, Hungary, Russia, Finland and Brazil. Salford's courses put brass bands firmly on the academic map and paved the way for other institutions to forge links with the brass band movement.

A course at Huddersfield Technical College catered for bandsmen at 'foundation' level, with individual instrumental lessons and the Tecol Band, directed by Phillip McCann. In 1980, with McCann on the teaching staff of the Polytechnic and directing its bands, a more positive move towards brass band studies was made. Without abandoning the traditional music degree course, a compromise was found which enabled those students who had an interest in bands to pursue it. This was achieved by including a Brass Band Studies module among the optional segments of the course. Students who opted for this studied brass band history and scoring in their second and third years. Brass band instruments were also now acceptable for first study. Symbolic of the link between Sellers Engineering

Works and the Tecol Band, an annual cash scholarship was awarded by the company to a selected student taking the band studies option. This was instituted in 1993, by which time the Polytechnic had become the University of Huddersfield.

A new two-year full-time band course, aimed primarily at 16-year-olds, began at Barnsley Technical College in 1987, with support from Boosey & Hawkes. Peter Parkes became head in 1988 and two years later the course was redesigned for older students and led to a Diploma in Higher Education. From 1992 Barnsley offered a BA in Band Studies, courses being validated by the University of Sheffield. By 1994 David Hirst (see page 265) was course coordinator. A number of high-profile bandsmen who had been unable to undertake serious musical studies earlier in their lives graduated at Barnsley in the late 1990s.

In 1988 the brass band of Birmingham School of Music was re-formed and brass band students encouraged to apply for music courses. By 1992 it had become Birmingham Conservatoire and with tutors including Steven Mead and Phillip McCann there was more emphasis on the brass band.

The Royal Northern College of Music (RNCM) became the first major Conservatoire to accept brass band instruments for first study on its four-year course, starting in 1990. Successful completion of this course was rewarded by a Graduate Diploma and now students who played brass band instruments could graduate at this high-profile institution. An RNCM Brass Band was formed, performing alongside the college's symphony orchestra and wind orchestra, and in the late 1990s the College unveiled a brass band option in its degree course. It also offers a one-year post-graduate course in Band Direction.

In 1992 a further band course opened, at Accrington & Rossendale College of Further Education. This was part-time, based on 'distance learning', whereby students met their tutors and each other monthly for an intensive weekend of studies, completing the bulk of their work at home. This was a boon to older students not in a position to study full-time. As with Barnsley, course validation was undertaken by Sheffield University. From 1993 there were two options, one leading to the Certificate in Higher Education and another leading to the Diploma in Higher Education. From 1994 the course was extended and offered a BA in Brass Band Studies.

Nineteen-eighty-nine saw at least three colleges giving more encouragement to students who were members of brass bands. These were Colchester Institute, the London College of Music and Leeds University, which now had a brass band. There was also a thriving brass band in the Guildhall's Junior School of Music.

## The brass band press

The *British Bandsman* reached its centenary in 1987. Included in the celebrations were a luncheon, a competition for municipal floral displays, a 72-page special edition of the magazine and the publication of *The British Bandsman Centenary Book* written by Alf Hailstone, a member of the editorial staff. There was also a special concert, held in Manchester's Free Trade Hall, featuring Black Dyke, Besses and Yorkshire Imperial as well as the Childs Brothers (see page 288) and four legendary principal cornet players of Black Dyke – Willie Lang, Maurice Murphy, James Shepherd and Phillip McCann. Moreover, the editor was given tickets for Royal Garden Parties for distribution amongst staff and leading personalities within the brass band movement. The centenary celebrations ended with a special Bandsmen's Service in London.

In the year 2000 Trevor Austin, the managing director of Austin Catelinet Ltd, and joint owner of *BB* with Peter Wilson for 23 years, transferred all rights to Kapitol Media and Events, whose principals were Philip Morris, now also manager of the National Championships, and Niki Bland, *BB*'s chief feature writer. Wilson, managing editor since 1977, retired, though he continued in the capacity of a consultant.

A new magazine appeared in 1991. The first issue was published in February and there were to be ten per year. The editor was Robert Mulholland, born in New Zealand and son of a former bandmaster of Fairey Aviation Works Band – also called Robert Mulholland. Harry Mortimer was invited to be the chief adviser and several other leading figures from the world of brass were enlisted either as contributors or consultants. The magazine introduced itself thus:

> We believe there is a marketing niche in Britain and overseas for a quality monthly magazine for the British brass band. Bright, colourful, controversial, but not stridently so, entertaining, informative and educative. Whatever your specific interest we hope you shall find something in *Brass Band World* for you. If not, let us know. It is a magazine designed for YOU.

*Brass Band World* quickly established itself as a valuable addition to the brass band press. It has certainly lived up to its declared intentions, has provided in-depth articles as well as lively comment, critical reviews, contest news and articles of international interest.

At around the same time *Brass Review* was also launched. Published by Kirklees Music, it is supplied free, production costs being covered through sales of advertising space. Dennis Wilby is the editor and he assembles a varied collection of articles plus a fairly substantial 'Critics Corner'.

## The year 2000

This year, hailed as 'The Millennium', has generally been portrayed as the first year in the third millennium. For the purpose of this book the author has viewed it as the final year of the second. It was quite a special year, with several events unique to it. For example, 17 young brass players from all over Britain flew to Sydney to become part of a large band featured in the opening ceremony of the Olympic Games. This year was also the centenary of Foden's Band. Following an impressive celebratory concert in Manchester's Bridgewater Hall the band released a video recording of the concert – possibly the first such commercial release.

Following the death of Mrs Margaret Mortimer in December 1999 the year 2000 saw a new generation of Mortimers – Martin and his wife Karyn, together with their three children – organising the Grand Shield and the British Open contests. With changes also in the administration of the National Championships, there really was an air of 'ring out the old, ring in the new'.

Whit Friday contests took on broader dimensions during the 1990s, with increased prize-money, more contests and more participating bands. During the early post-war years there were generally eight contests; by 1992 this had risen to 19, with more than 60 competing bands. These, formerly coming mainly from Yorkshire, Lancashire and Cheshire were now drawn not only from all parts of Britain, but also from overseas. The Whit Friday contests of the year 2000 set new records with no less than 164 bands on a circuit which now boasted 23 contests. A staggering 68 bands played in that held in the village of Uppermill.

Personal computers and websites developed rapidly during the 1990s. Many bands, associations and individuals opened websites, and communication and publicity took on new dimensions. There were chatlines and discussion groups – not always healthy – and there was to be an online magazine, '4bars rest'.

## Conclusion

Names from the brass band world continued to appear periodically in the Honours Lists, though, with the exception of Dean Goffin, knighted in 1983, and Harry Mortimer, 'promoted' from OBE to CBE a year later, they seem to have been almost exclusively the award of the MBE, of a lower standing than the OBEs regularly conferred in earlier times.

Despite many problems faced by many bands and despite a continuing decline in the number of bands active, the final 20 years of the century saw the movement reach a musical maturity unmatched in earlier times.

The repertoire had certainly matured, as had concert presentation, along with developments in the quality of teaching, and in the technical and reading standards of the players. There was a new breed of instruments, tonally superior to earlier ones and now in tune with the rest of the musical world. Percussion was now an integral part of the band and the standard of percussion playing had risen substantially. School and youth bands were reaching unprecedented levels – in quality of playing, presentation and entertainment.

The movement as a whole was less inward-looking than formerly and more people from the wider world of music were appreciating the quality of music-making achieved by the better bands. Extra cash input during the 1990s helped many bands replace old, worn-out instruments. A number of bands were able to have purpose-built bandrooms made and many more commissioned new music for their own individual use.

Perhaps the most significant factor was the thirst for education. This was not now restricted to schools, but was present in higher education. Further, many short courses and summer schools catered for the whole band community. Though there were social and recreational aspects to these, and perhaps little in the way of in-depth study, band people of all ages and abilities were being introduced to modern teaching methods and to an ever-widening repertoire.

# CHAPTER 10

# Contest developments and repertoire

### The demise of Belle Vue

Despite the threats of the closure of Belle Vue the Spring Festival survived, but in reduced form. In 1981 and 1982 there were just two sections – Grand Shield and Senior Cup. In 1983 the Senior Cup section was suspended and the Grand Shield contest held in Rochdale. It returned to Belle Vue for a year, being held in the Cumberland Suite as the King's Hall, hitherto the venue for the Grand Shield section, was now closed. From 1985 the Spring Festival, down to the Grand Shield only, moved to the Free Trade Hall – home of the Hallé Orchestra and Manchester's principal concert venue.

The final contest in the King's Hall was not, in fact, one of Belle Vue's own contests, but the annual contest of the North West Brass Band Association, held in February 1982. Following the contest there was a pageant featuring three bands – Glossop School, Besses and Rochdale – which ended with an emotional audience singing *Auld Lang Syne*.[1]

On Harry Mortimer's death in 1992 there was much speculation as to the future of the former Belle Vue contests, of which he had become the owner. However, his widow, Mrs Margaret Mortimer, who had played a leading role in their organisation, took charge. In 1995 the Free Trade Hall closed down and the Spring Festival moved to Bolton, held in the Albert Hall for one year and thereafter in the Victoria Hall, a spacious Methodist chapel built in the shape of a concert hall, complete with tiered stage, balcony and gallery.

Mrs Mortimer died in December 1999. Just as she had assisted Harry, in turn she had been helped by their son, Martin. Helped by his wife Karyn, Martin now took over, organising the eightieth Spring Brass Band Festival in 2000 and continuing into the twenty-first century.

### The British Open Championships

Sponsorship was now becoming a lifeline to many contests. During the early 1980s the *Daily Mirror* sponsored the prize money for the British

---

[1] Information taken from a programme in the writer's collection.

Open, amounting to £5400. Harry and Margaret Mortimer were 'organisers and sponsors' in 1985 and 1986, whilst British Coal donated the prizes in the following two years. From 1989 prize monies were increased, the winner now receiving £3000. Yorkshire Bank provided the cash for three years and from 1994 sponsorship was by JJB Sports – a leading sports outfitters whose managing director, multi-millionaire David Whelan, was himself a former bandsman and a product of Wigan Boys' Club Band.

The British Open Championships were held at Belle Vue for the last time in 1981, after which the contest moved to the Free Trade Hall, preceding the Spring Festival by three years. Hawthorne City Band from Australia competed in the first Free Trade Hall British Open Championships, won by Besses o' th' Barn.

In 1991 a number of extra bands were invited. In addition to three from the May contest, Desford was invited in recognition of a London hat-trick and CWS (Glasgow) as reigning National Champions. A number of special awards also appeared, including the 'Mortimer Maestro Statuette'. A new one was presented each year to the conductor of the winning band. Though Harry Mortimer died in 1992 the Open continued, organised, like the Grand Shield, by Mrs Mortimer. It remained at the Free Trade Hall until its closure in 1995.

Then followed a trying period for Mrs Mortimer. The natural successor to the Free Trade Hall as Manchester's premier concert venue was the newly opened Bridgewater Hall, and the British Open Championships of 1995 were held there. Alas, it proved unsatisfactory on a number of counts. Mrs Mortimer then made the brave decision to take the competition away from Manchester where it had been based for 144 years. Her choice was another new venue, Symphony Hall in Birmingham. Having made the decision, booked the hall, invited the bands and commissioned the test piece, days before the event Her Royal Highness Princess Diana died in a Paris road accident. The funeral was on the very day that the Open was to have its baptism in Birmingham. There was no alternative but to postpone the contest. Rescheduled for Saturday, 17 January 1997, it was an enormous success and the nomadic years of the British Open Championships were ended.

Following Harry Mortimer's death a charitable trust was set up, with funds invested to provide rewards and to help perpetuate his memory. The first was a scholarship worth £500, presented annually to each of five students nominated by the universities and colleges which encouraged brass bands.[2] The other award, established in 1995, was the Mortimer

---

[2] These were the Universities of Salford and Huddersfield, the RNCM, the GSM and Barnsley College.

Medal, awarded by the Worshipful Company of Musicians for services to youth bands. The first recipient was Nigel Boddice, for his work with West Lothian Schools Band.[3] The presentations were made during the British Open Championships.

From 1996 a new marking scheme was introduced at the Open. Hitherto all bands had been given a mark out of 200. From now only the top six bands were to be awarded these, others simply being given their order of merit.[4]

The death of Margaret Mortimer was mentioned earlier. As was the case with the Grand Shield, her son and daughter-in-law, Martin and Karyn Mortimer, continued to organise the British Open Championships (Figure 10.1).

Appendix C gives the results of the British Open Championships from 1975 to 2000. Earlier results may be found in Taylor, 1979; Brand, 1979; and the Belle Vue results sheets. See also Read, 2002, for the complete results from 1853.

## The Nationals – times of change

It was now the turn of Robert Alexander, owner of the Nationals since 1976 (see page 101), to go bankrupt, meaning that the National Brass Band Championships were heavily in dept. Boosey & Hawkes came to the rescue in 1981, paid off the debts – reportedly some £67 000 – and took over ownership of the Nationals, appointing an advisory panel to look after the contest details. This panel comprised Bram Gay, Edward Gregson and William Relton. The National Contesting Council (NCC) was now formed, replacing the NBBCC of Vaughan Morris's day. There were two representatives from Boosey & Hawkes and one from each Area.

Changes during the early 1980s included the return of the box to the arena and the dropping of the 'lap of honour'. Up to this point, the winning band had returned to the platform to give a further performance of the test piece. This was now discontinued.

The format of the day of the National Championships at the start of the 1980s was that in the Royal Albert Hall the championship section ran from around nine o'clock, was followed by the Butlins Youth Championships from four in the afternoon, and in the evening there was

---

[3] Subsequent recipients of this award were Leighton Rich, Hampshire Youth Band (1996); Gordon Evans MBE, Campbeltown Schools Band (1997); Christopher Wormald, Smithills School Band, Bolton (1998); Lynda Nicholson, St Helens Youth Bands (1999); and Derek Greenwood, St Keverne Youth Band, Cornwall (2000).

[4] In truth, adjudicators continued awarding points to all bands but only the marks for the top six bands were published.

Figure 10.1   The most famous brass band family – Margaret, Martin and Harry Mortimer CBE, c. 1990

229

the gala concert. Sections 2, 3 and 4 were held in nearby halls. The European Championships were held in the Royal Albert Hall on the following day.

In 1983 there was a major turnaround. The European Championships were now to be held at a different time of the year. This released the Royal Albert Hall on the Sunday, making it available to British bands for the whole weekend. Further, Butlins were no longer involved in the Youth Championships. The new format of the weekend was that all senior sections were held in the Royal Albert Hall over two days, the championship section being held on Sunday afternoon. The youth section was held on the Sunday in the Royal College of Music, just a few hundred yards away from the Albert Hall. The concert took place, as usual, on Saturday evening.

However, there were two major disadvantages. Attractive as it was for lower-section bands to perform in the awe-inspiring hall, they commanded only very small audiences which, apart from the financial implications, failed to create any atmosphere. It also meant that the Saturday evening concert audience was greatly reduced as there were far fewer band people in London. Therefore, from 1986 sections 1–4 were again taken elsewhere, the Youth Championships returned to the Albert Hall and all events were again held on the Saturday. The one change from the pre-1983 format was that the youth section now commenced at nine o'clock, with the championship section following at around midday.

Meanwhile, in 1985 there had been a radical change in the Areas. There were now nine instead of eight, with some boundaries redefined in an attempt to even out the numbers of bands in the various areas. This was not wholly successful and in 1994 the eight-Area format was restored.

From 1988, in addition to the normal qualification of two bands from each Area, any Area which had two or more bands in the top ten in the previous year's Finals would have extra bands qualifying. This was a method of guaranteeing that more of the better bands qualified for the Finals whilst also ensuring a good line-up in the Areas.

A new set of rules drawn up by the NCC in 1991 allowed professional musicians to play in contests. This was a controversial issue but it solved the question of at what point (financially) a bandsman might be deemed to be a professional musician. Military bandsmen and professional orchestral players were now eligible to play in contests.

The next major change came in 1992, when an extra section was added, the sections now being designated Championship, first, second, third and fourth. Concurrent with this development, the Finals of sections 1–4 were taken to Wembley Conference Centre on a separate weekend and spread over two days. There was also, from 1992, a new North Wales region, but it existed for only three years, after which the whole of Wales was merged into one Area.[5] In 1993 the Youth Championships were separated from the London event. (This is discussed at length below – see page 232.)

Bill Martin had managed the Nationals on behalf of Boosey & Hawkes since they became the owners in 1981. In 1989 he retired and was succeeded by Anne Marie Sizer. From 1995, though Boosey & Hawkes retained ownership of the Nationals, management was handed to the NCC as representatives of the brass band movement. Boosey's pledged £25 000 per year in sponsorship and a group of businesses associated with bands was enlisted as joint sponsors.

An agreement between the NCC and the Welsh associations meant that, in line with England and Scotland, the Welsh champions would henceforth be determined by the Welsh Area contest rather than by the series of independent events (see page 118). A further change to the qualification rule meant that the four highest-placed bands in the Finals would automatically qualify for those of the following year, though this was dependent on them appearing in their respective Area contests.

From 1997 the NCC's control of the Nationals was extended, but with reduced sponsorship. However, in the year 2000 it was announced that the contract would not be renewed but that Philip Morris, secretary of the NCC, would continue as administrator.

Lower-section Finals remained in Wembley until 1995, after which the NCC elected to move them around; from 1996 to 1999 they were held in Cardiff, Harrogate, Birmingham and Nottingham. In 2000, the final year of the NCC's stewardship, all sections were held in the Royal Albert Hall and spread over three days, Friday to Sunday, in the special Millennium Finals. Thus, though ending in style, the expiry of the contract between Boosey's and the NCC, meant that the Nationals again faced an uncertain future.

Appendix D gives the results of the National Championships from 1975 to 2000. Earlier results may be found in Taylor, 1979; and Brand, 1979.

## Gala concerts

During the 1980s these became less lavish. More use was made of English soloists, guest conductors were generally associated with brass bands and three bands became the standard line-up – occasionally with a fourth. In 1981 one of the highlights was a group of Phillip McCann solos, accompanied by Black Dyke, conducted by Harry Mortimer. Two years later Elgar Howarth was guest conductor, with James Shepherd as soloist. The programme this year included a 'Tribute to Eric Ball', celebrating his eightieth birthday and conducting the finale, Parry's *Jerusalem*.

---

[5] Prior to this bands from North Wales competed in the North West of England.

The year 1984 saw a partial return to the spectacular, with three bands, the Bach Choir and conductor Sir David Willcocks, and with the Childs Brothers as guest performers. Other guest conductors featured during the 1980s included Howard Snell, who appeared four times, Bram Tovey and Geoffrey Brand.

Audiences dwindled as enthusiasm for the concerts waned and in the early 1990s the full-length evening concert gave way to a mini-concert, played between the end of the contest and the announcement of results. In 1997 an attempt was made to revive the evening concert, with Black Dyke, the ISB and a remarkable Australian soloist, James Morrison, who played a whole range of instruments to virtuoso standard. The concert, sponsored by Egon, proved to be a one-off. In 1999 a group of soloists provided the 'interlude' whilst in 2000 the mini-concert was provided by Cory (now 'Buy as You View Cory'), conducted by Robert Childs and featuring his son, David.

*Youth band championships*

For some time there had been concern that October – almost the start of a new school year – was not a good time for school bands to be involved in the Finals. Many pupils who had been in the bands which were successful in the Area contests had now left school and the bands of the new school year had barely had time to settle in. A new system was, therefore, introduced following the 1992 Youth Championships, with regional contests in November and December, and Finals at the RNCM in the following April. There were two sections, West Lothian Schools winning the Open section and Wardle High School winning the Junior section.

From 1994 qualifying rounds were dispensed with and the Finals taken to Salford University. The Championships now gave school bands adequate time to prepare. There were three sections – Open, Intermediate and Junior – with open adjudication and the event spread over two days. The maximum age for the Junior class was 16 and for the other classes 19. A year later an Advanced section was added, with the competition now under the control of the BBHT. With but small changes the same format continued through to 2000, when a record 39 bands competed in the four classes. During the Salford years winners of the Senior section were West Lothian Schools (1993, 1995, 1996 and 1998), Gwent County Youth (1994 and 1999), Hampshire Youth (1997) and St Helens Youth (2000).

## Other contests of national significance

### Solo and Quartet Championships

The Oxford series came to an end in 1981 but was relaunched in Wigan in 1988 as the 'British Open Solo and Quartet Championships', presented jointly by the British Open Brass Band Championships and Wigan Borough Council. For the first event 40 soloists and 28 quartets competed, prize-money totalling £2000. Winners were invited to perform at the conclusion of both the Grand Shield and the British Open contests. The winning soloist also competed in New Zealand for the International Musician of the Year Award, the trip being funded by the British Open Championships.

Interest gradually waned and the quartet section was suspended in 1992 and 1993; however, from 1992 there was a section for junior soloists. The support of the Wigan Council was withdrawn after 1993. Nevertheless, with support from Yorkshire Building Society, the Championships were presented at Salford University in 1995, after which they received sponsorship from Tameside Council and moved into the Stalybridge area, remaining there until the end of the century and beyond.

A list of winning quartets and soloists is given in Appendix E.

### Pontin's

Harry Mortimer was musical adviser to Pontin's almost from the beginning. Following his death in 1992 James Scott took over. In 1993 the highest section became known as the 'Harry Mortimer Memorial Championships' and the Easter preliminaries were now gradually scaled down. Nineteen-ninety-four saw the demise of the Hemsby contest and from 1995 all the Easter contests were scrapped. For the next two years the Prestatyn event was spread over two weekends but finally settled as a single weekend competition. The Pontin's contest never attracted the very top bands but there was always a good spread of bands from the middle range of the championship section and throughout the other sections. With accommodation for the whole weekend – from Friday evening to Monday morning – 'Pontin's' became the most important 'social' contest in the brass band calendar. In the year 2000 the top section was renamed 'the Harry and Margaret Mortimer Championships'.

### Brass in Concert

This competition was founded in 1977 by the tobacco company Rothman's on the site of a newly-opened factory in Darlington. It was run on similar lines to the Granada contest, but without television. Entry was by invitation and 12 leading bands each performed a short programme. Roy Newsome was appointed music adviser and he composed a march which each band was required to include in its programme.[6] Prize-money was generous for the time at £1000, £700, £400 and £150. The adjudication system was different from that at Granada, with two adjudicators seated together, screened from the bands, and awarding an agreed mark for quality of performance. There were three more adjudicators, assessing the entertainment value of the programme and its presentation. These were, in effect, representatives of the general public.

The contest had been intended as a one-off but the directors of Rothman's were so impressed that it became an annual event. From the second year the BBC recorded all the bands and broadcast a programme of highlights on *Listen to the Band*. Through generous sponsorship the organisers were able to add new features. The draws for order of play in 1979 and 1980 were made respectively by André Previn and Harry Mortimer. Gordon Langford was commissioned to make a new arrangement, to be included in all programmes. He did this for two years prior to handing over to Goff Richards. In 1980 the prize-money was almost doubled. By now there was also a special prize for the best soloist, to which several other 'specials' were added during the ensuing years. During the early 1980s there was a composer's competition to find the set test piece, with a prize of £200 and a broadcast of the winning piece.

From 1983 the competition moved into central Darlington. Sponsorship by Rothman's ended a year later and the competition now became known simply as 'Brass in Concert'. Supported by the Musicians' Union and the Tobacco Workers' Union, it was also sub-titled 'A Trades Union Festival'. In 1986 the competition's venue changed again – to the small County Durham town of Spennymoor.

The next development, begun in 1995, was an award of £500 for what was considered to be the best composition or arrangement written especially for a first performance at Brass in Concert. This resulted in a considerable widening of the 'new music' aspect of the competition and contributed significantly to the concert repertoire in the closing years of the century. Winners up to 2000 were as follows:

| | | | | | |
|---|---|---|---|---|---|
| 1977 | Grimethorpe | 1985 | Desford | 1993 | Grimethorpe |
| 1978 | Hammond's | 1986 | Grimethorpe | 1994 | Grimethorpe |
| 1979 | Grimethorpe | 1987 | Britannia BS | 1995 | Yorkshire Imperial |
| 1980 | Grimethorpe | 1988 | Britannia BS | 1996 | Fairey |
| 1981 | Grimethorpe | 1989 | Leyland DAF | 1997 | JJB Sports |
| 1982 | Desford | 1990 | Britannia BS | 1998 | Fodens (Courtois) |
| 1983 | Grimethorpe | 1991 | Leyland DAF | 1999 | Grimethorpe |
| 1984 | Desford | 1992 | BNFL | 2000 | Fodens (Courtois) |

6  The march was named *King Size* after one of Rothman's brand names.

*The All England Masters*

This contest was instituted in Cambridge in 1989 by Philip Biggs and Richard Franklin[7] and, as the title implies, is open to English bands only. Black Dyke is the one top English band not to have supported the contest.[8] Established test pieces are generally used, though the organisers have from time to time commissioned a new work.

From 1992 bands were allowed to vote on their choice of test piece from a prescribed list and from 1993 the organisers presented a 'Masters Dedicated Service Award', honouring outstanding work in the brass band movement. In 1997 a 'split draw' was introduced, whereby it was determined in advance which bands would perform early, which in the middle of the day and which towards the end. This helped bands sort out sensible travel arrangements in advance. The final draws were then taken in the usual manner. This idea was requested by the bands themselves, as was, from 1998, adjudicators located in separate 'boxes', with aggregate results based on placings, not on points. The following is a list of winners:

| | | | |
|------|-------------|------|-------------|
| 1989 | Leyland DAF | 1995 | Britannia BS |
| 1990 | Britannia BS | 1996 | Fairey |
| 1991 | Britannia BS | 1997 | Fairey |
| 1992 | BNFL | 1998 | Brighouse |
| 1993 | Brighouse | 1999 | YBS |
| 1994 | Britannia BS | 2000 | YBS |

## The European Championships

From 1981 Boosey & Hawkes sponsored the European Championships. In 1982 Brighouse & Rastrick refused to defend their title, won the previous year, maintaining that competing in both the Nationals and the European Championships on the same weekend placed unacceptable pressure on British bands. Black Dyke also threatened not to compete unless there was closed adjudication and the contest was run in two halves – that is, with bands playing the set test in one session and the own-choice piece in the other. These latter requests were granted; Black Dyke competed and won. Probably partly as a result of Brighouse's stance,

---

[7] Franklin was a former member of Cambridge and GUS bands.

[8] The only contests attended by Black Dyke are the Area, the National Championships and the British Open and, when qualifying, the European Championships. They do not attend entertainment contests and have so far not been to the All England Masters. The reason is that the band is in such great demand for concert work that it neither has the time nor sees the need to attend other contests.

from 1983 the event was separated from the London weekend and travelled around Europe, beginning in Kerkrade, Holland. There was rejoicing here when the Dutch band Soli Deo Gloria took 2nd prize, the highest placing of a European band up to that time. In 1994 a 'B' section was introduced to encourage competitors from countries not rich in brass bands.

The first non-British Band to win the 'European' was Norway's Eikanger Bjorsvik, which they did in two successive years – 1988 and 1989. The first continental band to win on British soil was Brass Band Willebroek, from Belgium, in 1993.

From 1998 competitions were instituted for young composers, soloists and conductors, one held each year, so creating a triennial sequence. By now, Boosey & Hawkes had placed the management of the championships in the hands of EBBA. EBBA, in turn handed over the running of the competition of 2000 in Birmingham to the BFBB. An important feature this year was the founding of a European Youth Band. Comprising two players from each of the 16 competing countries, the band played in the foyer prior to the start of the competition, on stage at the presentation ceremony and in the gala concert.

Winners of the European Championships, set tests and venues are shown in Appendix F.

### Other contests of some importance

A new contest was founded in Leeds in 1982. With sponsorship from the brewer Tetley (hence known as Tetley's Championships), administrative support from Leeds Leisure Services and £3000 in prize money, it held much promise. It took place in Leeds Town Hall and was followed by an evening concert featuring one or more leading bands. Early winners were City of Coventry, Yorkshire Imperial and Hanwell. However, sponsorship for the contest ceased in 1986 and it survived as The Leeds Open for just two more years.

A new contest was attempted in 1982, to find the 'Champion of Champions'. It took place in Manchester and set out to put together the current holders of the Open, Nationals, Granada and Rothmans titles. Owing to the difficulty of finding dates when all relevant bands were available, the contest ran for only two years, the winner on both occasions being Desford.

As part of the bicentenary celebration of 1988, the Australian Band Council arranged a contest in Sydney, billed as the World Championships. Leading bands from around the world expressed interest – on condition that sponsorship could be found to cover the enormous costs. In the event, most had to withdraw and, though 11 countries were represented in the competition, no elite bands were there from Britain. Gothenburg and Stavanger were the principal prizewinners.

A 'UK Entertainments Contest' was held in Doncaster in 1990. Though a 1st prize of £5000 was offered, the response from bands was disappointing. The event survived for only one more year, the respective winners being Britannia Building Society and Grimethorpe.

\* \* \*

It is apparent that contesting was thriving at all levels by the 1980s, perhaps benefiting from a range of new music created in the 1960s and 1970s. Entertainment contests became popular. Difficult from an adjudicating point of view and obviously posing problems for those charged with selecting the material to be played, these were popular with audiences – more so to the general listener than to the brass band purist. For the connoisseur the test piece contest still held the greatest attraction. Many established contests continued to flourish; the number of events was constantly increasing, as was the prize-money offered and the number of bands attending.

The European Championships were the single most significant event to be started during the late twentieth century. Moving around Europe, despite enormous costs to bands and visitors, they provide a range of events to supplement the actual contest and the title 'European Champions' has become a symbol of high achievement.

## Repertoire

As in the previous references to repertoire in Chapter 6 (see page 120), it is recommended that constant reference be made to Appendix G when reading the following.

### Original works 1981–90

In this period there was again an escalation in the number of works composed, with further new composers writing for the medium. Of those having already written for band, Bourgeois and Sparke contributed the largest number of new works. From Bourgeois, *Blitz* and *Diversions* were outstanding major test pieces whilst *A Barchester Suite*, based on music originally composed for a television series, was an excellent work playable by most bands. There was also a very fine *Trombone Concerto*. Of the Sparke series, *The Year of the Dragon, Variations on an Enigma* and *Harmony Music* were outstanding championship test pieces, whilst *Music for a Festival* was an excellent example of music composed with talented youth in mind. Sparke became one of the most prolific and most popular of all test piece composers. In addition to his writing, he was also music editor for Studio Music and conducted a number of bands, including Hanwell.

Edward Gregson produced two more fine test pieces, each more extended than earlier ones. In *Dances and Arias* he calls for the use of a second flügelhorn and in *Of Men and Mountains* he requires a special effect created by sliding the bow of a string bass across the edge of a cymbal. Both works demand a large array of percussion instruments (see page 65 for percussion requirements in the 1984 work).

Arthur Butterworth's compositions now took on much larger proportions than his earlier band pieces. A prolific writer of orchestral music, with five symphonies to his credit, much of his work is influenced by Nordic composers, including Sibelius and Nielsen. *Odin*, commissioned by Black Dyke, was selected as the test piece for the National Championships of 1989. His *Passacaglia on a theme of Brahms*, a Desford commission, was later used for testing first-section bands.

Other composers who returned to the band scene during these years include Heaton, Horovitz, Howarth and McCabe. The Heaton *Partita*, a very substantial work, was rediscovered by Howard Snell and first performed over 30 years after it had been written. Horovitz and McCabe each produced memorable test pieces for the National Championships whilst the 1982 Howarth piece, originally called *Requiem for RK*, was composed as a tribute to Rudolf Kempe, the great German orchestral conductor who died in 1976. Kempe was one of Howarth's musical idols; he was an authority on the music of Richard Strauss and the brass band work is a pastiche in the style of the great German composer.

Sir William Walton, though never actually composing for brass band, allowed Elgar Howarth to revise a section from his 1935 ballet, *The First Shoot*, using brass band instrumentation. It was premiered in this form at a Promenade Concert in 1981.

The musical career of George Lloyd (1913–98) was seriously interrupted during 1942 when he was badly shell-shocked whilst serving in an Arctic convoy. Not for some 30 years was he able to return to composing but he then produced a large amount of orchestral music. During the early war years he had played in a military band and this may have influenced his decision to accept a BBC commission to compose *Royal Parks* for the 1985 European Championships. This and his later brass band works have all retained their popularity. Two other mainstream composers who accepted commissions to write for band were Sir Michael Tippett (1983) and Richard Rodney Bennett (1989).

Gareth Wood, a string bass player in the Philharmonia, was a popular composer of lower-section test pieces, two of his commissions finding their way into the contest repertoire in 1981. His *Hinemoa* was commissioned for the 1979 New Zealand Championships, whilst *Margam Stones* was commissioned by the West Glamorgan Youth Brass Band. It was in a 1981 West Glamorgan composers' competition that Peter Graham achieved his first success. *Dimensions* was the winner of the competition and three years later was selected as a test piece. Graham was in the SA and for a time worked in New York as an editor and staff arranger. Therefore, his first intended competition piece did not appear for some time. *Essence of Time* (1990) was the first of a number of highly successful major test pieces.

The SA composer Ray Steadman-Allen (b. 1922) lived much of his life under the restrictions imposed by that organisation and, though he composed ceaselessly for the SA, works for contesting bands did not appear until the late 1980s.

Michael Ball (b. 1946) composed *Frontier* for the 1987 European Championships. He was, however, essentially a brass band composer of the 1990s as, indeed, was Peter Graham.

One work of a special nature which appeared during this decade was for organ and brass band. Called *The Fenlands*, it was commissioned and first performed by Cambridge Co-op under David Read. The organist and composer was Arthur Willis, organist of Ely Cathedral.

*Original works 1991–2000*

Michael Ball followed *Frontier* with three more brass band works during this final decade. His style was of the twentieth century but distinctly approachable. Peter Graham likewise had the facility to write enjoyable test pieces and had a particular penchant for writing good melodies. He made three further notable contributions to the test piece repertoire (in 1994, 1997 and 2000) but his innovative *Shine as the Light*, though sometimes played in contests, is essentially a concert item. Written as a tribute to a colleague who had died, it portrays the passage of the soul through death into everlasting light.

Bourgeois and Howarth both added to contest repertoire in the 1990s. Sparke also wrote two more test pieces, both works of a high calibre, as well as several more instrumental solos. Bourgeois and Graham also added to the solo repertoire. Gregson composed his spectacular *The Trumpets of the Angels* for seven solo trumpets, brass band, organ and percussion in 2000. Lloyd and Steadman-Allen each produced at least one further work of note during the decade whilst Wilfred Heaton, inspired by Snell and Britannia Building Society, composed two instrumental solos of immense stature – a *Sinfonia Concertante* for cornet and a *Trombone Concerto*.

Turning to composers not previously mentioned, David Bedford (b. 1937) responded to a 1998 NYBB commission with his *Requiem*, portraying his own feelings of frustration at being held up in a traffic jam, followed by feelings of shame when he learned that the hold-up was caused by the death of a child. Judith Bingham, also a mainstream composer, produced a number of brass band works during the 1990s, including *Prague* (1996) – a musical portrayal of the city's political problems. John Pickard, writing in a modern idiom, composed his band works primarily for the NYBBW and Cory's.

Three SA composers each made significant contributions to the contest repertoire – Robert Redhead, Kevin Norbury and Kenneth Downie. The latter wrote a series of lower-section test pieces before becoming composer-in-residence at YBS.

Howard Snell and Goff Richards, though contributing mainly through arrangements of lighter pieces (as well as some heavyweight transcriptions in the case of Snell), each wrote compositions of some note. Richards had composed his *Oceans* in 1984 but it was not popularised for almost a decade. *Images of the Millenium* by Snell used a unique scoring technique and required a double band.

Without doubt, the 'discoveries' of the decade were Philip Wilby and Martin Ellerby. Both were from the wider world of music, both heavily involved in teaching composition – Ellerby at the London College of Music and Wilby at the University of Leeds. Ellerby's works were very approachable and suitable for contest or concert, though they generally had quite demanding percussion parts. Wilby's introduction to the brass band movement was via an NYBB commission in 1990 which led to a sequence of major works spread throughout the 1990s and beyond.

Reminiscent of Gilbert Vinter, both in the regularity of the appearance of new works and in the way each one seems to develop from its predecessor, Wilby leads bands constantly into new musical territories. Technical demands are usually very high and he often injects spatial elements into the music, demanding that players move to different positions on the stage. In *Dove Descending* a recording of a blackbird singing is required in part of the work. He describes his *Revelation* as a 'Symphony for Double Brass' and calls for a special seating formation. There have been several references to the music of earlier composers, for example in *Paganini Variations*, and there is often a spiritual message in the music. Both Wilby and Ellerby have composed instrumental solos and both are able to write for more modest bands.

## Choral works

The combination of brass and voices has for long been popular but has chiefly been the result of transcriptions of songs or choruses from opera or oratorio. The first major such transcription was Denis Wright's working of the accompaniments to Handel's *Messiah* in 1946. The English composer Thomas Wood (1892–1950) composed a work for massed brass bands and men's chorus called *The Rainbow*. It was based on a story of the Dunkirk evacuation and was commissioned by the Arts Council for the Festival of Britain in 1951. Possibly the first work specially composed for brass band and voices, it was performed in the Royal Albert Hall on 12 May, conducted by Sir Adrian Boult.[9]

Appendix G lists a number of later works for brass band and voices, the most important of which was undoubtedly Vinter's *The Trumpets*. For further information on this, see page 190; and for information about the Sir Peter Maxwell Davies's 1985 work, see page 216.

## Transcriptions

At least three further large-scale transcriptions were added to the repertoire during this period – Elgar's *Enigma Variations*, transcribed by Eric Ball in 1983; Stephen Roberts's 1996 reworking of Holst's *The Planets;* and the orchestral accompaniments of Mozart's opera *The Magic Flute*, transcribed by Bram Gay in the early 1990s. Other significant contributions were the transcriptions of Ray Farr and Howard Snell. Edward Watson's transcriptions of some Walton incidental music were also quite notable. A revised version of Elgar's *Severn Suite* was made by Geoffrey Brand and broadcast by Fairey's, and a further version edited by Bram Gay appeared in 1996. Like the Brand version it was a tone higher than that of the original 1930 edition. It was selected as test piece for the 1996 British Open.

## Middle-of-the-road music

The 1980s saw further arrangements by Goff Richards and Howard Snell. (The 'arrangement' differs from the 'transcription' in that there is usually an element of originality on the part of the arranger in terms of structure, harmony and rhythm.) Amongst the successes of Richards were *Songs of the Quay, Shepherd's Song* and two winners in the European Broadcasting Union's competitions for new band pieces – *Continental Caprice* and *Country Scene*. Snell's pieces in this category included the

---

[9] For further detail see Grove, 5th edition, Vol IX, p. 360.

*Air from Bach's Suite No. 3* featuring cornets and flugelhorn, *Winter* from Vivaldi's *The Seasons* and short, snappy pieces by Shostakovich, Khatchaturian and Monti. There was a celebrated arrangement by Ray Farr of Leoncavallo's *On With the Motley*, surprisingly successful as a soprano cornet solo. In the 1990s Peter Graham emerged as one of the leaders in this field, with his *Alloway Tales, Cry of the Celts* and *Windows of the World* – all commissioned by David King and YBS. These are just a few examples of an ever-increasing library of middle-of-the-road music for band.

*Popular music*

The popularity of the selection now waned. *Music* by John Miles and arranged by Sparke, and Goff Richards's *Disney Fantasy* both enjoyed much success but there were few others.

During the 1980s Howard Snell's witty arrangements came to the fore. *Tea for Two* – complete with cups and saucers; Rossini's *Duet for Two Cats* – with cornet and trombone soloists wooing each other; and *Love's Old Sweet Song* – in which the flugelhorn soloist pointed the instrument into the bell of a bass whilst the bass player moved the valves quickly up and down giving a kind of balalaika effect, were just three of them. Their visual and novelty effects made them ideal choices in entertainment contests.

Ray Farr was another successful arranger. Amongst his arrangements were *Holiday for Strings* – featuring the cornets; the pop group Sky's version of Bach's *Toccata in D Minor*; and Morricone's *The Good, the Bad and the Ugly*. Several other hits appeared, including Freddy Mercury's *Bohemian Rhapsody*, arranged by Darrol Barry; *Love Changes Everything* – American Stephen Bulla scoring one of many Lloyd Webber favourites; and *River Dance* – Bill Whelan's enormously successful offering, the band version made by Ray Farr. Wright & Round published a collection of film music, including *Jurassic Park, Star Trek, Mission Impossible, Batman the Movie* and, as the century came to a close, *Braveheart*. There were spectacular hymn tune settings by Wilby and Richards, and solos and instrumental features galore.

## Conclusion

The above constitutes a somewhat inadequate survey of brass band music of the last 20 years of the twentieth century. It would be foolish to say that all music published during this period was of outstanding quality, but a great deal of it was highly accomplished in content and imagination.

The divide between middle-of-the-road and popular music was becoming difficult to identify and with so many quality writers contributing to the serious and the non-serious repertoire the discerning conductor had a great deal of choice. Away from Britain, writers such as Aagaard Nielsen (Norway), Jan Van der Roost (Belgium), Jan de Haan (Holland) and Brenton Broadstock (Australia) all contributed significant pieces to brass band repertoire. There was also now a great deal of material from American writers. Indeed, writing for brass band had become truly international.

# CHAPTER 11

# Bands and their activities, and band personalities

## Banding in the 1980s and 1990s

Yet again, brass bands endured mixed fortunes during the early 1980s, many losing their sponsorships. Some found alternative support, some survived without, but a large number were disbanded. Several contests were cancelled through lack of support, as bands had to count the cost of attending such events.

One of the most serious situations imaginable was the discovery in 1981 that the National Championships were in danger of being abandoned (see page 228). Boosey & Hawkes came to the rescue and, though not everyone sees eye to eye with their managerial decisions, the backing of such a major company has brought stability and security to one of the movement's most prized institutions.

Many bands suffered during the 1980s through a phenomenon known as 'rate capping'. As a result of this, whilst many householders and certain organisations received rebates on their local taxes, bands were taxed to the limit on their rehearsal premises. In time some overcame the problem by becoming registered charities.

There were also problems for school bands when the Education Act of 1988 decreed that individual schools should henceforth provide funding. Severe cuts followed and in many cases instrumental lessons were terminated. Further, schools tended to buy only the smaller and therefore cheaper instruments, to the exclusion of the more costly larger ones. In 1998 the National Schools Band Association held a conference to consider instrumental teaching in schools. There were now 12 000 fewer children learning to play a musical instrument than three years earlier. The new National Curriculum placed little value on music and whilst interested middle-class parents were prepared to pay for lessons many under-privileged children lost out. Following pressure from the music industry and the profession, music was reinstated as a core curriculum subject.

Brodsworth Colliery was amongst the bands which now disappeared. It had represented Britain in the 1983 European Championships but collapsed in the aftermath of the 1988 strike; a decade later Kennedy's Swinton Concert Brass (see page 270) was disbanded through the withdrawal of sponsorship. The recession deepened and rampant unemployment created further hardships for bands throughout the length and breadth of the country. Imperial Metal Industries, Jaguar and the DAF vehicle manufacturers all withdrew the sponsorships of their bands during 1991 and 1992. Happily, these bands were able to find alternatives, but many others which lost their sponsors simply had to survive without.

Pit closures in 1992 were extremely serious for bands. Some 30 collieries were closed down, including Grimethorpe and Carlton Main. At Grimethorpe, 18 band members worked at the pit and were made redundant. However, this band was lucky as, because of its high profile, the Coal Board continued to support it. Though despondent about the future, the band won the 1992 Nationals in the most emotionally charged contest in living memory.[1]

In contrast to these seemingly insurmountable social problems so closely interwoven with the political life of the nation, the musical progress of bands was abundantly evident. A new generation of players, conductors and composers worked alongside and built on the foundations laid by those mentioned in Chapter 7.

Many bands benefited through grants from various arts bodies and for the elite bands there were generous sponsorships, high-class engagements and tours, and a pool of gifted players. The gulf between those and the remainder seemed to be widening, but these better bands were gaining respect from the musical world at large, as they made music in ever-widening styles and to different types of audiences.

Several bands emerged in the upper echelons of bands at this time which have previously been mentioned only en passant. Though they are discussed in some detail below, to avoid confusion here are some initial facts. Britannia Building Society Band grew from what could have been the ashes of Foden's. Its conductor, Howard Snell, was also connected with Desford Colliery, which was to become a leading band in the 1980s. The Yorkshire-based Hammonds Sauce Works Band was mentioned on page 139 as the band that Geoffrey Whitham took on after leaving Black Dyke in 1965. This band had a somewhat chequered history before becoming the Yorkshire Building Society Band – a pacemaker in the latter part of the century. As was seen earlier, Richard Evans left Fairey's for the relatively unknown Leyland Vehicles Band, a band which was to have a colourful history under various sponsorships.

Moving to two bands which did not quite reach the 'Top Ten' but which nevertheless won major titles: W.B. Hargreaves, as was seen on page 158, left Brighouse in order to concentrate on a band in Bristol. This was the Stanshawe Band, formed in 1972 and later to become known as Sun Life.

---

[1] There is a good account of the aftermath of pit closures in *BB* of 31 September 1992, p. 3.

This band had a brief but successful history. Finally to Marple; this was literally a village band that enjoyed a fairy-tale existence for a few years. These bands are all discussed below.

### The 'Top Ten' bands 1981–2000

*Table 11.1    The 'Top Ten' bands 1981–2000*

|    |                            | Prizes won | | | |
|----|----------------------------|-----|-----|-----|--------|
|    |                            | 1st | 2nd | 3rd | Points |
| 1  | Black Dyke Mills           | 9   | 11  | 1   | 50     |
| 2  | Fairey Aviation            | 5   | 7   | 6   | 35     |
| 3  | Desford Colliery           | 4   | 2   | 1   | 17     |
| 4  | Grimethorpe Colliery       | 3   | 1   | 6   | 17     |
| 5  | Foden's/Britannia Bdg Soc. | 1   | 5   | 4   | 17     |
| 6  | Cory's                     | 5   | –   | –   | 15     |
| 7  | Hammonds Sauce/YBS         | 2   | 3   | 2   | 14     |
| 8  | Brighouse & Rastrick       | 2   | 3   | 1   | 13     |
| 9  | Leyland/BNFL/JJB           | 1   | 3   | 4   | 13     |
| 10 | CWS (Glasgow)              | 2   | –   | 2   | 8      |

Despite the proliferation of contests of national significance, the Nationals and the British Open Championships remained the ultimate hallmarks of achievement and it is from the results of these that the top ten bands have again been determined (Table 11.1). Several bands underwent name changes and the totals given include prizes won between 1981 and 2000 under all their different names. As in Tables 2.1 and 7.1, the figures here are based on three points for a win, two for a 2nd prize and one for a 3rd. Though Black Dyke and Fairey's remain in the top two places, five new names appear – Desford, Cory's, Hammonds, Leyland and CWS (Glasgow).

GUS, Yorkshire Imperial, Carlton Main and Wingates were still active and will be reviewed later, but other bands had moved up to take their places in the hierarchy. There were also some name changes. CWS (Manchester) was in its death throes at the start of the 1980s and by 1984 the Board of Directors was considering withdrawing the sponsorship. The band made its final contest appearance in the Area contest of 1985, giving its last concert in March. The remnants of the band became the City of Manchester Band, making its only appearance at the British Open

Championships under that name in the same year. By 1991 it was in the third section, a year later was down 14 members and soon faded.

Though the bands in the table undoubtedly were the top ten based on the given statistics, their respective overall reputations by the year 2000 were not necessarily in the order indicated. Black Dyke was certainly the biggest box-office attraction, but in terms of engagements attracted and versatility Grimethorpe were close rivals. Fairey's remained a powerful force, but were later rivalled by YBS, whose seemingly modest ranking conceals the fact that its successes were achieved during the later years of the period. Foden's/Britannia Building Society built an excellent reputation in concerts and were adept in a wide range of styles, from the most serious avant-garde composition to light-hearted and highly entertaining 'lollipops'. Leyland also had an enviable reputation as a concert band, their forte undoubtedly coming under the heading of 'entertainment'. Brighouse, though perhaps less versatile, well merited a place in the table, while Cory's, after a dip in the middle years of the period, made a late bid for competition glory and were to come very much to the fore. Desford Colliery, after a brilliant start, had an odd kind of existence during the closing years of the period whilst CWS (Glasgow), though maintaining a quality band, were not well-placed geographically in terms of concert engagements and this was reflected in their perceived status. The following reviews are made in the order of contest ranking, but they attempt also to paint a wider picture of each band's activities and personnel.

## Black Dyke Mills

Black Dyke again topped the list of competition winners by a substantial margin. There were five wins at the British Open and four at the Nationals. In the new European Championships, Black Dyke won for four years in succession from 1982 to 1985 and again in 1987, 1990 and 1991. Their peak year was in 1985, the band winning the Yorkshire Area, the European Championships, the British Open and the Nationals, and also being declared 'BBC Band of the Year'. There were three major overseas tours – Japan in 1984 and 1990, and Australia in 1988 – whilst European countries visited included Spain, Austria, Switzerland and Holland. From 1986 the band became known as John Foster Black Dyke Mills Band.

There was a succession of resident conductors during the 1980s, including Trevor Walmsley, Derek Broadbent, David Hirst and Kevin Bolton. Phillip McCann and John Clough, both long-serving key players, left in 1988 and were replaced by Roger Webster and Robert Childs. Peter Parkes remained as professional conductor until 1989.

From his entry into brass bands in 1975, Peter Parkes became one of the most successful contest conductors of all times. The European

Championships took on increased significance and between 1975 and 2000 Parkes collected 21 titles from the Nationals, the Open and the European. He was probably the most sought-after brass band conductor throughout the 1980s. For example, he conducted five bands in the Area contests of 1984 – Grimethorpe, Fairey's, Whitburn, Ever Ready and Ransome's, all of which qualified for the Finals. This was in addition to Black Dyke, given a bye in its Area, but with which in the same year he obtained a win in the European Championships and 2nd prizes at both the Open and the Nationals.

Parkes was succeeded at Black Dyke by David King. He was an Australian who, in 1982, came to England to study at Salford and, two years later, on completion of his studies, became a lecturer at the College. Soon after his arrival he joined the solo cornet section of Black Dyke. Having been the Australian Cornet Champion in 1981, he was North of England Solo Champion in the years 1984–85–86 and when the British Open Solo Championships were founded in 1988 he had an immediate impact, becoming Cornet Champion in five successive years from 1988 to 1992. In this last year, as the British Open Solo champion, he flew to New Zealand and won the title 'International Brass Musician of the Year'. Passionately interested in conducting, King built the highly successful but short-lived Kennedy's Swinton Concert Brass before, in 1989, becoming the youngest ever professional conductor of Black Dyke and leading the band to its European titles of 1990 and 1991.

Phillip McCann's successor at Black Dyke, Roger Webster, began his playing career with Grimethorpe Juniors. He played with a number of South Yorkshire bands, including Grimethorpe, before being appointed principal cornet player of Carlton Main in 1983. In 1987 he became the North of England Solo Champion whilst playing principal cornet with Brighouse. He remained with Black Dyke from 1988 until 1993 when, already in demand both at home and abroad, he left in search of a solo career. Despite a contract with CWS (Glasgow) in 1993, his solo career blossomed and he produced several solo CDs. In the year 2000 he returned to Black Dyke, having built a reputation as one of the finest soloists of his era.

John Clough was replaced by Morgan Griffiths (see 'Personalia') but from 1992 Robert Childs was Black Dyke's solo euphonium player. Born in South Wales where his father conducted Tredegar Town Band, Childs began his playing career in Tredegar Juniors, graduated into the seniors and became a member of the NYBB. Leaving Tredegar, he played successively with GUS, Grimethorpe, Hammonds and Brighouse & Rastrick before joining Black Dyke, where he also became assistant conductor. In 1990, as an instrumental teacher in Hull, Childs formed and conducted the City of Hull Band – later named EYMS (see Glossary).

In May 2000 he resigned from Black Dyke to become musical director of Cory's.

In 1992 David King was replaced at Black Dyke by James Watson. This heralded a somewhat turbulent period when, following the dismissal of two players, several others resigned. A period of rebuilding ensued. Later in the year the band visited Sierre Leone. Though the tour was successful musically, the band left in haste just before a coup which led to looting and general lawlessness, and the deposition of the president.[2] A highlight for the band in 1993 was a visit to New York to perform in the prestigious Carnegie Hall and to give masterclasses at the renowned Julliard School of Music.

Watson's personal 'double' as Junior Champion and Champion Soloist of Great Britain (see page 110) remained unique in the history of the two competitions, as did the sequence of Junior Solo Champion titles in 1965–66–67–68. He was principal cornet player with Desford Colliery Band until 1971, after which he held a similar position with the newly formed City of London Band (see Glossary), whilst studying at the Royal Academy of Music. On completion of his studies he became principal trumpet with the Royal Philharmonic Orchestra, later also joining the PJBE.

A highly successful professional trumpet player, Watson also became keenly interested in brass band conducting. After 'guesting' with a number of bands his first important appointment was as professional conductor of Brighouse & Rastrick, from 1983. He resigned in 1986 due to commitment clashes with his position as principal trumpet at the Royal Opera House. From 1987 he conducted Desford, leading his former band to its four National titles (see page 253).

James Watson was principal conductor of Black Dyke from 1992 to 2000. He helped secure changes in the management structure of the band and guided it through the trauma of the loss of support when the firm of John Foster & Son plc closed down in 1994. In concerts he featured both traditional music and music in the big band idiom, and also featured himself as trumpet soloist. He procured several television contracts for what had now become The Black Dyke Band. He also helped add more titles to his own and the band's lists. Other bands to benefit from Watson's experience included Parc & Dare, Sun Life, the NYBB and the NYBBW.

Black Dyke's colourful history continued and after the unfortunate demise of the parent company – a further reflection of Britain's economic plight – the band gratefully accepted the backing of Bradford & Bingley Building Society (reportedly £210 000 over a three-year period). Another peak in the competitive field was reached in 1995, the band winning the European, British Open and National Championships – a mere three years after the start of the rebuilding process.

---

2 See *BB* of 13 June 1992, p. 8 for further detail.

In 1996 composer Philip Wilby became a musical associate, advising on musical matters such as commissions, and occasionally conducting. He was joined a year later by the composer Peter Graham. In this year, the band became band-in-residence at the Royal Academy of Music (where Watson was a trumpet professor). Residencies such as this took on a variety of forms. There would be occasional concerts in the establishment concerned, and master classes given to students by leading members of the band.

Watson resigned in 2000 and Nicholas Childs (see pages 257–8), brother of Robert, became principal conductor. Sponsorship by the Bradford & Bingley Building Society ceased at this time but Black Dyke won 2nd prize in the Nationals – a good start with the new conductor.

*Fairey Aviation*

Across the Pennines, Fairey Engineering Works Band also faced conductor changes during the 1980s, being led in turn by W.B. Hargreaves, Geoffrey Brand, Howard Williams, Roy Newsome and Peter Parkes. Brian Broadbent resigned as resident conductor in 1983 and amongst his successors were Kevin Bolton, Alan Lawton (a long-serving cornet player at Fairey's) and Garry Cutt (see page 254). In addition, Denzil Stephens conducted at the 1983 Nationals. In this same year the band appeared in the Hong Kong Music Festival, giving the premiere of a new work by Sir Michael Tippett, *Festal Brass with Blues*, under the orchestral conductor Howard Williams.

In 1985 there was a name change to Williams Fairey Engineering Band, Williams now being the name of the parent company. In the major contests Fairey's produced two winning performances during the 1980s – at the 1986 Nationals and the 1987 Open (Figure 11.1). In 1987 it celebrated its fiftieth anniversary with visits to Holland, Germany and Switzerland, and with the award of the title 'BBC Band of the Year'. This title was awarded again in 1989. At around this time Newsome left, and was replaced by Peter Parkes.

In 1991 Phillip McCann returned as principal cornet player, a position he had held earlier before moving to Black Dyke. He also took on the role of resident conductor, but left later in the year due to pressure of other commitments. Derek Broadbent now became resident conductor. Under Parkes, Fairey's took the Open and National titles in the autumn of 1993 and completed a 'triple' by becoming European Champions in the following spring. The band was now renamed Williams Fairey Band. In 1995 Peter Graham was appointed composer-in-residence and Bryan Hurdley resident conductor. Hurdley was a former student of Birmingham School of Music and an accomplished euphonium player. He had also served as resident

Figure 11.1  Williams Fairey celebrates its 1986 Nationals win outside the Royal
Albert Hall

conductor with Sun Life (see page 271). Peter Parkes was now succeeded
as professional conductor by James Gourlay.

A product of the Scottish brass band scene, Gourlay had played as a
boy in Tullis Russell Band. In 1974, after studies at the Royal College of
Music, he became principal tuba player with the CBSO, five years later

transferring to the BBC Symphony Orchestra. He was also a member of the PJBE. He began his conducting with the brass band of the London College of Music and by 1987 was conducting both Hanwell and BTM (see Glossary). A year later he moved to Switzerland to join the orchestra of Zurich Opera, also becoming principal conductor of the highly successful Brassband Berner Oberland (BBO). By 1995 Gourlay was back in Britain. He appeared as guest conductor with the NYBB and the NYBBW and towards the end of the year became the principal conductor of Fairey's.

Here he had early successes in the Area contests. At national level there was a win at the British Open in 1998, following 2nd prizes at the 1995 Open and in both major contests of 1997. Other highlights of the Gourlay years included wins at Brass in Concert in 1996 and the All England Masters in 1996 and 1997. Away from Fairey's, Gourlay worked for a time with Stavanger Brass in Norway, leading them to victory at the Norwegian Nationals in 1998. In this same year he became Director of Brass Studies at the RNCM.

Gourlay remained with Fairey's until December 2000, when he was succeeded by Howard Snell. In 1997 composer Martin Ellerby joined Peter Graham and yet another composer, Rodney Newton, took on a new role, as 'co-ordinator of light music'. Andrew Duncan, the Hallé Orchestra's principal tubist and an up-and-coming composer/arranger joined forces with the band in 1999. Fairey's toured Sweden in 1996, Switzerland in 2000 and also mounted the highly successful Acid Brass concerts and CD (see page 278).

*Desford Colliery*

Desford is located in Leicestershire. Ernest Woodhouse and Albert Chappell were amongst the band's early conductors. It was then conducted from 1977 to 1987 by Howard Snell, highlights in traditional contests during this period being a win in the European Championships of 1986 and 2nd prizes at the 1979 British Open and the 1985 Nationals. However, these years brought even greater success in entertainment contests, with wins in Granada Band of the Year, the BBC series *Best of Brass* and a hat trick at Brass in Concert.

Solo euphonium player Steven Mead was a key figure at Desford during these years and was to become an important person worldwide in the recognition of his instrument. A graduate of Bristol University, Mead first came to attention with the Stanshawe Band in 1983 when voted the most popular soloist in *Best of Brass*. He played for Desford from 1984 to 1989, whilst also taking on important teaching appointments and overseas engagements. He regularly visited all the principal European brass band centres as well as the USA, Canada, Japan and New Zealand. He also made several solo CDs. In 1991 Mead formed the British Tuba Quartet (comprising two euphoniums and two tubas) which performed serious compositions and transcriptions as well as lightweight pieces which relied on slick presentation as much as virtuoso playing. In 1993, along with Roger Webster, Mead became attached to the CWS (Glasgow) Band.

Kevin Dye was Desford's principal cornet player during the early Snell years. He was both a fine leader and a noted soloist. Having been Champion Soloist of Great Britain in 1977 prior to joining Desford, he went on to become CISWO's Champion Soloist in 1981 and 1982, and to win the soloist's prize at Brass in Concert a year later. He was succeeded as principal cornet player by Martin Winter (see 'Personalia').

Desford's most productive period in straight contests came under Snell's successor, James Watson, who led them to a hat-trick at the Nationals in 1987–88–89. Here was another well-travelled band, with trips to Germany, Norway, Switzerland, Holland, Austria and Belgium, in 1989 a concert tour in Russia and in the following year a visit to the USA. As a result of sponsorship changes, the band was known from 1981 as Desford Colliery Dowty and from 1989 as Desford Colliery Caterpillar.

The 1990s began well for Desford with a triumphant return and a win at the Nationals in 1991 bringing it, effectively, four wins in succession. Following Watson's departure in 1992, a professional french horn player, Stephen Roberts (see 'Personalia'), was appointed as his successor, leading the band to second place in the Nationals of 1992.

Financial problems saw the band on the brink of folding in 1994 and the word 'Caterpillar' disappeared from its name. However, there was an upturn in the following year – musically with the assistance of Peter Parkes and Ray Farr, and financially with sponsorship from Coal Investments plc. Nevertheless, the second half of the 1990s saw Desford facing perpetual financial problems and the break-up of the band's normal social structure. Instead of 28 permanent members the band had about half of that number and called upon other players to bring it up to full strength for contests, tours and other special engagements. Some of these were ex-members who had turned professional but who wished to continue their banding on an occasional basis. There were three European tours during 1996, a visit to America in the following year and in 1999 a tour encompassing Singapore and Thailand. The band's hey-day in major contests was now over, though they won the premier class in the Kerkrade competition of 1997.

Long term, Desford was a powerful force at Area level; despite five byes owing to successes in the Finals, they were winners eight times during 1981–2000.

*Grimethorpe Colliery*

Returning to Yorkshire: Grimethorpe Colliery Band became one of the most successful of all bands on the concert platform. Its former obsession with changing conductors abated somewhat during the 1980s with Ray Farr remaining as resident conductor until 1984, then a four-year residency by David James (see 'Personalia') and two years under John Anderson, a former Opera North timpanist, seeing it through until 1990. Elgar Howarth remained as musical adviser but Geoffrey Brand, Howard Snell and Peter Parkes were also involved, particularly in contests. The band travelled less frequently during the 1980s, though in 1982 there was a month-long tour of Australia. Also, in 1989 Grimethorpe played in the Berlin Music Festival and in the following year spent some time in the Orkneys. The only major contest win during the 1980s was at the British Open of 1984, conducted by Geoffrey Brand.

In 1991 Garry Cutt was appointed resident conductor, a position he held until well into the twenty-first century. As a young bandsman Cutt had been a cornet player, playing with CWS (Manchester) in its closing years, and was also a student at Salford in the early days of its Band Studies course. From 1981 he was resident conductor of Wingates and in 1983 became musical director of Marple. After spells with Fairey's and JSVB, he became resident conductor of Yorkshire Imperial. His first major contest success was leading the fledgling Kennedy's Swinton Concert Brass to victory in the 1989 British Open Championships, becoming the youngest winning conductor in the history of the contest and the first recipient of the Mortimer Maestro Award. He had a long-standing commitment to Marple, directing their title-winning performance in the 1996 Open.

As resident conductor at Grimethorpe, Cutt conducted most of the band's concert engagements and occasionally directed the band in contests, leading them to victory at Brass in Concert in 1993, 1994 and 2000. However, he preferred the freedom to conduct other bands, which the engagement of a 'professional' at Grimethorpe facilitated, and he did this with much success, both in Britain and overseas. In 1995 he was conducting Stavanger in Norway and Flowers Gloucester (see Glossary), and in 2000 led Sandefijord to victory in the Norwegian Championships.

Nineteen-ninety-one was a momentous year for Grimethorpe, with a five-day engagement in Cologne and a win at the British Open Championships under the newly appointed professional conductor, Frank Renton. Nineteen-ninety-two was the year of the big shut-down by British Coal (see page 207). However, the band proceeded to win the National Championships – again under Renton – and continued independently, retaining its instruments and music library (Figure 11.2).

Figure 11.2 Grimethorpe Colliery, 1992 National Champions, being photographed by the 'National Press' – who were more concerned with the impending closure of the pit and the possible demise of the band than with its outstanding musical achievement

As a youth Frank Renton had played the cornet in Black Dyke, later taking up the trumpet and, after studies at the RNCM, joining the army. He won the NABBC's Young Conductor's competition in 1966 and did some freelance conducting during the early 1970s. His first important appointment came in 1977 when he became musical director of Wingates and later of the JSVB. Meanwhile, he had become Director of Music of the Band of the Parachute Regiment. During 1978 he conducted some concerts with Grimethorpe, but remained with JSVB until early in 1979, when his name was associated with two more bands – CWS (Manchester) which he took to the British Open, and then Roneo (Hanwell) where he became musical director.

In 1982 Renton became Director of Music of the Royal Artillery Mounted Band and two years later took over the regiment's renowned Woolwich Band. Promoted to lieutenant colonel, in 1987 he took the army's top musical job as Director of Music of the Royal Military School of

Music (Kneller Hall). Lieut.-Col. Renton was musical director of Grimethorpe from 1988 to 1993.

Following the Grimethorpe tenure he worked with a number of bands, in particular conducting Desford in the late 1980s. He retired from the army in 1992, by which time he had become professional conductor at Kirkintilloch (see Glossary). In 1999 he became professional director of Stavanger Band in Norway. Frank Renton was also a well-known adjudicator, broadcaster and writer.

Back with Grimethorpe, Garry Cutt took the band to its contests in 1994, securing wins at CISWO and Brass in Concert, following a tour in Switzerland and Germany. During the next year formal sponsorship was secured from British Coal. The second half of the 1990s saw much activity, largely due to the success of the film *Brassed Off* (see page 277). This attracted worldwide attention, leading to radio, television and recording contracts and several tours. There was a five-day tour of France and Germany in 1997 and a week in Paris in the following year. A 23-day tour of Japan and Australia was partly due to the success of the film in both countries. There was a further Japanese tour in 2000 and the award of a Gold Disc for UK sales of the *Brassed Off* record.

A new sponsor was acquired in 1998 and the band became Grimethorpe Colliery RJB Band. Also in this year the band became the ensemble-in-residence at the Royal College of Music and (in contrast) performed during the interval at the Eurovision Song Contest.

Alan Morrison was the principal cornet player of Grimethorpe for over a decade. He had held several similar appointments with bands in the North East but moved to Grimethorpe in 1982. A former leader of the NYBB, he first made his mark by becoming the Solo Champion of Great Britain in 1977. As a result of this, he enjoyed two trips to Australia, first competing in the Queensland solo championships and then for the Australian 'Champion of Champions' title, both of which he won. He recorded the first of several solo albums in 1983, being one of the first brass band soloists to do so. He was in great demand as a teacher and in 1995 issued a video course on Cornet Technique. Morrison was also an able composer and conductor, and was becoming a respected adjudicator. In the later 1990s he took up conducting, directing Sellers, BTM and two Norwegian bands. However, in 1999 he returned to his cornet playing as principal with JJB Sports.

*Fodens/Britannia Building Society*

Moving now into Cheshire: at the beginning of the 1980s the famous band was still known as Foden's Motor Works. However, as was seen in Chapter 7, the parent company went bankrupt. Fortunately, as with

Grimethorpe, the band was allowed to continue using the instruments and the music library. In 1983 Foden's found a new benefactor, Richard Carlton Tickell, who agreed to sponsor it through his company, Overseas Technical Services. It was therefore renamed Foden OTS Band. Foden OTS had an auspicious start, playing on Buckingham Palace forecourt, by Royal Command.

Howard Snell was now musical director and John Hudson became principal cornet player. He had been with CWS (Manchester), first as assistant to Derek Garside and then as principal. In 1977 he became principal cornet player with Leyland and in 1983 moved to Foden's, where there was promise of some conducting as assistant to Snell. By 1988 Hudson's conducting reputation was spreading and he did some work in Norway.

Tragically, Richard Tickell died within weeks of signing the agreement with the band. It was, nevertheless, honoured, until its expiry in 1986, after which the band acquired another sponsor, becoming the Britannia Building Society Foden Band. To the consternation of the brass band world the name 'Foden' was dropped in 1988.

The all-out win at the top level eluded the band, though it took 2nd prizes at the Nationals in 1988, 1990 and 1991. However, Snell's flair for arranging and his achievements in entertainment contests were of great benefit to 'Britannia' and from 1987 there were regular successes in major entertainment contests. Nineteen-ninety proved to be a peak contesting year, with wins at Brass in Concert, the UK Entertainment Contest and the All England Masters, plus a 2nd prize in the Nationals. The band also earned the title BBC Band of the Year.

The early 1990s were good years, with highly acclaimed concerts and recordings, further successes in entertainment contests, 2nd prize in the Nationals of 1991 and a win at the European Championships in the following year. Also in 1992 Philip Wilby was appointed composer-in-residence (the earliest such appointment). Britannia again won the All England Masters title in 1994 and 1995.

Following Snell's departure in 1996, Phillip McCann took over. In 1997 fellow Scotsmen Alan Fernie and Andrew Duncan became respectively arranger- and composer-in-residence. However, later in the year a double change was announced when, following a new sponsorship by the French instrument makers Antoine Courtois, Nicholas Childs was appointed musical director and the band became 'Fodens (Courtois)'.

Nicholas Childs was the younger brother of Robert and like him, played with Tredegar Juniors, Tredegar Town Band and the NYBB. On leaving Tredegar he played with Brodsworth, Carlton Main and Yorkshire Imperial before succeeding Robert as principal euphonium with Grimethorpe in 1982. In 1988 he took up a similar position with Britannia Building Society, staying until 1993, when he became resident conductor of YBS, before returning to Britannia – now Fodens (Courtois) – as musical director. He had also conducted several other bands, including Ever Ready, Desford and Wingates, and had notable successes as professional conductor of Tredegar.

The respective entries of the Childs brothers into conducting at the top level is the stuff of which fairy tales are made. In 1999 Nicholas led Fodens to 1st prize in the Nationals and then in 2000 Robert led Cory's to the double, winning both the Open and the Nationals, with Nicholas taking 2nd prize in the British Open – this time conducting Black Dyke, of which he had become principal conductor earlier in the year.

Fodens (Courtois) were passing through a relatively golden patch, with a 3rd prize in the 1997 Nationals, 2nd at the Open and a win at Brass in Concert a year later, and in 1999 its first win at the National Championships since 1958.

Under Childs, Barrie Forgie took over the arranging residency; he was conductor of the BBC Big Band and made a number of spectacular arrangements in big band style for Foden's. In 1999 the band became ensemble-in-residence of the University of Leeds. Following an impressive centenary concert and the departure of Childs in 2000, Bramwell Tovey became the band's professional conductor and Bryan Hurdley resident conductor, though Ray Farr was engaged to take Foden's to Brass in Concert. His flair for this type of concert brought its reward – 1st prize (Figure 11.3).

After studies at the University of London and the Royal Academy of Music, Tovey made his professional conducting debut in 1975, though it was not until 1986 that he attracted international attention by conducting the opening concert of an LSO Festival – at 24 hours' notice. Appointments with Scottish Ballet, Sadler's Wells and D'Oyly Carte followed. From 1989 he was Artistic Director of the Winnipeg Symphony Orchestra but was also regularly appearing as guest conductor with several major British orchestras. In 1999 he became music director of the Vancouver Symphony Orchestra.

Tovey's interest in brass bands stems from his SA background and the fact that he played tuba professionally for a short time before taking up the baton. He received his brass band conducting baptism with Hanwell, being their professional conductor from 1974 to 1976. His first major appointment was with GUS where, in 1985, at eight days' notice, he conducted in the National Finals. Three years later he directed their winning performance in the Open, as Rigid Containers (see page 269). He also conducted Desford for a short time.

Spending much of his time in Canada, Tovey has conducted both the Canadian Staff Band of the Salvation Army and Toronto's Hannaford

Figure 11.3   Foden's with the National Championship trophy and resident
conductor Bryan Hurdley in 1999

Street Silver Band. In great demand on the orchestral scene, he remains
enthusiastic about his connection with brass bands. He directed two courses
with the NYBB and one with the NYBBW.

*Cory's*

The Welsh band Cory's were conducted early in the period by Denzil
Stephens but then Major Kenney returned, leading the band to a Nationals
hat-trick in the years 1982–83–84. The 1984 win was particularly felicitous
as it coincided with the band's centenary. There were also further titles,
such as 'Radio Wales Band of the Year' and 'Champion Band of Wales'.

It was also in 1984 that the band said goodbye to its long-serving
principal cornet player. Solo Champion of Wales at 15, Jim Davies made
his reputation as principal cornet with Cory's, a position he took up in

1967 at the age of 20, then serving for 17 years before moving north to become principal cornet player with Fairey's. Then, after a short spell of conducting, he became principal cornet player of Brighouse & Rastrick, where he remained from 1989 to 1998 before once again turning to conducting, as resident with Carlton Main.

In 1988 Kenney again retired from Cory's, on health grounds, and during the final years of the decade the band came under the baton of a number of conductors. In 1989 they found a sponsor in a firm of furniture makers, becoming Christie Tyler Cory Band. Disaster struck a year later when the bandroom was destroyed by fire resulting in a substantial loss, not only of instruments and uniforms, but also of irreplaceable music and valuable memorabilia.

During the early 1990s both Stephens and Kenney returned but, symbolic of the unsettled period through which Cory's was passing, it was a local man, David Thomas, who helped the band to the title of Welsh Champions in 1992 and Michael Antrobus, flying in from Norway, who took them to the Grand Shield contest of 1993. However, the band had to wait another year, with further conducting changes, before winning the 'Shield' and returning to the British Open Championships.

In 1998 a deal was struck with a local television rental company amounting to a three-year sponsorship, the band being renamed Just Rentals Cory. A year later the firm expanded, changed its name and the band now became Buy As You View Cory. Jeremy Wise (see page 286) became musical director in 1997 to be followed in 2000 by Robert Childs.

Cory's remained strong at Area level, with six wins and two 2nd prizes during the 20-year period, but there was no further success nationally after the London hat-trick until the year 2000 when, as Buy As You View Cory, the band became British Open Champions for the first time in its history. It then went on to complete the 'double', by also winning the Nationals – a magnificent achievement that put the band back in the ranks of the elite (Figure 11.4).

*Hammonds Sauce/YBS*

Hammonds Sauce Works Band was relegated from the British Open Championships[3] in the early 1980s. This proved to be a turbulent period, precipitated by the death, in 1983, of Horace Hawley, the band's president and the company's managing director. Geoffrey Whitham remained as musical director, though a number of guest conductors were employed, with Denzil Stephens appointed as 'professional'. However, differences now occurred between the new management and the band, particularly

---

[3] Just as there was promotion for winners of the Grand Shield, there was demotion for bands doing least well in the Open.

Figure 11.4   Members of Buy As You View Cory with Robert Childs – Double Champions in 2000

with regard to the appointment of conductors, and in 1984 Whitham and many band members resigned, as did Stephens.

Whitham then worked periodically with several other bands, including Grimethorpe, JSVB, Fairey's and Desford. In 1988 he returned to Hammonds, meeting with immediate success in the Grand Shield. He remained here until 1993, after which he had spells with Wingates and Ever Ready.[4] He now also became more involved with adjudicating than conducting, though he was a co-conductor of 'Kings of Brass' (see Glossary).

The former Hammonds players now formed a new band, finding a sponsor in the shape of an instrument dealer, Bill Lewington. Part of Lewington's business was as the main British dealer for Yamaha. He provided a set of new instruments and agreed to underwrite all running costs of the new group, called Lewington Yamaha Band. It enjoyed a measure of success, but towards the end of 1989 Lewington lost the Yamaha franchise. As he was unable to continue with the sponsorship, in 1990 the band closed down.

Meanwhile, Hammonds had a junior band, which was renamed Hammonds Sauce Works Band and continued to function as such. In 1987 Richard Evans was appointed musical director but in the following year Whitham returned, leading the band to victory in the Grand Shield at Belle Vue. In September Hammonds took 2nd prize – narrowly missing a place in the record books as the only band to win the Grand Shield and the British Open in the same year. A new company took over the sauce works in the early 1990s and in 1993 the 33-year-long sponsorship ended.[5]

Fortunately, a deal was struck with the Yorkshire Building Society (YBS) which had its headquarters quite close to the site of the sauce works. There were, in fact, three Hammonds bands and YBS took them all under its wing, naming them Yorkshire Building Society Brass Band, YBS Hawley Band and YBS Juniors. Whitham continued as musical director of the senior band for a time but later in 1993 he retired.

David King then became principal conductor, with Nicholas Childs as resident. Two years later Childs relinquished his position but, following a further relegation, King led the band to another victory in the Grand Shield. He was to become the most successful of the younger generation of conductors. Following his two and a half years at Black Dyke (see page 248) he was appointed musical director of YBS, moulding them into a top-class contesting unit (Figure 11.5). King was also in demand to conduct other bands and did particularly well in Norway where he led

---

[4] There is an informative interview with Whitham in *BB* of 18 December 1993, p. 7.
[5] There is a good history of Hammonds Sauce Works Band in *BB* of 3 July 1993, pp. 7 and 9.

Figure 11.5    Yorkshire Building Society with David King in Huddersfield Town Hall. Trophies on display include the All England Masters trophy (*left*), the British Open Shield (*right*) and the European trophy (*centre*)

Manger Musiklag to four successive Norwegian Championship titles
(1994–97). He had also, meanwhile, become Head of Band Studies at the
University of Salford. In 1999 King visited his native Australia as chief
adjudicator of the National Championships and in the year 2000 achieved
his Doctorate of Musical Arts (DMA).[6]

The YBS/King partnership produced the most successful band of the
late 1990s, with four European titles (1996, 1997, 1999 and 2000) and
two British Open Championship wins (1997 and 1999). Further, with
King's imaginative programme-planning the band acquired a fine
reputation for its individualistic concert presentation, also producing a
series of highly acclaimed CDs. King championed SA music and in 1996
YBS became the first contesting band to broadcast an entire programme
of SA music and also the first to make an entire CD of it. In the field of
secular music he became adept at planning the all-inclusive sequence of
pieces based on a theme, with choreography and sometimes the necessity
for players to memorise their parts. Two of these sequences, *Cry of the
Celts* and *Windows of the World*, came from the pen of Peter Graham,
with a third, *This Sceptred Isle*, from Edward Watson – all commissioned
by King and YBS, and premiered in major concerts. In 1998 Kenneth
Downie became the band's composer-in-residence, preparing a number of
works for YBS during the remaining years of the century.

### Brighouse & Rastrick

Another Yorkshire band, Brighouse & Rastrick, maintained its reputation
as the most successful unsponsored band – still surviving on donations/
subscriptions and the band's own earnings through concerts, recording
fees and prize-moneys. The 1980s began well, with a 2nd prize in the
1981 Nationals with Derek Broadbent conducting, and a win at the
European Championships under James Scott. Scott was in charge for most
of the band's contests during the early 1980s. In 1983 Broadbent left after
ten years' service. James Watson then took the band to the British Open,
helping it win 2nd prize, after which he was appointed professional
conductor. He remained until 1986, when Adrian Leaper, a young
orchestral conductor, took Brighouse to the two major contests. Broadbent
then returned as musical director with a brief to conduct at major contests,
which he did until 1989. Overseas visits saw the band in Germany, Norway
and Switzerland, and also in the Channel Islands.

---

6 In June 2003 David King was appointed Professor of Music – Performance, a unique
honour for a member of the brass band movement. This was announced in *BB* of 21 June,
with a full-length account of Professor King's career in the issue of 28 June (pages 6–8).

In 1991 Allan Withington was appointed professional conductor. Coming from a well-known Lancashire banding family, Withington had played cornet with Wingates and Foden's. He was a member of the first cohort of students on the Band Studies course at Salford College of Technology, after which he took up the trumpet. On completion of postgraduate studies at the RNCM, he undertook freelance work and also played in the orchestra of the Royal Festival Ballet in London prior to moving to Norway as a member of the Bergen Philharmonic Orchestra. Withington conducted a number of brass bands in Norway, his successes there leading to his appointment as professional conductor at Brighouse. He remained in Norway, playing in the orchestra but making regular trips to England to fulfil his commitments.[7]

He was to remain with Brighouse for the rest of the decade, bringing considerable success, including National Championship wins in 1997 and 1998 (narrowly missing the hat-trick by being placed second in 1999), and also winning the All England Masters in 1993 and both that and the European Championships in 1998. Les Beevers, a former bass player, served as resident conductor for a time and was replaced, in 1993, by Jeremy Wise and later by David Hirst, who was to become one of the band's longest-serving resident conductors.

Hirst had played soprano cornet with Black Dyke from 1970 to 1973 and again during 1979–80 but was also gaining experience as a conductor with lower-section bands. His first conducting appointment of note was with Lewington Yamaha, of which he became resident conductor in 1986. A number of similar appointments followed, at Black Dyke, Yorkshire Imperial and Ransome's, but from 1994 he was with Brighouse & Rastrick. He had also become co-ordinator of the Barnsley courses in band musicianship (see page 222) and was building a career as an adjudicator.

Brighouse & Rastrick enjoyed a Swiss tour in 1991 and a visit to Norway – courtesy of its professional conductor – in 1993. Then 1995 witnessed the opening of a new, purpose-built bandroom costing some £160 000, a remarkable acquisition for an unsponsored band. In the Yorkshire Area contest Brighouse's record stood supreme, with six wins and three 2nd prizes during the period 1981–2000

## *Leyland / BNFL / JJB Sports*

In May 1946 Leyland Motors (based in the Lancashire town of Leyland) had formed a band. Though winning the Grand Shield in 1952 under Harold Moss (see 'Personalia') the band continued as a second-section band until 1978, when the company decided that, if the band was to

---

[7] There is a good biography of Withington in *BB* of 18 April 1991, p. 10.

continue, it must aspire to the top flight. Richard Evans was appointed full-time musical director, charged with bringing the band to the required level. By winning the second-section Finals in 1979 they gained entry into the championship section. This year also saw the band on a highly prestigious tour of Japan. In 1980 Leyland won a BBC North West television knockout competition (Figure 11.6).

By winning the Grand Shield in May 1981, Leyland gained re-entry into the 'September'. Like Hammonds some years later, they narrowly missed achieving the 'double', taking 2nd prize at the following Open. Due to a company name-change in 1987 the band became 'Leyland DAF'. There were several overseas tours during the 1980s.

In 1985, playing an avant-garde work which involved the use of a computer, Leyland became 'BBC Band of the Year', an important accolade. Two more significant successes came in 1989 – winning the first All England Masters and Brass in Concert.

When the DAF sponsorship ceased early in 1992, a new company became involved with the band, which was now renamed the 'BNFL Band' (British Nuclear Fuels Ltd). Despite a clutch of wins at Area level, there were no prizes in the National Finals during the 1990s. The band's record in the British Open Championships was better, with two 3rd prizes, a 2nd and, in 1994, a win. As Leyland DAF the band had won the All England Masters competition in 1989; it repeated the success three years later as BNFL. There were several overseas tours during the early 1990s, in particular one in 1993 on behalf of BNFL, encompassing Korea and Japan. Both 1994 and 1997 saw American tours.

The BNFL sponsorship ended in 1997 and the band became 'JJB Sports Leyland' – JJB being the company owned by David Whelan who also now sponsored the British Open Championships (see page 227). Under this name the band won Brass in Concert, having also won in 1991 as Leyland DAF and in 1992 as BNFL. Yet again this sponsorship ended and in the final year of the century the unsponsored band reverted simply to the name 'Leyland'. Despite only modest major contest successes during the period, the band built a reputation second to none as a highly entertaining band in concert, enhanced by its charismatic musical director, Richard Evans.

Evans remained with Leyland until the end of the century, guiding it through its various sponsorships and name changes. Away from his band, he was in great demand as a guest conductor and adjudicator. In addition to many adjudicating assignments in Britain he was frequently on the continent and twice adjudicated the New Zealand Championships (1992 and 1997). He succeeded Geoffrey Brand as music director of NYBBS in 1992 and in the same year helped found, and became head of, the course in Band Studies at Accrington and Rossendale College.

Figure 11.6    Leyland Vehicles in a television studio, with Richard Evans (conductor) and John Hudson (cornet soloist)

Leyland, under its various names, was the most successful band in North West Area contests, with seven wins and six 2nd prizes between 1981 and 2000. From 2000 it was announced that Evans would no longer be conducting Leyland in test piece contests; Howard Snell took over, though Evans led the band to second place at Brass in Concert.

### CWS (Glasgow)

Moving north: the successes of CWS – now CWS (Glasgow), formerly Scottish CWS – during the 1980s were inconsistent to say the least. There were Area wins under Howard Snell in 1988 and 1989, and a spectacular win in the National Championships in 1990 under John Hudson, the newly appointed resident conductor. For much of the period under review Howard Snell was the band's professional conductor. His association began in 1984, and in 1988, by winning the Grand Shield, the band gained re-entry into the British Open Championships. There were also wins at the Edinburgh International contest in 1982, 1987 and 1989. Overseas visits during the 1980s included two trips to Norway and a visit to Belfast.

A number of conductors were involved during the early 1990s. Stephen Sykes (see page 290) was resident conductor for a time. From *circa* 1988 he had been developing his conducting skills, with residencies at Camborne, BTM and Sun Life. Ray Farr took CWS to the 1991 Nationals, whilst Frans Violet (conductor of the Belgian Brass Band Willebroek) led them to third place in the 1993 Open, following which Allan Withington took them to the Nationals. Roger Webster and Steven Mead were engaged at this time to play respectively principal cornet and solo euphonium in major contests and concerts. During the summer of 1993 there was a tour of Australia and New Zealand, with concerts in Perth, Fremantle, Sydney and Brisbane in Australia, and Auckland, Wellington, Invercargill and Christchurch in New Zealand. Nineteen-ninety-six was the band's peak contesting year in the 1990s, David King leading it to first place in the Area competition and Howard Snell directing the title-winning performance in the National Championships.

Webster and Mead, who had stayed only for about two years initially, returned in 1996, and in 1998 CWS completed a hat-trick of wins in the Area contest. Though Snell remained as professional conductor, the band took the unusual step of engaging a Japanese conductor to take them to the British Open. He was Kazuyoshi Uemera, musical director of the Breeze Brass Band of Osaka.

\* \* \*

These top ten bands were now the elite of the brass band movement. They were well organised, could play virtually anything to a very high standard, regularly produced CDs and commanded the best engagements. Better players tended to gravitate towards them and there was a considerable gap between them and the bands on the next rung down. Nevertheless, many other bands also maintained a high standard, were capable of delivering good quality concerts and CDs and formed an important link between average local bands and those in the upper echelons.

### Other winners of the British Open Championships

City of Coventry had its finest hour in 1981, winning the British Open Championships – conducted by Major Arthur Kenney, more generally associated with Cory's. During 1984 it acquired sponsorship and became known as Jaguar Cars (City of Coventry). There was a succession of conductors, including Peter Parkes and Ray Farr. The latter was resident conductor from 1987 and took the band to Holland in 1990. There was one Area win (1986) and four runner-up positions but the only top-three placing at the Nationals was 3rd prize in 1988. Despite a number of sponsorship changes the band faded. Its final appearance at the Open was in 1992; a year later it had gone.

Besses o' th' Barn had just two more years of relative success – in particular, a win at the British Open Championships in 1982 under Roy Newsome. Besses undertook a Swiss tour in 1981, and in both 1983 and 1986 flew to Finland to participate in a festival known as the Lieksa Brass Week. In 1988 Besses faced relegation from the British Open but returned following a third place at the Grand Shield contest of 1990. There were a few prizes in the Area contests, including one win. Alec Evans remained as resident conductor for a time, after which there were several resident and guest conductors. In 1990 Paul Hindmarsh, the BBC producer in charge of bands on Radio 3, became musical director. He brought a number of prestige engagements to the band. From 1992 Besses accepted sponsorship from a local brewery and was known for a time as 'Besses o' th' Barn (J.W. Lees)'.

As was seen on pages 154–5, Keith Wilkinson was already the musical director of GUS at the start of the 1980s. In 1985 he resigned; John Berryman then became resident conductor and Bram Tovey was appointed professional conductor. Following a new sponsorship agreement, in 1987 GUS became the 'Rigid Container's Group Band', celebrating this by winning the 1988 British Open Championships under Tovey. During the 1980s the band visited Holland and undertook three Swiss tours. Area wins included two under Wilkinson and one under Tovey, whilst a 1990 win was directed by Robert Watson (brother of James). Berryman returned in 1991 but, despite some success at Area level, there were no further successes at national level. The existing sponsorship ceased in 1998 and the band, for a time, reverted to the name GUS. Berryman resigned and was replaced by Melvin White (see page 286). In 2000 a sponsorship deal was struck and the band became Travelsphere Holiday Band.

Kennedy's Swinton Concert Brass was formed, by a group of enthusiasts in the early 1980s, from the former Swinton Town Youth Band. David King was the founding conductor. They had a rapid rise, winning each of the four sections in the highly competitive North West Area between 1984 and 1987, and in the latter year taking fifth place in the championship section of the Finals. They were runners-up in the Grand Shield of 1988, thus gaining access to the British Open Championships. By 1989 King had left for Black Dyke but, conducted by Garry Cutt, Swinton took the band movement by storm, becoming British Open Champions. There were two further appearances at the Open, a 2nd prize in the Area in 1992 and an appearance at the Nationals. However, in 1993, on losing both the sponsorship and a number of players, rather than move down the sections, the members agreed to disband. Thus, its descent was even swifter than its ascent!

The Stanshawe band was formed in Bristol in 1968 by a group of enthusiasts who were determined that the South West should have a band which could compete on equal terms with those from other regions. Within three years it had reached the second section, achieving 2nd prize in the Finals. W.B. Hargreaves was professional conductor and good-quality players were being attracted.

Brian Howard, a highly experienced local musician, became resident conductor in 1972, which proved to be a remarkable year for the band. It won the Grand Shield, thereby qualifying for an invitation to the British Open, and later in the year won the Edinburgh International contest. These achievements were almost dwarfed when the band took 2nd prizes at the British Open in 1974 and 1976, and at the National Finals in 1975, having won its Area championships in 1974 and 1975. Missing a major title by one place in each of three consecutive years, disappointing as it must have been, reflected a phenomenal achievement.

'W.B.' left at the end of 1977. Almost simultaneously with the news that, through sponsorship from the insurance giant, the band had become 'Sun Life Stanshawe', Roy Newsome became its professional conductor. The band was now broadcasting, making commercial recordings and attracting some interesting engagements. In 1979, under Brian Howard, the band won the BBC's Best of Brass competition. Newsome left early in 1980 and was succeeded by composer and Bristol University lecturer, Derek Bourgeois.

Bourgeois remained as conductor until 1983, during which year the band became 'The Sun Life Band'. Several guest conductors were now engaged, including W.B. Hargreaves, who returned to lead an Area contest win in 1984. Geoffrey Brand and James Watson also helped for short periods. At national level Sun Life secured 2nd prize at the 1984 Nationals and 3rd two years later. In 1989 Bryan Hurdley became resident conductor and Roy Newsome returned as principal conductor. The band's peak came in 1990 with a win at the British Open Championships.

Engagements were never easy to come by in a region where the public perception of brass bands was not high, but the band itself promoted a number of concerts locally, as well as visiting Switzerland, Holland, Scotland and the Isle of Man. In 1990 it received the *British Bandsman* award for the promotion of new original music. Senior members of Sun Life now acted as tutors for Hampshire Youth Band's annual weekend residential course and from 1992, in an attempt to stimulate some enthusiasm for brass banding in the Bristol region, the band organised workshops for young local brass players.

One of Sun Life's finest hours came in 1993 when it won the open brass band section at Kerkrade (WMC). Always searching for new initiatives, Sun Life set up its own recording company in 1994, using its original name – 'Stanshawe' – for the label, and in the following year claimed to be the first brass band to open a website. In this year Newsome left, following major surgery. In 1996 the 18-year sponsorship ceased and for a short time the band continued under its old name of Stanshawe. Amongst its final engagements was another visit to the Isle of Man.

Sadly, due to shortage of players and engagements, and mounting debts, the band folded in 1997. It had dominated the West's Area contests, between 1981 and 1996 achieving 11 wins and two 2nd prizes.[8]

Marple is a small town located south-west of Manchester. Its band, formed in 1965, functioned as a community band for 25 years before, in 1990, earning 2nd prize in the Grand Shield competition. They were conducted on this occasion by Garry Cutt, who was to be the band's father-figure. Though Marple were never likely to become a leading band, this nevertheless opened the door to an amazing sequence of successes at the British Open, with four consecutive 4th prizes between 1992 and 1995, crowned with a win in 1996. The 1996 Open win led to a concert in St John's Smith Square, London, with Elgar Howarth conducting. In 2000 Garry Cutt resigned, unable to bear the weight of both Grimethorpe and Marple as well as other freelance engagements. David Hirst then took the band to the All England Masters and the Open.

---

[8] This information is taken from sleeve notes in the triple album *Legacy*, from the band's website, from articles in *BB*, and from author's own notes.

*Bands no longer in the top league*

Following its 1980 win at the British Open, Yorkshire Imperial Metals Band made only a small mark during the remainder of the 1980s, with but two third places and a fourth in the Nationals, along with two Area contest wins. In 1984 the band became IMI Yorkshire Imperial. Conductors between 1981 and 1990 included the orchestral conductors John Pryce-Jones and Howard Williams, along with several brass band specialists. In 1982 the band toured Denmark and throughout the decade continued to attract recording contracts and good concert engagements, including an appearance at the 1989 Harrogate Festival and a Swiss tour in 1990.

In 1992 the band found a new sponsor – the owner of a national coach company, David Urquhart Travel. With an eye on the past as well as on the present, it was now known as DUT Imperial Band. One of its conductors in the early 1990s, Allan Exley, a former principal cornet player of both Yorkshire Imperial and Brighouse & Rastrick, led the band to wins in the 1993 Area contest and at Brass in Concert in 1995. However, despite a 2nd prize at Kerkrade, all was not well and in 1998 an 'alliance' was announced between DUT Imperial and another band, both being short of players. This 'alliance' was short-lived and a different partnership was sought, following 14 transfers to a third band, Rothwell. This band now appeared at the 1999 British Open as DUT Rothwell. However, the eventual compromise was to re-form as the DUT Yorkshire Imperial Rothwell Band.

Carlton Main Frickley Colliery Band was one of a number of bands whose success rate seems to have been inversely proportional to the number of conductor changes. The band engaged at least eight different conductors during the 1980s but their total tally of contest successes was a win in the television knockout competition Best of Brass and three prizes in Area contests, including a win in 1982. The early 1990s were extremely difficult, largely due to the miners' strike. Following this, the band was reportedly down to six members and out of the championship section. However, by regrouping and winning the new first-section Finals, it regained championship status. Worse was to come, however, with the closure of the pit in 1993. After further struggles and changes of conductor a process of rebuilding began, with imaginative programming and a highly acclaimed CD. By 1999 the work was bearing fruit and the band was rewarded with an Area contest win, and victory in the Grand Shield, enabling re-entry into the British Open Championships.

As was seen earlier, in 1980 Wingates dropped the word 'Temperance' from its name, becoming simply, The Wingates Band. Paradoxically, its first sponsor was the brewery company Bass. This sponsorship began in 1982 and lasted for three years, after which Bass Wingates became British Aerospace Wingates.

In 1981 Garry Cutt became the resident and Denis Carr the professional conductor. Carr left a year later, however, to be succeeded by James Scott, who accompanied the band on a successful American tour. There was a second American tour in 1989, but a somewhat unsettled period followed. Major contest successes eluded Wingates during the 1980s, except for a 2nd prize at the Open in 1985. In 1991 the Aerospace sponsorship ended but the band, since then, has enjoyed modest financial help from a local company. The band's highest achievement during the 1990s was an Area win in 1995, conducted by John Hudson. Nicholas Childs took Wingates to the Grand Shield contest in 1996 which they won, regaining access into the British Open. John Maines then became musical director, but Howard Snell took the band to the All England Masters and picked up 2nd prize. Michael Fowles, a protégé of Snell's and a Junior Fellow at the RNCM School of Wind and Percussion, now became resident conductor. However, this was temporary and there were several other conductors during the closing years of the period.

Ransome's enjoyed only modest success during the early 1980s, even at Area level. It did, nevertheless, manage to secure two sponsorships. The first, somewhat short-lived, began in 1982. However, Brown's Musical Ransome Band became Airquick (Newark) Ransome Band in 1984. Retaining the name 'Ransome' was crucial and helped maintain a reasonable status in the engagement market. Conductors at this time included Peter Parkes and Trevor Walmsley. The Airquick sponsorship ceased in 1992, after which the band survived thanks to joint sponsorship with Newark Town Council and some local companies. However, in 1994 a new five-year deal was struck and the band became RHP-NSK Ransomes. Under its various names the band enjoyed several Area contest successes between 1985 and 2000, with two wins and three 2nd prizes. The later 1990s saw a slight resurgence, with 4th prizes in the 1997 British Open and the 1999 Nationals, conducted by Brian Grant (a former principal cornet player of GUS and resident conductor at Ransome's from 1996), and ending on a high note with 2nd prize in the 2000 Nationals, conducted by Russell Gray (see 'Personalia'). The band enjoyed a good relationship with the parent company, NSK, undertaking a Japanese tour to celebrate the company's eightieth anniversary. In 2000, though still sponsored, the name was changed to The Ransome Band.

In 1981 composer Philip Sparke became resident conductor of Roneo Vickers, the former Hanwell Band, and Eric Bravington returned as musical director. He was already a sick man, however, and W.B. Hargreaves took the band to the 1982 Area contest. In August the musical world mourned Bravington's death, at the age of 61. In the following year sponsorship ceased and the band reverted to the name Hanwell.

Interesting engagements continued to come its way and in 1982 the band visited Holland and Belgium. However, its only Area contest win during these 20 years was in 1987. Several conductors fronted the band during the next few years but the loss of sponsorship and, more particularly, the loss of Eric Bravington, combined to bring about the demise, in 1989, of what had once been London's most consistently successful brass band. However, the band was re-formed as a second-section band in 1991 and is still functioning as such.

Parc & Dare maintained its consistency during the 1980s, becoming the Radio Band of Wales and Best of Brass Champions in 1981. Between then and 1990 it was amongst the top three bands at the Area contests seven times, with three wins – leading to three appearances in the European Championships. In 1984 Ieaun Morgan retired after 42 years with the band – 19 of them as musical director. In 1990, through sponsorship, the band became National Fuel Distributors Band (Parc & Dare). Following its second place in the 1991 Area contest, the band had no further successes in this competition, though it again became Radio Band of Wales in 1994.

Of the many other bands that could be mentioned under this heading, seven are reviewed in the Glossary. These are Ever Ready, Whitburn and Tredegar – important bands in their respective regions of the North East, Scotland and Wales; two London bands – Hendon and First City; and Flowers Gloucester and William Davis Construction Group Band from the Midlands.

### Concerts – an upgrade in activities

Sponsorship was the key to many events of the 1980s and 1990s. Capitol Radio sponsored London Festivals of Brass in 1983–84–85. These took place on the South Bank and in the final event ten local bands played during the day whilst Hanwell, Hendon and Desford combined under Howard Snell for the evening concert.

There were also many charity concerts. For example, in 1985 former Prime Minister Edward Heath was guest conductor at a concert in Coventry Cathedral with Besses o' th' Barn and the NYBB. A substantial donation was made to 'Opportunities for the Disabled' as a result of this event. This was nothing new, but such concerts now received more publicity, bands often announced how much profit their concerts had made for the charity and the charities themselves assisted with promotion.

A Huddersfield journalist and *BB* feature writer, Ron Massey, organised a series of concerts in the Royal Albert Hall on behalf of the Yorkshire Cancer Research Campaign. These involved bands and male voice choirs and took place in 1987, 1991 and 1994. The latter concert featured

Brighouse & Rastrick, Sellers Engineering Band and a massed choir of 800 voices. One further concert took place in the Albert Hall, in 1997, after which, due to the expense of taking the bands to London the event was moved to the Sheffield Arena for the concert of the year 2000. Over £100000 had already been contributed and the fifth concert in the series saw Grimethorpe, YBS and Sellers bands, along with a choir of 2500, all performing under William Relton – musical director of the series from the outset.

Several concerts now featured combinations of leading bands – generally playing individually. One series, held annually from 1989 to 1991 in Bristol's Colston Hall, was organised by Bram Gay, who also ran a Festival at the Manchester Palace Theatre with six quality bands. Other series which ran for a time appeared in Blackburn, Nottingham and Birmingham. There were also open-air concerts in various locations, including Kenwood Lakeside, as part of the English Heritage series. Some attracted audiences of upwards of 10000. Amongst the earlier ones were concerts by Grimethorpe and Sun Life (1985), and by Brighouse & Rastrick, Grimethorpe and GUS (1987), both concerts being conducted by Geoffrey Brand.

One of the most important sequences of concerts was that organised by the BBC in its newly opened Studio 7 in Manchester. These also began in the late 1980s and generally involved eight or more bands, each giving its own afternoon or evening concert, over a period of several Sundays. The BBC Festival of 1991 included not only the regulars – Grimethorpe, Black Dyke, Leyland, Sun Life, Fairey's and Britannia Building Society – but also the ISB and Norway's Eikanger Bjorsvik. All the BBC concerts and most of the others mentioned featured the serious repertoire. A Sheffield Festival of Brass, also in 1991, featured Leyland, Grimethorpe, Britannia and Desford, as well as Howard Snell Brass (see page 282), the Childs Brothers and Desford's quartet. They all performed during the day, whilst the evening concert was devoted to youth bands and school choirs.

The BBC Festivals were gradually phased out but in their place came the RNCM Manchester Festival, organised by James Gourlay and featuring leading bands giving full-length programmes, again spread over a few weekends and with budget-priced tickets. In its 1999 Festival of Brass the RNCM paid tribute to two composers – Philip Wilby in his fiftieth year and John McCabe in his sixtieth – whilst in the following year the event incorporated an International Tuba and Euphonium Festival.

An old idea now given a new look was the promotion of musical instruments through the artists who played them. In former times this was largely restricted to the publishing of photographs of those who played the various instruments. During the 1990s Boosey's and Yamaha in particular went further, paying fees to soloists or groups for appearing under the company name. Thus the events received extra publicity as well as having the benefit of star players without cost to the organisers.

There was now a preference for bands to play separately – possibly massing for the finale. It also became normal to mix bands with other kinds of groups – for example, orchestral brass and brass ensembles – and with soloists from the worlds of symphonic brass and big bands. The Barbican (London), Symphony Hall (Birmingham) and the Bridgewater Hall (Manchester) became popular venues, but use was also made of concert halls in various colleges of music. A 'Brass Explosion' in Symphony Hall during 1996 featured not only three leading bands, but also internationally renowned soloists, the British Tuba Quartet and the Fine Arts Brass Ensemble. In the same year the seventy-fifth birthdays of Sir Malcolm Arnold and Robert Simpson were celebrated at The Barbican in a concert featuring Desford and the LSO Brass.

North of the border, Nigel Boddice and Bryan Allen began a series of 'Brass Spectaculars' in the Royal Scottish Academy of Music and Drama, featuring leading Scottish bands and (mostly) English soloists.

By 1998 entrepreneur Philip Biggs was advertising his Great Northern Brass Arts Festival. This was to become an annual event held in Manchester in early September and filling the gap left by moving the British Open Championships to Birmingham. Its main sponsors were SP&S – the SA's own publishing company. Featured in the first event were the RNCM Brass Band, Hallé Brass, Stockport Schools, Fairey's, Marple and Enfield Citadel (SA) bands. Each gave its own mini-concert. For good measure John Wallace (trumpet) and James Gourlay were amongst the featured soloists. Thus school, college, Salvation Army and contesting bands were mixed with professional soloists and ensembles in a single event.

Black Dyke gave an early evening Prom in the Royal Albert Hall in 1997 and in the same year Britannia Building Society became the first brass band to play at the famous Snape Maltings in Aldeburgh, whilst Grimethorpe appeared in London's Barbican. During 1998 Black Dyke produced CDs with both Halifax Choral Society and the renowned percussionist Evelyn Glennie, and appeared in concert in Birmingham with the BBC Big Band and an Australian jazz specialist, James Morrison. These were further examples of mixing the brass band with music from other genres.

Bram Gay tried his entrepreneurial skills again towards the close of the century, organising a number of spectacular concerts featuring a range of bands. His 'Concert of the Century' of 1999 featured Tredegar, Grimethorpe, Marple, Foden's, JJB Sports, Fairey's and the All-Star Girls of Brass (see Glossary) in a marathon concert in Symphony Hall on the day following the British Open Championships. He was back again in 2000 with a 'Bands of the World' concert. This featured seven bands from four different countries – England, Belgium, the USA and New Zealand. Sandwiched in between the 'Open' and this concert was a Saturday evening event celebrating the Quincentenary of the Worshipful Company of Musicians. This was in the same venue and featured Grimethorpe and YBS playing individually under their own conductors, and massed under Elgar Howarth.

Thus, there was a range of prestigious concerts, all helping raise the profile of brass bands. They generally contained a mixture of serious and light pieces, and attracted large audiences.

Normal local concerts and park engagements were also relatively plentiful during the 1990s, though, as always, this varied from region to region. A nationwide activity in which many bands participated was the annual National Music Day, organised during the summer and which received much publicity. Many of the events were featured on radio or television. In 1992 it was claimed that some 65 000 musicians participated, aged mainly between five and 21. A substantial number of these were members of brass bands.

In 1997 the BBC organised a 'Brass Day' at the huge G-Mex Centre in Manchester. The massed blow, though not achieving the anticipated 1500 'blowers' was quite successful and the day also included a traditional-type massed band concert featuring Britannia Building Society, Brighouse & Rastrick and Wingates. It was brought to a close with a gala concert by Black Dyke, broadcast live.

By now there was a long list of overseas tours and many average bands seemed to spend their winters participating in contests and fund-raising, and travelling abroad at some point during the summer. European tours were now almost commonplace as more bands went to such faraway places as Canada and the USA, Australia and New Zealand, Japan and Korea. International travel for bands and other musical groups became big business, with a number of tour operators vying for that business.

## Brass bands and the media in the 1990s

There was an escalation in the interest of the media for brass band activities towards the close of the century. Early in 1996 Phillip McCann recorded the theme music for the BBC television series *Hetty Wainthrop Investigates*. The music became extremely popular and the series, commanding an estimated audience of some 13 million, made his individualistic sound very well known.

The most spectacular brass band event of the late twentieth century, however, was the release, in November 1996, of the film *Brassed Off*. The story was set against the backdrop of the pit closures in 1992. It was set in the fictitious village of Grimley and highlighted the human issues brought about by the destruction of its mining community. Top-line film stars involved included Tara Fitzgerald and Peter Postlethwaite. The sound track featured playing of the highest calibre by Grimethorpe Colliery Band, members of which also portrayed the players in the Grimley Band. The film was to do for Grimethorpe and the whole brass band movement what Brighouse and the *Floral Dance* had done some 20 years earlier. It was, nevertheless, somewhat controversial, some people criticising certain aspects of it – such as the over-use of bad language and an exaggerated emphasis on beer-drinking. A stage production appeared in Sheffield in 1998 and, following a nationwide tour, reached London later in the year, with local bands providing the music.

Another film, *The Full Monty*, appeared in 1997. It not only featured, but virtually rescued from extinction Stocksbridge Engineering Band. Like *Brassed Off*, this film later appeared as a stage production. However, though immensely popular, it did not achieve the fame of its predecessor.

A musical play was devised by Michael Brand (son of Geoffrey). An adaptation of the famous *Ragged Trousered Philanthropist* by Robert Tressel, it was called *In the Red*. Because of its political implications Brand felt that the sound of a brass band would enhance the storyline and he scored the music accordingly. A backing track was recorded by Fairey's in 1998 and by the following year the whole play was available on CD. The first London performance took place in 2000, with Geoffrey Brand as musical director and Fairey's playing in Her Majesty's Theatre, Haymarket.

Back in 1997 the band had crossed into the realms of pop music by performing and recording *Acid Brass* – ten acid house anthems,[9] arranged for the band by its musical-associate, Rodney Newton. Fairey's had a big success with this music, performing it in various centres including Liverpool and London, and appearing on television as well as producing a CD.

In 1999 James Watson and Black Dyke moved in with the media, recording background music for *Ground Force*, a popular gardening programme. At around the same time they made recordings with a number of pop stars, including Sir Elton John.

*The Salvation Army*

For some time there had been divided views within the SA regarding its policy of not allowing contesting bands to perform its music. Many devotees had come to feel that the spiritual message within its music could be communicated to an audience by any band – whether attached to the SA or not. There was also concern at the continuing loss of bandsmen

---

[9] Acid house music is the pop equivalent of minimalism. Very repetitive, it was a popular form of dance music in the 1980s.

who, over many years, had 'defected' to 'outside' bands so that they could perform a wider range of music. By 1985 SA musicians were allowed to play with non-SA bands providing that this did not interfere with their commitment as Salvationists. In 1989 the SA made some of its music available to church and school bands, and in 1992 all restrictions on the sale of SA music to other bands were lifted.

This widened the serious repertoire available to bands and, though it happened slowly at first, many bands were to take advantage of the 'new' repertoire in concerts, broadcasts and recordings. Salvationist Publishing and Supplier (SP&S) sponsored a number of brass band festivals, and concerts primarily for contesting bands also featured bands and soloists from the SA. The first time an SA band actually combined with a contesting band was at the Gala Concert of the 1997 National Championships, when Black Dyke and the International Staff Band (ISB) appeared on stage together.

## More on personalities

### *Three farewells – to Eric Ball, Harry Mortimer and W.B. Hargreaves*

The brass band world mourned the death, on 1 October 1989, of Eric Ball. He had been the most prolific writer of brass band music ever and had contributed immeasurably to the repertoires of both contesting and Salvation Army bands. He had also been a great influence through his writing, lecturing, conducting and in his role as editor of *BB*.[10]

Still the undisputed doyen of the brass band movement, Harry Mortimer celebrated his eightieth birthday in 1982 with a television programme featuring a composite 'All-Star' band. Many honours were to come his way during the 1980s – the first Honorary Graduate of Salford in 1983, Honorary Fellow of the RNCM in 1987, Honorary Doctor of Letters at Salford University in 1988 and, most important of all, the CBE, announced in the New Year Honours list of 1984. Though less physically active as an octogenarian, he had his finger on the metaphorical pulse of the brass band world. He was president of several organisations and in constant contact with leading figures in all areas of banding.

There were three broadcasts in honour of his eighty-fifth birthday during 1987 and, as a kind of birthday treat, in 1989 the BBC organised a recording of Denis Wright's transcription of Handel's *Messiah*. With

---

[10] There is a good biography of Eric Ball in *BB* of 7 October 1989, p. 3, with tributes in the editions of 14 October, p. 5; 21 October, p. 7; and 28 October, p. 7. See also Peter Cooke's *Eric Ball – The Man and His Music* (1991).

Mortimer on the rostrum, Huddersfield Town Hall echoed to the strains of this music, sung by Huddersfield Choral Society and with Black Dyke and Britannia Building Society bands providing the accompaniments. This was to fulfil a long-held dream of Mortimer's.[11]

With the help of his wife Margaret, 'H.M.' continued to mastermind the British Open Championships and the Grand Shield. However, he was hospitalised towards the end of 1992 and died on 23 January 1993 at the age of 89.[12] As his body had been donated to medical research there was no actual funeral. There was, however, on the day following the next British Open Championships, a Service of Thanksgiving in Manchester Cathedral at which a composite band of leading players was conducted by Elgar Howarth.

In his will, Harry Mortimer donated £50 000 to British Open Championships Ltd, to be called the Harry Mortimer Memorial Fund. It was to be invested and used for the encouragement of brass band music in the United Kingdom. The Trustees set up a number of grants and awarded various commemorative medals, to be financed from the Fund. Many concerts were organised as tributes to his memory.

W.B. Hargreaves conducted Fairey's for the last time in 1981 and then, after short periods with Carlton Main and Roneo (Hanwell), had two very successful years in his native Scotland as professional conductor of Kirkintilloch, leading them to Scottish Championship titles in 1984 and 1985. He then bowed out of contesting, leaving behind many fond memories as one of the most lovable characters the brass band world had produced.[13] His disappearance from the band scene indicated the end of an era. Walter B. Hargreaves died on 24 June 1998, aged 91. Tributes were paid to him in *BB* of 11 July, on page 2.

*A later generation of conductors*

Geoffrey Brand continued to exert considerable influence on and off the contest platform, both at home and abroad. In 1981 he was appointed musical director of Fairey's but was also working with Wingates and Carlton Main. Leaving Fairey's in 1983, he took Grimethorpe to the major contests for two years. He regularly appeared as a guest conductor, directed masterclasses and continued with his work as managing director of R. Smith & Co. He was also taking on more work abroad, particularly in

---

[11] For further information about this event, see *BB* of 18 March 1989, pp. 1 and 7; and 25 March, p. 7.

[12] *BB* of 1 February 1993 contains many tributes and appraisals of Harry Mortimer and his life's work.

[13] There is an interesting and informative interview with Hargreaves in *BB* of 25 April 1987, pp. 8–9.

Australia where, in 1982, he became the first 'Visiting Musician' of the University of Western Australia, working with students, choirs and bands. En route to Australia he attended a band directors' clinic in Japan, a country of which he was to become a frequent visitor. He returned to the University of Western Australia in 1984, residing there for three months and becoming a regular visitor. There were also visits to Europe and engagements in Malaysia and Singapore, as well as further adjudicating appointments worldwide. In 1991 Geoffrey Brand celebrated 21 years as the permanent conductor of NYBBS. Even with reduced commitments to contest conducting, he remained one of the most dominating influences on the brass band stage.

Elgar Howarth continued his association with Grimethorpe. However, as he became more deeply entrenched in his work with orchestras and opera, he became less actively involved with brass bands than formerly. He was, nevertheless, still a strong influence and remained first choice as guest conductor in prestigious concerts. He was the recipient of many awards, including honorary doctorates at the Universities of Keele and York, a Fellowship of the Royal College of Music and, in 1997, the prestigious Oliver Award for achievement in the field of opera.

*Further successful conductors*

Some of the conductors mentioned earlier in this chapter in connection with specific bands had a wider overall influence on the scene. Their respective careers are taken up here.

Howard Snell's early musical career was outlined in Chapter 7. He resigned as conductor of the Wren Orchestra in 1982 but continued as musical director at Desford until 1987. From 1981 he held a similar position with Foden's/Britannia Building Society. In 1984 he began an association with CWS (Glasgow) and from 1987 built up a highly successful partnership with Eikanger Bjorsvick in Norway, leading them to wins in the European Championships of 1988 and 1989, the first non-British band to achieve this. He also occasionally conducted Grimethorpe and Yorkshire Imperial. The partnership with Britannia Building Society lasted until 1996.

Snell was never wildly enthusiastic about traditional contests though he recognised their value. Regularly steering his bands into the prize-lists, he nevertheless collected only one title from the two major British contests – with CWS (Glasgow) in the Nationals of 1996. He was more successful in the European Championships and at the All England Masters, with four wins in each. However, he had an exceptional flair for arranging and made some first-rate transcriptions, the most popular being *Elsa's Procession to the Minster* (from Wagner's *Lohengrin*). He also developed programme-building to a high degree, earning many titles for his bands at major entertainment contests and creating a fine concert band at Britannia.

He directed the NYBB's Easter course in 1993, his work with Eikanger continued – especially in concert work and recording, and during 2000 he took Leyland to the major contests.

In 1983 Snell became Head of Brass at the RNCM. At around the same time he formed a publishing company called Rakeway Music, with the primary object of publishing his own arrangements. Though a highly respected adjudicator he did not officiate very often, but he did make the journey to New Zealand in 1989 to adjudicate at the National Championships. In the same year he formed his 'Howard Snell Brass', an all-star ten-piece group which broadcast, made recordings and undertook concert work.

He relinquished his post at the RNCM in 1994 but in 1999 became a professor of trumpet at the Royal Academy of Music and published a highly acclaimed book, *The Trumpet – Its practice and performance*.

Away from contests Snell exerted considerable influence, particularly through his transcriptions and arrangements. He also championed new serious music for brass bands, in particular promoting the music of John McCabe and Wilfred Heaton. Snell's forthright views on how banding could be improved were frequently expressed in the band press and his founding of a brass band course at the RNCM was of international importance. Howard Snell's professional orchestral background has enabled him to take a wide view of the brass band movement – the value of which he passionately believes in.

Peter Parkes left Black Dyke in 1989. He was the professional conductor of Fairey Engineering until 1995 and of Grimethorpe from then until 1998. In 1995 he led Desford to victory in the Area contest and also conducted them into third place in the Finals. In addition to these 'permanent' appointments he took on numerous others with a wide range of bands. He developed a highly successful partnership with the Swiss band Treize Etoiles, beginning in 1998. He was also in demand as an adjudicator both in Britain and Europe, adjudicating at the Australian Championships in 1982 and 1983, and the New Zealand Championships in 1983 and 1989. He succeeded Harry Mortimer as president of the British Federation of Brass Bands in 1984 and during 1988 helped build the course in Band Studies at Barnsley College.

Shortly after his return from Tripoli (see page 173), in 1981 Arthur Kenney led City of Coventry to its only major title of British Open Champions. Following this he returned to Cory's, where he remained for six years, leading them through their Nationals hat-trick (1982–83–84) and also working with other Welsh bands. During 1987 Kenney visited New Zealand to conduct the reigning champions, Continental Airlines

Auckland, but towards the end of the following year he suffered a stroke and retired from Cory's on health grounds. He returned briefly in 1992 but, following more periods of ill-health, he died on 20 July 1994 aged 75.

James Scott conducted Brighouse in 1981–82 (winning the European Championships with them in 1981) and Grimethorpe in 1983. From 1984 he was conducting Wingates and two years later, though still with Wingates, was appointed professional conductor of Yorkshire Imperial, having conducted them spasmodically since 1979. Scott also worked with other bands and adjudicated regularly, both in Britain and abroad. Towards the end of the 1980s he relinquished much of his conducting work in order to concentrate more on adjudicating and in 1990 he retired from his full-time post as Head of Brass and Senior Instrumental Teacher for Wirral Schools' Instrumental Services. From 1993, following the death of Harry Mortimer, Scott became music adviser to the Pontin's Championships. He was a co-conductor of Kings of Brass from its formation in 1995. In the year 2000 James Scott flew south to adjudicate at the Australian and New Zealand Championships.

Denzil Stephens was a wartime refugee from Guernsey. As was seen on page 7, his evacuation led to him becoming a member of Black Dyke, eventually playing solo euphonium. In 1950 he joined the RAF. By 1955 he was at its Music School at Uxbridge and by 1972, as Director of Music of the RAF Cranwell Band, had reached the rank of Squadron Leader. Although serving in various locations, he never lost touch with brass bands and enjoyed conducting appointments with several, including Ransome's and Carlton Main. He also became musical director of Cory's in the late 1970s and then, after leaving the RAF, musical editor of Wright & Round.

Stephens left Cory's in 1981, but not before he had led them to first place in the European Championships of 1980. He had associations with many other bands over the next few years, including Carlton Main, Point of Ayr, Fairey's, Hammonds, BTM and Parc & Dare. In 1985 he founded his own music publishing company, having severed his connections with Wright & Round. Called Sarnia Music, its catalogue contained many of his own compositions. From 1987 he was again associated with Cory's and during 1989 directed some Britannia Building Society concerts. During the early 1990s Denzil Stephens moved to Cornwall, there working with several local bands.

Roy Newsome was musical director of Besses from 1978 to 1985. During this period he became something of a globe-trotter, adjudicating three times at the Australian National Championships (1978, 1981 and 1987) and twice in New Zealand (1982 and 1990). He visited the USA several times to conduct River City Brass Band (see page 316) and in 1984 was chief adjudicator at the second contest of the North American

Brass Band Association (NABBA). Whilst with Besses, Newsome worked with several other bands. He also regularly visited Switzerland to conduct and adjudicate, and in 1987 was appointed adviser to the music committee of the Swiss Championships.

In 1986 he became professional conductor of Fairey Engineering, with title-winning performances both in the Nationals and the British Open. However, in 1989 he returned to Sun Life, where the two main successes were wins at the British Open in 1990 – Newsome's fifth success at the Open – and at the WMC contest in Kerkrade in 1993.

Nineteen-eighty-nine saw his retirement from Salford, the presentation of an Honorary Graduate Diploma and his appointment as Conductor Laureate. At around this time he did further conducting with several leading English bands and also visited Gothenburg Brass Band. In 1992 he made one of several visits to Japan, working mainly with the Breeze Brass Band of Osaka. Between 1986 and 1994 he was presenter of the BBC's weekly programme, *Listen to the Band*.

Leaving Sun Life in 1995, Newsome became more involved in adjudicating and did little further contest conducting. From 1984 to 2000 he was music director of the NYBB and in 1993 succeeded Harry Mortimer as president of the NABBC. In 1999 Roy Newsome graduated as a PhD, his thesis being titled 'The 19th Century Brass Band in Northern England'.

Trevor Walmsley was resident conductor of Black Dyke during 1982, but in the following year was appointed consultant to a newly formed Boosey & Hawkes Advisory Services. He nevertheless retained his conducting interests and conducted both Ransome's and Point of Ayr during these years. He published a booklet in 1986 – *You and Your Band*. During 1992 he became musical director of Carlton Main. However, now in his seventies, he became less involved with bands. He died on 25 March 1998 aged 76.

Derek Broadbent's residency with Brighouse & Rastrick lasted until 1983, when he took a similar appointment at Black Dyke. After two years there he returned to Brighouse as musical director, conducting the band at all contests as well as in most of its engagements. In 1988 he became musical editor for Wright & Round. He left Brighouse at the end of 1989 and for a time concentrated more on composing, editing and adjudicating, though in 1990 he became professional conductor of Wingates. Youth bands figured quite heavily in Broadbent's schedule – he conducted the Manx Youth Band on a tour of New Zealand and directed the highly successful summer courses of the Wessex Youth Band. In 1992 he became resident conductor of Fairey's, but between 1996 and 1998 was professional conductor of Besses. He also worked with other bands – including Flowers and Ransome's – as well as producing a steady stream of compositions and arrangements and becoming a much sought-after adjudicator.[14]

Remaining as musical director of GUS until 1985, Keith Wilkinson then took up a similar post with William Davis Construction. Under his direction these two bands won the Midlands or North Midlands Area contest nine times. Several other bands also came under his influence and in 1991 he gave up his academic career in order to devote all of his time to brass band work. In 1996 he moved to Ohio in the USA, taking up an appointment as Divisional Music Director with the SA. He left this position in 1999 and in the following year became professional conductor of the St Louis Brass Band. He had a number of successful published arrangements.

The William Davis and GUS bands were also conducted by John Berryman.[15] In 1985 Berryman returned to the band of which he had been principal cornet player, GUS – about to be renamed Rigid Containers Group – remaining there until 1998. He directed three winning performances in the Area contests: one with William Davis and two with Rigid Containers. As a brass teacher for the Northampton County Council, he conducted the County Youth Band, retiring from this in 1997 after 22 years' service. John Berryman remains a well-respected adjudicator.

In 1990 John Hudson stood down as principal cornet player of Britannia Building Society and was appointed resident conductor of CWS (Glasgow), which he conducted in the National Championships in 1990 – winning 1st prize. In 1993 he took Tredegar to runner-up position in the Nationals and two years later led Wingates to a win in the North West Area contest. Hudson then left Wingates and for a time was musical director of William Davis Construction Works Band, whilst also conducting a number of local bands in Lancashire. However, he was now spending much time in Norway and early in 2000 he moved there.

With his Radio Orchestra background and a flair for arranging, Ray Farr was highly successful in entertainment contests. As resident conductor of Grimethorpe he led it to four wins at Brass in Concert and one in the Granada Band of the Year. Leaving in 1984 he took Parc & Dare to the European Championships and then moved to Yorkshire Imperial, staying until 1986. He worked with several other bands and was musical director of City of Coventry from 1987 to 1989. In 1990 he moved to Norway where he became resident conductor of Eikanger, but also had associations with several other Norwegian bands. In 1995 he began renewing his links with English bands, conducting Desford at the Open and Fairey's at the Nationals. In 1997 he had a brief association with DUT Yorkshire Imperial and in 2000 led Foden's to victory at Brass in Concert.

---

[14] See biography in the British Open programme of 1988.
[15] See biography in the British Open programme of 1987.

Phillip McCann, Black Dyke's principal cornet player until 1988, worked initially as a conductor with his Huddersfield students, forming them into the Tecol Band. Chandos Records produced a very popular series of CDs featuring McCann on cornet, playing 'The World's Most Beautiful Melodies'. The series had been begun whilst he was at Black Dyke and was continued with Sellers, which grew out of Tecol and of which he had become musical director. In addition to his work at Huddersfield, he played principal cornet with Brighouse & Rastrick in both the Open and the Nationals of 1998, then became principal cornet of Leyland and accepted a part-time teaching appointment at Birmingham School of Music. In 1997, having won the Grand Shield with Sellers, McCann made his debut as a conductor in the British Open Championships.

In addition to his work with Sellers, McCann made numerous appearances as a guest soloist and in 1991 returned to Fairey's for a short time as principal cornet and resident conductor. In 1992 he took Whitburn to the National Finals; he later conducted them periodically and became their musical director in 1999. In 1995 he resigned from Sellers and conducted Britannia Building Society for some time, but in 1999 he returned to the Huddersfield-based band. In this same year he joined the Boosey & Hawkes instrumental research team, helping with the design of new models of cornet.

Living in various locations in the South, Kenneth Dennison became less actively involved with practical band matters, though he did some conducting in the 1980s and was still in demand as an adjudicator. In the 1990s he became involved in administration, as president of the Southern Counties Amateur Bands Association and for a time as general secretary of the BFBB.

Denis Carr also took a less active role from about 1987, prior to which he had held conducting appointments with Brodsworth, CWS (Glasgow), Wingates and Lewington Yamaha. His work with the BBC precluded him from devoting much time to banding and he faded into the background.

Other conductors with an input during this period include Paul Cosh, a professional trumpet player; Bryan Hurdley; and Melvin White and Jeremy Wise, both with SA backgrounds. Cosh is found in the records of Parc & Dare, Sun Life, Hanwell and Ransomes and Hurdley came to the fore as resident conductor of Sun Life in the late 1980s. He held a similar position with Fairey's from 1991 to 1998, when he moved to Cornwall to work with the Mount Charles group of bands. He moved back north in 2000 to become resident conductor of Foden's. White was very active in the South throughout the period and amongst the bands with which his name was linked were Newham, Cory's, Hendon, BTM, Woodfalls and GUS/Travelsphere. He had a very good record in Area contests. Wise came on the scene as a conductor in the 1990s, having spells with Hendon, Brighouse, Cory's and First City Brass (see Glossary). Details of some other conductors will be found in 'Personalia'.

*Some other notable personalities*

Bram Gay continued to combine his professional career with his interests in bands but was unable to be involved on a week-to-week basis due to commitments at Covent Garden. His influence during the latter part of the twentieth century was mainly through his work as editor of Novello's brass band publications, as an arranger, as an adjudicator and in his various advisory capacities. He was a major driving force behind Granada Band of the Year, which ran from 1971 to 1987, and also became something of an entrepreneur, organising many concerts. Gay was a frequent visitor to Sweden as guest conductor of both the Solna and Gothenburg bands. Along with composer Edward Gregson, he was a founding editor of the magazine *Sounding Brass*, and the two of them were joined by William Relton on the Boosey & Hawkes advisory panel, convened when the company took over the Nationals.

Though never active with any particular band (except as a player in the 1940s), William Relton, through his work at the BBC, became an influential figure not only with brass bands but in the musical world at large. In 1970, after 13 years as a music producer – many of them looking after band programmes – he was appointed orchestral manager of the BBC Symphony Orchestra. Five years later he became general manager, responsible for concerts, tours, and the appointment of conductors. He was on the Council of the Royal Albert Hall and actively involved with the Arts Council of England. In the brass band world, in addition to a number of advisory positions, he regularly accepted guest-conducting appointments and probably adjudicated at more of the leading competitions in Britain and Europe than any other person.

David Read continued with his work in education and as conductor of Cambridge Co-op Band (from which he retired in 1988 after 14 years). During the 1980s he became a leading adjudicator, regularly officiating at the highest level both in Britain and abroad. By the year 2000 he had officiated in 11 British Open Championships and 12 Nationals. Always keenly interested in developments in education, he became Education Officer for the British Federation of Brass Bands.

## Players

*Soloists who have championed their particular instruments*

Whilst it is true that all quality players help raise the status of their instrument there are a few who have not only performed to a high level, but have commissioned new solos, given recitals and masterclasses, and literally crusaded to widen their instrument's acceptance.

The band-playing and conducting of Robert and Nicholas Childs has already been outlined, but there is another dimension to their careers – as The Childs Brothers (Figure 11.7). This began in the 1980s, at first almost as a family affair, sometimes involving their father/conductor John,[16] and other members of the family. Their international reputation developed from 1987 with engagements in Europe, America and Russia, and with regular appearances in the Nationals gala concerts. Their tours promoted the British style of euphonium-playing – considerably different from the traditional American style. They were also responsible for commissioning and premiering new works for euphonium, including several concertos. Under the name Childs Play – the title of a piece composed for them by John Golland – they made recordings and edited albums of solos for euphonium.

More than any other brass band player, however, Steven Mead has become a professional soloist with a worldwide reputation. During the second half of the 1990s he did little band-playing other than on an occasional basis with CWS (Glasgow), concentrating on recitals, masterclasses and teaching. He has also been responsible for the commissioning of many new works for euphonium, not only with brass band, but also with wind band, with orchestra and with piano accompaniment.

The tenor horn is almost unique to the brass band. One of its finest exponents, Gordon Higginbottom, won his first solo contest at the age of eight and joined Besses Boys' Band at 13. At 16 he was a member of CWS (Manchester) Band. A tenor horn player *par excellence*, he was a key figure in gaining recognition for this as a solo instrument, several solos being composed specially for him. He played with several leading bands, but achieved his greatest fame as the tenor horn and mellophonium player with JSVB, with whom he played until 1989. This despite already being recognised worldwide as a soloist/entertainer, with appearances throughout Britain, Europe, America and Japan. He was able to combine his artistic life with his professional career, which had moved into the development and marketing of brass instruments, first for Boosey & Hawkes and later for Yamaha. In 1991 Higginbottom was one of the founders of the Tenor Horn Society.

Other tenor horn soloists devoted to promoting the instrument included Sandy Smith (of Black Dyke, Fairey's and Grimethorpe) and Sheona White (of YBS). The latter, as a result of winning the title of 'BBC Radio 2 Young

---

[16] John Childs left Tredegar in 1978; amongst other bands which he conducted were Brodsworth, Carlton Main and Ever Ready. He died in 1985, aged only 52.

Figure 11.7   The Childs Brothers – Nicholas and Robert – in the Yorkshire village of Dobcross, *c.* 1980

Musician of the Year' in 1996 became known worldwide, touring in Europe, Australia and New Zealand.

The other instrument which is virtually unique to the brass band is the baritone. A number of individuals have helped it achieve wider recognition through solo work, recording and commissioning. These include Carole Crompton, associated with Desford and Britannia Building Society; Peter Christian – of Foden's, Fairey's and Black Dyke; Stephen Booth – of Leyland, Black Dyke and YBS; and Robert Blackburn, associated with Black Dyke and Yorkshire Building Society.

Another pioneer for his instrument was Stephen Sykes. From 1978 he was E♭ bass tuba soloist with Grimethorpe Colliery, where he achieved an international reputation as a brilliant exponent of the instrument – not really regarded up to that time as a solo instrument. In 1982 he left Grimethorpe and began developing his career as soloist, clinician and arranger, and founding his own publishing company. The inspiration behind many solo works for tuba, Sykes has performed in all the major brass band countries. He has also performed with leading wind bands and has produced a range of solo CDs.

James Gourlay, though a leading conductor, has also remained dedicated to the tuba, appearing regularly as soloist and clinician, crusading for it as a solo instrument and being responsible for a number of commissions and premieres.

*Some other leading players – a summary*

This section is a kind of overview, intended to tie up a few loose ends. Because more bandsmen play cornet than any other instrument more of them become well-known personalities. Many have become professional trumpet players, though more have stayed in brass bands. Some have already been discussed, and the careers of several others are outlined in 'Personalia'.

Soprano cornet is an important position in any band. Often referred to as the 'piccolo of the band', it plays high, exposed parts and demands total control of both technique and nerve. There have been several legendary 'soprano' players down the years; four who were living legends by the end of the century are discussed in 'Personalia' – Brian Evans, Peter Roberts, Roy Roe and Allan Wycherley.

The flugelhorn came into its own as a solo instrument quite late in the century and has so far produced few, if any, legendary players. As there is only normally one such instrument in a band, it is called upon to play many solo passages within band pieces and has been increasingly featured in stand-up solos and duets. Amongst those who have given good service to the instrument are David Pogson who held the position for some 25 years at Black Dyke and Mark Walters who played with great distinction for a number of years at Grimethorpe. Amongst several solo prizes won by Walters was the British Open Solo Champion title in 1989. A predecessor of Walters at Grimethorpe was Stan Lippeatt. He also did much to bring the flugelhorn to the fore as a solo instrument, later following in his father's footsteps as a conductor.

The tenor horn achieved prominence rather earlier than the flugelhorn. A number of horn soloists have already been commented on. Two others deserving of a mention are Kevin Wadsworth, solo horn player with Black Dyke for many years and later with Brighouse & Rastrick, and William (Billy) Rushworth, a remarkable player who played with several leading bands before, like Wadsworth, taking an interest in conducting. Amongst legendary baritone players, the name John Slinger, of Black Dyke, is first and foremost.

The trombone is one of the most versatile of all brass instruments and is found not only in brass and wind (military) bands but also in jazz and the symphony orchestra. Many trombonists have begun their playing careers in brass bands and then moved on. Four who remained faithful to their roots are discussed in 'Personalia' – Nicholas Hudson, Chris Jeans, John Maines and Chris Thomas.

The euphonium, 'the cello of the band', is primarily a band instrument and its exponents are likely to stay in the band scene. Never having played with any of the leading bands, Barrie Perrins is less well-known than other euphonium players so far discussed. His career is outlined in 'Personalia'.

Lyndon Baglin became 'Euphonium Player of the Year' in 1984, though by then he was becoming involved in conducting. He made something of a comeback when, in 1989, he became solo euphonium player with Cory's, a year later switching to the same position with Sun Life and helping this band to its 1990 title of British Open Champions. After a further period of 'retirement' he was back with Sun Life in 1994 – playing E♭ bass.

Other great euphonium players during this period included Trevor Groom, associated with Munn & Felton's/GUS for most of his top-class playing days; John Clough, solo euphonium with Black Dyke for almost 25 years; David Moore, principally with Grimethorpe but also playing with JSVB and Yorkshire Imperial; Stephen Lord, of Wingates and Brighouse; and Bill Millar (see page 85), who played with several bands, including Wingates, Leyland, Grimethorpe and JSVB. Clough later took up the baritone, playing with various bands. The award of Euphonium Player of the Year went to Groom in 1981 and Clough in 1987, whilst Moore was Champion Soloist of Great Britain in 1969 and 1970. Robin Taylor had a brief but spectacular career in brass bands prior to joining the RAF in the late 1990s. Playing with Grimethorpe, he was voted Euphonium Player of the Year and British Open Soloist in 1995. There was also Mike Kilroy, whose bands have included CWS (Manchester), Wingates, Yorkshire Imperial, Leyland, Brighouse and Grimethorpe.

Other instrumentalists whose input warrants a mention include Kevin Crockford, a former NYBB member who played soprano with several bands, including City of Coventry, Leyland, Carlton Main, Desford, Grimethorpe and Fairey's and, for good measure, spent two periods with Black Dyke. Two younger players who each found their way to Black Dyke were trombonist Brett Baker and David Thornton, another star of the euphonium. Baker played for some time with Flowers and had already acquired a reputation as a recitalist before moving to Fairey's in 1992 and then to Black Dyke in 2000. He had made two CDs and undertaken a recital tour of Australia and New Zealand. Thornton also reached Black Dyke in 2000, via Wingates and Fairey's. He was a student at the RNCM and won a number of prestigious prizes and scholarships. Baker and Thornton were both former principal players with the NYBB.

## Conclusion

Despite the problems outlined early in this chapter, brass bands made incredible progress, particularly in the 1990s. Though bands themselves create their players, it is obvious that it is the players who, in turn, enable their bands to reach new heights of achievement.

It is also obvious that the increased professionalism within the movement has found new musical pathways for bands to explore.

Most of the leading conductors have, as will have been noted, been attached to a range of bands. They seem to fall into three basic categories: those who have been brought up in the movement and remained there; those who began their music-making in bands, went into the music profession and returned to inject new ideas; and those who have not previously been connected with bands but have created new horizons for banding. All three groups have contributed to the progress of bands, helping bring them into their years of maturity.

The fruits of all this have been increased acceptance in the wider world of music, compositions by more mainstream composers and a dramatic increase in the number of high-quality concert openings.

# Part Four
# Overseas Developments

# CHAPTER 12

# Brass bands outside mainland Britain

## Introduction

The first moves towards international status for brass bands were initiated by the Salvation Army, starting in the 1880s. They were said to exist in 63 different countries by 1916, in 97 by 1941 and in 103 by 1997,[1] but many of these 'bands' were merely small brass ensembles. The Boys' Brigade also played its part. It boasted several brass bands in Britain, and the origins of brass bands in Ireland are attributable to this organisation. However, the biggest factor in the early spread of the British-style brass band was the large number of mid-nineteenth-century emigrants who took their skills and enthusiasms into other parts of the world, in particular to Australia, New Zealand and Canada.

Though pockets of interest existed in some other countries, the brass band as we know it, even in the 1930s, was substantially a British phenomenon. In post-war years it was to become a major 'export', first of all to mainland Europe. Holland, Switzerland, Norway, Denmark, Sweden, Belgium and Luxembourg all became areas of development for British-style brass bands. Though France and Germany were regularly visited by bands, it was not until late in the twentieth century that those countries became seriously interested. There was also a growing interest in countries as diverse as the Faroe Islands and the USA.

The growth of British-style bands in America began in the 1960s and gave encouragement to the small group of bands in Canada. The final developing area of any significance was Japan, where British-style banding took root in the 1970s.

## Other parts of the British Isles

### Northern Ireland

Due to an industrial environment and regular visitors from England, brass bands became a significant part of local culture in Northern Ireland. They

---

[1] Herbert, 2000, p. 215.

featured in the Irish Championships during the 1930s. In 1938 there were eight brass bands in the senior brass section. Lisburn Silver – one of the oldest – were winners; five more participated in the junior brass section. By 1939 there were some 16 brass bands in the North, some having recently converted from flute bands. Information on the war years is almost non-existent, but the Northern Ireland Bands Association advertised for an adjudicator in May 1945.

It was inevitable that Northern Ireland bands would wish to measure their standards against those of their counterparts in mainland Britain and some began attending the Belle Vue May contest. The first was Agnes Street which, in 1949, secured 3rd prize in Class B.

By 1951 Northern Ireland had two major brass band contests, one for brass bands only, organised by the newly formed Brass Band League, and the Irish Championships – catering for all kinds of band and spread over six evenings.[2] The 55th Old Boys and Laganvale Silver dominated during the 1950s, when it was estimated that there were about 100 bands – mainly brass – with more conversions from flute bands.

An interesting event, indicative of the progress being made, took place in January 1955. This was a 'Brass and Voices' concert with the massed bands of Agnes Street and Laganvale. The programme included Denis Wright's transcriptions of the Grieg *Piano Concerto* (first movement) and excerpts from his transcription of *Messiah*. The League Championships this year attracted 21 brass bands, in four sections. In the following year 32 competed, including Stedfast from Dublin (see below).

Visitors to Belfast during the early post-war years included William Halliwell and Harry Mortimer. In 1957 Denis Wright travelled there to conduct the Templemore Avenue band in the first Northern Ireland performance of the complete version of his *Messiah* transcription. The band was made up of pupils of Templemore Avenue School, having been founded by the music master, A.E. (Alfie) Bell, who also conducted. In 1957 the average age was said to be 15. Templemore's first visit to Belle Vue was in 1956, when it took 1st prize in the Senior Cup. As a result of its consistency in May contests over a few years, the band was invited to participate in the September contest of 1958. Probably the youngest band ever to play at this event, it certainly received the greatest ovation of the day. It returned the following year to take 5th prize.

During 1964 a Northern Ireland Youth Brass Band was formed, W.B. Hargreaves directing the course.[3]

---

2 In addition to those for brass bands, there were classes for flute bands, accordion bands and military bands. All had senior, intermediate and junior sections. See also *BBN* January 1951, p. 3, and *The Conductor*, October 1951, p. 6.

3 *BB* 5 October 1963, p. 2, and 6 June 1964, p. 6.

As the political problems escalated in the North, bands survived under difficult circumstances. In 1972 it was reported that Templemore had been bombed out of its bandroom twice. Despite this, it continued to be the most pro-active of the Northern Ireland bands, winning the Championships several times in the late 1970s and early 1980s.

From 1985 Agnes Street again became the leading Northern Ireland band. As Irish Champions in 1988 it was invited to the European Championships but, unfortunately, could not raise sufficient funds to attend. Regrettably, it folded in 1994. Formed in 1921, it had been Irish Champions seven times, and competed in the British Open Championships during the 1960s. Fortunately, the remnants of the band joined forces with other local bands to become CWA Brass.[4]

Meanwhile, Strabane Concert was coming to the fore, becoming League Champions in 1992 and 1993, and Northern Ireland Champions in 1994. Nevertheless, interest in brass bands had waned somewhat by now and, in an attempt to revive it and also to strengthen bonds between North and South, a new Irish National Youth Band was formed in 1998, performing under the direction of Dennis Wilby. However, this suffered from lack of support and survived for only two or three years.

## Southern Ireland

Southern Ireland (Eire) was predominantly agricultural and, though pockets of interest exist, these have never developed into a 'movement'. It had strong traditions in flute and military bands, but one of the earliest Irish brass bands was formed there, growing out of the Boys' Brigade movement.[5] This emanated from Glasgow and its arrival in Dublin in 1891 was marked by the formation of the 1st Dublin Company's brass band. A second band appeared in 1898, attached to the 14th Company of the Boys' Brigade. In 1936 past members of the 14th Company formed an Old Boys' Band and called it St George's.

The 6th Old Boys, whose band was not founded until 1942, did the same in 1951, forming the Stedfast Band. This was the first band from Eire to compete at a Belle Vue contest, entering the May contest of 1955. It also competed in the Northern Ireland League Championships of 1956 and in the second section of the *Daily Herald* North West Area contest of 1960. It made its first broadcast on Radio Eireann in August 1956.

St George's won 1st prize at the Irish National Music Festival in 1955, and in December 1957 the three Southern bands combined for a Festival

---

[4] CWA are initials for Carrick, Whitehouse and Agnes Street.
[5] The Boys' Brigade was formed in Glasgow in 1883, and within a few years had a brass band with similar instrumentation to that of other early British brass bands.

of Carols. A further joint concert was given in the following year to celebrate the seventy-fifth anniversary of the Boys' Brigade, whilst in 1960 Templemore travelled south and combined with Stedfast in a 'Bands Across the Border' concert.

An Irish Association of Brass & Military Bands was formed in 1959; by 1966 there were 30 member bands, including Concord, a brass band recently formed in Dublin. Regional committees were formed and there was an annual Summer School in Drogheda, some 25 miles north of Dublin, directed by Allan Street.

Between 1966 and 1978 Stedfast won the Irish National Championships eight times, achieving two hat-tricks. It attended the Belle Vue Spring Festival seven times and competed in the North West Area contests on four occasions.

Brass bands in Eire now struggled for some years but there was a revival in the late 1990s with new names coming to the fore, some of them competing as Irish Champions in the B section of the European Championships (begun in 1994). These included Loch Garmon, Arklow Silver and Drogheda. Arklow was founded in 1968 and entered its first contest five years later. From 1977 it competed regularly at Pontin's, appeared on radio and TV and also produced recordings. It first competed in the European Championships B Section in 1988, earning fourth place. Drogheda has roots going back to 1886, but did not become all-brass until 1964. It has several Irish National titles to its name and first competed in the European B section in 2000.

## The Isle of Man

Due to its close proximity to North West England and its consequent attraction to British holidaymakers, the Isle of Man was a virtual beehive of banding activity during the 1930s. Manxland notes in *BBN* were teeming with information about the island's bands, of which there were eight in addition to the Douglas SA Band.[6]

The Isle of Man's bands struggled during the war. However, the Manxland correspondent reappeared in *BBN* in March 1945 with news that bands on the Island were re-awakening. Nevertheless, news was sparse and a report in *BBN* of May 1951 indicated that the level of activity was still low. One group had disbanded through lack of interest and the brass band section of the Manx Guild contest was cancelled, only two bands having entered.

---

6 The eight bands were Douglas Town, St Matthew's Douglas, Castletown Metropolitan, Crosby Village, Ramsey Town, Laxey Village, Peel and Onchan, the last-named being formed in Coronation year.

Visits by British bands during the 1970s aided a rejuvenation and during this decade a Manx Youth Brass Band was formed, its founder and conductor being Jim Crosbie MBE, a local enthusiast who died in 1981.

There was a gradual renaissance during the 1980s, with the reappearance of the Manx Festival, a local radio programme called *Time for Brass*, a three-day course directed by James Shepherd and organised by Ramsey Town Band, and, in 1986, a visit by Black Dyke.

Nineteen-eighty-seven was a momentous year for banding on the island, with the Manx Youth Band touring Holland, Sun Life giving a concert in Douglas, the hosting of the last Granada contest and the commencement of the Isle of Man Brass Band Festival. This was supported by the Manx Tourist Board and attracted 18 bands from the mainland to a two-section entertainment contest in Douglas, with bands also marching along the promenade. This competition, known as 'The Friendly Festival', flourished for a decade but was cancelled in 1997 due to a low entry, and was never revived. On a happier note, Kings of Brass gave a concert in Douglas later in the year.

The biggest event during the latter part of the century was a tour of New Zealand by the Manx Youth Band during August 1990. This was quite extensive and concentrated to a large extent on the promotion of music in schools. Derek Broadbent was musical director for the tour.

The island's bands have all progressed during the 1990s no doubt encouraged by the continuation of the radio programme *Time for Brass*.

## The Channel Islands

Pre-war brass band activity in the Channel Islands seems to have been confined to bands of the SA. During the early post-war years several top British bands visited fairly regularly, usually playing in the Howard Davies Park in St Helier. Outside of the SA the Band of the Isle of Jersey, a band of 29 plus a corps of six drummers, became a brass band in 1962 and was fulfilling 12 engagements per year for the Jersey Tourism Committee, besides making regular trips to France.[7]

The Guernsey Concert Band was formed in 1965, and in 1978 a Guernsey Youth Band gave a concert conducted by composer Robert Farnon. Derek Broadbent visited this band in 1979 and in the following year Brighouse & Rastrick Band were its guests. Denzil Stephens, a native of Guernsey, returned to conduct the Youth Band in 1981. By 1995 the Concert Band, now 30 years old and 52 strong, was giving 50 concerts per annum. From 1997 it began an annual pilgrimage to Lancashire to

---

[7] Further details of the Band of the Isle of Jersey are to be found in *BB* of 21 September 1968, on p. 6.

participate in the Whit Friday march contests. There was also a band on the island of Alderney, formed in 1991 after the first of several visits by Redbridge.

## The Antipodes

*The early years*

On the other side of the world National Championships were held annually in New Zealand from 1890. In Australia there were State Championships only at first, with the Nationals founded early in the twentieth century. Interchange between British and Antipodean band people has a long history. Besses o' th' Barn Band toured both countries early in the twentieth century, various Australian bands have visited Britain and for many years English adjudicators have officiated both in Australia and New Zealand.

The New Zealand Brass Bands Association was formed in 1931 to organise the annual National Championships, which alternate between North and South Islands. Though New Zealand is some 2000 miles east of Australia, there has long been rivalry between bands of the two countries. This began in 1935 when New Zealand's Woolston Brass competed successfully in the Australian Championships in Ballarat.[8]

Former Australian cornet champion Frank Wright settled in England in 1934. In February 1940 he adjudicated at New Zealand's Centennial Contest in Wellington. Brass band activities in both countries were minimal during the war.

*After World War II*

The New Zealand Nationals were reinstated in 1946 and by 1952 Australian bands were under the control of the Australian Band Council which was now responsible for organising the National Championships. In an attempt to spread the enormous cost of travelling these are nowadays rotated through the six states where brass bands exist – South Australia, Queensland, New South Wales, Victoria, Tasmania and, over 3000 miles away, Western Australia. In both Australia and New Zealand the National Championships are spread over five days and include solo and ensemble playing as well as own choice and set test categories for full band. There are also spectacular marching competitions. Instead of the 'first section', 'second section' designations used in Britain, both countries use the terms 'A Grade', 'B Grade' and so on.

---

[8] Newcomb, 1980, p. 47.

Denis Wright developed an affinity with New Zealand. He was the first post-war British adjudicator to officiate there and made four visits – in 1951, 1956, 1959 and 1961. Typically, the 1956 visit lasted four months, taking in both New Zealand and Australia. He gave a series of lectures at University College, Canterbury,[9] and after the five-day championships undertook about 100 engagements. He also travelled to Australia to adjudicate the Queensland Championships.[10]

Other English adjudicators officiating at New Zealand's Nationals during this period were Eric Ball (1952 and 1955) and Harry Mortimer (1953). Ball's 1955 trip also took in Australia, where he adjudicated in Ballarat. In 1956 Mortimer was chief adjudicator at the Australian Championships.

Several ex-Fairey's men conducted bands in New Zealand in the late 1950s, including Elgar Clayton, Frank Smith and Robert Mulholland. There was also the influential Ken Smith (see page 147). Bands regularly advertised in the British band press for players and conductors, free passage and assistance with housing and employment generally being offered.

The National Band of New Zealand undertook its first tour in 1953. This cost around £30 000, most of it raised in New Zealand before the start of the tour, including a government grant of £10 000. The country had a population of a mere two million and yet 130 contesting bands were now registered with its Association,[11] which organised the National Band and its tours and took responsibility for New Zealand's National Youth Brass Band, as well as being responsible for the Nationals.

The 1957 Australian Championships were held in Tanunda, South Australia. Ken Smith was the chief adjudicator and 21 bands participated – five in A Grade. Malvern Municipal, Hawthorne City and Preston Municipal – all from Victoria, the strongest banding state at the time – were the prizewinners. The 1958 New Zealand Nationals in Dunedin attracted 41 bands, ten of them in A Grade. The chief adjudicator was again Ken Smith, and the winning band St Kilda. These figures suggest that banding – or at least contesting – was taken more seriously in New Zealand than in Australia.

There was little news of activity from either country during the 1960s, though in 1968 there were further articles and advertisements inviting British bandsmen to emigrate to Australia.

News in the 1970s was more plentiful. Geoffrey Brand made the first of many trips to the southern hemisphere in 1972, adjudicating in both Australia and New Zealand. He was back in Australia for a month in

---

[9] Canterbury is the most heavily-populated region of South Island. Christchurch is its principal city.

[10] For fuller details of Denis Wright in the Antipodes, see Newsome, 1995, pp. 184–90.

[11] *The Conductor*, January 1954, p. 8.

1975. In addition to adjudicating, he undertook a training programme for conductors in several centres under the auspices of the National Council. He returned to New Zealand during 1977 – adjudicating, directing seminars and working with the National Youth Brass Band.

W.B. Hargreaves went to Australia to adjudicate the 1973 Nationals, also directing seminars and workshops; whilst in the same year Eric Ball adjudicated the New Zealand Championships. He awarded 1st prize to Skellerup Woolston who were to come to Britain in 1975 – and win the Edinburgh Contest.

By the 1970s Sydney was one of Australia's brass band strongholds, with two of its bands directed by professional brass players: Willoughby, conducted by trumpet player Peter Walmsley, and Waverley, conducted by tuba player Cliff Goodchild. Both bands gave high-profile concerts and in 1972, as 'Sydney Brass', combined for a concert in the newly built Sydney Opera House.

In addition to the Sydney bands there were two highly successful bands in the Melbourne area of Victoria. These were Hawthorne City and Footscray-Yarraville. Footscray were Australian Champions in 1972–73–74, Hawthorne City in 1975–76–77, Willoughby in 1979, then Hawthorne again in 1979, but New Zealanders Skellerup Woolston became Australian Champions in 1980. Roy Newsome was chief adjudicator at the 1978 Australian championships, when 50 bands competed in four sections. Hawthorne were conducted for a number of years by a former Black Dyke cornet player, Ken McDonald; his principal solo cornet player was Tom Paulin (see page 150 n.26). Hawthorne continued to dominate the Australian National Championships during the 1980s and 1990s.

In 1975 Footscray-Yarraville went on a three-week tour of Canada, and won an international competition. Hammonds Sauce Works Band undertook a historic two-week tour in Australia during 1976, being the first British non-SA band in the Antipodes since the Besses tour of 1911. Concerts were given in Perth, Sydney and Melbourne. Footscray then visited Switzerland and Britain in 1984, whilst Black Dyke toured Australia in 1988, the bicentennial year. They performed in Sydney Opera House and were guests at the National Championships. River City Brass Band, from the USA (see pages 316–17), also toured Australia in 1988.

CWS (Glasgow) undertook a substantial tour of both Australia and New Zealand in 1993. Two years later Stocksbridge Engineering Band made a 20-day tour. Manx Youth Band toured New Zealand in 1990, Skellerup toured Japan in 1993 and the National Band of New Zealand toured the USA in 1995. In the same year another band, Waitakere, visited Denmark and Britain, competing at the Pontin's Championships. The world had become a smaller place!

The New Zealand Championships were dominated by Skellerup Woolston during the 1970s, with wins in 1971–72, 1974–75–76 and 1978–79. The winners in 1980 were the newly sponsored Continental Airlines Auckland Brass. The 1980 Championships celebrated a century of contesting in New Zealand and were sponsored by Boosey & Hawkes. Amongst the special features were two newly composed test pieces, *Land of the Long White Cloud* by Philip Sparke and *Hinemoa* by Gareth Wood. These were used as set tests in grades A and B and both titles had a special significance for New Zealand's Maori connections.

Skellerup continued to dominate in the 1980s and early 1990s, though there were several other champions including Continental Airlines Auckland and Wormald Brass. Ten British bandsmen joined up with Wormald Brass in 1989, helping it to its win in the following year, whilst Nigel Weeks, former conductor of Tredegar (see Glossary), emigrated in 1993 to become its musical director.

During the 1990s, following sponsorship changes, Wormald Brass was renamed Television New Zealand Brass, and Continental Airlines became Foster's Auckland Brass.

## Canada

Canada had been a haven for British immigrants since around 1840. Many chose to settle in Ontario, Canada's second largest province. Its capital, Toronto, developed into a major industrial region and could have become rich in brass bands. The Household Troops Band of the SA toured in 1888,[12] and both Black Dyke and Besses o' th' Barn were there in 1906, following which there were pockets of enthusiasm. These were later encouraged by the Canadian National Exhibition (CNE) in Toronto, which had classes for brass bands in its annual competition and, during the early 1930s, featured both St Hilda's and Besses o' th' Barn on its bandstand. However, because of the influence of America and its wind bands, there were few secular brass bands – about ten seniors and possibly a dozen junior and intermediate ones.

News of Canadian brass bands during the 1930s came from a *BBN* correspondent. During a holiday in Canada he had spent some time with Toronto Silver, its 30 members said to be mostly from Britain. Having won the CNE contest three years in succession (1934–35–36), they claimed to be Champions of Canada. Ontario Regiment, based in Oshawa on the shores of Lake Ontario, were Champions in 1939 and 1940. Other bands which regularly competed included Weston Silver and Metropolitan Silver.

---

12 Boon, 1978, p. 61.

Moving into the 1950s, Metropolitan Silver was now the dominant band. This was attached to the Metropolitan United Church and in 1955 celebrated its twenty-first anniversary by completing a hat-trick at the contest.[13] Metropolitan won again in 1956 and 1957 but in the following year it took second place, Ontario Regiment winning. This band contained several recent British immigrants. Others had also joined bands in Weston and Whitby. Bands outside of the SA had survived on a slender thread during the early years of the twentieth century but due to this influx of brass band-minded immigrants they were becoming more active. There are parallels here with the Australian and New Zealand scenes, though on a smaller scale. Many bands were attached to part-time militia-type regiments.

Men o' Brass visited the CNE during 1961 and the National Band of New Zealand toured Canada in 1964. During the 1960s several English school bands visited both Canada and the USA.

The big event of the early 1970s was the Canadian Brass Band Festival of July 1972. Black Dyke, CWS (Manchester), GUS (Footwear) and Fairey, together with their respective resident conductors – Newsome, Garside, Boddington and Dennison – and three guest conductors – Mortimer, Ball and Brand – were flown across the Atlantic along with another plane full of supporters. They were based in Niagara Falls during their ten-day stay. There were two massed band concerts, one to open the Festival and the other to close it. Additionally the bands gave concerts with their own conductors, one each in Niagara Falls and others in places such as Toronto, Buffalo (USA) and Hamilton.

Hammonds Sauce Works Band spent a week in Canada during 1979, playing at the CNE. At around the same time *BB* carried reports of Metropolitan Silver[14] and Weston. As part of this latter band's sixtieth-anniversary celebration, it formed a composite band to rehearse with Edward Gregson, who was holidaying in Canada.

The CNE contest seems to have waned in the early 1980s, though new bands were being formed. The University of Toronto Brass Choir was instituted as a brass band in 1982 and two years later the now famous Hannaford Street Silver Band was formed. Made up of professional brass players and sponsored by Boosey & Hawkes, this was one of seven bands then functioning in Toronto, apart from the SA. There was also Chester Brass, located in Nova Scotia, some 1600 miles away. Nevertheless, Weston seems to have been one of the most active in the late 1980s, fulfilling some 25 engagements annually.

---

[13] Professor Ron Holz, of Asbury College Music Department, Wilmore, Kentucky, tells me that Metropolitan Silver was formed in 1930 on the resignation of the bandmaster and 29 bandsmen from a local Salvation Army band.

[14] *BB* 1 September 1979, p. 6 – including a good history.

Canadian bands received a boost in 1983 with the formation of the North American Brass Band Association (NABBA – see page 318). A number of them attended annual contests organised by this Association.

In 1988 composer Edward Gregson[15] embarked on a lecture tour across Canada, working with both SA and non-SA bands.

### Brass bands in Europe

Whilst there were many British-style brass bands in the Dominions, the only such ensembles in Europe before the war were attached to the SA. It was noted on page 160 that Foden's had visited Belgium, Holland and France in 1945. The Dutch part of the tour was of most significance because it was here that the European brass band movement began.

Many European countries are rich in amateur bands, but these are mainly either mixed wind bands or a rather hybrid combination known as the 'fanfare' (pronounced fan-far) – a combination of brass, percussion and saxophones. In these, trumpets and/or flugelhorns are preferred to cornets. Their early repertoire was mainly light.

### *The Netherlands*

There had been SA bands in Holland since the 1890s but the visit by Foden's exhibited new dimensions in brass-playing. Fairey Aviation also made a number of trips to Holland in the late 1940s, whilst Carlton Main had three successful tours (1949, 1950 and 1952), amazing audiences with their wide-ranging repertoire.

Denis Wright was in Holland during 1951, rehearsing three of the country's earliest British-style brass bands. All located in the North – at Groningen,[16] Leeuwarden and Drogenham – the bands combined at the end of the week in a massed band concert. Holland was sufficiently close to Britain to be able to hear the BBC's brass band broadcasts. The Royal Albert Hall Championships also attracted Dutch visitors and these two factors, along with the availability of recordings, paved the way for the development of the brass band. Enthusiasm was not universal, however. Many of those involved with wind bands or fanfares placed every possible impediment in the way of the progress of 'the British disease'.

---

[15] Edward Gregson's brother Bramwell conducted one of Canada's most prominent SA bands, in London, Ontario.

[16] Groningen Crescendo band claimed to be the first British-style brass band in Holland. It was formed in 1946 with 25 members, 15 of whom were ex-Salvation Army. The conductor was A. van Kammen, also ex-SA.

An international band contest was held in Kerkrade in the South Netherlands in 1951. This become known as the World Music Festival or WMC,[17] and eventually took place every four years. Details of the third event were announced in *BB* of 18 August 1956. To be held in 1958, it was specifically for amateur bands and orchestras and was subject to the rules of the Netherlands Music Federation. Free board and lodging was offered to groups resident more than 200 kilometres from Kerkrade.

WMC remained the leading music event in Holland and continued to attract British bands. Frank Wright was a regular adjudicator and wrote informative articles about the Festival.[18] The National Band of New Zealand won the 1953 contest with a record number of marks. GUS (Footwear) Band won in 1966 – again with a record mark, and the New Zealanders won again in 1970. At the 1974 festival the opening concert was given jointly by Brighouse & Rastrick and Fairey's – a singular honour for brass bands.

Dutch tours by British brass bands became more common during the 1950s. In 1954 Foden's were there again, having been invited to participate in a contest organised by a newly formed Dutch Brass Band Association. Whilst there, Foden's also gave four highly acclaimed concerts. Munn & Felton's spent two weeks in Holland during 1955, playing everywhere to full halls, fêted with civic receptions, and broadcasting from Hilversum.

The Dutch publisher Molenaar issued a number of pieces, transcribed for fanfare. The head of this company, Piet Molenaar, was a great enthusiast who regularly visited England and was an avid collector of brass band recordings.[19] Molenaar published a number of brass band works in editions for fanfare, which helped popularise British brass band music.

Two later visits were by Wingates (1969) and Black Dyke (1970). The former was organised by Gordon Higginbottom and Frank Wolff whilst the latter was at the invitation of Piet Molenaar to commemorate the twenty-fifth anniversary of the liberation of Holland. Another historic occasion was the first visit by a Dutch brass band to England – in 1970. This was Soli Deo Gloria, one of the early leading Dutch brass bands and based in Leeuwarden.

A Brass Band Club of The Netherlands was formed in 1968 by Jurien de Koning and a Dutch National Band was formed in the following year. The first Dutch brass band contest took place in Utrecht during June 1971

---

[17] The WMC (World Music Concourse) was founded as a result of the success of the early tours by Carlton Main.

[18] *BB* 1 August 1970, p. 1, and 15 August, pp. 1 and 8.

[19] The writer stayed with Mr Molenaar for a few days during Black Dyke's tour and can testify personally to his enthusiasm.

with 30 bands playing in two sections, the premier section being won by Concordia.[20] Another contest took place in June 1972. This was known as Vara after a broadcasting company which, through the enthusiasm of its management, regularly offered engagements to visiting British bands. Fifteen bands competed and Harry Mortimer was guest conductor in the evening concert. This contest also ran annually and in 1976 moved from Hilversum to Amsterdam. A leading British band generally took part in the evening concert and from 1977 the panel of adjudicators included at least one member from Britain. De Waldsang was the most successful band at Vara, its regular wins including two hat-tricks. The contest ran until 1986, when Sun Life were guests at the last of the gala concerts.

The Utrecht contest became the Dutch National Championships and, in order to avoid a clash with Vara, was moved to November. The most successful band here during the early years was Brass Band Rotterdam, which completed a hat-trick in 1976–77–78. However, such is the fragility of bands in their early years that, having been selected to appear in the first European Championships (1978), it was quite suddenly disbanded. De Waldsang continued, however, remained a leading Dutch band and visited England early in 1978.[21]

From 1981 the Utrecht event became the Netherlands Championships. In 1986 it was renamed the Dutch National Brass Band Festival and ran in parallel with a new Dutch Open Brass Band Festival, which attracted bands from Norway, Switzerland, Belgium and England. De Waldsang remained the most successful Dutch band, with Soli Deo Gloria a close second, under their respective conductors Tjeerd Brouwer and Jan de Haan. Other winners of the Nationals included Brassband Limburg from the southern part of the Netherlands and De Bazuin. Winners of the Dutch Open contest included Eikanger from Norway, Willebroek and De Bazuin from Belgium, and Soli Deo Gloria.

The 'Open' survived until 1998, when De Bazuin became champions. De Waldsang continued in their winning ways, with successes at the Dutch Nationals of 1998 and the newly instituted French Open Championships of 2000 (see page 314).

High-profile British bands to tour Holland during the 1980s included GUS, Black Dyke, Yorkshire Imperial and Fairey's. Visiting bands in the 1990s included BNFL, Desford and Stocksbridge. No leading British band participated in the eleventh WMC in 1989, but in 1993 Sun Life won the open brass band class, Desford achieving the win in 1997.

---

[20] Concordia was formed in 1898, becoming all-brass in 1966 (*BB* 5 February 1971, p. 1).

[21] For a good history of De Waldsang, see *BB* 11 October 1980, p. 7.

*Switzerland*

Switzerland was the second European country to take a serious interest in the British brass band, the seeds being planted in 1951 when Derek Garside appeared as a guest soloist. He was there again two years later with CWS (Manchester) and Eric Ball.

CWS returned to Switzerland in 1955 under Alex Mortimer and now came the first indication that the British-style brass band might develop into a European movement. An article in *BB* reported that H. de Vries of Leeuwarden and André Winkler of Thun, Switzerland, had each persuaded a number of bands in their respective localities to adopt British instrumentation.[22] However, the first British-style brass band in Switzerland was formed in Speicher in 1956 by Ernst Graf who had lived for a time in Northern Ireland.

More brass bands now began to appear, formed by members of individual fanfares who were interested in playing a more serious repertoire. They remained members of their fanfares but met periodically to rehearse music by composers such as Eric Ball and Denis Wright.

Several British bands toured Switzerland during the early 1960s. Following the pioneering work done by CWS (Manchester), there were successful tours by Morris Motors, GUS and several youth bands. In 1963, for the first time, a Dutch band undertook a Swiss concert tour. This was Soli Deo Gloria.

Towards the end of the 1960s there were yet more Swiss tours by leading English bands – Brighouse & Rastrick in 1969 and CWS (Manchester) in 1969 and 1970. The CWS tours were organised by Ernst Obrecht, a leading Swiss figure in the move to foster British-style bands.[23] Swiss enthusiasts were now visiting London to attend the National Championships.

Hendon toured Switzerland in 1970, perhaps because several Swiss bandsmen had actually played with them whilst living in England. One of these was Markus Bach, destined to become one of the most prominent brass band figures both in Switzerland and, as president of EBBA, in the European band movement. Major band tours continued during the 1970s, including those by Black Dyke in 1971, 1973 and 1976, and by Hanwell and Brighouse in 1975.

The first Swiss all-brass band championships were held in Lausanne in 1972. Rules were similar to those in Britain, but there were five adjudicators. There was just one section, with ten bands. A second contest was held in the following year with an original test piece, *Rondo for Brass Band* by

---

22 *BB* 9 April 1955, p. 3.

23 The Obrecht family runs the Swiss brass band music publishing company Obrasso and has organised many concerts and festivals.

the Swiss composer Albert Benz. For the third, the adjudication panel included Geoffrey Brand and William Relton.

In April 1974 Markus Bach founded the Swiss Quartet and Solo Championships which have been run annually ever since, attracting literally hundreds of competitors. Bach also formed the Brassband Berner Oberland (BBO), which was to become a leading Swiss band. The group visited Britain in 1976, giving concerts and attending the National Championships, as observers. The National Youth Brass Band of Switzerland (NJBB) was founded by Bach in 1976. For the NJBB course of the following year he invited Phillip McCann and Ian Craddock (solo euphonium player of Yorkshire Imperial Metals) as soloists and tutors. This set a trend for future years.

The Swiss Brass Band Association was formed in 1978. There were now two sections in the championships, the winners of the premier section this year being Treize Etoiles, from a mountainous region in the canton of Valais and destined to become another leading Swiss band. In 1979 the Association restricted the number of competing bands to 11 in order to maintain a high standard. It was now customary to engage an English conductor to join the adjudication panel and to be guest conductor at the evening concert. Peter Parkes fulfilled these roles in 1980, when Treize Etoiles completed their hat-trick.

Brassband Burgermusik Luzern competed in Kerkrade in 1981 and was awarded a gold medal.[24] Following its first win in the Swiss Championships of 1987, BBO became the most successful Swiss band, not only in the Nationals but also in the early years of a major entertainment contest – U-Brass, started in 1987. Following the example of Holland, a Swiss Open contest was founded in 1990. This competition was held in Luzern and from 1999 an extension was introduced, called the European Open. BBO were the first winners followed, in 2000, by Treize Etoiles.

BBO, Treize Etoiles and Luzern were the three most successful Swiss bands, though Brass Band Bienne won the Championships in 1984 and 1985. Their conductors, up to the later 1980s, were Markus Bach (BBO), Geo-Pierre Moren (Treize Etoiles), Ives Illy (Luzern) and Paschal Eicher (Bienne). These were Switzerland's leading brass band specialist conductors. In later years some Swiss bands adopted the English tradition of engaging professional conductors. Amongst these have been James Gourlay, who worked for a time with BBO; Allan Withington, who had a short association with Luzern; and Richard Evans and Peter Parkes, who both conducted Treize Etoiles.

---

[24] This band was founded in 1892 and became all-brass in 1968 under André Winkler. Ives Illy took over in 1979 and established it as one of Switzerland's leading brass bands.

In 1987 Roy Newsome was appointed Adviser to the Music Committee of the Swiss Brass Band Association, charged with bringing the Swiss adjudication system into line with that of Britain and also advising on choice of test pieces and adjudicators.

Bands which toured Switzerland during the 1980s and 1990s included GUS, Desford, Black Dyke, Brighouse & Rastrick, Britannia Building Society and Yorkshire Imperial. BBO toured Japan and Hong Kong in 1985, and the NJBB performed in Russia during 1994.

## Denmark and Sweden

As in other countries discussed, the SA was active in Denmark and Sweden from the 1890s, but the mature British-style brass band did not reach Scandinavia until the late 1950s. Bands here had been influenced by the German style due to occupation during the war. The amateur band movement in Denmark owed much to an organisation similar to the Boy's Brigade, called the FDF.[25]

The development of a brass band movement in Denmark and Sweden has been less successful than in Holland or Switzerland, although both Scandinavian countries have produced good bands, have been visited by British brass band personalities, and have participated in the European Championships.

The brass band was pioneered in Denmark by Herbert Møller, a music teacher inspired by the visit of an English SA band. He changed the instrumentation of his own band, Concord, during the late 1940s but by the mid-1950s needed further help. He contacted Denis Wright, who now became involved in yet another bout of missionary work with visits to both Denmark and Sweden. The first was in 1958, when he conducted Concord in Denmark and a church youth band, LKU, in Malmö, Sweden. Working in the same way as he had done with the three Dutch bands a decade earlier, he ended the week with a concert in the Tivoli Concert Hall.

Visits by English personalities escalated during the early 1960s, with regular appearances by Geoffrey Brand and Bram Gay. Letters to *BB* during 1962 indicated that brass bands were making progress and in 1963, after being runners-up in the Danish National Championships for three years, Concord actually won, even though competing against the country's best wind bands. The Championships were still organised for bands of all kinds, playing in the one group, though there were now over 30 brass bands. Harry Mortimer adjudicated at the Danish Championships of 1970. Of the 21 bands which competed, 18 were all-brass and, for the fifth time, Concord were winners.

---

25 Frivilligt Drenge-Forbund – Boys' Voluntary Organisation.

Little was reported about brass band activities in Denmark during the early 1970s other than visits by the NYBB in 1971 and by Geoffrey Brand during 1975. However, progress continued. The 1976 championships, spread over two days and attracting an audience of over 1000, had three brass band classes, with a total of 27 bands varying in size from ten to 35. In 1978 four bands competed for the title and a place in the new European Championships – Copenhagen Brass Band were winners. In the following year Brass Band Concord became champions.

Møller formed Denmark's National Youth Brass Band in 1978. Geoffrey Brand was its first guest conductor, with Harry Mortimer officiating in 1981. In 1980 the NYBB made its second visit to Denmark. Brighouse & Rastrick also toured, with financial support from Boosey & Hawkes.

In Sweden, LKU celebrated its Golden Jubilee in 1968. A year later it won the brass band section of the Swedish Amateur Band Association contest, receiving the highest mark in the competition. Now in great demand throughout Sweden, the band also toured in France and Holland.

Sweden was now regularly in the news, primarily through the formation of Solna Brass in 1970. This was made up of players from Stockholm bands, about half of them from the SA, and founded by the director of Solna School of Music and Ballet. Early visitors included Howarth, Brand and Gregson. During 1976 Solna were visited by Harry Mortimer and in 1977 the band came to London to make a commercial recording.

Swedish bands were now on the move, LKU coming to England as part of their sixtieth-anniversary celebrations and Solna visiting Oslo. Solna also had a special weekend in London in October 1978, being featured in the gala concert of the Nationals and competing in the European Championships the following day, where they were were rewarded with 3rd prize. The band performed in Switzerland during 1981 and won the Swedish Championships in 1982 and 1983.

A second major Swedish band – Gothenburg Brass – was formed in 1983. Bengt Eklund, a professional trumpet player and professor of trumpet at Gothenburg Conservatoire, was the founder and conductor, and the membership included several professional brass players. Brand, Gregson and Newsome visited the band, which became Swedish Champions for the first time in 1986. During the next few years the band travelled extensively, visiting Japan, Estonia, Lithuania, Russia and France. Bram Gay now became a regular visitor and Gothenburg became regular Swedish Champions. They were also winners at the World Championships in Sydney, Australia, in 1988 and continued as one of Europe's leading bands throughout the 1990s.

*Norway*

The first Norwegian Band Championships were held in Hamar in 1966 – a three-day event at which Harry Mortimer was an adjudicator. At that time there were 1300 bands in membership of the Norwegian Bands Federation, but a mere 60–70 were all-brass. Each of them had about 30 members, but had not yet adopted British instrumentation.

A few lesser-known British bands toured Norway during the late 1960s but it was not until towards the mid-1970s that Norwegian interest in the British brass band really dawned. In 1973 Geoffrey Brand went to Oslo, conducting and appearing on the radio. He returned in 1974 with City of London Band for an eight-day tour, visiting Bergen, Oslo and Hamar.

In 1977 Eikanger Bjorsvik from near Bergen undertook a ten-day tour of England. Bergen, a seaport on the western side of Norway, was to become the principal location for Norwegian brass bands and this band's conductor Tom Brevik, a trombonist with an SA background, provided the necessary enthusiasm. Eikanger and near neighbours Manger Musikklag, which Brevik also conducted, became two of Norway's leading brass bands. Manger won the brass section of the 1977 Championships, qualifying for a place in the first European Championships. Founded as a wind band in 1922, it was now all-brass and had 35 members (of whom 16 were female), with an average age of 24.

The arrival in Bergen of Rod Franks[26] as principal trumpet player with the Bergen Philharmonic Orchestra was a key factor in the development of Norwegian brass bands. Between them, Brevik and Franks founded the Brass Band Club of Norway. For its first event, in May 1978, they brought Roy Newsome from England to conduct a massed band concert featuring Eikanger, Manger and three other Bergen-based bands. In the following year he returned as adjudicator in the first Norwegian Brass Band Championships. Despite the strength of the Bergen bands, it was a band from Oslo – 1st Metronome 66 – which won the 1978 title and represented Norway in the 1979 European Championships.

Of several British band tours during this period one of the more important was by Black Dyke. This took place during the summer of 1979. In the following year Wingates also toured.

Eikanger and Manger were Norway's leading bands but a third was now making a mark – that of Stavanger, founded in 1981. Also located on the west coast but about 100 miles south of Bergen, Stavanger itself became an important centre for brass, with annual weekend training courses for

---

26 Franks, a former member of both Brighouse & Rastrick and Black Dyke, was later to become a member of the PJBE and also joined Maurice Murphy leading the trumpet section of the LSO.

its many school brass bands and the founding, in 1983, of an entertainment contest called 'Siddis' run on similar lines to Britain's 'Brass in Concert'.

From the beginning the Norwegians were eager to take advice from leading British personalities. Michael Antrobus, an ex-Black Dyke resident conductor, moved there in 1981, to be followed by Ray Farr in 1990 and later by others, including Allan Withington and John Hudson. During 1985 the Norwegian Band Federation organised a series of seminars for would-be adjudicators, engaging Farr, Newsome and Gregson to each spend a weekend in Manger directing them. For the 1987 Championships no fewer than six of the competing bands engaged British conductors, two of the adjudicators were from Britain and Stephen Sykes was the guest soloist at the evening concert.

Howard Snell was by now the professional conductor of Eikanger and under his direction they became Norway's most successful band, not only in the National Championships but also in Siddis, and winners of the European Championships in 1988 and 1989. Eikanger also won the 1988 Dutch Open and were very popular on the concert platform, on radio and through their many CDs.

In the early 1990s David King became professional conductor of Manger and created a record by leading them to four successive wins in the Norwegian Championships – 1994–95–96–97.

## Belgium

Though Belgium had been one of the first countries visited by a leading British brass band (Foden's, 1945) and was moreover the birthplace of Adolphe Sax, inventor of the saxhorn – the foundation of the British brass band – it was one of the later countries in Western Europe to host British bands. Hendon seems to have been the first to visit Belgium with any regularity, playing in Brussels in 1968, 1969 and 1970. The first Belgian British-style brass band was formed late in 1972 when enthusiast Roger de Pauw formed the Brass Band Brabant. By early 1975 five of Belgium's fanfare-style bands had changed to British instrumentation. A rare visit by a leading British band took place in 1976 when GUS played there.

The Belgian National Championships were founded in 1978, the first winners being St Cecilia, Nossigen. Bands played a set test and an own choice, and there was an evening concert. Shortly after this a Federation of Belgian Bands was formed. Further afield, Belgium's Brass Band Buizingen won the 1979 Dutch Championships and Midden Brabant were runners-up in Denmark in 1980.

De Pauw became a leading figure, helping with the Championships and also editing a monthly brass band magazine. The growth of brass bands in Belgium was reflected by the entries in the Belgian Championships –

with four in 1978, rising to 12 in 1979 (in two sections) and 16 in 1980 (in three). Prizes in the highest section this year went to Midden Brabant, Kortrijk and Buizingen. Visitors to Belgium now included Hendon in 1978 and Black Dyke, as part of a three-country tour sponsored by Boosey & Hawkes, in 1980.

From 1985 Brass Band Willebroek became Belgium's leading band, dominating the Championships and in 1993 winning both the European Championships – in England – and the Dutch Open. They collected five other prizes at the European Championships between 1991 and 2000. The band was formed in 1979 by Franz Violet, a professional trumpet player and head of brass in a local academy, who became its permanent conductor.

Another successful Belgian band was that of Kortrijk, founded in 1976 and regular prize-winners in the Championships. In 1995 this band travelled to Folkestone to compete in the Southern Counties Amateur Band Association's annual contest – and won. Willebroek did the same in 1999.

## Luxembourg

Luxembourg's first brass band came into existence as a direct result of the formation of the Brass Band Brabant in Belgium. It was formed in 1973 by Fred Harles, professor of trumpet at the conservatoire at Esch-sur-Alzette. The band gave its inaugural concert late in 1974 and made its first recording in 1977. The only brass band of any standing in Luxembourg, it has fought the proverbial lone battle. It has appeared from time to time in the European Championships and Harles has been an influential member of EBBA. Luxembourg actually hosted the European Championships in 1995.

## Elsewhere in Europe

France hosted several visiting British brass bands during the post-war years, but the visits were generally social rather than cultural. Not until 1969 was the sound of a leading brass band heard in France. In this year, both Black Dyke and Cammell Laird crossed the Channel. Though the bands were well-received in their respective town-twinning ceremonies, interest was superficial. Even as late as 1980 a tour by Whitburn and Peter Parkes, with 12 concerts over five days, had little impact.

However, greater enthusiasm was eventually aroused and by 1991 there were reportedly five British-style brass bands in existence. The French Open contest was founded in the town of Amboise in the Loire Valley in 1995. This became an annual event, attended by a number of British bands and with England strongly represented on the panel of adjudicators. The

B Section of the European Championships was won in both 1996 and 2000 by France's Brass Band Normandie – formed in 1994 specifically to promote the British-style brass band.

Early reaction in Germany was almost as negative as that in France. Following several visits during the 1950s and 1960s, mainly by school bands, Germany's first brass band appeared in 1969. This was an Auxiliary Fire Brigade Band, located near Hamburg. A few more appeared during the 1970s but they were isolated examples. In 1981 Boosey & Hawkes financed a Black Dyke tour as part of a sales drive. Even this drew little response.

However, the coming of the B Section in the European Championships had an effect, as the winner in 1995 was Germany's Brass Band Oberschwaben-Allgäu. Further, a band from near-neighbours Austria – Fröschl Hall – were winners in 1994, 1997, 1998 and 1999. The 1999 European Championships were held in Munich.

## The United States of America

Though there were literally thousands of all-brass bands in America at the time of the American Civil War, since then the mixed brass, wind and percussion band had become the norm. There were not only fine professional bands, both military and civilian, but there were thousands more formed in high schools, colleges and universities. The oldest American British-style brass band is probably Buffalo Silver, formed in 1915.[27] It enjoyed success during the 1970s by winning the brass competition at the CNE on the four occasions when it competed.

Eric Ball was in the USA during the early 1960s and sensed a growing appreciation of the British-style all-brass band. The first such American band to be reported in the 'modern' era was up and running by 1963 at the Sylvania High School, Ohio. A second one appeared in 1966 in Florida – the Clewston Sugarland Band, comprising 33 boys and girls. Its conductor was Jack L. Scott, a tuba player whose interest in brass bands began in 1953 when he heard a Canadian SA band. He later came to England where, in 1970, he completed a PhD at Sheffield University.[28]

Philip Catelinet (see 'Personalia') moved to the USA in 1956. His work was mainly as a teacher at Carnegie Melon University, Pittsburgh, but he also played tuba professionally. In 1968 he formed a university brass ensemble, calling it an 'American Brass Orchestra'. Though not using

---

[27] *BB* 10 January 1981, p. 7.

[28] Scott's unpublished thesis was entitled 'The Evolution of the Brass Band and its Repertoire in Northern England' and is a standard reference for brass band historians.

British instrumentation he introduced British repertoire, laying foundations which were to be built on some 20 years later.

American interest in British brass bands became more widespread during the 1970s. Educationalists in particular were attracted. Bemoaning the fact that, whilst billions of dollars were spent on instrumental teaching in schools and colleges, the number of people who continued playing in adulthood was minuscule, many saw the British brass band as more conducive to amateur music-making than their wind bands.

The bicentennial of the Declaration of Independence fell in 1976. To mark the affinity which now existed between America and Britain there were many cultural events, one of which was a visit by two British brass bands – Grimethorpe and Cory's. As both were connected to the mining industry, the tours, which covered a wide area in the Mid-West and on the Eastern Seaboard, were sponsored by American mining unions.

Robert Bernat of Boiling Springs, Pennsylvania, met and heard both bands and took a keen interest. In the following year he came to England to investigate the British brass band movement. Like Scott, he stayed in Sheffield and spent much time with a number of bands – in particular, Grimethorpe and Black Dyke. His experiences in Britain suggested that the focal point of a brass band movement should be an industrial region and he chose as his centre Pittsburgh, the place where Catelinet had worked. This was a steel-producing town, situated at the confluence of two rivers which combine to make the Ohio River.

Bernat's strategy was to form a British-style brass band of professional players who would quickly adapt to the style and instrumentation. He would mount concerts to acquaint the public with the sound of the band, hopefully instilling an enthusiasm in the players who would, he anticipated, go into the outlying districts where they lived and form amateur bands. In this way Bernat believed he could build a successful brass band movement within Greater Pittsburgh, with its population of some 2.2 million. The band was to be run like a professional orchestra and he established a board of directors which included influential people capable of attracting sponsorship. André Previn, at that time principal conductor of the Pittsburgh Orchestra, was co-opted onto the Advisory Committee.

Bernat had some difficulties in attracting players for his band – which he called the River City Brass Band (RCBB). Trombones, tubas and percussion posed no problems; cornettists had to be trumpet players, prepared to play cornet. This worked to a certain extent, but those earning most of their living playing trumpet would go only so far in adapting to the style of the cornet. Horns were even more difficult. He was obliged to employ french horn players and as this instrument was pitched in F the players transposed from E♭ tenor horn parts. More significantly, the sound was quite different from that of the tenor horn. Bernat's biggest problem was finding euphonium and baritone players as these were not called for professionally, so he made use of the best players from the SA. The band produced a sound quite different from that of the true British brass band. Nevertheless, it worked and RCBB became very popular.

The inaugural concert was in 1982 and Robert Childs appeared as guest soloist. Bernat had secured a series of paid engagements in six different venues and, with programmes of popular music, the band was greeted enthusiastically. Having made a success of these, he then secured another series, and another, and so on, so that within a few years his players were earning around 50 per cent of their income through rehearsals and engagements with RCBB. A number of band members also undertook additional administrative duties. Concerts were given imaginative titles such as 'Mediterranean Ports of Call' and 'A Pennsylvania Sampler'.

In 1988 RCBB went on tour, visiting Australia, New Zealand and the Hawaiian Islands. At an estimated cost of half a million dollars, the band performed in 20 venues. In 1992 it completed its tenth season, giving 87 performances and playing to an estimated 125 000 listeners. A year later Bernat died, but the organisation was strong and the band continued.

The second part of the project, the building of a brass band movement throughout Greater Pittsburgh never happened. One or two players took up the challenge of forming amateur bands, but most had neither the time nor the enthusiasm for such a project.

Nevertheless, by the late 1970s there were several British-style brass bands in America. Up to this point they each worked independently in a country where they could be separated by thousands of miles. In 1978 the Director of Music of North Carolina State University, Perry Watson, came to England on a fact-finding mission. He visited many bands, including Black Dyke and Besses – both with long histories which included American tours early in the twentieth century. By 1980 he was organising events of interest to any American involved with or contemplating the formation of a British-style brass band. Watson's first major venture was a two-day workshop in his university, which attracted 37 delegates from a wide catchment area. He also organised a concert within the University – 'Music from the British Isles'.

The formation of an American Brass Band Association was now being seriously considered and a concert given by the Penn State Brass Chorale in May 1980 was presented 'in association with the nascent American Brass Band Association'. In 1981 Watson organised a 'British Brass Band Showcase', inviting Peter Wilson and Denzil Stephens to help promote the idea of the British-style brass band[29] and there were now thought to be about 12 of them in America. A concert given by the Capitol English

---

[29] Reported by Peter Wilson in *BB* of 11 April 1981, p. 9.

Brass Band, in Salt Lake City, Utah, in the western part of the United States, was reported. The guest soloist was euphonium player Glenn Call, a member of the United States Marine Band and a strong advocate of British instrumentation.

Perry Watson planned a 'North Carolina Brass Band Summer Course', to take place at Lancaster University, England, in the late 1970s. Designed specifically for American enthusiasts, it was to last three weeks, with activities supervised by leading English brass band figures. In the event, rising air fares and a falling American economy meant there were insufficient applicants to make the project viable. However, 12 delegates from America and Canada attended that year's 'Sounding Brass' summer school at Marlborough. Several of these contributed to the development of an American brass band movement.

The forming of the North American Brass Band Association (NABBA) was Watson's next target. The Association was primarily intended to run an annual competition and to publish a bimonthly magazine, *The Brass Band Bridge*. The first NABBA Championships took place in 1983 in Raleigh, with Peter Wilson (who had drawn up the rules for the competition), Robert Bernat and Derek Smith (Bandmaster of the New York Staff Band of the SA) as adjudicators. There were two sections and bands were required to play a short programme containing a prescribed test piece. Weston and Whitby bands from Canada were amongst the competitors in the early years. Brass Band of Columbus (Ohio), formed in 1984 dominated the Championships from 1986, with a hat-trick between then and 1988 and further success in the 1990s. However, the Illinois Brass Band came to the fore in the last few years, with a hat-trick in 1996–97–98 and a further win in 2000.

New bands were being formed all the time but one dating from 1993 calls for special mention. It was the Band of Battle Creek, lavishly sponsored by Kellogg's. All the American members were top-class professionals and leading players were flown out from England to boost their twice-yearly concerts. In 1998 the band came to England and played in the Royal Albert Hall at the conclusion of the National Championships – to great acclaim.

## Japan

In Japan the band scene was based on the American system, with a strong leaning to the mixed brass and wind band. The first sign of interest in British brass bands did not appear until 1964, when the President of the Tokyo Band League visited Britain to learn about the movement. More Japanese visitors arrived during the next few years. One couple in particular,

Mr and Mrs Inoue from Tokyo, made their first trip in 1972, as a direct result of which the Tokyo Brass Society (TBS) formed a brass band which was soon giving monthly concerts.[30]

However, it was not until 1977 that things really began to move, with more Japanese visitors coming to Britain, including members of TBS and their conductor Professor Takeo Yamamoto. They visited Fairey's and Hanwell. In 1979 Richard Evans spent a few days in Japan coaching and advising; he returned the following year with the Leyland Band.

More bands were formed during the early 1980s as Professor Yamamoto became involved. In addition to conducting the TBS brass band, in 1985 he founded the Tamagawa University Masters Brass Band. In 1988 he came to England on an eight-month study tour, being attached to University College, Salford.

In 1987 the first Japanese Brass Band Festival was held. This was a non-competitive event – each of four bands played a short programme, followed by a massed band concert. At around this time Gordon Higginbottom spent some time in Japan, working for Yamaha and also becoming involved with a number of brass bands.

Black Dyke undertook two substantial Japanese tours in 1984 and 1990, both funded by Boosey & Hawkes. In 1991 Gothenburg Brass also toured Japan. Geoffrey Brand is still a frequent visitor, conducting both brass bands and wind bands. Other regular visitors include the Childs Brothers, Steven Mead and Roger Webster. In addition to those already mentioned, active brass bands have included Black Colt and Concord, both in Tokyo, Breeze Brass Band of Osaka and Suzume Youth Band. This last band, based some 60 miles north of Tokyo, was formed in 1983 and has visited England twice.

Visits in both directions continued. In 1996 Breeze visited England, France and Switzerland, whilst Ransome's toured Japan. Three years later the Australian champions, Kew, flew to Japan. In this same year, 1999, the film *Brassed Off* attracted great interest in Japan, resulting in two tours for Grimethorpe and the formation of more bands. The Japanese Brass Band Festival is steadily growing and there is also a weekly radio programme of brass band recordings, hosted by the newly formed Japanese Brass Band Association.

However, the growth of the brass band movement in Japan has been restricted, largely through the education system. For, whilst there are brass bands in many primary schools, at high school level wind bands are the norm.

---

[30] *BB* 28 April 1973, p. 8; and 9 July 1977, *International Bandsman* (part of *BB*), with an interesting history of banding in Japan.

**Elsewhere**

There were small brass ensembles in the Faroe Islands as early as the 1920s, and the Havnar Hornorkestur, originally founded in 1903, was re-formed as a brass band after World War II through the influence of the Salvation Army and British soldiers. By 1951 there were three brass bands plus a SA band in the islands and in 1956 Havnar offered a six-month contract to a suitable conductor to live in the Faroes and work with the band. In 1961 the same band offered travelling expenses, board, lodging and a salary to a cornet player willing to live there for a year, playing with, training and conducting the band and teaching beginners. Robert Oughton (see page 170) took up Havnar's offer, staying for two years and transforming it into a modern brass band, later known as Tórshaven Brass Band.

Wynne Moore, a former Grimethorpe solo cornet player, succeeded Oughton. He also stayed for two years, during which time other guests were invited, including Major Jaeger, James Shepherd and Derek Garside. Havnar Hornorkestur celebrated its seventieth anniversary in 1973. By now there were eight brass bands in the Faroes, not counting the SA band. Every year there was a festival, each band playing a 20-minute programme. Oughton returned in 1978, organising a course for boys and girls. In 1989 a report stated that there were still eight brass bands plus one wind band and a National Youth Band. Two years later Alan Fernie was asked to write a piece for a National Band. In the late 1990s visitors included Peter Parkes and Goff Richards. The National Band competed in the B section of the European Championships of 2000.[31]

Finland was visited twice by Besses, in 1983 and 1986. The Töölo Band had been formed in 1980. Its conductor was a professional trumpet player. This band also attended the B section of the European Championships in 1998 and 2000, gaining 3rd prize on its first attempt.

There were a number of reports in the band press of brass bands in South Africa, in Malta and of one in Hong Kong. Many other countries have been visited by British brass bands, but there is nothing to suggest that British-style brass bands were formed there.

**Conclusion**

Though pockets of interest in brass bands existed in a small number of other countries, the brass band as we know it, even in the 1930s, was

---

[31] For a good history, see *BB* of 22 April 2000, p. 12. (Tórshaven was to win the European B section in 2004.)

substantially a British phenomenon. Following serious problems during the 1920s and 1930s, bands in the Antipodes regrouped just before World War II, laying foundations which were built upon during the post-war era. From the mid-1950s a further influx of bandsmen from Britain gave a boost, particularly in New Zealand where a number of high-profile conductors and players settled, enjoying much success.

A brass band movement now appeared in Northern Ireland, as many flute bands converted to all-brass. Again, a number of English conductors helped. Banding in Canada survived by a thread. Struggling against the dominance of the American-style wind band, it managed only one contest per year. During the late 1950s, as was the case in the Antipodes, an influx of bandsmen from Britain helped the few Canadian brass bands to consolidate.

Brass bands were slow to develop in Europe, partly because of language differences, but also because many European countries had their own band movements, comprising wind bands and 'fanfares'. However, they gradually came into existence – from the late 1940s in Holland, from the mid-1950s in Switzerland, from 1958 in Denmark and Sweden, and later in Norway, Belgium and Luxembourg.

Thus, by the 1960s the British-style brass band was becoming a far more international phenomenon than in earlier periods. The principal developments in the 1970s were in America and Japan, particularly in the former. Interest by the end of the century could reasonably be described as worldwide.

# Finale: A personal view

The writing of this history has been a fascinating exercise for me, especially as I have been involved in much of the history as it was made. As I write this, in June 2004, it is difficult to realise that more than three years have elapsed since the official end-date of the book. However, that allows me to stand at the close of the year 2000 and look into the future.

A tendency towards longer test pieces has, inevitably, made for longer contests. The new owners of the two major British competitions have created no major changes though they have brought about two welcome add-ons – a return to the full evening gala concert following the Nationals and, to the 'sister' contest of the British Open – the Spring Festival – the addition of one and then two more sections to the Grand Shield, so that there are now Senior Trophy and Senior Cup sections. There has also been a change of venue for this event, which is now held in the Winter Gardens, Blackpool.

The National Youth Brass Band Championships continue to generate great enthusiasm. Up to 2003 they were held at Salford University but from 2004 have returned to the RNCM. The other major youth competition, now known as the Youth Brass Band Entertainment Festival of Great Britain, continues to stimulate extravaganzas created by the young bands. Still held in Blackpool, it now supports Action Medical Research. All other major competitions are still active.

Richard Evans remains as music director of NYBBS, whilst Robert Childs now looks after the musical interests of the NYBBW. On the NYBB front, I retired from the post of music director at the end of 2000. Elgar Howarth was appointed as my successor, with the title Artistic Director. A National Children's Brass Band of Great Britain is to be formed in July 2004. It will be a parallel organisation to the NYBB and will be governed by the same Council. Philip Biggs continues as administrator of both bands, as well as fulfilling his other entrepreneurial activities. He has also founded a new quarterly magazine, *The Brass Herald*. This appeared in 2003 and caters for all types of brass player.

The hierarchy of bands remains much the same, but a worrying – and growing – shortage of players means that the very top bands are tending to pull even further away from those lower in status. The best players gravitate upwards, as they always have done, but vacancies lower down become increasingly difficult to fill. There is now also a projected crisis through a shortage of lower brasses – partly as a result of policy changes in school education through which fewer large instruments are being bought. On a more positive note, female players are now to be found in most of the top-flight bands.

In the media, band broadcasts and appearances on television have almost dried up. From the late 1990s there has been only one dedicated weekly brass band broadcast, the late Friday evening programme *Listen to the Band*, and that lasting a mere half-hour. Bands on television are almost completely limited to spasmodic appearances in programmes such as *Songs of Praise*.

On the other hand, brass band recordings have again escalated. During the 1980s the LP gave way to the CD (compact disc). The first-ever brass band CD was made by Black Dyke; it appeared in 1985. Titled *Blitz*, it included a studio performance of the spectacular test piece composed by Derek Bourgeois for the 1981 National Finals and was released by Chandos. Brass band CDs have not been taken seriously by the major recording companies, but have been produced in abundance by the brass band specialist firms, notably Chandos and Polyphonic, along with Doyen (a company founded by the Childs Brothers) and Kirklees Music, whose managing director is David Horsfield. SP&S have maintained a steady flow of CDs made by SA bands.

The recently-launched 'World of Brass' is a subsidiary of SP&S and a recent catalogue shows the current availability of well over 300 brass band CDs – most of which have been produced within the last five years. Some 60 albums feature a particular soloist and more than 50 are recordings of SA bands. Of the 50 or so featuring more than one band, a substantial number include both contesting bands and an SA band – usually that of the ISB. As in previous eras, Black Dyke is the most recorded band; but Fodens, Grimethorpe, YBS, Fairey, Cory and Brighouse & Rastrick have each produced a substantial number of CDs. The quality of playing, of repertoire, and of the presentation of the CDs is at a consistently high level. There are also facilities for bands lower in status to produce commercial recordings – on either CD or cassette.

High-quality concerts and festivals in prestigious venues continue, though we still await the first twenty-first-century brass band Promenade Concert.

In higher education, in addition to colleges and universities already discussed, the Welsh College of Music & Drama has now opened its doors to brass band-minded students and has appointed Robert Childs to teach and to run the college's brass band. The Royal Scottish Academy of Music & Drama, though perhaps not going as far as its Welsh counterpart, has forged strong links with the Scottish brass band movement. In the universities, higher degrees such as MA, PhD and DMA with leanings towards brass bands are becoming more readily available, and the most recent university brass band course has appeared at Durham, where Ray Farr is in charge of activities.

Competition continues to be a major part of banding. The Association of Brass Band Adjudicators (ABBA) has made much progress and is becoming accepted as the 'voice' of adjudicators. Sadly, criticisms of adjudicators and adjudicating systems persist. These have not been mentioned previously but, like the proverbial poor, they have always been with us.

The British Federation, though still not universally accepted, is seen by many as an important cornerstone in the developing network of banding.

The European Championships go from strength to strength and have become part of a week-long festival which attracts a large number of visitors from all over Europe. Markus Bach remains the president and driving force. There are representatives on EBBA from all participating countries, but the two who have borne the lions' share of the work along with Bach are Norway's Tom Brevik and Jappie Dijkstra from the Netherlands. YBS remains the most successful British band in this event and in 2004 achieved its sixth consecutive win. Brass Band Willebroek is the most consistently successful continental band. There is now the prospect of a World Championships, to be held in Kerkrade in 2005.

In the course of writing this book I have deliberately avoided going into detail about Salvation Army bands, because that is a separate and equally extensive topic; yet it has been impossible to avoid the subject. Throughout their respective histories the religious and secular wings of the brass band movement have been interrelated and interactive, though in recent years the crossover has been both more marked and more deliberate.

Another trend has been toward increasing links with the wider world of music. No longer is it of special significance if a mainstream composer writes for brass band; nor is it unusual for orchestral conductors or instrumentalists to be involved. There are also frequent links between bands and the 'pop' world.

In concluding, may I say how much I have enjoyed writing this book. I am sure that I have left many gaps and I hope that I will not have lost too many friends in so doing. There are always lessons to be learned from history and I hope that the book will serve as a reminder of some of the events of the past, particularly as they impinge on the present and the future. To have spent a lifetime in brass bands has been a privilege. Brass bands have become one of the highest, if not the highest, form of amateur music-making and yet they are peopled by folk who I can unashamedly describe as 'the salt of the earth'. I hope that *The Modern Brass Band* will bring pleasure to those who read it and, to any younger readers, may I express the hope that you will enjoy your banding as much as I have enjoyed mine. No one could wish for more.

# Glossary of brass bands

The Glossary aims to fill some of the gaps left in the main text of the book, by giving concise accounts of bands that have been mentioned only in passing.

**All-Star Girls of Brass** – *see* Girls o' Brass.

**AMOCO** – *see* Crookhall Colliery.

**Barrow Shipyard Band,** formed in 1892, was frequently used by the company to provide music at the launching of its ships. It regularly appeared at the 'September', but its only reward there was 4th prize in 1947. It won the North West Area championships in 1946. During 1958 the band was renamed Vickers-Armstrong Works Band, but has since reverted to its original name.

**Baxendale's Works Band** enjoyed some national successes during the 1930s. The parent company was a plumbers' merchants, located in Manchester. Its band, though never winning a major title, appeared in the 'September' prize-lists in 1930s. The firm was destroyed by an enemy bomb during the Manchester blitz and the band went out of existence, some of its members joining CWS (Manchester).

**Birmingham School of Music** – *see* Jones & Crossland

**BTM** (the initials of Bedwas, Trethomas and Machen, three small Welsh villages) first made its mark at the Area championships when it took 3rd prizes in 1985 and 1986 before completing a hat-trick of 2nd prizes in 1988–90 and winning in 1991 and 1993. It became Radio Band of Wales in 1990 and 1991. Amongst BTM's later conductors was Alan Morrison, who directed the band's 2nd-prizewinning performance in the 1998 Area contest.

**Burton Construction (Newhall)** earned 3rd prizes at the Area contests of 1973, 1978 and 1979. In 1978 they became Webb Ivory (Newhall), broadcasting, making LPs, undertaking overseas tours and winning the Edinburgh International Contest. The band ceased to exist in 1982, following the withdrawal of sponsorship due to the recession.

**Callender's Cable Works Band** was based in Erith, Kent. There were actually three bands – Callender's Seniors, Callender's 'A' and Callender's

'B'. Callender's Cable Works Band (the 'Seniors') came to the fore as a contesting band in 1924. The high point came in 1927, with 2nd prizes at both major contests. Callender's then benefited from an influx of players from St Hilda's, following the closure of that pit. Going for all-out wins in 1928, 2nd and 5th prizes led Callender's to the conclusion that they were being unfairly judged. They ceased contesting, boycotted the publications of R. Smith & Co – the main publishers of contest pieces – and commissioned pieces by well-known composers for their own use (see page 45). After the war Callender's maintained its stance as a non-contesting band and in April 1952 completed its 200th broadcast. However, the band's closure was announced early in 1961, after 54 years and 250 broadcasts. The reason given was that not all members were employees of the company.

**Camborne Town** was the premier band of Cornwall during the early post-war years, winning the Area Championships of 1948–49–50, 1952–53–54 and 1956–57–58. Each hat-trick attracted a bye and guaranteed an invitation to the Finals, so Camborne remained unbeaten in Area contests until 1960. The conductor in the early post-war years was A.W. Parker. Following his death in 1951 he was succeeded by Fred Roberts (see page 148). Camborne slipped somewhat in the 1960s, managing only two Area wins. Roberts retired in 1970 and Derek Greenwood, a Yorkshireman and former principal euphonium player with the Grenadier Guards, was appointed musical director in 1976. This helped put Camborne back on the brass band map, with Area contest wins in 1977 and 1978, and 2nd prize in 1980. Camborne thus ended the decade as once again the most successful West of England band. However, between 1981 and 2000, due largely to the supremacy of Sun Life (Stanshawe), they won ten 2nd prizes but only one 1st. From 1988 another Yorkshireman, the tuba virtuoso Stephen Sykes, was the conductor. The band received sponsorship from the South West Electricity Board for a few years, but this was withdrawn in 1995.

**Cammell Laird Shipbuilding & Engineering Band**, based in Liverpool, was founded in 1957. Rex Mortimer was appointed professional conductor and in 1960 James Scott became musical director. It won the Area contests in 1964, 1965 and 1970, the 1965 Area win leading to 2nd prize in the Nationals. However, in April 1972 it was tersely announced that the band had been closed down, instruments and uniforms called in, and future engagements cancelled.

**City of Hull** – *see* EYMS.

**City of London Band** was formed by Geoffrey Brand in 1971, and comprised mainly students from the London music colleges who were former members of brass bands. The inaugural concert took place in the SA's Regent Hall. The band made broadcasts from time to time. It also undertook some educational work in Norway. During 1975 it became known as Morley College Brass Band. There was a further name-change in 1976, to London Collegiate. Around the same time Edward Gregson became its conductor.

**Clayton Aniline Works Band**, based near Manchester, was formed in December 1943 and by 1946 was giving regular concerts. In 1949 it made its inaugural broadcast, and in December 1951 became one of the first bands to appear on television. Though never reaching the top, it made several appearances at the 'September' and it came as a great surprise when the company closed the band down in 1956. E.C. Buttress (see 'Personalia') was the band's major driving force.

**Craghead Colliery** – *see* Ever Ready.

**Crookhall Colliery**, based in the Northern Area (formerly North East Area) was the region's most successful band during the early post-war years. It won the Area contest seven times, with hat-tricks in 1950–51–52 and 1958–59–60, and celebrated its 100th broadcast in 1957. Following the closure of the pit in 1963, as Crookhall Bradley (Bradley being the name of some local mining workshops), it was still the dominating band, winning the Area contest in 1963 and completing a hat-trick in 1965–66–67. In 1968, following the closure of the Bradley workshops, Patchogue-Plymouth, an American-owned company which had moved into the area, offered sponsorship. After several name-changes it settled on AMOCO. During the 1970s the band was runner-up in the Area contests five times and in 1973 it won the Grand Shield.

**Crossley's Carpet Works Band** was formed in Halifax during 1950. A group of workers in the factory, all bandsmen, approached the directors about forming a company band, to which they readily agreed. Instruments, uniforms and a rehearsal room were provided and under the baton of one of the workers, the new band won 1st prize at its first contest – the 1951 Area fourth section. Crossley's achieved instant success largely through attracting good players. Under John Harrison, Crossley's took 2nd prize at the 1955 Area Championships and so qualified for the National Finals. Harrison left following the Area success and Willie Wood (see 'Personalia') took over. Harrison returned in 1958, but in the following year Rex Mortimer conducted the band at the Area contest, winning 3rd prize and an invitation to the Finals. Bernard Bygraves (see 'Personalia') was now the principal cornet player. The early 1960s were the best years for Crossley's, with 3rd prizes at both the Area and the Finals in 1961; 1st in the Area, 2nd in the Nationals and 3rd in the British Open in 1962; and

2nd at the 1964 Area contest. In 1969 the company closed the band down on the grounds that there were too few band members now working for the company; it also wished to widen the scope of its sponsorship.

**Dalmellington**, located in the wilds of Ayrshire, was formerly a mining town. Dalmellington Silver Band's history goes back to 1864 when it was able to find employment for the bandmaster and key players. In 1967, under local conductor Hugh Johnstone, it won 1st prize in the second section of the Scottish Area. Two years later he led it to the title of 'Scottish Champions'. In 1970 Allan Street became professional conductor, taking Area 2nd prizes in 1972 and 1973, and 4th prize in the National Finals of 1973. The band returned to take first place in Scotland again in 1976 under Johnstone. Richard Evans was appointed professional conductor in 1978, taking the Scottish title on his first attempt and securing 2nd prize two years later.

**David A. Hall Whitburn** – *see* Whitburn.

**Ever Ready** dominated the North East for most of the last 30 years of the century. As Craghead Colliery it came to the fore in the latter part of the 1960s with a hat-trick at the Area contests in 1968–69–70. Winning the Grand Shield at Belle Vue in 1966, it gained access to the British Open Championships, being conducted throughout by its resident conductor Eric Cunningham. In 1969 it became the Ever Ready Craghead Band. From late 1975 a succession of conductors was imported for major contests and in 1979 Trevor Walmsley became musical director. Of 13 Area contests attended up to 1980, Ever Ready had won 12. There were 12 more wins and five second places between 1981 and 2000, most of them under the baton of the professional conductor Peter Parkes. There was also a win at the 1983 Edinburgh International Contest. In 1989 Eric Cunningham retired. Three years later Ever Ready lost its sponsorship but continued to use its well-established name, retaining Peter Parkes until 1998.

**EYMS** (East Yorkshire Motor Services) **Band** made a bid for regional superiority in the North East in the later 1990s, winning three Area contests in succession, 1996–97–98. Formed in 1989 as the City of Hull Band by Robert Childs, it was sponsored by EYMS from 1992. Childs left in 1997 due to pressure of work at Black Dyke and yet this year saw the start of a hat-trick of wins in the Area championships.

**First City Brass** was formed in 1997 in Hendon, London. Under Jeremy Wise it went on to win 1st prize in the London Area contest of 1999 and 2nd prize in 2000.

**Flowers Gloucester** (Flowers being the name of a brewery) became the leading band in the West of England following the demise of Sun Life.

They first appeared in the West of England Area Championships in 1988, winning 3rd prize under Derek Broadbent, who led them to victory in the following year. Garry Cutt helped Flowers win again, in 1994, 1995 and 1997, whilst Richard Evans steered them into first place in 2000.

**Friary Brewery**, based in Guildford, Surrey, was formed in 1926 and came into prominence in 1935. With good employment prospects the band attracted players from the North. However, following a dispute with the management, in 1937 the conductor (David Aspinall) left to establish Ransome & Marles Works Band. Several key players went with him. Soon 'Friary' was down to 14 and in November 1938 the brewery called in all instruments and uniforms.

**Girls o' Brass** was formed in 1981 by Elaine Wolff (see 'Personalia') and a group of friends. Many of its members were ex-NYBB and its first rehearsal was directed by the then music adviser, Arthur Butterworth. Drawing on players from a wide range of bands, it could meet only occasionally. Nevertheless, under various conductors, in addition to a number of 'ordinary' concerts, it played in the Royal Albert Hall prior to the announcement of results at the 1981 European Championships and also in the festival concert of the Dutch Vara contest of 1984. More engagements were reported in 1985 and the band was still extant in 1988.

A completely new band was formed in 1999 and came to the fore with an appearance at the Concert of the Century (see page 276). Called The All-Star Girls of Brass, it represented a new generation of female players.

**Heart of England Hyundai** – *see* Jones & Crossland.

**Hendon Band,** formed in 1956, came to the fore during the 1970s. It won the Area contest in 1975, took runner-up position on four other occasions and also earned quite a reputation for its concert work. The conductor, Don Morrison, had a flair for making arrangements in the style of the big band and several commercial recordings were made featuring these. Hendon was a well-travelled band and by 1978 had completed 17 continental tours. Through sponsorship it became John Laing (Hendon) during 1985. In 1988 Morrison retired after 31 years. Though losing its sponsorship in 1998, Hendon benefited from the temporary demise of Hanwell in the following year, as it welcomed some of the players to its ranks and in 1990 won the Area contest. Jeremy Wise became musical director in the early 1990s and there were further Area wins in 1993 and 1995. However, with the formation of First City Brass in 1997, also based in Hendon, Wise and several players moved, and the remaining members of Hendon amalgamated with another local band.

**John White Footwear Band,** formed in 1954, was located in Higham Ferrers, near Rushden. Under George Thompson it enjoyed a brief run of successes, with 3rd prize at Belle Vue in 1954 and 2nd in 1955. However, it was closed down in 1957, petrol rationing and rising costs being blamed for its demise.

**Jones & Crossland Band** was the re-formed Birmingham School of Music Band. Created in 1974 by Roy Curran, it hit the headlines by taking 3rd prize in the 1979 Nationals. In 1981 it was taken over by a local musical instrument firm, Jones & Crossland, Curran remaining as conductor until 1982. He was a professional trumpet player, member of the CBSO, a former member of the NYBB and a future conductor of several bands. Stephen Roberts succeeded him and in 1983 the band qualified for entry into the British Open Championships. Sponsorship ceased in 1986 and 'J & C' was disbanded. Many of the players stuck together, however, and, with the help of a new sponsor, became Heart of England Hyundai then, from 1989, PMG Heart of England. Area successes included wins in 1988 as the former and in 1989 as the latter.

**Kings of Brass** was a group of older players, which came together in 1995, initially to give a one-off concert in the Lancashire town of Uppermill. This was so successful that other concerts were arranged and a CD made. The conductors were James Scott and Geoffrey Whitham. All playing members either had been or still were attached to leading bands. The band existed for a few years, making recordings, before giving its final concert in the Isle of Man in May 2001.

**Kinneil Colliery** dominated the Scottish Area contests during the 1960s, winning four times and failing to secure a prize only twice. It played under John Kirkwood, Scotland's most successful conductor of the time. The young Phillip McCann spent some of his formative years at Kinneil, seeing it progress from the fourth section to championship level.

**Kirkintilloch** was the third most successful Scottish band during the latter part of the century, coming to the fore in 1984 by winning the Area Championships under W.B. Hargreaves. This was actually the first win at this event by both band and conductor and the same partnership again tasted victory in the following year. In 1989 and 1990, the band's centenary year, 'Kirky' gained the title yet again, under Frank Renton. The band continued to make its mark in the 1990s when, following a third place at the 1997 Area contest, it took 4th prize at the Finals.

**London Collegiate** – *see* City of London.

**Markham Main Colliery Band**, from South Yorkshire, won three 2nd prizes in the Area contests – in 1963 under its bandmaster, and in 1965 and 1966 with W.B. Hargreaves as 'professional'. Markham's only success in the Finals was a fifth place in 1965. During 1966 Allan Street was appointed musical director. Under him, Markham Main earned a good reputation for its modern outlook in concert programmes, but during the late 1960s made no further mark in the championship section.

**Morley College Brass Band** – *see* City of London.

**Murray International Whitburn** – *see* Whitburn.

**Patchogue-Plymouth** – *see* Crookhall Colliery.

**PMG Heart of England** – *see* Jones & Crossland.

**Point of Ayr** – a colliery band founded in 1966 – was Radio Band of Wales in 1983, 1984 and 1986. In 1985 it took second place in the Grand Shield and made its British Open debut. Along with other bands from North Wales, from 1992 it competed in the Welsh Area contest instead of, as formerly, in the North West. It was the most successful of the bands from the North and won the Welsh Area contest twice (1997 and 1999). Michael Fowles, a graduate of the RNCM, took over the musical directorship in 1995 and, despite constant financial problems, created a good contesting band, directing the two Area contest wins and gaining a highly commendable 3rd prize in the European Championships of 1998. The year 2000 saw a serious cash crisis, causing the band to withdraw from the National Finals and to cancel all future engagements.

**St Dennis Silver** was Cornwall's second most successful band. It was conducted by a number of local men during the early post-war years, then by John Harrison in 1955, George Thompson two years later, and from 1958 by Eddie Williams (see page 80). He brought a wealth of experience to St Dennis, from which the band benefited until his death in 1983. In 1951 – when Camborne was enjoying a bye – St Dennis won the Area Championships for the first time, but did not win again until 1960 when it inflicted the first-ever Area defeat on Camborne. St Dennis took over temporarily as the leading West Country band during the 1960s, with five Area contest wins and two other prizes, and appearances in the British Open Championships in 1964, 1965 and 1968. The 1970s, however, were years of rebuilding and not until its win of 1976 did the band again figure in the prizes at Area contests. Nevertheless, St Dennis regularly appeared in the National Finals, achieving sixth place in 1978.

**St Hilda's** – the following announcement appeared in the June issue of *BBN*, 1944: 'Sponsored by J. Squires, late secretary of Brighouse & Rastrick and H.B. Hawley[1] of Saltaire, and one or two other gentlemen, an attempt is being made to get a band together to compete at Odsal [Bradford] under

---

[1] Hawley was the founder of Hammonds Sauce Works Band and managing director of the company.

the name of St. Hilda's . . .' This band, taking the name of one of the most famous of all bands (see page 26) did, in fact, come to fruition and met with some success for a few years. Its sponsors had bought the rights to the name from the earlier band's owner. Though not a works band it enjoyed strong financial backing. Experienced players were 'bought' and George Hespe appointed conductor. Success was immediate, with a 2nd prize at the 1945 Area contest. This attracted an invitation to the Finals but here the band was unsuccessful. In fact, during its six-year existence St Hilda's failed to secure any prize at national level. In August 1951 the band was taken over by the Shipley-based Yorkshire Engineering and Welding Company and became known as Yewco. Ken Aitken-Jones (see page 158) became principal cornet player and later in the year Maurice Murphy joined as his assistant. When Aitken-Jones moved on Murphy became principal. Without warning the company closed the band down during the early part of 1956.

**Sankey's Castle Works Band**, based in Wellington, Shropshire, was frequently in the news in the post-war years. A 'regular' at the 'September', it made its 100th broadcast in 1953. Towards the end of the year the conductor, Cyril I. Yorath (see 'Personalia') and several players left, and by 1955 the band had lost its first-class status. However, a new conductor was appointed and within little more than a year Sankey's had bounced back, passing a BBC audition and appearing, for the first time in a number of years, at the 1956 'September'. It survived only until March 1963, however, when it was disbanded owing to the difficulties of recruiting and retaining high-class soloists.

**Sellers Engineering Band** had its root in the Tecol Band, formed in Huddersfield in January 1986 by Phillip McCann from students at the Technical College. The band progressed quickly and was promoted to the second section. It toured Spain in 1987 and 1988 and in this year, through sponsorship by a local engineering firm, became The Sellers College Band. Runner-up in the 1988 Grand Shield, it made its debut in the Open later in the year. By 1990 it had achieved championship status, taking 2nd prize in the formidable Yorkshire Area contest and 3rd in the National Finals. There was a further Area contest 2nd prize in 1995, but the strength of Sellers lay in its concert work. The company's managing director was very supportive and with his help, and with McCann not only conducting but regularly featured as cornet soloist, £70 000 had been raised for charity by 1996. During 1995 McCann resigned and was replaced by Alan Morrison, but in 1998 McCann returned. Many quality engagements came the band's way, including appearances at the prestigious Huddersfield Contemporary Music Festival and on television's *Songs of Praise*. In 1998, owing to a company name-change, the band became Sellers International Band.

**Sellers International** – *see* Sellers Engineering.

**Tecol** – *see* Sellers Engineering.

**Tredegar Town Band** was promoted to the Championship section after winning the second-section Finals in 1973. It achieved two wins and three 2nd prizes in Area Championships between 1974 and 1980. During this period John Childs, the band's former euphonium player, was the conductor and driving force at Tredegar (see page 83 n.28). Tredegar were Welsh Champions in 1975 and won the Grand Shield in 1976, the band's centenary year. They remained in the forefront of Welsh bands during the 1980s and 1990s, with five Area wins and four 2nd prizes, and becoming Champion Band of Wales in 1990. Following its 3rd prize in the European Championships of 1991, Tredegar became Radio Band of Wales in 1992 and 1993. A former Tredegar trombonist, Nigel Weeks, became musical director in 1985 but he left in 1993, emigrating to New Zealand. The band had, however, qualified for the Finals, where John Hudson steered them into second place. Nicholas Childs, John Child's son, then returned to his roots, becoming professional conductor in 1995 and leading the band again to the titles of Champion Band of Wales and Radio Band of Wales. Tredegar again represented Wales in the 1997 European Championships, earning fourth place. After this, Childs left to take up his position with Foden's. There were then a number of conductors, with Thomas Wyss, a Swiss expatriate, helping Tredegar to its 3rd prize in the Nationals of 1999.

**The Virtuosi Band** was founded in the early 1970s, primarily as a recording combination. Eric Ball was its first conductor and directed the band's first four LPs, released during 1973 and 1974. Players were drawn from leading brass bands and the JSVB, with James Shepherd on principal cornet. There were 28 players (not always the same) and later conductors included James Scott, Harry Mortimer, Maurice Handford and Stanley Boddington. The band produced nine LPs and gave one concert, in Portsmouth in July 1979.

**Whitburn** is a small town midway between Glasgow and Edinburgh and located in a former mining area. Up to 1961 its band was known as Whitburn Miners, but by 1963 the mining connection had gone and the band had changed its name to Whitburn Burgh. Its first major successes came under a well-known Scottish conductor, Alex Fleming, with wins in the Area championships of 1968, 1970 and 1972. John Harrison then became professional conductor, leading Whitburn to a further win in 1974. A flurry of later conductors included Peter Parkes, who was appointed music adviser in 1979 and brought Whitburn its next win the following year. Because of his involvement at Black Dyke it was often necessary to call in alternative conductors and James Scott conducted Whitburn's 3rd prize-winning performance in the 1989 Nationals. The band also regularly did well in BBC Scotland's competition 'Fanfare', completing a hat-trick in 1983. From 1983, through sponsorship, the band became known as Murray International Whitburn. In 1995 the band lost this sponsorship but almost immediately began another association, becoming the David A. Hall Whitburn Band. It remained Scotland's leading band in Area contests, with seven wins and seven 2nd prizes in the 20-year period. Phillip McCann first became associated with Whitburn as conductor in 1992 when he took them to the Finals. Towards the end of the century he took over from Peter Parkes and became musical director.

**William Davis Construction Group Band** (formed from the former Snibstone Colliery in 1970) won a succession of lower prizes at Area contests in the 1970s. In 1976 John Berryman became musical director. He left in 1985, to be replaced by Keith Wilkinson. Based near Leicester the band shared honours with Desford in the North Midlands during the period of the split region (see page 230). During the decade when Wilkinson was at the helm the band was highly successful at Area level, with six wins (four in successive years) and two second places. However, there were no successes at national level, though the band acquired a good reputation for its concerts, broadcasts, recordings and overseas tours. After Wilkinson's departure in 1996 John Hudson conducted for a while, but following the loss of its sponsorship the band took on local band status.

**Yewco** – *see* St Hilda's.

# Personalia

This section aims to fill some of the gaps left in the main text, providing additional information about personalities perhaps mentioned there but not featured.

**Betty Anderson** (b. 1929) followed in the footsteps of her father Jim as a tenor horn player, both of them winning numerous solo competitions. She won the tenor horn section in the All-England Solo Championships of 1947. Later she presented a trophy in memory of her father, for annual award to the highest-placed tenor horn player in the Solo Championships of Great Britain and in 1964 won the award herself. Earlier she had played in the Leicester Imperial Band, becoming its conductor in 1956 – the only lady conductor in brass bands at the time. Moving to Kibworth, she became its first lady 'bandmaster' in 1964. During the early 1970s her interest in teaching and conducting began to outweigh that in playing and she became musical director of the Ratby Band (Ratby being a small town a few miles from Leicester). This became a fruitful partnership, with many successes in local contests and much involvement in the community. In 1978 the band won the Grand Shield and later in the year Betty Anderson became the first lady to conduct in the British Open Championships. She retired from conducting Ratby in 1982. Her interest in youth led to her being chairman of the NYBB from 1974 to 1994.

**Alfred Ashpole** (1892–1990) was a well-known adjudicator, composer and writer on musical topics, probably best known for his correspondence courses. Particularly successful with candidates for conducting examinations, he published a book of specimen questions likely to be asked in viva voce tests (with its companion book of 'model answers'). He was a key figure during the early years of the NABBC and for a time was in charge of its Adjudicator's Training Scheme. Ashpole composed a number of pieces – both serious and light – some of which he published himself.

**Nigel Boddice** (b. 1952), a former leader of the NYBB, studied trumpet at the Royal Academy of Music. In 1975 he joined the BBC Scottish Symphony Orchestra as principal trumpet player. He combined this with conducting various Scottish bands, in particular Clydebank Burgh and CWS (Glasgow). Due to heavy commitments, both professionally and to a teaching programme at the Royal Scottish Academy of Music, he became less involved with bands during the 1980s. His interests during the 1990s swung towards younger players and following an involvement with NYBBS – mainly with the training band – he took a keen interest in West Lothian Schools Band, leading it to many successes (see page 213).

**Kevin Bolton** was principal cornet of Fairey's from 1973 to 1977, following a spell with Carlton Main. In 1981, after early conducting experience with several other bands, he returned to Carlton Main as resident conductor before taking a similar position with Fairey's in 1983–84 and later returning to Carlton Main as 'professional'. In 1990 he became resident conductor of Black Dyke, but left in the following year, becoming more involved in teaching and lecturing. He presided over several sessions for the NABBC and directed seminars in Japan. In 1992 he conducted Kennedy Swinton's 2nd prize-winning performance in the North West Area contest. Ill-health curtailed his further practical involvement for some years, though he made some successful transcriptions.

**E.C. (Ted) Buttress** (1917–94) was chiefly associated with Clayton Aniline Works Band (see Glossary), which he conducted from November 1944 until its demise in 1956. He was also a leading figure in the North West Area Brass Band Association, being chairman from 1950 to 1965. He organised several courses, for both players and conductors, in conjunction with Lancashire Education Authority, and he adjudicated regularly. He was a key figure in COBBA and was for many years editor of *British Mouthpiece*.

**Bernard Bygraves** joined Creswell Colliery at the age of 17, was appointed principal cornet at Brighouse in the following year and in 1951 took up a similar position with Black Dyke. He played with various other bands, including Ferodo and Crossley's Carpet Works, before emigrating to Australia.

**Philip Catelinet** (1910–95) was a product of the Salvation Army. His studies were mainly at Guildhall's evening classes, through which he became an accomplished pianist and studied composition with Henry Geehl. For a time he worked alongside Eric Ball in the SA's Editorial Department. Later he became a freelance musician, playing euphonium with the BBC Wireless Military Band from 1938. After war service he played tuba with various London orchestras and had the distinction of giving the première of the Vaughan Williams *Tuba Concerto*, with the LSO. Catelinet was a founder member of both the NABBC and the NSBBA and never lost his enthusiasm for bands. As a composer he wrote a great deal of SA music and a few test pieces; he was also an adjudicator. In 1956 Catelinet sailed for America (see page 315), but returned to Britain some years later. He was editor of *The Conductor* from 1978 to 1990.

**David Childs** (b. 1981), son and pupil of Robert, developed rapidly as a euphonium player. He was appointed principal euphonium of Brighouse & Rastrick in 1997 at the age of 16, and at 18 enrolled as a student at the RNCM. In the year 2000 he left Brighouse, succeeding Steven Mead at CWS (Glasgow), in a position which enabled him to remain prominent in the brass band scene whilst pursuing his studies in Manchester. In this year he also made a CD titled 'Prodigy', was declared Euphonium Player of the Year and won the brass Semi-finals in the BBC Young Musician of the Year.

**Leonard Davies** (1910–66) conducted Crystal Palace Band from 1935 to 1939, coming under the influence of Denis Wright, its then professional conductor. Following this he moved to Manchester to conduct Baxendale's Works Band (see Glossary). After war service, Davies conducted the newly-created St Hilda's for a time, but in 1948 became principal of the Parr School of Music (see page 85). Along with his teaching duties here, he accepted adjudicating appointments and worked as an examiner for the AOMF Scholarship, where the Director of Examinations was Denis Wright. When the latter formed the NYBB in 1952, Davies became its first secretary, a position he held until 1964, when he retired through ill health.

**Brian Evans** (1943–2005) began a top-class banding career in the late 1950s with CWS (Manchester), where he played soprano cornet for ten years. He then spent two years with Fairey's and six with Brighouse before, in 1979, joining Black Dyke. He had to relinquish this position for business reasons, but in the mid-1980s he joined Wingates. In 1988, he made a highly acclaimed solo LP.

**Gregor J. Grant** (1887–1966) was a Glaswegian. After military service he played euphonium with a number of bands and orchestras before taking up the baton, mainly with Govan Burgh Band, with whom he won the Scottish title in 1929 and 1932 (and again in 1951 and 1953). He later conducted Scottish CWS, but was unable to give the commitment required as he was now playing tuba with the Scottish Orchestra. He was also well-known as a composer and arranger. Grant combined his professional work with brass band conducting and adjudicating until his death in 1966.

**Russell Gray** (b. 1968) spent his formative years with Clydebank Burgh in his native Scotland. In 1985 he was the British Junior Cornet Champion and by 1989 was leader of NYBBS. He had been assistant principal with both Leyland and Black Dyke before becoming principal cornet player at Britannia Building Society in 1990. In 1994, he became the British Open Solo Champion and also received a *BB* award as the 'Top Cornet Player of the Year'. He embarked on a world tour as a soloist, that lasted from

August to December 1999. On his return he took up the baton, leading Ransome's to 2nd prize in the Nationals of 2000.

**John A. Greenwood** (1876–1953) was born in Winsford, Cheshire, and as a boy came under the influence of brass pioneers Henry Round and William Rimmer, succeeding the latter as musical editor for Wright & Round in 1936. As a conductor he lived under the shadow of William Halliwell, despite which he had some notable successes, winning the Belle Vue September contest with Black Dyke in 1914 and with Horwich RMI in 1916, 1917 and 1922. In 1925, he achieved a personal 'double' by winning the 'September' with Creswell, and the Nationals with Marsden Colliery. He also led Scottish CWS Band to victory in the Scottish Championships of 1937 and 1938. Greenwood was a prolific composer and arranger and was in constant demand as an adjudicator.

**Morgan Griffiths** (b. 1971), a pupil of Geoffrey Whitham, moved from 2nd euphonium at Hammonds Sauce Works to principal euphonium at Black Dyke in 1989. He returned to Hammonds three years later, saw it through the change to YBS and quickly became one of the country's leading exponents of the instrument. He was declared Euphonium Player of the Year in 1999.

**George Hawkins** (1876–1967) was born in Middlesbrough, though he lived in Scotland from 1926. He conducted over 50 bands, including St Hilda's, Harton (whom he led to victory at Belle Vue in 1919) and Parc & Dare. He worked with several Scottish bands and became professional conductor of Scottish CWS in 1931, winning the Scottish Championships in that year – and subsequently in 1934 and 1935. In June 1936 he had a serious accident which curtailed his conducting activities for a time. Hawkins finally retired from conducting in 1951. He regularly adjudicated, however, and was a prolific composer and arranger.

**Nicholas Hudson** became the solo trombone player of Foden's in 1982 at the age of 14. He built a fine reputation both as a section leader and as a stand-up soloist. His intention in 1996, when leaving what had become Britannia Building Society Band, was to build a solo career. Though he succeeded in doing this, he also found time to play with a number of bands – firstly with BNFL, then with Fairey's and finally with YBS. He left YBS in 1999 to devote himself full-time to his career as a soloist and clinician, on the way making several highly acclaimed CDs.

**Enoch Jackson** was a former principal cornet player of Besses and Creswell, and in 1934 became a professional trumpet player. He played principal trumpet with the BBC Symphony Orchestra, Liverpool Philharmonic and the Scottish National Orchestras. Whilst in Scotland he conducted Scottish CWS Band but had to leave because he could not give the commitment required. He became a regular adjudicator at premier brass band contests.

**David James** (b. 1942), a former leader of the NYBB, had played cornet in his town band in South Wales. He then studied trumpet at the Royal Academy of Music, also playing with Hanwell for a time. On completing his studies he became principal trumpet of the BBC Scottish Symphony Orchestra, combining this with conducting various Scottish brass bands. In 1978 he relinquished his position with the orchestra and moved south to conduct Carlton Main. He maintained his connections in Scotland, however, leading Bo'ness & Carriden to a win at the 1980 Edinburgh International Contest. Resigning from Carlton Main a year later, he became musical director of Yorkshire Imperial before moving to Grimethorpe, where he had four successful years, led the band to wins at Granada in 1985 (but see page 112) and Brass in Concert in 1986. During the later 1980s he had associations with several bands. In 1991 he led Point of Ayr to a win in the new North Wales Area contest and Rigid Containers to second place in the South Midlands. Later in the year he returned to Scotland to teach for the Grampian Authority.

**Chris Jeans** (b. 1960) played with Sun Life before moving to Desford and sharing in their greatest successes. This period was followed by two years with Rigid Containers during which time he twice became Brass in Concert Solo Champion. He then joined Black Dyke, remaining there until 1995. At this time Jeans became interested in conducting and had much success with Youthbrass 2000. In the year 2000 he had the opportunity to combine his two loves, becoming resident conductor and principal trombone with Ransome's.

**John Maines** (b. 1948) began his playing in Wigan Boys' Club Band and then lived for a time in Cornwall, playing with some of the county's leading bands. He achieved a hat-trick as Trombone Champion of Great Britain, in 1971–72–73. Later he played solo trombone for Stanshawe, Fairey's and Men o' Brass before, in 1982, becoming solo trombone with Black Dyke, a position he held for two years. By this time he was becoming interested in conducting, serving for several years as musical director of British Telecom Band. Playing was still important to him, however, and in 1987 he became solo trombonist of Wingates. He then relinquished his conductorship of BT and was musical director at Wingates from 1996 to 1998.

**Richard Marshall** (b. 1976) was one of the younger stars of the cornet in the approach to the end of the twentieth century. He began playing at the age of nine, in 1985. Grimethorpe Juniors was one of his earlier bands but at 15 he was playing principal cornet with Rothwell. From 1989 he was regularly winning solo competitions and in both 1992 and 1993 was declared British Open Junior Champion. In 1996, he became principal cornet player of Grimethorpe but was also in great demand as a soloist and, during 1999, undertook a 14-day solo tour in Canada.

**Dennis Masters** (b. 1923) was a cornet player in his youth and, after conducting for some years at a local level, in 1964 became musical director of Ransome & Marles, directing a number of prizewinning performances in the Midlands Area contests. His last place in the record books came with an Area win in 1971, though he remained with Ransome's until 1974, by which time he was on the teaching staff of Birmingham School of Music and in demand as an adjudicator.

**Harold Moss** (1891–1960) was one of the finest trombonists of his generation before taking up the baton. His greatest conducting successes were with Wingates, conducting them from 1909 to 1936 and winning the 1931 Crystal Palace contest. He then became musical director of Creswell Colliery, remaining there until 1948, when he moved back to Lancashire to take Leyland Motors Band. He composed several solos and made many arrangements for his bands, mostly unpublished. In his later years he became a leading adjudicator.

**Lynda Nicholson** (b. 1957) is a former leader of the NYBB. Amongst bands with which she played were Hendon and Hanwell, being principal cornet with the latter from 1982 to 1985. She then moved north to become assistant principal cornet player with Foden's and to teach in Cheshire. In 1989–90 she played principal cornet with Wingates, moving to a similar position at Desford in 1992. Later she returned to Wingates and was now teaching in Merseyside where she formed the highly successful St Helens Youth Band, winner of the National Youth Brass Band Championships in 2000.

**Barrie Perrins** was the Euphonium Champion of Great Britain in 1964, 1969, 1970 and 1971. He played solo euphonium with Hendon for 19 years, acquiring an international reputation, particularly in Switzerland and the USA. He was a regular contributor to band press and in 1984 published *Brass Band Digest*, a collection of articles he had written over the years. He was the first recipient, in 1979, of the award of 'Euphonium Player of the Year'.

**Ian Porthouse**, a former NYBB leader, moved to Leyland in the mid-1980s as assistant principal, later becoming principal cornet player. He held this position for three years before taking up a similar appointment at Desford and playing in two of the band's National Championship successes. He left in 1992 and lived for a time in New Zealand. In 1993, he became principal cornet of Black Dyke, a position he relinquished a year later, following a motor car accident. He then took the principal's chair at Tredegar, winning the 'Best Soloist' award at the British Open of 1998. He moved to YBS a year later, but left in 2000 and, after a short break, returned to Tredegar. During these later years he was also gaining experience as a conductor.

**T.J. (Tom) Powell** (1897–1965) was born in Tredegar and played with the SA band there before joining the Royal Marines. From 1920, back in civilian life, Powell conducted Melingriffith Works Band in Cardiff, having considerable success at local level. He became the leading brass band conductor in Wales during the 1950s and was appointed musical director of Cory's in 1959. Known as the 'Welsh March King', amongst his 50 or so compositions there were a number of well-known contest marches and some test pieces. Powell was a leading adjudicator, officiating at both the major contests. He died of a heart attack whilst conducting Cory's during a broadcast in 1965.

**Gareth Pritchard** (b. 1955) was a product of Parc & Dare, for whom he played principal cornet, and was the Cornet Champion of Great Britain in 1977 and 1979. He later played principal cornet with several other bands, including Fairey's and Ransome's. Amongst a number of conducting appointments, he held the residency at Carlton Main. He then moved to Norway where he enjoyed successes with several more bands. He later returned to England and became professional conductor of a number of bands.

**William Rimmer** (1861–1936) was the leading brass band conductor in the early twentieth century. He regularly conducted up to six bands in the 'September' and in 1909 his bands took five of the six prizes. From 1905 to 1909 he conducted every winning band at both major contests. He then retired from contesting in order to concentrate on arranging and composing. Rimmer's death was announced in *BBN* of March 1936. He had been musical editor of Wright & Round since 1913 (following appointments with F. Richardson and R. Smith).

**Peter Roberts** (b. 1950) was a product of Grimethorpe Juniors, where he came under the influence of George Thompson. He joined the senior band in 1965 on soprano cornet, playing which he won numerous solo awards, becoming the Granada Soloist in 1983 and the British Open Solo Champion in 1988 (its inaugural year). The latter led to a trip to New Zealand, participation in an international solo competition and winning 3rd prize. In 1989 Roberts retired from playing on medical advice. However, he overcame the problem and by 1991 was again banding. He played with a number of bands before settling down with YBS in 1997, with them winning the solo prize at Brass in Concert a year later. He became British Open Solo Champion again in 1999, once more qualifying for the New Zealand solo contest – this time winning and becoming the International Musician of the Year. In 2003 he published his autobiography, *A Legend in His Own Lifetime*.

**Stephen Roberts**, a french horn player with the Fine Arts Brass Ensemble until October 2004. He also has great skills as an arranger, producing many highly entertaining pieces and also some more serious transcriptions, notably one of the complete *Planets* suite of Holst. He has worked successfully with a number of Midlands bands, including Jones & Crossland and Desford.

**Roy Roe** (b. 1943) was playing soprano cornet with Foden's at the age of 17. He did this for four years before moving to Fairey's, staying there for a further five. During this time he was also in Men o' Brass. He next moved to his native Yorkshire, to Yorkshire Imperial. In 1980 he began a six-year appointment with Brighouse & Rastrick, at the end of which he had completed almost 20 years playing at the highest level. He was also, by now, taking an interest in conducting and adjudicating.

**William (Bill) Scholes** (1907–1991), though having an SA background, was appointed conductor of Rushden Temperance Band in 1947. He also conducted other bands but his name was very much associated with Rushden until his departure in 1963, after which he became musical director of Kibworth Band where he remained throughout the 1960s and early 1970s. In 1975, at the age of 70, he returned to Rushden.

**Dennis Smith** (1927–93) had an SA background. He began playing at the age of 11, played with SP&S and Rosehill bands before moving into the contesting sector where, first of all he played with CWS (Manchester) and then, in 1958, joined Foden's. Whilst still solo euphonium player here he also took up the baton, initially with local bands but in 1967 taking on Creswell. By 1970 he had left Foden's and become musical director at Wingates where he had a spectacular start, with 1st prizes both in the Area contests and in the National Finals of 1971. He remained with Wingates only until 1972 after which he moved around quite a lot. His later years were dogged by ill health.

**Chris Thomas** played with both BTM and Tredegar before becoming British Open Solo Champion in 1992 and 1993, and International Musician of the Year in 1992, winning the prestigious award in Auckland, New Zealand. He spent some with Fairey's before returning to his native Wales, later becoming the solo trombone player with Cory's.

**Dennis Wilby** (b. 1934), a former professional trumpet player, conducted a number of bands during the late 1970s and early 1980s, including Wingates and Grimethorpe. In the 1990s he became founding editor of the quarterly magazine *Brass Review* (see page 223). He was conductor of the Irish National Youth Band (founded in 1998) and for over 20 years has been a frequent visitor to Norway.

**Mark Wilkinson** (b. 1971) was a product of Besses Boys' Band and a former leader of the NYBB. At the age of 19 he became principal cornet with Wingates, shortly after which he accepted (in 1992) an invitation to take on a similar role at Britannia Building Society. He remained in this position through its various name changes until the end of the century and beyond.

**Martin Winter** (b. 1965), another former leader of the NYBB, was principal cornet player with Loughborough Youth Band (Butlin's Champions 1978). In 1982 he moved to near-neighbours Desford, where he progressed to the principal's chair three years later, but left in 1988 to study trumpet at the RNCM. Here he won several major awards and also played for a time with Britannia Building Society. In 1993, he was appointed associate principal trumpet of the BBC Philharmonic Orchestra but then moved to Norway to become co-principal of the Bergen Philharmonic Orchestra. He has played with and conducted several Norwegian bands.

**Elaine Wolff**, yet another former leader of the NYBB, played with Hanwell and was winner of the Brass Semi-finals of the BBC Young Musician of the Year competition in 1980. During the early 1980s she was with Desford but in 1986 moved south again to join Newham and in 1989 (now as Mrs Elaine Williams) became principal cornet with Hendon. One of her long-standing preoccupations was as principal cornet with the Young Ambassadors. She was also the main driving force behind the original Girls o' Brass (see Glossary).

**William (Willie) Wood** (1887–1981) first played at Crystal Palace contest in 1904. He joined Black Dyke in 1907, initially playing flugelhorn, then becoming assistant principal and, for a short time, principal cornet. He turned professional in 1912, playing trumpet and french horn with the Carl Rosa Opera Company, but returned to brass bands as a conductor after the 1914–18 War, gaining early successes with Brighouse & Rastrick and Horwich RMI. He came to prominence in 1920 when, following Alexander Owen's death a fortnight before the Belle Vue September contest, he led Besses to victory. Wood also conducted their winning 'September' performance in 1937, repeating the feat two years later with Wingates. In the post-war years Besses struggled for survival but, thanks to the existence of Besses Boys' Band, Wood was able to mould a combination of the two into a championship-winning team, taking them to the British Open title in 1959. He also conducted Creswell and Yorkshire Copper Works for a time, was musical director of Crossley's Carpet Works Band between 1955 and 1958, and professional conductor of Brighouse & Rastrick at about the same time. He retired from Besses early in 1963 but continued working with Besses Boys. In 1970, at the age of 83 and regarded by many as the Grand Old Man of the band movement, he finally retired after giving 20 years' valuable service to the Boys' Band, with connections with the senior band going back 50 years and with bands in general for over 70.

**Ernest Woodhouse** (1921–83) became musical director of Creswell Colliery in 1954 and was an influential personality in the Midlands, working for a time with Desford Colliery. He had a successful period with Burton Construction in the 1970s (see Glossary), followed by a spell as resident conductor at Grimethorpe. A well-respected adjudicator, Woodhouse was also Director of Examinations for the Bandsman's College of Music for a time.

**Allan Wycherley** (b. 1957) began his playing at the top level with a 15-year stint at Fairey's, starting in 1972. He then joined Desford but was there for only a short period, followed by a brief spell with Leyland, joining JSVB in 1988. Following this, he moved to Foden's, remaining in the top flight of soprano cornet players to the end of the twentieth century and beyond.

**Cyril I. Yorath** (1907–85) was born in South Wales, though his early banding experience was gained in Somerset. He was appointed conductor of Sankey's Castle Works Band in September 1936, remaining there until the end of 1953 and directing them in more than 100 broadcasts. After a dispute with the management, he became musical director of Enfield Central, staying there for about two years. He conducted a number of Midlands bands, including City of Coventry, and was a leading figure in the Midlands.

# Recipients of the Iles Medal, 1947–2000

The Iles Medal is awarded to the Brass Bandmaster or Conductor of unquestioned musical ability who has given outstanding service to the Movement for many years.

| | | | |
|---|---|---|---|
| 1947 | Arthur O. Pearce | 1974 | Albert Chappell |
| 1948 | No award | 1975 | Bernard Adams (SA) |
| 1949 | Fred Mortimer | 1976 | Roy Newsome |
| 1950 | J.A. Greenwood | 1977 | James Scott |
| 1951 | Herbert Bennett | 1978 | Kenneth Dennison |
| 1952 | George Hawkins | 1979 | Geoffrey Whitham |
| 1953 | Harry Mortimer | 1980 | John R. Carr |
| 1954 | Eric Ball | 1981 | Eddie Williams |
| 1955 | Stanley Boddington | 1982 | Denis Carr |
| 1956 | Denis Wright | 1983 | David Read |
| 1957 | Frank Wright | 1984 | Ieuan Morgan |
| 1958 | T.J. Powell | 1985 | Dennis Masters |
| 1959 | Alex Mortimer | 1986 | Richard Evans |
| 1960 | Drake Rimmer | 1987 | John Berryman |
| 1961 | George Hespe | 1988 | Derek Broadbent |
| 1962 | Rex Mortimer | 1989 | James Shepherd |
| 1963 | William Wood | 1990 | Norman Ashcroft |
| 1964 | W.B. Hargreaves | 1991 | Peter Wilson |
| 1965 | Leonard Lamb | 1992 | Bram Gay |
| 1966 | E.C. Buttress | 1993 | Elgar Howarth |
| 1967 | Geoffrey Brand | 1994 | Peter Parkes (Major) |
| 1968 | Tom F. Atkinson | 1995 | Howard Snell |
| 1969 | William Scholes | 1996 | James Watson and Margaret Mortimer |
| 1970 | George Thompson | 1997 | James Williams (SA) |
| 1971 | Albert Coupe | 1998 | Edward Gregson |
| 1972 | No award | 1999 | David King |
| 1973 | Trevor Walmsley DFC | 2000 | Philip Sparke |

# AOMF Scholarship winners, 1922–90

Initially the Scholarship was meant to be bi-annual, but was soon established as an annual event until the disruption caused by the war. With the exception of the years between 1961 and 1971, when it ceased to function temporarily, it was held every year, subject to a satisfactory number of candidates entering.

1922   Herbert White (son of J.H. White) – cornet, one-time conductor of Besses o' th' Barn

1924   Joe Farrington – cornet – played with and conducted Creswell Colliery

1926   Elgar Clayton – principal cornet Munn & Felton's, Fairey's; conducted SCWS and Forfar; emigrated to New Zealand; MBE 1884

1928   Willie Clegg – soprano cornet Brighouse & Rastrick, St Hilda's professional band, Bickershaw

1929   Harold Hall – cornet with St Hilda's professional band 1930–37 and trumpet with BBC Northern Orchestra

1930   Thomas Berry – cornet, Skelmersdale

1931   Bramwell Allington – cornet, Wombwell; became Bandmaster of Canadian Staff Band (SA)

1932   James Haighton – cornet, Darwen

1933   Thomas Pickford – cornet, Openshaw; became professional musician

1934   Joseph Smith – cornet, Bamber Bridge; played with Luton

1935   James Harrison – cornet, played with Wingates

1936   George Etheridge – cornet, Rochdale (SA)

1937   Bertram Humphries – euphonium, Rushall, Staffs

1938   C. Smith – trombone, Walsall Wood, Staffs; RAF Pilot Officer, killed 23 September 1943

1939 { Alan M. Pockock, Street, Somerset
Arthur Butterworth – principal trumpet, Hallé Orchestra; composer, conductor, adjudicator

1942   Gracie Cole – Firbeck, cornet soloist, became professional trumpet player, Ivy Benson's Band

1944   Ronald Yarwood – euphonium ICI (Alkali) Northwich

1945   Bram Gay – principal cornet Foden's, principal trumpet Hallé Orchestra, conductor of several bands, Orchestral Director Covent Garden, leading figure in brass band movement

1946   Kenneth Dennison – principal trombone, later musical director, Fairey Band; adjudicator and leading figure in brass band movement

1947   Tom Atkinson – euphonium Bradford Victoria, tuba, BBC Northern Orchestra

1948   Bryon Whiteside – cornet, Besses Boys and CWS (Manchester)

1949   Norman Burnham – euphonium Highfield Modern School, NYBB and Yewco Works

1951   Elgar Howarth – leading trumpet player and internationally renowned classical conductor; musical advisor Grimethorpe Colliery, Artistic Director NYBB

1952   G.M. Dutton – trombone, Derby

1954   William Peter Boyle – cornet, Arbroath; became music master at Dundee Academy

1955   W.A. Gillett – cornet, Preston

1956   Adrian Barrett – assistant principal cornet CWS (Manchester)

1957   John C. Hayes – flugelhorn, Bradford; NYBB

1958   Bryce Ford – cornet, Manchester

1959   D. Demack – cornet, Hoggarth's Works

1961   John Hardy, Bradford – became professional trumpet player, orchestra of Royal Opera House, Covent Garden

1971   Stephen Corbett – Manchester, solo cornet Brighouse & Rastrick and CWS Manchester

1972   Peter Pollard – cornet, Kibworth

1973   Christopher Joynes – Grimethorpe; moved to Switzerland as brass teacher

1975   Russell Howarth – became principal trombone with BBC Big Band

1976   David Lancaster – Pemberton Old; lecturer in higher education and conductor

1977   Graham McEvoy, Manchester – solo euphonium Besses and Fairey

1978   William (Bill) Millar – Wingates; solo euphonium Grimethorpe, JSVB and Leyland

1979   John Allmark – became professional trumpet player; emigrated to USA

1980   Beverley Vaughan – solo horn Hanwell/Roneo

1981   Richard Grantham – cornet, NYBB, Yorkshire Imperial

1982   Michael Wildgust, Manchester – solo cornet Besses, member of JSVB

1983   Kirsten Thomas, Dobcross – flugelhorn NYBB, Fodens, Wingates

1984   Jason Glover – trombone, William Davis Construction, Desford; professional musician and composer

1985   Mark Vause – cornet, Morcambe; head of school music department in Cambridge

1986   Paul Lawler – euphonium, Manchester

1987   David Welsh – Wingates, solo euphonium Fairey; moved to Switzerland

1989   Richard Wood – cornet

1990   Rachael Morris – soprano cornet, Ifton Welfare

# The British Open Championships, 1975–2000

**1975    Fireworks: Elgar Howarth**
| | | |
|---|---|---|
| 1st | Wingates Temperance | Richard Evans |
| 2nd | The Fairey Band | Kenneth Dennison |
| 3rd | Yorkshire Imperial Metals | Trevor Walmsley |
| 4th | The Cory Band | Arthur Kenney |

**1976    An Epic Symphony: Percy Fletcher**
| | | |
|---|---|---|
| 1st | Black Dyke Mills Band | Peter Parkes |
| 2nd | Stanshawe (Bristol) | W.B. Hargreaves |
| 3rd | Brighouse & Rastrick | Maurice Handford |
| 4th | The Cory Band | Bram Gay |

**1977    Diadem of Gold: G. Bailey, arr. Frank Wright**
| | | |
|---|---|---|
| 1st | Black Dyke Mills Band | Peter Parkes |
| 2nd | Brighouse & Rastrick | Derek Broadbent |
| 3rd | Fairey Enginering Works | Richard Evans |
| 4th | Hammonds Sauce Works | Geoffrey Whitham |

**1978    Overture Benvenuto Cellini: Berlioz, arr. Frank Wright**
| | | |
|---|---|---|
| 1st | Brighouse & Rastrick | Geoffrey Brand |
| 2nd | Black Dyke Mills Band | Peter Parkes |
| 3rd | Ransome Hoffman Pollard | Stephen Shimwell |
| 4th | Fairey Engineering | W.B. Hargreaves |

**1979    Overture Le Carnaval Romain: Berlioz, arr. Frank Wright**
| | | |
|---|---|---|
| 1st | Fairey Engineering | W.B. Hargreaves |
| 2nd | Desford Colliery | Howard Snell |
| 3rd | Grimethorpe Colliery | Elgar Howarth |
| 4th | Black Dyke | Peter Parkes |

**1980    Energy: Robert Simpson**
| | | |
|---|---|---|
| 1st | Yorkshire Imperial Metals | John Pryce-Jones |
| 2nd | GUS (Footwear) | Keith Wilkinson |
| 3rd | Desford Colliery | Howard Snell |
| 4th | Sun Life | Derek Bourgeois |

**1981    Variations on a Ninth: Gilbert Vinter**
| | | |
|---|---|---|
| 1st | City of Coventry | Arthur Kenney |

| 2nd | Leyland Vehicles | Richard Evans |
| 3rd | Fodens Motor Works | Howard Snell |
| 4th | Hammonds Sauce Works | Geoffrey Whitham |

**1982  Three Figures: Herbert Howells**

| 1st | Besses o' th' Barn | Roy Newsome |
| 2nd | Fairey Engineering | Geoffrey Brand |
| 3rd | GUS (Footwear) | Keith Wilkinson |
| 4th | Desford Colliery Dowty | Howard Snell |

**1983  Connotations: Edward Gregson**

| 1st | Black Dyke Mills Band | Peter Parkes |
| 2nd | Brighouse & Rastrick | James Watson |
| 3rd | Grimethorpe Colliery Institute | James Scott |
| 4th | City of Coventry | Don Blakeson |

**1984  A Comedy Overture: John Ireland**

| 1st | Grimethorpe Colliery Institute | Geoffrey Brand |
| 2nd | Black Dyke Mills Band | Peter Parkes |
| 3rd | Fairey Engineering | Howard Williams |
| 4th | Brighouse & Rastrick | James Watson |

**1985  Salute to Youth: Gilbert Vinter**

| 1st | Black Dyke Mills Band | Peter Parkes |
| 2nd | British Aerospace Wingates | James Scott |
| 3rd | Fodens OTS | Howard Snell |
| 4th | Leyland Vehicles | Richard Evans |

**1986  An Epic Symphony (Mvts 1 & 2): Percy Fletcher
and Fusions: Howard Blake**

| 1st | Black Dyke Mills Band | Peter Parkes |
| 2nd | Fairey Engineering | Roy Newsome |
| 3rd | GUS (Kettering) | Bramwell Tovey |
| 4th | Britannia Building Society | Howard Snell |

**1987  Freedom: Hubert Bath**

| 1st | Williams Fairey Engineering | Roy Newsome |
| 2nd | Britannia Building Society Foden | Howard Snell |
| 3rd | Grimethorpe Colliery | David James |
| 4th | Ever Ready | Eric Cunningham |

**1988  Contest Music: Wilfred Heaton**

| 1st | Rigid Containers Group | Bramwell Tovey |
| 2nd | Black Dyke Mills Band | Peter Parkes |
| 3rd | Williams Fairey Engineering | Roy Newsome |
| 4th | Leyland DAF | Richard Evans |

**1989 Diversions: Derek Bourgeois**
| | | |
|---|---|---|
| 1st | Kennedy's Swinton Concert Brass | Garry Cutt |
| 2nd | Hammonds Sauce Works | Geoffrey Whitham |
| 3rd | Leyland DAF | Richard Evans |
| 4th | Black Dyke Mills Band | David King |

**1990 Overture Le Roi d'Ys: Lalo, arr. Frank Wright**
| | | |
|---|---|---|
| 1st | Sun Life | Roy Newsome |
| 2nd | Leyland DAF | Richard Evans |
| 3rd | Grimethorpe Colliery | Frank Renton |
| 4th | Hammonds Sauce Works | Geoffrey Whitham |

**1991 Paganini Variations: Philip Wilby**
| | | |
|---|---|---|
| 1st | Grimethorpe Colliery | Frank Renton |
| 2nd | Williams Fairey Engineering | Peter Parkes |
| 3rd | Leyland DAF | Richard Evans |
| 4th | Britannia Building Society | Howard Snell |

**1992 Cloudcatcher Fells: John McCabe**
| | | |
|---|---|---|
| 1st | Black Dyke Mills Band | James Watson |
| 2nd | BNFL | Richard Evans |
| 3rd | Williams Fairey Engineering | Peter Parkes |
| 4th | Marple | Garry Cutt |

**1993 Masquerade: Philip Wilby**
| | | |
|---|---|---|
| 1st | Williams Fairey Engineering | Peter Parkes |
| 2nd | Black Dyke Mills Band | James Watson |
| 3rd | CWS (Glasgow) | Frans Violet |
| 4th | Marple | Garry Cutt |

**1994 Salamander: John McCabe**
| | | |
|---|---|---|
| 1st | BNFL | Richard Evans |
| 2nd | Black Dyke Mills Band | James Watson |
| 3rd | Grimethorpe Colliery | Garry Cutt |
| 4th | Marple | Derek Broadbent |

**1995 Revelation: Philip Wilby**
| | | |
|---|---|---|
| 1st | Black Dyke Mills Band | James Watson |
| 2nd | Williams Fairey Engineering | James Gourlay |
| 3rd | Yorkshire Building Society | David King |
| 4th | Marple | Derek Broadbent |

**1996 Severn Suite: Edward Elgar, ed. Gay**
| | | |
|---|---|---|
| 1st | Marple | Garry Cutt |
| 2nd | Tredegar | Nicholas Childs |
| 3rd | BNFL | Richard Evans |
| 4th | Williams Fairey Engineering | James Gourlay |

**1997    Whitsun Wakes: Michael Ball**

| | | |
|---|---|---|
| 1st | Yorkshire Building Society | David King |
| 2nd | Williams Fairey Engineering | James Gourlay |
| 3rd | CWS (Glasgow) | Howard Snell |
| 4th | NSK-RHP Ransome | Brian Grant |

**1998    Diversions on a Bass Theme: George Lloyd**

| | | |
|---|---|---|
| 1st | Williams Fairey Engineering | James Gourlay |
| 2nd | Fodens (Courtois) | Nicholas Childs |
| 3rd | Brighouse & Rastrick | Allan Withington |
| 4th | Grimethorpe Colliery | Peter Parkes |

**1999    Dove Descending: Philip Wilby**

| | | |
|---|---|---|
| 1st | Yorkshire Building Society | David King |
| 2nd | Black Dyke Band | James Watson |
| 3rd | Williams Fairey Engineering | James Gourlay |
| 4th | Brighouse & Rastrick | Allan Withington |

**2000    Ceremony: Michael Ball**

| | | |
|---|---|---|
| 1st | Buy As You View Cory | Robert Childs |
| 2nd | Black Dyke Band | Nicholas Childs |
| 3rd | Grimethorpe Colliery | Garry Cutt |
| 4th | Williams Fairey Engineering | James Gourlay |

# The National Championships, 1975–2000

**1975   Un Vie de Matelot: Robert Farnon**
1st   Black Dyke Mills Band          Peter Parkes
2nd   Stanshawe                     W.B. Hargreaves
3rd   Brighouse & Rastrick          James Scott
4th   Yorkshire Imperial Metals     Trevor Walmsley

**1976   Sinfonietta for Brass Band – The Wayfarer: Eric Ball**
1st   Black Dyke Mills Band          Peter Parkes
2nd   Yorkshire Imperial Metals     Trevor Walmsley
3rd   Wingates Temperance           Richard Evans
4th   Ever Ready (GB)               Eric Cunningham

**1977   Connotations for Brass Band: Edward Gregson**
1st   Black Dyke Mills Band          Peter Parkes
2nd   Grimethorpe Colliery          Gerard Schwarz
3rd   Yorkshire Imperial Metals     Denis Carr
4th   Camborne Town                 Derek Greenwood

**1978   Four Dances from 'Checkmate': Sir Arthur Bliss, arr. Ball**
1st   Yorkshire Imperial Metals     Denis Carr
2nd   Besses o' th' Barn            Roy Newsome
3rd   Grimethorpe Colliery Institute   Stanley Boddington
4th   Fairey Engineering            W.B. Hargreaves

**1979   Volcano: Robert Simpson**
1st   Black Dyke Mills Band          Peter Parkes
2nd   The Cory Band                 Denzil Stephens
3rd   Birmingham School of Music    Roy Curran
4th   Carlton Main Frickley Colliery   David James

**1980   Overture – Carnival: Antonín Dvořák, arr. Brand**
1st   Brighouse & Rastrick          Derek Broadbent
2nd   Black Dyke Mills Band          Peter Parkes
3rd   Fairey Engineering            W.B. Hargreaves
4th   The Cory Band                 Denzil Stephens

**1981   Blitz: Derek Bourgeois**
1st   Black Dyke Mills Band          Peter Parkes

| 2nd | Brighouse & Rastrick | Derek Broadbent |
| 3rd | Whitburn Miners' Welfare | Geoffrey Whitham |
| 4th | Yorkshire Imperial | John Pryce-Jones |

**1982 Contest Music: Wilfred Heaton**

| 1st | The Cory Band | Arthur Kenney |
| 2nd | Black Dyke Mills Band | Peter Parkes |
| 3rd | Brodsworth Colliery | Denis Carr |
| 4th | Camborne Town | Derek Greenwood |

**1983 Ballet for Band: Joseph Horovitz**

| 1st | The Cory Band | Arthur Kenney |
| 2nd | Black Dyke Mills Band | Peter Parkes |
| 3rd | GUS (Footwear) | Keith Wilkinson |
| 4th | Grimethorpe Colliery | James Scott |

**1984 Dances and Arias: Edward Gregson**

| 1st | The Cory Band | Arthur Kenney |
| 2nd | Sun Life | Christopher Adey |
| 3rd | Leyland Vehicles | Richard Evans |
| 4th | Fairey Engineering | Roy Newsome |

**1985 Cloudcatcher Fells: John McCabe**

| 1st | Black Dyke Mills Band | Peter Parkes |
| 2nd | Desford Colliery Dowty | Howard Snell |
| 3rd | IMI Yorkshire Imperial | James Scott |
| 4th | Sun Life | Geoffrey Brand |

**1986 Diversions: Derek Bourgeois**

| 1st | Fairey Engineering | Roy Newsome |
| 2nd | Black Dyke Mills Band | Peter Parkes |
| 3rd | Sun Life | Rob Wiffin |
| 4th | GUS Band | Bram Tovey |

**1987 Harmony Music: Philip Sparke**

| 1st | Desford Colliery Dowty | James Watson |
| 2nd | Black Dyke Mills Band | Peter Parkes |
| 3rd | IMI Yorkshire Imperial | James Scott |
| 4th | Williams Fairey Engineering | Roy Newsome |

**1988 Seascapes: Ray Steadman-Allen**

| 1st | Desford Colliery Dowty | James Watson |
| 2nd | Britannia Building Society Foden | Howard Snell |
| 3rd | Jaguar Cars (City of Coventry) | Ray Farr |
| 4th | IMI Yorkshire Imperial | James Scott |

**1989   Odin: Arthur Butterworth**

| | | |
|---|---|---|
| 1st | Desford Colliery Caterpillar | James Watson |
| 2nd | Black Dyke Mills Band | David King |
| 3rd | Murray International Whitburn | James Scott |
| 4th | Britannia Building Society | Howard Snell |

**1990   English Heritage: George Lloyd**

| | | |
|---|---|---|
| 1st | CWS (Glasgow) | John Hudson |
| 2nd | Britannia Building Society | Howard Snell |
| 3rd | Sellers Engineering | Phillip McCann |
| 4th | Leyland DAF | Richard Evans |

**1991   Energy: Robert Simpson**

| | | |
|---|---|---|
| 1st | Desford Colliery Caterpillar | James Watson |
| 2nd | Britannia Building Society | Howard Snell |
| 3rd | Grimethorpe Colliery | Frank Renton |
| 4th | Scottish Brewers (Newtongrange) | Raymond Tennant |

**1992   The New Jerusalem: Philip Wilby**

| | | |
|---|---|---|
| 1st | Grimethorpe Colliery | Frank Renton |
| 2nd | Desford Colliery Caterpillar | Stephen Roberts |
| 3rd | Williams Fairey Engineering | Peter Parkes |
| 4th | CWS (Glasgow) | Howard Snell |

**1993   The Devil and the Deep Blue Sea: Derek Bourgeois**

| | | |
|---|---|---|
| 1st | Williams Fairey Engineering | Peter Parkes |
| 2nd | Tredegar | John Hudson |
| 3rd | Sun Life | Roy Newsome |
| 4th | Grimethorpe Colliery | Frank Renton |

**1994   Theme and Co-operation: Joseph Horovitz**

| | | |
|---|---|---|
| 1st | Black Dyke Mills Band | James Watson |
| 2nd | Williams Fairey Engineering | Peter Parkes |
| 3rd | Yorkshire Building Society | David King |
| 4th | Sun Life | Roy Newsome |

**1995   Songs for B.L.: Elgar Howarth**

| | | |
|---|---|---|
| 1st | Black Dyke Mills Band | James Watson |
| 2nd | Yorkshire Building Society | David King |
| 3rd | Desford Colliery | Peter Parkes |
| 4th | Brighouse & Rastrick | Allan Withington |

**1996   Isaiah 40: Robert Redhead**

| | | |
|---|---|---|
| 1st | CWS (Glasgow) | Howard Snell |
| 2nd | Grimethorpe Colliery | Peter Parkes |
| 3rd | Black Dyke Mills Band | James Watson |
| 4th | Williams Fairey | James Gourlay |

**1997  On Alderley Edge: Peter Graham**
| | | |
|---|---|---|
| 1st | Brighouse & Rastrick | Allan Withington |
| 2nd | Williams Fairey | James Gourlay |
| 3rd | Fodens (Courtois) | Nicholas Childs |
| 4th | Kirkintilloch | Frank Renton |

**1998  Between the Moon and Mexico: Philip Sparke**
| | | |
|---|---|---|
| 1st | Brighouse & Rastrick | Allan Withington |
| 2nd | Yorkshire Building Society | David King |
| 3rd | Williams Fairey | James Gourlay |
| 4th | Fodens (Courtois) | Nicholas Childs |

**1999  Concerto No. 1 for Brass Band: Derek Bourgeois**
| | | |
|---|---|---|
| 1st | Fodens (Courtois) | Nicholas Childs |
| 2nd | Brighouse & Rastrick | Allan Withington |
| 3rd | Tredegar | Thomas Wyss |
| 4th | NSK-RHP Ransome | Brian Grant |

**2000  Harrison's Dream: Peter Graham**
| | | |
|---|---|---|
| 1st | Buy As You View Cory | Robert Childs |
| 2nd | NSK-RHP Ransome | Russell Gray |
| 3rd | Fodens (Courtois) | Bram Tovey |
| 4th | Brighouse & Rastrick | Allan Withington |

# Quartet and Soloist Championships, 1944–2000

**Champion quartets (1944–81)**

*Morris Motors' Quartet Contest*

1944   Hanwell, Callender's, RAF Bomber Command

*Brass Quartet Championships of Great Britain*

1945   Hanwell, Fairey's/RAF Bomber Command
1946   Creswell, Black Dyke No. 2, Leicester Imperial
1947   Black Dyke, Luton, Creswell
1948   Black Dyke 'A', Munn & Felton's, Black Dyke 'B'
1949   Black Dyke, Barry Ostlere & Shepherd Trombones, Horsham Borough
1950   Foden's, Barry Ostlere & Shepherd Trombones, Langley Silver
1951   Foden's, Barry Ostlere & Shepherd Trombones, Black Dyke 'A'
1952   Barry Ostlere & Shepherd Trombones
1953   Foden's No. 2, Fairey's, Foden's No. 1
1954   Barry Ostlere & Shepherd Trombones, John White Footwear, Rushden Temperance
1955   Rushden Temperance, Foden's, Barry Ostlere & Shepherd Trombones
1956   Foden's, Fairey's, Barry Ostlere & Shepherd Trombones
1957   Wingates, Fairey's, Foden's
1958   Fairey's, Edge Hill, Langley Silver
1959   Grimethorpe, Rushden Temperance, Munn & Felton's Basses
1960   Rushden Temperance, Crookhall Colliery, Grimethorpe 'A'
1961   CWS (Manchester), Brighouse & Rastrick, Edge Hill British Railways
1962   Brighouse & Rastrick, Carlton Main, CWS (Manchester)
1963   Edge Hill British Railways, Brighouse & Rastrick 'B', Brighouse & Rastrick 'A'
1964   Black Dyke, Edge Hill British Railways, GUS (Footwear)
1965   Black Dyke 'B', Black Dyke 'A', Cammell Laird
1966   GUS (Footwear), Slaithwaite, Foden's

1967  GUS (Footwear), Desford, Grimethorpe
1968  GUS (Footwear), Wingates, Fairey's
1969  Wingates, Fairey's, Ransome & Marles
1970  Ransome & Marles, City of Coventry, Grimethorpe
1971  Hamworthy Engineering, Edge Hill British Railways, Broxburn
1972  Broxburn, Linthwaite, Ever Ready
1973  City of Coventry, Ever Ready, Brighouse & Rastrick
1974  City of Coventry, Brighouse & Rastrick, Stanshawe
1975  Thoresby, City of Coventry, Loughborough
1976  Foden's, Loughborough, Linthwaite
1977  Wingates, Fairey's, William Davis
1978  City of Coventry, Wingates, Foden's
1979  Wingates, City of Coventry, Desford
1980  City of Coventry, Fairey's, Loughborough
1981  City of Coventry, Jones & Crossland, Loughborough

*A Section Winning Quartets*

1955  Crookhall Colliery
1956  Wingates Temperance
1957  High Wycombe
1958  Crookhall Colliery

## Champion soloists (1959–81)

*Cornet Air Varié Championships*

1959  James Scott (M & F), Cliff Sayers (Crookhall), John Berryman
      (Camborne)
1960  James Scott (M & F), Lloyd Landry (M & F), Brian Mather
      (Ransomes)

*Euphonium Air Varié Championships*

1960  T. Graham (Galashiels), L. Baglin (Lydbrook), E. Dougall (Dalkeith)

*Solo Championships of Great Britain*

1961  L. Baglin (euph, CWS), A. English (tbn, Foden's), B. Rankine
      (cornet, B O & Shepherd)
1962  J. Shepherd (cornet, Carlton Main), J. Gray (tbn, Dalkeith),
      K. Tinsley (cornet, C. Laird) and G. Hirst (horn, Brighouse &
      Rastrick) tied in third

1963 J. Shepherd (cornet, Carlton Main), R. Davidson (euph, B & R), B. Cooling (cornet, Grimethorpe)

1964 J. Shepherd (cornet, Black Dyke), B. Perrins (euph, Hendon), B. Rankine (cornet, Bowhill)

1965 B. Rankine (cornet, Scot. Ch.), S. Thornton (cornet, Black Dyke), A. Rutherford (cornet, Bowhill)

1966 J. Watson (cornet, Bedworth), L. Baglin (euph, Lydbrook), B. Rankine (cornet, Kinneil)

1967 K. Tinsley (cornet, Edge Hill), T.C. Jennings (euph, City of Bristol), J. Watson (cornet, Desford)

1968 P. McCann (cornet, Fairey's), D. Read (cornet, GUS), L. Landry (cornet, Welsh Ch.)

1969 D. Moore (euph, Grimethorpe), P. McCann (cornet, Fairey's), B. Perrins (euph, Hendon)

1970 D. Moore (euph, Grimethorpe), B. Perrins (euph, Hendon), J. Pollard (tbn, Grimethorpe)

1971 G. Walker (cornet, Yorks Imps), D. Moore (euph, Grimethorpe), Miss S. Carlin (horn, Shirland)

1972 L. Landry (cornet, GUS), N. Thompson (cornet, City of Coventry), A. Fawbert (euph, Shirland)

1973 D. Read (cornet, GUS), A. Fawbert (euph, Shirland), R. McDowell (euph, Irish Ch., Agnes St)

1974 R. McDowell (euph, Irish Ch., Agnes St), L. Baglin (euph, S'shawe), A. Evans (euph, Ystalyfera)

1975 R. McDowell (euph, Agnes St), B. Crookes (euph, Hammonds), D. Morris (cornet, Rochdale)

1976 A. Morrison (cornet, AMOCO), R. McDowell (euph, Agnes St), R. Childs (euph, GUS)

1977 K. Dye (cornet, Shirland), D. Hall (euph, GUS), S. Lippeatt (flugel, Thoresby)

1978 E. Capron (sop, Luton), K. Bradley (horn, St Mary's, Australia), T. Halliwell (cornet, Wingates)

1979 T. Halliwell (cornet, Wingates), N. Childs (euph, Brodsworth), G. Pritchard (cornet, Brodsworth)

1980 G. McEvoy (euph, Besses), Howard Wilson (horn, City of Coventry), D. Bonvin (tbn, Switz.)

1981 D. Maplestone (cornet, Grimethorpe), Howard Wilson (horn, City of Coventry), G. Call (euph, USA)

**British Open Quartet, Solo and Junior Championships (1988–2000)**

| | Quartet | Senior Champion | Junior Champion |
|---|---|---|---|
| 1988 | Jaguar (City of Cov.) | Peter Roberts (sop, Grimethorpe) | |
| 1989 | Desford | Mark Walters (flug, Grimethorpe) | |
| 1990 | Desford | Mark Hutcherson (euph, BTM) | |
| 1991 | Kennedy's Swinton | David King (cornet, Black Dyke) | |
| 1992 | No contest | Chris Thomas (tbn, BTM) | Richard Marshall (cornet, Rothwell) |
| 1993 | No contest | Chris Thomas (tbn, BTM) | Richard Marshall (cornet, Stocksbridge) |
| 1995 | BNFL | Sheona White (horn, YBS) | Owen Farr (horn, BTM) |
| 1997 | JJB Sports Leyland | Mark Ruddock (sop, Laganvale) | David Geoghegan (cornet, Besses) |
| 1998 | JJB Sports Leyland | Jonathan Leedale (tbn, Marple) | David Geoghegan (cornet, Marple) |
| 1999 | Drighlington | Peter Roberts (sop, YBS) | Anna Spedding (cornet, Trinity Girls) |
| 2000 | BTM | Andrew King (tbn, Leyland) | Chris Gomersall (tbn, Newc Br Ale) |

# The European Championships, 1978–2000

| Year | Winner | Set test piece | Venue |
|------|--------|----------------|-------|
| 1978 | Black Dyke (Parkes) | Introduction, Elegy & Caprice (Calvert) | London |
| 1979 | Black Dyke (Parkes) | Symphonic Music (Huber) | London |
| 1980 | Cory (Stephens) | Land of the Long White Cloud (Sparke) | London |
| 1981 | Brighouse (Scott) | Caliban (Butterworth) | London |
| 1982 | Black Dyke (Parkes) | Journey into Freedom (E. Ball) | London |
| 1983 | Black Dyke (Parkes) | Ciacona Seria (Badings) | Kerkrade |
| 1984 | Black Dyke (Parkes) | Refrains and Cadenzas (Wilson) | Edinburgh |
| 1985 | Black Dyke (Parkes) | Royal Parks (Lloyd) | Copenhagen |
| 1986 | Desford (Snell) | The Year of the Dragon (Sparke) | Cardiff |
| 1987 | Black Dyke (Parkes) | Frontier (M. Ball) | Nottingham |
| 1988 | Eikanger (Snell) | Connotations (Gregson) | Lucerne |
| 1989 | Eikanger (Snell) | Trittico (Curnow) | Bergen |
| 1990 | Black Dyke (King) | The Essence of Time (Graham) | Falkirk |
| 1991 | Black Dyke (King) | A London Overture (Sparke) | Rotterdam |
| 1992 | Britannia Bdg Soc. (Snell) | Five Blooms in a Welsh Garden (Wood) | Cardiff |
| 1993 | Willebroek (Violet) | Sounds (Golland) | Plymouth |
| 1994 | Fairey (Parkes) | Le Chant de l'Alpe (Balissat) | Montreux |
| 1995 | Black Dyke (Watson) | Red Earth (Wiltgen) | Luxembourg |
| 1996 | YBS (King) | Seid (Aagaard-Nilsen) | Bergen |
| 1997 | YBS (King) | Salamander (McCabe) | London |
| 1998 | Brighouse (Withington) | Burlesque for Brass Band (Goorhuis) | Kerkrade |
| 1999 | YBS (King) | Odyssey (Norbury) | Munich |
| 2000 | YBS (King) | Tallis Variations (Sparke) | Birmingham |

## 'B' Section

| Year | Winner | Set test piece |
|------|--------|----------------|
| 1994 | Frösch Hall (Buchegger) | Resurgam (E Ball) |
| 1995 | Oberschwaben (Kurat) | Three Musketeers (Hespe) |
| 1996 | Normandie (Gervais) | Occasion (Gregson) |
| 1997 | Frösch Hall (Buchegger) | Entertainments (Vinter) |
| 1998 | Frösch Hall (Buchegger) | Fantasy (van Dijk) |
| 1999 | Frösch Hall (Buchegger) | The Bandsman's Challenge (Moren) |
| 2000 | Normandie (Gervais) | Corpus Christi (Redhead) |

# Principal works for brass bands, 1913–2000

As well as the name of the composer and the title of each piece, this table also gives their origins or the occasion on which they were first played.

## Original works

### 1913–60

| | | |
|---|---|---|
| Percy Fletcher | Labour and Love | Crystal Palace 1913 |
| Cyril Jenkins | Life Divine | Crystal Palace 1921 |
| Percy Fletcher | An Epic Symphony | Crystal Palace 1926 |
| Thomas Keighley | Lorenzo | Belle Vue September 1928 |
| Gustav Holst | A Moorside Suite | Crystal Palace 1928 |
| Sir Edward Elgar | Severn Suite | Crystal Palace 1930 |
| Denis Wright | Tintagel | 1930; republished 1956 |
| John Ireland | A Downland Suite | Crystal Palace 1932 |
| Sir Granville Bantock | Prometheus Unbound | Crystal Palace 1933 |
| John Ireland | Comedy Overture | Crystal Palace 1934 |
| Herbert Howells | Pageantry | Belle Vue September 1934 |
| Sir Arthur Bliss | Kenilworth | Crystal Palace 1936 |
| Denis Wright | Overture for an Epic Occasion | National Championship Finals 1945 |
| Henry Geehl | Sinfonietta Pastorale | 2nd section Area & Finals 1947 |
| Eric Ball | Divertimento | 4th section Area & Finals 1947 |
| Eric Ball | Petite Suite de Ballet | 3rd section Area & Finals 1949 |
| Dean Goffin | Rhapsody in Brass | Belle Vue September 1949 |
| Eric Ball | Indian Summer | 3rd section Area & Finals 1950 |
| Eric Ball | Resurgam | Belle Vue September 1950 |
| Eric Ball | Rhapsody on Negro Spirituals | Senior Trophy, Belle Vue May 1952 |
| Henry Geehl | Scena Sinfonica | Belle Vue September 1952 |
| George Hespe | The Three Musketeers | Belle Vue September 1953 |
| Eric Ball | Tournament for Brass | Belle Vue September 1954 |
| Denis Wright | Glastonbury | 3rd section, Area & Finals 1954 |
| Gordon Jacob | Suite in B flat | BBC commission 1955 |
| William Alwyn | The Moor of Venice | BBC commission 1956 |
| Denis Wright | Tam o' Shanter's Ride | Belle Vue September 1956 |
| Eric Ball | Festival Music | National Championship Finals 1956 |
| Helen Perkin | Carnival | Belle Vue September 1957 |
| R. Vaughan Williams | Variations for Brass Band | National Championship Finals 1957 |
| Eric Ball | Sunset Rhapsody | Belle Vue September 1958 |
| Edmund Rubbra | Variations on 'The Shining River' | National Championship Finals 1958 |
| Herbert Howells | Three Figures | National Championship Finals 1960 |
| Peter Yorke | The Shipbuilders | BBC commission 1960 |

## 1961–70

| | | |
|---|---|---|
| Gilbert Vinter | Salute to Youth | National Championship Area 1962 |
| Gilbert Vinter | James Cook, Circumnavigator | Comp. 1969 for 1970 NZ Champs |
| Malcolm Arnold | Little Suite for Brass | NYBBS commission 1963 |
| Arthur Bliss | Belmont Variations | National Championship Finals 1963 |
| Gilbert Vinter | Symphony of Marches | National Championship Area 1964 |
| Gilbert Vinter | Variations on a Ninth | National Championship Finals 1964 |
| Gilbert Vinter | Triumphant Rhapsody | National Championship Finals 1965 |
| Thea Musgrave | Variations for Brass Band | NYBBS commission 1966 |
| Malcolm Arnold | Little Suite No. 2 | Composed for Cornwall Youth 1967 |
| Eric Ball | Journey into Freedom | National Championship Finals 1967 |
| Allan Street | Rococo Variation on a Theme of Tchaikovsky | 2nd section Finals 1967 |
| Thomas Wilson | Sinfonietta | NYBBS commission 1967 |
| Arthur Butterworth | Three Impressions for Brass | Mid-Northumb. Arts comm. 1968 |
| Gilbert Vinter | John o' Gaunt | Belle Vue September 1968 |
| Gilbert Vinter | Spectrum | Belle Vue September 1969 |
| Bryan Kelly | Divertimento for Brass Band | NYBBS commission 1969 |
| Phyllis Tate | Illustrations | York Festival commission 1969 |
| Eric Ball | High Peak | National Championship Finals 1969 |
| Eric Ball | Youth Salutes a Master | Youth Championships 1970 |
| Allan Street | Embassy | Wills Championship Finals 1970 |

## 1971–80

| | | |
|---|---|---|
| Edward Gregson | Essay | Wills Championship Finals 1971 |
| Robert Simpson | Energy | World Championships 1971 |
| Joseph Horovitz | Sinfonietta for Brass Band | 2nd section Area 1972 |
| Eric Ball | A Kensington Concerto | National Championship Finals 1972 |
| Wilfred Heaton | Contest Music (comp. 1973) | National Championship Finals 1982 |
| Arthur Butterworth | Caliban (comp. 1973) | 2nd section 1975 |
| Bryan Kelly | Edinburgh Dances | NYBBS commission 1973 |
| Thomas Wilson | Refrains and Cadenzas | Cheltenham Festival commission 1973 |
| Edward Gregson | The Plantagenets | National Championship Area 1973 |
| Edward Gregson | Patterns | Butlins Finals 1974 |
| Harrison Birtwistle | Grimethorpe Aria | Grimethorpe commission 1974 |
| Malcolm Arnold | Fantasy for Brass Band | National Championship Finals 1974 |
| Derek Bourgeois | Concerto No. 1 | Adapted 1974 |
| John Golland | Sounds | Swiss commission 1974, first performed Holland; revised 1989 |
| Hans Werner Henze | Ragtimes and Habaneras | Grimethorpe commission 1975 |
| Robert Farnon | Un Vie de Matelot | National Championship Finals 1975 |
| Elgar Howarth | Fireworks | British Open 1975 |
| Paul Patterson | Chromoscope | Besses commission 1974 |
| Paul Patterson | Cataclysm | NYBB commission 1975 |
| Eric Ball | Sinfonietta – The Wayfarer | National Championship Finals 1976 |
| Derek Bourgeois | Concerto No. 2 | Composed 1976 |
| John McCabe | Images | Besses commission 1977 |
| George Benjamin | Altitude | Howarth commission 1977 |

| Edward Gregson | Connotations | National Championship Finals 1977 |
|---|---|---|
| William Mathias | Vivat Regina | Arts Council commission for Silver Jubilee 1977 |
| Edward Gregson | Variations on Laudate Dominum | SA composition 1978 |
| Derek Bourgeois | Concerto for Brass Band and Brass Quintet | Composed 1979 |
| Robert Simpson | Volcano | National Championship Finals 1979 |
| Philip Sparke | Land of the Long White Cloud | New Zealand Championships 1979 |

## 1981–90

| Derek Bourgeois | Blitz | National Championship Finals 1981 |
|---|---|---|
| William Walton | The First Shoot | Premiered at Proms 1981 |
| Peter Graham | Dimensions | Young composer's winner, Glamorgan 1981 |
| Gareth Wood | Hinemoa | 3rd section Area 1981 (NZ comm.) |
| Gareth Wood | Margam Stones | Butlins Finals 1981 |
| Elgar Howarth | In Memoriam R.K. | Composed 1982 |
| Elgar/Brand | Severn Suite (revised) | Broadcast by Fairey's 1982 |
| Philip Sparke | Jubilee Overture | GUS comm. 1983 (50th anniversary) |
| Joseph Horovitz | Ballet for Band | National Championship Finals 1983 |
| Michael Tippett | Festal Brass with Blues | Hong Kong Festival commission 1983 |
| Philip Sparke | A London Overture | Netherlands commission 1984; European Championships 1991 |
| Philip Sparke | Year of the Dragon | Cory commission 1984 |
| Edward Gregson | Dances and Arias | National Championship Finals 1984 |
| Wilfred Heaton | Partita (comp. in 1950s) | First performed 1984 by BBS (Snell) |
| Derek Bourgeois | A Barchester Suite | 3rd section Area 1985 |
| Derek Bourgeois | Diversions | Skellerup commission 1985 |
| John McCabe | Cloudcatcher Fells | National Championship Finals 1985 |
| Philip Sparke | Music for a Festival | Youth Finals 1985 |
| George Lloyd | Royal Parks | European Championships 1985 (BBC commission) |
| Philip Wilby | Revelation | British Open 1985 |
| Philip Sparke | Variations on an Enigma | Desford commission 1986 |
| Arthur Butterworth | Odin – from The Land of Fire and Ice | Black Dyke commission 1986, National Championships 1989 |
| George Lloyd | Diversions on a Bass Theme | CISWO 1986, Bass North/CISWO commission |
| Philip Sparke | Harmony Music | National Championship Finals 1987 |
| Ray Steadman-Allen | The Beacons | *BB* Centenary Concert 1987 |
| Michael Ball | Frontier | European Championships 1987 |
| Ray Steadman-Allen | Seascapes | National Championship Finals 1988 |
| Philip Sparke | Endeavour | Australian World Championships 1988 |
| George Lloyd | English Heritage | English Heritage commission 1988 |
| Richard Rodney Bennett | Flowers of the Forest | BBC commission for NYBB 1989 |
| Edward Gregson | Of Men and Mountains | Netherlands commission 1990 |
| Arthur Butterworth | Passacaglia for Brass | Desford commission 1990 |
| Peter Graham | The Essence of Time | European Championships 1990 |
| Philip Wilby | The New Jerusalem | NYBB commission 1990 |

## 1991–2000

| | | |
|---|---|---|
| John Pickard | Wildfire | NYBBW commission 1991 |
| Philip Wilby | Paganini Variations | BBC commission 1991 |
| Philip Sparke | Cambridge Variations | All-England Masters 1992 |
| Derek Bourgeois | Forest of Dean | 1st section Area 1993 (Swiss commission) |
| Derek Bourgeois | The Devil and the Deep Blue Sea | National Championship Finals 1993 |
| Goff Richards | Oceans | 2nd section Area 1993 |
| Martin Ellerby | Natalis | Hampshire Youth commission 1993 |
| Philip Wilby | Masquerade | British Open 1993 |
| Philip Wilby | A Lowry Sketchbook | Britannia Building Soc. commission 1993 |
| Peter Graham | Montage | All-England Masters 1994 |
| Kenneth Downie | Music from Kantara | Composed 1994 |
| Philip Wilby | Dance Before the Lord | NYBB commission 1994 |
| Elgar Howarth | Songs for B.L. | BBC commission Championship Finals 1995 |
| John Pickard | Men of Stone | Welsh Am. Mus. Federation 1995 |
| Kenneth Downie | Purcell Variations | Composed 1995 |
| Martin Ellerby | Vistas | BBO commission 1995 |
| Philip Wilby | Revelation | British Open 1995 |
| Elgar/Gay | Severn Suite (revised) | British Open 1996 |
| Judith Bingham | Prague | BBC commission 1996 |
| Peter Graham | Shine as the Light | Composed for Star Lake, USA, 1996 |
| Robert Redhead | Isaiah 40 | Commission 1996* |
| Goff Richards | The Aeronauts | 2nd section Finals 1996 |
| Martin Ellerby | Evocations | NYBB commission 1996 |
| Ray Steadman-Allen | Hymn at Sunrise | All-England Masters 1996 |
| Michael Ball | Whitsun Wakes | BBC commission 1997 |
| Peter Graham | On Alderley Edge | National Championship Finals 1997 |
| Elgar Howarth | Hymns at Heaven's Gate | European commission 1997 |
| Philip Wilby | Jazz | All-England Masters 1997 |
| David Bedford | Requiem | NYBB commission 1998 |
| Kenneth Downie | Capriccio | 2nd section Finals 1998 |
| Kevin Norbury | Odyssey | European Champs 1999 |
| Howard Snell | Excelsior | St Helens Youth commission 1999 |
| Martin Ellerby | Tristan Encounters | All-England Masters 1999 |
| Philip Wilby | Dove Descending | British Open 1999 |
| Howard Snell | Images of the Millennium | JJB commission 2000 |
| Michael Ball | Ceremony | British Open 2000 |
| Michael Ball | An English Suite | Comm. BBHT and Fodens for NYBB Championships 2000 |
| Peter Graham | Harrison's Dream | National Championship Finals 2000 |
| Philip Sparke | Tallis Variations | European Championships 2000, BFBB commission |
| Edward Gregson | The Trumpets of the Angels | Fodens commission and premiere 2000 |

---

* This work was jointly commissioned by Boosey & Hawkes and the National Championships of The Netherlands, Norway and Switzerland.

# Original solos

## *1941–80*

| | | |
|---|---|---|
| Denis Wright | Cornet Concert | 1941, with orchestra, mil. band and br. band |
| Denis Wright | Trio Concerto (cornet, euph, tbn) | Composed for NYBB 1967 |
| Edward Gregson | Concerto for French Horn and Brass Band | Arts Council commission 1971 |
| Edward Gregson | Prelude and Capriccio (cornet) | Composed 1972 |
| Joseph Horovitz | Euphonium Concerto | National BB Festival commission 1972 |
| Ernest Tomlinson | Cornet Concerto | National BB Festival commission 1974 |
| Elgar Howarth | Trombone Concerto | Composed 1974 |
| Elgar Howarth | Trumpet Concerto | Composed 1974 |
| Edward Gregson | Concerto for Tuba and Brass Band | Besses commission 1976 |
| Gordon Langford | Rhapsody for Trombone | National BB Festival commission 1976 |
| Philip Sparke | Fantasy for Euphonium | Composed 1978 |
| Gareth Wood | Concerto (trumpet) | Composed 1980 |

## *1981–2000*

| | | |
|---|---|---|
| Derek Bourgeois | Concerto Grosso | Composed 1981 |
| John Golland | Euphonium Concerto | Composed for Uster Music Festival, Switzerland, 1981 |
| Arthur Willis | The Fenlands (organ and brass band) | Funded by Eastern Arts 1981 |
| Gareth Wood | Dance Sequence (trombone) | Composed 1981 |
| Gordon Langford | Cornet Rhapsody | Recorded by Besses 1982 |
| Philip Sparke | Pantomine (euph) | 1991 – BB accompaniment (piano 1986) |
| John Golland | Euphonium Concerto No. 2 | First played Nick Childs and Grimethorpe 1988 |
| Martin Ellerby | Tuba Concerto | Hampshire Youth commission 1988 |
| Joseph Horovitz | Tuba Concerto | Premiered by Besses 1988 |
| Philip Sparke | Masquerade (tenor horn) | Composed for Gordon Higginbottom, 1988 |
| Philip Sparke | Concerto Grosso | CWS (Glasgow) commission 1988 |
| Philip Sparke | Concertino for Tuba and Brass Band | Composed 1988 |
| Derek Bourgeois | Trombone Concerto | Composed 1989 |
| Philip Sparke | Rhapsody for Baritone | Composed 1990 |
| Derek Bourgeois | Euphonium Concerto | Comm. and premiered Wendy Picton 1991 |
| Wilfred Heaton | Sinfonia Concertante (cornet) | Composed for BBS and M. Winter 1991 |
| Philip Sparke | Concerto for Trumpet and Brass Band | Carnegie Mellon University comm. 1991 |
| John Golland | Concerto for Flugelhorn | Stan Lippeatt commission 1992 |
| Wilfred Heaton | Concerto for Trombone | First performed BBS and N. Hudson 1992 |
| Gareth Wood | Tuba Concerto | Composed 1994 |
| Martin Ellerby | Euphonium Concerto | Comp. for and first performed by S. Mead/ BBO 1995 |
| Philip Sparke | Horn Concerto | RCBB commission 1995 |
| Philip Sparke | Euphonium Concerto | Composed 1995 |

| Martin Ellerby | Tenor Horn Concerto | First performed Smith and Fairey's, 1997 |
| Gareth Wood | Trombone Concerto | NYBBW commission 1999 |
| Martin Ellerby | Trombone Concerto | First performed Hampshire Youth, 2000 |

## Choral works

| Thomas Wood | The Rainbow | Arts Council commission 1945 |
| Gilbert Vinter | The Trumpets | Brass, percs, choir and bass soloist, BBC commission 1965 |
| Malcolm Arnold | Song of Freedom | NSBBA commission 1971 |
| Joseph Horovitz | Sampson | Brass, choir and baritone soloist, Nationals commission 1977 |
| Peter Maxwell Davies | The Peatcutters | NYBBS commission 1985 |

# Name-changes of some leading bands

**Black Dyke Mills Band, est. 1855**
1986   John Foster Black Dyke Mills
1994   Black Dyke Band

**City of Coventry, est. 1939**
1984   Jaguar Cars City of Coventry

**Cory, est. 1884 as Ton Temperance**
1895   Cory Workmen's Band
1979   The Cory Band
1989   Christie Tyler Cory
1998   Just Rentals Cory
2000   Buy As You View Cory

**Desford, est. 1863 as Snibstone Colliery**
1973   Desford Colliery
1982   Desford Colliery Dowty
1989   Desford Colliery Caterpillar

**Fairey Aviation Works Band, est. 1937**
1960   The Fairey Band
1976   Fairey Engineering Works Band
1985   Williams Fairey Engineering Band
1993   Williams Fairey Band

**Foden's Motor Works Band, est. 1900**
1900   Elworth Brass Band
1903   Foden's Motor Works
1983   Foden OTS
1986   Britannia Building Society Foden
1988   Britannia Building Society
1997   Fodens (Courtois)

**Hammonds Sauce Works Band, est. 1946**
1993   Yorkshire Building Society

**Hanwell Silver, est. 1891**
1979   Roneo Vickers
1983   The Hanwell Band

**Leyland Motors Band, est. 1946**
1980   Leyland Vehicles
1987   Leyland DAF
1992   BNFL
1997   JJB Sports Leyland
2000   The Leyland Band

**Munn & Felton's Works Band, est. 1933**
1958   Munn & Felton's (Footwear)
1962   GUS (Footwear)
1975   GUS (Kettering)
1978   The Great Universal Band
1980   The GUS Band
1987   Rigid Containers Group
1998   GUS
2000   Travelsphere Band

**Parc & Dare, est. 1875**
1989   Parc & Dare (NFD)
1990   National Fuel Distributors (Parc & Dare)

**Ransome & Marles, est. 1937**
1970   Ransome, Hoffman & Pollard
1972   RHP (Newark)
1979   The Ransome Band
1982   Brown's Musical Ransome
1984   Airquick (Newark) Ransome
1994   RHP-NSK Ransome
2000   The Ransome Band

**Stanshawe, est. 1968**
1978   Sun Life Stanshawe
1983   Sun Life Band
1996   Stanshawe

**Wingates Temperance, est. 1873**
1980   The Wingates Band
1982   Bass Wingates
1985   British Aerospace Wingates
1991   Wingates

**Yorkshire Copper Works, est. 1936**
1959   Yorkshire Imperial
1980   Yorkshire Imperial Metals
1984   IMI Yorkshire Imperial
1992   DUT Yorkshire Imperial
1999   DUT Rothwell
2000   DUT Yorkshire Imperial Rothwell

# Select bibliography

**Books and booklets**

Andrews, Frank (1997), *Brass Band Cylinder and Non-microgroove Disc Recordings 1903–1960*, Winchester: Piccolo Press.

Bainbridge, Cyril (1980), *Brass Triumphant*, London: Frederick Muller Ltd.

Barrett, F. (1963), *A History of Queensbury*, Queensbury: Queensbury Centenary Celebration Committee.

Blom, Eric (ed.)(1954), *Groves Dictionary of Music and Musicians*, 5th edn, London and New York: Macmillan.

Boon, Brindley (1978), *Play the Music Play!*, 2nd edn, London: SP&S Ltd.

Brand, Violet and Geoffrey (1979), *Brass Bands in the 20th Century*, Letchworth: Egon.

Brighton, Charlie (1983), *The Hanwell Band 1891–1983* [no publisher or place given].

Calder, Angus (1992 edn), *The People's War – Britain 1939–45*, London: Pimlico.

Cook, Kenneth (ed.)(1950), *The Bandsman's Everything Within*, London: Hinrichsen.

Cook, Kenneth (ed.)(1950), *Oh, Listen to the Band*, London: Hinrichsen.

Cook, K. and Caisley, L. (1953), *Music Through the Brass Band*, London: Hinrichsen.

Cooke, Peter M. (1991), *Eric Ball – The Man and His Music*, Baldock: Egon.

Cooke, Peter M. (1992), *Eric Ball – His Words and His Wisdom*, Baldock: Egon.

Dean, Frank (1980), *The Magic of Black Dyke*, Brighouse: Kirklees.

*The Directory of British Brass Bands* (2003), Volume 17, Barnsley: British Federation of Brass Bands.

Donnelly, M. (1999), *Britain in the Second World War*, London: Routledge.

Evans, Vaughan (comp.) (1992), *Durham County Brass Band League, 50 Golden Years*, Durham: County Durham Books.

Gammond, P. and Horricks, R. (eds) (1980), *Music on Record 1 – Brass Bands*, Cambridge: Patrick Stephens.

Grace, Harvey (ed.), *The New Musical Educator*, 4 vols, London: Caxton.

Greenalgh, Alec (1992), *Hail Smiling Morn: Whit Friday Brass Band Contests 1884 to 1991*, Oldham: Oldham Leisure Services.

Hailstone, Alf (1987), *The British Bandsman Centenary Book*, Baldock: Egon.

Hampson, Joseph N. (1893), *Origin, History and Achievement of the Besses o' th' Barn Band*, Northampton: Rogers.

Herbert, Trevor (ed.)(1991), *Bands – The Brass Band Movement in the 19th and 20th Centuries*, Milton Keynes: The Open University.

Herbert, Trevor (ed.)(2000), *The British Brass Band – A Musical and Social History*, Oxford: Oxford University Press.

Hill, Samuel (1994), *Bygone Stalybridge*, 3rd edn, Guisley: Rigg Publications.

Hind, Harold (1952), *The Brass Band*, 2nd edn, London: Hawkes & Son.

Hollinshead, Keith (1994), *The Major and His Band, The Story of Abram/Bickershaw Colliery Band*, Bradford: Kirklees Music.

Horwood, Wally (1980), *Adolphe Sax 1814–1894 – His Life and Legacy*, Bramley: Bramley Books.

Howarth, Elgar and Patrick (1988), *What a Performance – The Brass Band Plays*, London: Robson Books.

Littlemore, Allan (ed.)(1987), *The Rakeway Brass Band Yearbook 1987*, Hollington: Rakeway.

Littlemore Allan (ed.)(1988), *The Rakeway Brass Band Yearbook 1988*, Hollington: Rakeway.

Littlemore, Allan (1999), *Fodens Band: One Hundred Years of Musical Excellence*, Chapel-en-le-Frith: Caron Publications.

Livings, Henry (1975), *That the Medals and the Baton be Put on View – The Story of a Village Band 1875–1975*, Newton Abbot: David & Charles.

*The Macmillan Encyclopaedia* (1986 edn), Aylesbury: Macmillan.

Massey, Ron (1996), *Meltham and Meltham Mills Band – Celebrating 150 Years of Music 1846–1996*, Meltham: Burnhouse.

Merriday, F. (1899), *A Pictorial, Historical and Literary Souvenir of Whitefield, Besses and the Neighbourhood*, Radcliffe: Hayhurst.

Mortimer, Harry (with Alan Lynton) (1981), *Harry Mortimer on Brass*, Sherborne: Alphabooks.

Mutum, Tim (1991), *Brass Band Recordings – A Complete Guide to Brass Band Recordings since 1957*, Baldock: Egon.

Newcomb, S.P. (1980), *Challenging Brass: 100 Years of Brass Band Contests in New Zealand 1880–1980*, Takapuna, NZ: Powerbrass Music Co Ltd.

Newsome, Roy (1995), *Doctor Denis: The Life and Times of Doctor Denis Wright*, Baldock: Egon.

Newsome, Roy (1998), *Brass Roots, A Hundred Years of Brass Bands and their Music, 1836–1936*, Aldershot: Ashgate.

Nicholls, Robert (1989), *Looking Back at Belle Vue Manchester*, Altrincham: Willow Publishing.

*The Oxford Companion to Popular Music* (1991 edn), ed. P. Gammond, Oxford: Oxford University Press.

*The Oxford Dictionary of Music* (1986 edn), ed. M. Kennedy, Oxford: Oxford University Press.

Perrins, Barrie (1984), *Brass Band Digest*, Baldock: Egon.

Roberts, Peter (2003), *A Legend in His Own Lifetime – an Autobiography*, Stockport: Jagrins Music Publications.

Russell, Dave (1987), *Popular Music in England, 1840–1914*, Manchester: Manchester University Press.

Russell, J.F. and Elliot, J.H. (1936), *The Brass Band Movement*, London: Dent.

Sadie, Stanley (ed.)(1980), *The New Grove Dictionary of Music and Musicians*, London: Macmillan.

Steadman-Allen, Ray (1980), *Colour and Texture in the Brass Band Score*, London: SP&S.

Stevenson, J. and Cook, C. (1994), *Britain in the Depression, Society and Politics 1929–39*, Harlow: Longman.

Taylor, A.J.P. (1975), *English History 1914–1945*, Oxford: Oxford University Press.

Taylor, Arthur R. (1979), *Brass Bands*, St Albans: Granada.

Taylor, Arthur R. (1983), *Labour and Love, an Oral History of the Brass Band Movement*, London, Elm Tree.

Tiratsoo, Nick (ed.)(1997), *From Blitz to Blair – a New History of Britain Since 1939*, London: Phoenix.

Toms, Carel (2000), *Hitler's Fortress Islands*, Guernsey: Burbridge Publications.

Trethewey, Linda (1988), *St Dennis Band 150 Years 1838–1988*, St Dennis: [no publisher given].

Wade, Ralph (1980), *The First Hundred Years of Brighouse & Rastrick Band*, Brighouse: Brighouse Echo.

Walmsley, Trevor (1986), *You and Your Band – A Practical Guide to Better Banding*, Bradford: Printissimo.

Wright, Denis (1948), *The Brass Band Conductor*, Joshua Duckworth.

Wright, Denis (1963), *The Complete Bandmaster*, London: Pergamon Press.

Wright, Denis (1967 edn), *Scoring for Brass Band*, London: John Baker.

Wright, Frank (ed.)(1957), *Brass Today*, London: Besson.

## Booklets (un-named authors)

*31st Crystal Palace National Band Festival 1936 – Souvenir Programme.*

*British Open Championships – a record of results and test pieces since its commencement in 1853* (compiled by David Read).

*Championships Contest Records from 1985–1994* (compiled by the Scottish Amateur Brass Band Association Executive Committee).

*Cory Band 1884–1984 – Souvenir Centenary Brochure.*

*Floral Dance 25th Anniversary 1977–2002 – Souvenir Brochure.*

*National Fuel Distributors Band (Parc & Dare) Centenary 1893–1993.*

*Rothwell Temperance Band 1881–1981.*

*St Hilda's Band – Premier Band of England (c. 1935).*

*Slaithwaite Band: Golden Jubilee Year 1925–1975 – 50 Years at the Band Pavilion at Ing Head.*

*Slaithwaite Band Jubilee Souvenir 1892–1942.*

*South West Brass Band Association 1946–1996 – Fifty Years of Service.*

*Stalybridge Old Band 1814–1914.*

*Sun Life – A Celebration of Sun Life's 20th Anniversary Year.*

*Williams Fairey Engineering Band – Fifty Golden Years 1937–1987.*

## Other sources

*Brass Band News*

*Brass Band Review*

*Brass Band World*

*Brass Review*

*British Bandsman*

*British Mouthpieces*

*The Conductor*

*Halifax Courier*

*The Guardian*

*List of Prize Winners (with Selections of Music) of the Brass Band Contests from the commencement in 1853*, Belle Vue – 1973 edition.

'Origins and Promotion of Brass Band Contests' – a series of articles by Enderby Jackson in *Musical Opinion and Musical Trade Review*: April, July, September and November 1896.

*Sounding Brass*

# Subject index

Page numbers in *italics* refer to photographs. The most important page numbers in lengthy entries are shown in **bold** type.

## Principal bands and ensembles

## Principal competitions

## Personalities and composers

# General index

Acid Brass 252, **278**

Accrington & Rossendale College **222**, 266

Alexandra Palace xiii, 15, 17, 18, 49

America (USA) 34, 73, 81, 83, 166, 175, 217, 218, 266, 273, 283, 285, **295**, 302, 303, **315–18**, 321, 341

AOMF Scholarship **19–20**, 37, **66**, 208, 338 (*see also* Appendix B)

Association of Brass Band Adjudicators (ABBA) **209**, **325**

Australia 34, 66, 129, 150 n.26, 157, 224, 254, 256, 264, 295, 300, 301, 312, 317, 337

Bandsman's College of Music/BBCM: **20–21**, 37, **66**, 137, 164, 208, 345

Barnsley College **222**, 265, 282

BBC/Broadcasting 3, 11, 13, 22, 24, 29, 37, 44, 70, 71, 93, 100, 108, 122, 129, 130, 131, 153, 159, 184, **187–93**, 219, 275, 277, 305

  BBC Band of the Year 190, **191**, 250, 257, 266

  *Friday Night is Music Night* 187, 188, 193

  Light Music Festival 130, 190, 193

  *Listen to the Band* 187, 234, 284

  Local Radio **192–3**

  Radio Wales Band of the Year 191, 326, 334

  Young Musician of the Year 219, 338, 344

Belgium 295, 305, **313–14**, 321

Belle Vue xiii n.2, 15, 17, 33, 34, 44, 67, 89, 90, 92, 94, 95, 119, **226**, 227

Birmingham School of Music 87, **222**, 286, 341

Blitz 8, 9, 10, 16, 24, 42

Booŝey & Hawkes 56, 62, 145, 199, **220**, 222, 228, 231, 236, 244, 275, 286, 303, 304, 315, 319

Brass Band Heritage Trust **210**, 232

*Brass Band News* xii, xiii, 59

*Brass Band Review* xii, 56

*Brass Band World* xii, **223**

*Brassed Off* 256, **277**, 319

*Brass Review* xii, **223**, 344

*British Bandsman* x, xii, 17, **54**, 55, 60, 75, 96, 98, 132, 133, 160, **223**

British Federation **69–71**, **97–8**, **209–11**, 218, 282, 325

*British Mouthpiece* xii, **61**, 97, 337

Canada 34, 45, 73, 81, 129, 175, 295, **303–5**, 321, 341

Canadian Brass Band Festival 141, 147

Canadian National Exhibition (CNE) 34, 130, 303, 304, 315

Canford Summer School **221**

Channel Islands 7, 155, 184, **299–300**

Chappell & Co 37, 75, **126**

COBBA **61**, 67, 69, **96–7**, 99, 337

Crystal Palace xiii, 15, 17, 18, 29, 34, 35, 36, 49, 133, 341, 344

Denmark 75, 82, 134, 160, 216, 272, 295, 302, **310–11**, 321

ENSA **13**, 146, 160

Euphonium Player of the Year 57, 291, 338, 339, 341

European Brass Band Association (EBBA) 210, 211, 236, 314

Faroes 295, **320**

Feldman's **126**

Festival of Britain 58, **183**, 241

Finland **269**, 320

Floral Dance **159**, 278

Foundation for Sport and the Arts **207**, 210, 214

France 81, 141, 295, 305, 311, **314**, 319

*Full Monty, The* 278

Gala concerts (Nationals) 91, **102–3**, 131, 141, 197, 202, 230, **231–2**, 279, 311, 323